Audiovisual Input and Second Language Learning

Language Learning & Language Teaching (LL&LT)

ISSN 1569-9471

The LL&LT monograph series publishes monographs, edited volumes and text books on applied and methodological issues in the field of language pedagogy. The focus of the series is on subjects such as classroom discourse and interaction; language diversity in educational settings; bilingual education; language testing and language assessment; teaching methods and teaching performance; learning trajectories in second language acquisition; and written language learning in educational settings.

For an overview of all books published in this series, please see *benjamins.com/catalog/lllt*

Editors

Nina Spada
Ontario Institute for Studies in Education
University of Toronto

Laura Gurzynski-Weiss
Indiana University Bloomington

Volume 61

Audiovisual Input and Second Language Learning
Edited by Carmen Muñoz and Imma Miralpeix

Audiovisual Input and Second Language Learning

Edited by

Carmen Muñoz
Imma Miralpeix
University of Barcelona

John Benjamins Publishing Company
Amsterdam / Philadelphia

DOI 10.1075/lllt.61

Cataloging-in-Publication Data available from Library of Congress:
LCCN 2024031278 (PRINT) / 2024031279 (E-BOOK)

ISBN 978 90 272 1593 2 (HB)
ISBN 978 90 272 1592 5 (PB)
ISBN 978 90 272 4649 3 (E-BOOK)

John Benjamins Publishing Company · https://benjamins.com

Table of contents

Introduction

The chapters in this volume present a selection of studies conducted within the framework of the SUBTiLL (Subtitles in Language Learning) research project at the Universitat de Barcelona (Spain) by members of the GRAL (Grup de Recerca en Adquisició de Llengües) research group and colleagues. The project has been ongoing for the past decade and has facilitated various lines of research within the area of learning through viewing. A number of factors combined to spark our interest in this domain of second language learning. First of all, the quest to increase the amount and authenticity of input for learners of English in input-limited classrooms led to the recognition of the benefits of undubbed English-language audiovisual input as an unlimited and freely accessible source. In our specific context of a traditionally dubbing country, this meant taking a public stance in favor of subtitling or captioning over dubbing in television and cinemas. This occurred as the influence of the Internet in our daily lives, both for work and leisure, became omnipresent, changing people's attitudes towards original version viewing and enhancing students' awareness of its language learning potential through their lived experience. From a more general research-oriented point of view, the interest was sparked by the recognition that exploring the benefits of viewing for language learning enriches our perspectives of second language acquisition, as it sheds light on the multimodal nature of communication. Studying the effects of audiovisual input on language learning can also provide valuable insights into effective teaching methods, the role of technology in language education, and how individuals process and internalize linguistic information in diverse contexts.

The studies conducted within the framework of SUBTiLL present some distinguishing characteristics. These include the emphasis on young learners; the incorporation of participants with elementary levels of proficiency, and even with no previous knowledge of the target language (*ab initio* learning); the commitment to longitudinal studies in the classroom; the multiple foci, from vocabulary and comprehension to pronunciation, grammar, and pragmatics; and the attention to the role of individual differences in learning through viewing.

The studies in this volume stand out for their diverse methodologies, comprising mixed-methods designs that allow for qualitative analyses of participants' perceptions, and the use of eye-tracking methodology to examine participants' attention, either as the primary focus or as a supplementary tool. It is also worth noting that the perspectives explored here vary in terms of the type of learning under examination. In some chapters, participants engaged in incidental learning while watching videos with a focus on meaning and comprehension (*learning while watching*). In other chapters, participants were explicitly led to focus on form (*viewing for learning*). In studies involving enhanced captions or post-viewing tasks, neither purely incidental nor purely intentional learning can be assumed to have taken place.

The first three chapters report on longitudinal studies with primary school students. In Chapter 1, titled "Language learning from watching cartoons in the Primary EFL classroom", Montserrat Casulleras and Imma Miralpeix analyze the possible benefits of prolonged exposure to cartoons in English. Given the typically low proficiency levels among young learners in a foreign language, a question often raised is whether (L1) subtitles or (L2) captions can provide good support for understanding the programs and for language learning. This study compares two groups of primary school students who watched 20 episodes of an animated cartoon either with subtitles or captions over a five-month span. Additionally, individual variables such as linguistic aptitude, L2 vocabulary size, and reading speed were controlled for with the aim of evaluating their potential impact on comprehension and vocabulary acquisition resulting from the viewing experience.

In Chapter 2, titled "The development of L1 and L2 reading skills from captioned-video viewing in primary school EFL learners", Daniela Avello and Carmen Muñoz bring to the fore the importance of primary school children's reading skills within the context of captioned video viewing. The study focuses on a group of primary school learners in grades 4 and 5 at a Chilean school, whose reading skills in their first language, Spanish, were still developing, and who reported infrequent reading in their L1. These students watched 11 episodes of an animated cartoon with audio and on-screen text in English. The study examines the influence of both L1- and L2-related factors on the development of reading skills. A noteworthy aspect of this classroom-based study is its exploration of not only the development of L2 reading skills but also L1 reading skills as a result of the viewing experience.

In Chapter 3, entitled "The effects of textual enhancement on young learners' attention and vocabulary acquisition through captioned cartoons", Rebeca Finger-Bou and Carmen Muñoz explore the potential effect of caption enhancement on vocabulary learning among a group of primary school learners of English with Catalan and Spanish as their first languages. A notable contribution of this study is the use of enhanced captions with young learners. Like the study reported in Chapter 2, the participants in this study watched 11 episodes of a children's animated cartoon, one group with regular captions and one with enhanced captions.

Figure 3. Creation of Art Releases Tension (acrylic on paper)

or closed to the children. How might tutoring be a shaping influence on future educational opportunities?

Figure 4. Wondering about open or closed educational doors for the children's futures

The children's journals also informed our research conversations, our wonders, our book selections and our literature searches. The children's journals (see Figure 5) included images, sketches, words lists, sentences, and first attempts at paragraphs. When a child grew frustrated with what they perceived as the slow pace of improvement, we would return to the early pages of their journal and encourage them to describe the improvement.

Figure 5. An example of an individual sketchbook created by a child

Collaboratively composing research texts

When creating research texts[11] we did so collaboratively. This was purposeful because we wanted to acknowledge the uniqueness of multiple voices and shaping influences on experiences. Before coming to a collaborative session, we read and reread field notes, we listened to recordings, we viewed the children's work and we lingered with images and comments embedded in our field notes. In draft format, we shared our writing with trusted peers and our research assistant and asked for responses. We read individual sections and we read the work in its entirety. This collaborative approach helped us to identify tensions and themes. It also allowed us to imagine future, educative stories for ourselves and for the participants. Finally, the collaboration helped us to appreciate how the children's lives were interconnected and shaped by many influences as they struggled to live meaningful lives at school, with families and in the community.

---

11. Clandinin and Connelly (2000) described research texts as those texts which result when the inquirer, utilizing the three-dimensional narrative inquiry space "composes a text that at once looks backward and forward, looks inward and outward, and situates the experiences within the place" (p. 140).

Applied and theoretical challenges and assets with a narrative inquiry methodology

We experienced challenges related to the methodology. In this section we summarize and provide examples of some of the challenges.

Negotiating relationships takes time and access: History matters

We began by reaching out to the principal; she agreed to meet to discuss how we might contribute to the school. Sandra worked with her previously. Together we co-designed the study and wrote the funding application. Once we received notice of provincial funding, we began the process of navigating three separate ethical approvals for the research: university, Mi'Kmaq Ethics Watch (MEW), and the chief and council. University and MEW approval were familiar and therefore straightforward. Janet and Sandra had previously completed multiple, successful applications. When we applied for in-community, approval, the process slowed because we did not have previous experience, nor did we have a relationship history with community leaders.

One day, while having tea with an Indigenous colleague, we described our efforts. Our colleague said they would investigate. The next day we received an email, containing an attached letter of approval to proceed. We were simultaneously delighted and curious. Why had our colleague been able to do what we could not? We read Hall et al. (2015) and Smith (2008), which shed light on the notion of smash and grab and the resulting lack of trust encountered by subsequent academics wanting to conduct in-community research (Kovach, 2009; Regan, 2010). This was a powerful reminder that the proposed research and we ourselves were entering multiple and complex stories that were threaded to past, present, and future experiences. Through this experience we understood more fully the lives that we compose as we interact and intertwine with each other (Clandinin et al., 2018). Co-developing initiatives and research studies takes time as they are not occuring in a fixed space or place. "Our experiences, too, are multiple, shaped over time and place and relationship" (Clandinin et al., 2018, p.19).

Navigating competing stories

The research included methodological challenges related to the ongoing need to attend to the relational. We began with our individual positionings and stories and then engaged in the complex work of negotiating relationships with participants. There were times when the multiplicity of the children's stories resulted in moments of tension because once the children valued the tutoring tables, they each wanted to be first, and they each wanted to lengthen the time they spent tutoring. Furthermore, there were children in the classroom who sat in proximity of the tutoring tables, who were not part of the study and who asked the classroom teacher if they could participate. There were days when we experienced this as the need to continually attend to multiple lives, participants and non-participants as they unfolded in the classroom (Clandinin et al., 2006).

In response to this challenge and as part of our collaborative and sustained research conversations we reminded ourselves that the children were living complex and sometimes competing stories (Clandinin et al., 2006). The children's lives did not begin nor end as we entered and left the classroom. This was important because it allowed us to appreciate the experiences the children had outside of school. Also, it reminded us to think deeply before questioning the children's experiences from the perspective of our privileged and economically secure lives. We returned to this when we experienced COVID and the resulting school closure. When the school reopened, visitors were restricted to essential personnel. The abruptness to the end of the study was complex. We wondered how the children were. We wanted to be there with them; we missed them. The losses we experienced were a result of the meaningful relationships we were developing; relationships made possible by the research methodology. We waited and wondered about our next steps. We also knew that within the frame of narrative inquiry we lived one of the "most pressing methodological challenges for contemporary narrative inquiry...a means of respecting individual experience as a site of research and knowledge generation that on the one hand acknowledges the limits of the reach of personal reflection and on the other refuses to sit comfortable within those limits" (Rosiek, 2018, p. 205).

Connections between theory and methodology

We were interested in understanding children's experiences with learning to read. With Dewey as the theoretical core and narrative inquiry as the methodology we were able to study children's experiences learning to read while also attending to social, institutional and personal shaping influences (Clandinin & Connelly, 2000). By attending to narratives, we heard and participated in experiences and stories as the children worked to be fluent readers. Furthermore, because we were working in-community it was important that the methodology be grounded in a concern for "relational accountability" (Wilson, 2001, p. 177). This methodological concern created a link between Dewey's theoretical focus on experience, life and education and the inquiry. The theory allowed us to attend to the "context in which research problems are conceptualized and designed, and with the implications of research for its participants and their communities." (Smith, 2012, p.ix). As we moved in and out of the research site, we were cognizant of and directed by the theoretical and methodological affordances. We attended to the dance of entering the research in the midst of "our own li[ves], in the midst of participants' lives, and in the midst of institutional, social, familial, linguistic, and social narratives" (Clandinin, 2013, p.203). We know that we were only part of the story, as there "would never be a final story" (p.203).

Narrative inquiry's contributions to applied linguistics

Our intention was to live out a two-year narrative inquiry. We planned to engage teachers, families and children identified as struggling readers as participants. Unfortunately, this was not the case because of COVID. The data we collected, however, hint at potential contributions narrative inquiry can make to the field of reading remediation for youngsters identified as struggling readers.

By the time children reach grade three, they know who can read and who is struggling to read. Complex struggling reader identities become central characters in each classroom. Children live out the identity of struggling readers through interactions with self, classmates, teachers, curriculum, and researchers. Narrative inquiry allowed us to wonder about the connections between reader identity stories and attendance, mandated curriculum, unmet learning expectations, family involvement, behaviors, history, culture, and culturally relevant pedagogy. From our inquiries we began to understand that struggling readers do not experience school as a place where they spend a year in a classroom, learn, meet expectations and then successfully pass to the next grade. Rather children identified as struggling readers live with the uncertainty they might fail and spend another year in the same grade. They believe passing or failing is entirely a reflection of themselves. They do not think to wonder if the teaching methods are a best fit for their learning styles or if they might have learned to read if other pedagogical approaches were deployed. Success or failure then is singularly a reflection of the individual child.

Charlotte knew this and shared it when she called herself dumb. Inquiring into Charlotte's stories allowed us to understand this, which in turn helped us to understand her desire to be first and to linger the longest. On days when some children were absent and we completed the tutoring before the morning was over, Charlotte would quietly slip back into a vacant chair. She knew every child had been tutored and she knew there was time remaining therefore she wanted a second turn. Connelly and Clandinin (1988) described how an individual works to unite her experiences in efforts to make her life meaningful. We understood this was what Charlotte was doing, making her life meaningful by becoming a reader. She was also struggling to shift her story such that her excellent attendance resulted in met learning outcomes. We understood this as Charlotte's efforts to negotiate her school experiences such that they were educative (Dewey, 1938). As we understood Charlotte's efforts, our respect, care and relationship with her deepened. As often as we could we tutored her twice a morning. She responded joyfully, with humor, eagerness, openness, lengthened attention and slow and steady improvement to her reading. She was shifting her identity; she was working to unite her stories and a narrative inquiry methodology supported her efforts and it supported and directed the work we did with her. We began to appreciate that a narrative inquiry methodology was scaffolding for the children and for ourselves. When we thought system wide, we knew the methodology could support counterstories (Lindemann Nelson, 1995, p.171) to push against the taken for granted narrative of 32% (2023) of the children not meeting learning outcomes. In discussion with the classroom teacher and the children we began to compose a counterstory, a story of a particular school year where every child met the outcomes and passed into grade four.

Other contributions the methodology has to offer to the field of Applied Linguistics (particularly struggling readers) includes a vocabulary for describing efforts to shift identity stories. This is important because it allows researchers to attend to more than skill-set development. Also, alongside relationships provide support as the children struggle to shift their identity stories. In addition, "the narrative inquiry three-dimensional space and the elements of interaction, continuity and situation enable the deepening of analysis of field texts and the improvement of research design" (Baddeley & Singer, 2007, p.178).

Furthermore, the use of images to illustrate the complexity and nuance of stories makes the children's experiences accessible for analysis and understanding. Finally, narrative inquiry supports researchers to wonder, to move off the pedestal of expert, one who discovers things towards one who embraces wonders and complexities (context, history, worldviews) and how shifting amongst them expands our understandings of the children's complex efforts to become readers. The methodology also supports researchers and readers to "avoid arrogance or totalizing" (Baddeley & Singer, 2007, p.179) while letting us linger in wondering if Charlotte is now a fluent reader.

Ethical issues

Narrative research involves humans and therefore is complex and involves contextual particularities (MacIntyre, 1984). As noted by Clandinin (2007), "Because we are dealing with the real lives of real people, we can never know for sure at the outset that we will not have an impact on them that could be in some way painful" (p.559). This point was particularly relevant because this study included children. We endeavored to research alongside the children, in relation with them and not conduct research on them; however, there are no guarantees that harm did not result. Josselson (2006) helped us understand the importance of leading with ethical responsibility when she wrote:

> We must interact with our participants humbly, trying to learn from them. We must protect their privacy. What we think might do harm we cannot publish... There will always be dilemmas because virtue in this work stems from contextual ethics that are best specified in each situation through discussion with informed colleagues.
>
> (p.560)

Moreover, Park et al. (2016) described our understanding and "the responsibility, we fel[t] toward participants did not stem from obligation, but a genuine sense of relationship" (p.5).

In our quiet drives to and from school we often used this time to make field notes and discuss the justification for the study. We also returned to the literature and the early narrative inquiry foundations by Connelly and Clandinin. We considered the place and space in which the study was occurring. We wondered about the close working relationship with the principal, the teachers and the children and the stories they told and re-told about books, reading, and the support they received. We paused and wondered about the importance of our relationships as the foundation to building trust, trust on which their stories would emerge. Clandinin (2018) states, "relationship is key to what it is that narrative inquires do" (p.187). Our attitudes, questions, wonders and openness framed our journey into the classroom.

In conclusion, this narrative inquiry took months to secure the required three layers of ethical approval. Once we were in the classroom working with the children and teacher, the methodology guided us; it focused our attention on the relational. Branches of trust were beginning to develop, children were taking reading risks, attention span was lengthening and children were beginning to describe themselves as improving readers. We began with much promise; the children were eager to be known as readers. The global pandemic slammed the door on the research and on our relationships with these remarkable children. For months we experienced a loss. On occasion we would discuss the methodology and wonder if it might help us understand and deal with the abrupt end of the research and the relationships we were in the midst of developing.

Conclusion

Time and trust were key to the journey of co-designing and living out this narrative inquiry study in partnership with the principal, classroom teacher, and children, a structured literacy intervention for struggling readers. The process of beginning the study and then stopping the study because of the COVID pandemic left us in a place of quietness, heaviness and of worrying about the children and their reading progress. Yet, we were able to be attentive to the responsibilities of working within the process of narrative inquiry. We attended to the three-dimensional narrative inquiry space of sociality, place, and temporality (Clandinin, 2013). As well, we grew our understanding of relational ethics and in turn we were able to respond and make changes to the tutoring process (Clandinin et al., 2018). We grew in our ability to pivot as a result of the relational. Through the children's involvement in reading activities and in creative spaces, they were able to begin, albeit tentatively, to consider knowing themselves as readers, a story they so clearly wanted to tell.

References

Al Dahhan, N. Z., Kirby, J. R., & Munoz, D. P. (2016). Understanding reading and reading difficulties through naming speed tasks: Bridging the gaps among neuroscience, cognition, and education. *AERA Open, 2*(4), 1–15.

Augustine, S. (2016). The Mi'Kmaw creation story. In M. Battiste (Ed.), *Visioning a Mi'Kmaw humanities* (pp. 18–28). Cape Breton University Press.

Baddeley, J., & Singer, J. A. (2007). Charting the life story's path narrative identity across the life span. In D. J. Clandinin (Ed.), *Handbook of narrative inquiry* (pp. 177–202). Sage.

Brown-Jeffy, S., & Cooper, J. E. (2011). Toward a conceptual framework of culturally relevant pedagogy: An overview of the conceptual and theoretical literature. *Teacher Education Quarterly, 38*(1), 1010.

California Department of Education. (2022). *Culturally relevant pedagogy.* https://www.cde.ca .gov/pd/ee/culturalrelevantpedagogy.asp

Carr, D. (1986). *Time, narrative, and history.* Indiana University Press.

Clandinin, D. J. (2007). *Narrative inquiry.* Sage.

Clandinin, D. J. (2013). *Engaging in narrative inquiry.* Routledge.

Clandinin, D. J., Cabe, M. T., & Berendonk, C. (2016). Narrative inquiry: A relational research methodology for medical education. *Medical Education, 51*(1), 89–96.

Clandinin, D. J., Caine, V., & Lessard, S. (2018). *The relational ethics of narrative inquiry.* Routledge.

Clandinin, D. J., Caine, V., Estefan, A., Huber, J., Murphy, M. S., & Steeves, P. (2015). Places of practice: Learning to think narratively. *Narrative Works: Issues, Investigations & Interventions, 5*(1), 22–39.

Clandinin, D. J., Huber, J., Huber, M., Murphy, M. S., Orr, M. A., Pearce, M., & Steeves, P. (2006). *Composing diverse identities.* Taylor & Francis.

Connelly, F. M., & Clandinin, D. J. (1990). Stories of experience and narrative inquiry. *Educational Researcher, 19*(5), 2–14.

Connelly, F. M., & Clandinin, D. J. (1999). Shaping a professional identity. In F. M. Connelly & D. J. Clandinin (Eds.), *Shaping a professional identity: Stories of educational practice.* Teachers College Press.

Connelly, F. M., & Clandinin, D. J. (2006). Narrative inquiry. In J. L. Green, G. Camilli, & P. Elmore (Eds.), *Handbook of complementary methods in education research* (3rd ed., pp. 477–487). Routledge.

DeWalt, D. A., & Hink, A. (2009). Health literacy and child health outcomes: A systematic review of the literature. *Pediatrics, 124*(Suppl 3), S265–S274.

Dewey, John. (1938a). *Logic: The theory of inquiry.* Henry Holt and Company.

Dewey, J. (1938b). *Experience and education.* Simon & Schuster Press.

Encyclopedia of Children's Health. (2022). *Retention.* Retrieved on 8 October 2024 from http://www.healthofchildren.com/R/Retention-in-School.html#:~:text=The%20term%20%22retention%22%20in%20regards,peers%20regardless%20of%20academic%20performance

Enriquez, G., Johnson, E., Kontovourki, S., & Mallozzi, C. A. (2016). *Literacy, learning, and the body.* Taylor & Francis.

Etherington, K. (2004). *Becoming a reflexive practitioner.* Jessica Kingsley Publishers.

Fecho, B., & Meacham, S. (2007). In C. Lewis, P. Enciso, & E. B. Birr Moje (Eds.), *Introduction: Reframing sociocultural research on literacy (pp. 163–188).* Routledge.

Fisher, D., Frey, N., & Haddie, J. (2016). *Visible learning for literacy impact.* Corwin Literacy.

Fisher, L., & Fisher, L. (2020). *2019 report card on child and family poverty in Nova Scotia: Three decades lost.* (pp. 1–49). Canadian Centre for Policy Alternatives, Nova Scotia Office. Retrieved on 8 October 2024 from https://policyalternatives.ca/sites/default/files/uploads/publications/Nova%20Scotia%20Office/2020/01/2019%20report%20card%20on%20child%20and%20family%20poverty.pdf

Fountas & Pinnell Literacy. (2019). *Home page.* https://www.fountasandpinnell.com/

Freire, P. (1985). Reading the world and reading the word: An interview with Paulo Freire. *Language Arts, 62*(1), 15–21.

Frontier College. (2022). *President and chief executive officer.* https://www.frontiercollege.ca/Get-Involved/Job-Opportunities/Current-Positions/President

Gee, J. (1996). *Social linguistics and literacies: Ideology in discourses.* Routledge.

Greene, M. (1995). *Releasing the imagination.* John Wiley & Sons.

Hall, L., Dell, C. A., Fornssier, B., Hopkins, C., Mushquash, C., & Rowan, M. (2015). Research as cultural renewal: Applying two-eyed seeing in a research project about cultural interventions in First Nations addictions treatment. *International Indigenous Policy Journal, 6*(2), 1–15.

Hollingsworth, S. (1994). *Teacher research and urban literacy education: Lessons and conversations in a feminist key.* Teachers College Press.

[doi] Huber, J., Caine, V., Huber, M., & Steeves, M. (2013). Narrative inquiry as andragogy in education: The extraordinary potential of living, telling, retelling, and reliving stories of experience. *Review of Research in Education, 37,* 212–242.

Indigenous Corporate Training. (2022). *Eight First Nation reserve facts.* Retrieved on 8 October 2024 from https://www.ictinc.ca/blog/8-first-nation-reserve-faqs

[doi] Jack-Malik, S. (2012). *Literacies and three women's on-going stories to shift identities: A narrative inquiry.*

[doi] Jack-Malik, S., & Kuhnke, J.L. (2020). Narrative inquiry as relational research methodology and andragogy: Adult literacies, identities and identify shifting. *Language and Literacy, 22*(2), 43–63.

Josselson, R. (2007). The ethical attitude in narrative research: Principles and practicalities. In J.D. Clandinin (Ed.), *Narrative inquiry,* (pp. 527–566). Sage.

Knight, S.D. (2009). The power of student' stories: Narrative inquiry in English education. *Journal of Language and Literacy Education* [Online], 5(1), 45–58.

Kovach, M. (2009). *Indigenous methodologies: Characteristics, conversations, and contexts.* University of Toronto Press.

[doi] Ladson-Billings, G. (1995). Toward a theory of culturally relevant pedagogy. *American Educational Research Journal, 32*(3), 465–491. Retrieved on 8 October 2024 from http://lmcreadinglist.pbworks.com/f/Ladson-Billings.

[doi] Lessard, S., Caine, V., & Clandinin, D.J. (2015). A narrative inquiry into familial and school curriculum making: Attending to multiple worlds of Aboriginal youth and families. *Journal of Youth Studies, 18*(2), 197–214.

Lewis, C., Enciso, P., & Moje, E.B. (2007). *Introduction: Reframing sociocultural research on literacy.* Routledge.

Lindemann Nelson, H. (1995). *The patient in the family.* Routledge.

Lindamood, P.C., & Lindamood, P.D. (2011). *The Lindamood phoneme sequencing program for reading, spelling, and speech.* Retrieved on 8 October 2024 from https://lindamoodbell.com/program/lindamood-phoneme-sequencing-program

Lindamood, P.C., & Bell, N. (2022). *Seeing stars program.* Retrieved on 8 October 2024 from https://lindamoodbell.com/program/seeing-stars-program

[doi] Metsala, J.L., David, M.D., & Brown, S. (2017). An examination of reading skills and reading outcomes for youth involved in a crime prevention program. *Reading & Writing Quarterly, 33*(6), 549–562.

Mi'Kmaw Kina'matnewey Member Community. (2021). *Serving Mi'kma'ki.* Retrieved on 8 October 2024 from https://www.kinu.ca/about-us

[doi] Miles, S.B., & Stipek, D. (2006). Contemporaneous and longitudinal associations between social behavior and literacy achievement in a sample of low-income elementary school children. *Child Development, 77*(1), 103–117.

Moats, L.C. (2020 Summer). Teaching reading is rocket science. *American Educator,* 4–9, & 39.

Moats, L.C. (2010). *Speech to print.* Paul Brooks.

Moon, C.H. (2010). *Materials and media in art therapy.* Routledge.

Nova Scotia Government. (2021–2022). 2021–2022 Nova Scotia assessment literacy and mathematics in grade 3. Retrieved on 8 October 2024 from https://plans.ednet.ns.ca/sites /default/files/documents/2021-22-LM3.pdf

Nova Scotia Government. (2017). Nova Scotia provincial literacy strategy (pp. 1–9). Retrieved on 8 October 2024 from https://www.ednet.ns.ca/docs/nsprovincialliteracystrategy.pdf

Nova Scotia Government. (2022, September). *Student assessment policy.* Retrieved on 8 October 2024 from https://www.ednet.ns.ca/docs/studentassessmentpolicyen.pdf

Nova Scotia Government. (2022). *Nova Scotia early childhood development intervention services.* Retrieved on 8 October 2024 from https://www.ednet.ns.ca/earlyyears/families /earlyinterventionprograms.shtml

Park, E., Caine, V., McConnell, D., & Minaker, J. (2016). Ethical tensions and educative spaces in narrative inquiry. *Forum Qualitative Sozialforschung / Forum: Qualitative Social Research, 17*(2), Art. 25, 1–19.

Regan, P. (2010). *Unsettling the settler within.* UBC Press.

Rosiek, J. L. (2018). Afterword: The ethical and politics of narrative inquiry. In J. D. Clandinin, V. Caine, & S. Lessard (Eds.), *The relational ethics of narrative inquiry* (pp. 204–209). Routledge.

Shahid, R., Shoker, M., Chu, L. M. et al. (2022). Impact of low health literacy on patients' health outcomes: a multicenter cohort study. *BMC Health Services Research, 22*(1), 11–48.

Shaywitz, S. E., & Shaywitz, B. A. (2005). Dyslexia (Specific reading disability). *Biological Psychiatry, 57,* 1301–1309.

Shaywitz, S. E., & Shaywitz, B. A. (2008). Paying attention to reading: The neurobiology of reading and dyslexia. *Development and Psychopathology, 20*(4), 1329–1349.

Smith, T. L. (2008). *Decolonizing methodologies.* Zed Books.

Tanaka, M. T. D. (2016). *Learning and teaching together: Weaving Indigenous ways of knowing into education.* UBC Press.

Wilson, S. (2001). What is an indigenous research methodology? *Canadian Journal of Native Education, 25*(2), 1–6.

Coda

CHAPTER 14

Contemporary Applied Linguistics Research
Between reflection and reflexivity

Matthew T. Prior
Arizona State University

In this commentary, I will offer some thoughts on the preceding chapters and their contributions to reflective and reflexive research in Applied Linguistics. We must, of course, first acknowledge that contemporary Applied Linguistics is a multidisciplinary field — no longer confined to linguistics, nor reducible to second (i.e., additional or foreign) language acquisition or English Language Teaching (ELT).[1] I will begin with a brief historical snapshot of developments across the field to locate this volume in relation to ongoing scholarly conversations. I then examine some of the ways reflection and reflexivity have been defined and applied in qualitative inquiry, before concluding with some suggestions for advancing both theory and practice.

> [R]eflexivity includes both acknowledging and critiquing our place and privilege in society and using the stories we tell to break long-held silences on power, relationships, cultural taboos, and forgotten and/or suppressed experiences.
> (Adams, Holman Jones, & Ellis, 2015, p. 103)

Reflections on applied linguistics

When telling the story of Applied Linguistics, scholars often cite the various "turns" said to reflect our evolving concerns and commitments (see also Prior, 2019). This list includes *the social/discursive turn* (Coupland et al., 2001), *the critical turn* (Basturkman & Elder, 2004), *the identity turn* (Block, 2007), *the narrative turn*

---

1. In keeping with preceding chapters, I will use the label *Applied Linguistics* to include English Language Teaching (ELT); however, I ask the reader to keep in mind the scope of contemporary Applied Linguistics extends well beyond language teaching or even English.

https://doi.org/10.1075/rmal.8.14pri

(Pavlenko, 2007), *the affective turn* (Pavlenko, 2013), *the translanguaging turn* (García & Wei, 2014), *the interpretivist turn* (Talmy, 2014), *the dynamic turn* (de Bot, 2015), *the ethical turn* (De Costa, 2016), *the ecological turn* (De Costa & Norton, 2017), and *the bi/multilingual turn* (Ortega, 2017). Although the labels vary, together they reflect applied linguists' interests in investigating and understanding language life in the "real world" — which encompasses, inter alia, individual language learners and users, language in the home or community, language in the classroom or other institutional settings, societal discourses and ideologies, and, increasingly, language in digital spaces.

The influences of these various turns across Applied Linguistics and cognate fields and disciplines reflect the flourishing of qualitative inquiry and discursive-dialogic approaches. We are also witnessing the decentering of conventional and hegemonic "Western" and English-centric views of language and research, the legitimization of feminist, Indigenous, and critical perspectives, the acknowledgment of subjectivities and real-world inequalities, greater attention to the modes of data generation and knowledge production, the pursuit of transdisciplinarity and alternative approaches, and the recognition of the moral imperative to address the social utility (Ortega, 2005; Ushioda, 2020) of our research. Alongside such epistemological and methodological pluralism have come renewed calls for critical reflection and reflexivity, especially in the interrogation of practice, policy, power, and privilege. We may, then, add to our growing list, a *social justice turn* (Ortega, 2017), an *anti-racism* and *decolonizing turn* (Friedrich, 2023; Motha, 2020; Rosa & Flores, 2017), and a *methodological turn* (Byrnes, 2013; Li & Prior, 2022). More recently, applied linguists have heralded the emergence of a *reflexive turn*, [2] which "has caused the grand notions of 'methodological perfection', 'neutral validity', or 'objectivity' in knowledge production to lose some ground" (Consoli & Ganassin, 2023, p. 6).

As an outcome of the convergence of these various developments — mirroring also sociopolitical movements within and outside the academy — language researchers, practitioners, and other knowledge generators and gatekeepers are urged to acknowledge how they perpetuate "epistemological racism" (Kubota, 2019) and analytic violence in their work by privileging some voices and forms of knowledge while ignoring or erasing others. We are becoming conscious of our complicity in the "political-epistemic violence of modernity" (Walsh & Mignolo, 2018, p. 1), including the spaces of our research. As many scholars have observed, "It is not just that applied linguistics research always reflects the cultural and

---

2. However, we can trace various instantiations of a "reflective turn" in education to the 1990s (Schön, 1991) and a "reflexive turn" to anthropology and sociology in the 1970s–80s (e.g., Ashmore, 1989).

political contexts in which it is done, however, but that the knowledge it produces is always part of larger interests" (Pennycook, 2017, p. 139).

Both novices and experts face challenges when navigating what Leung et al. (2004) call the 'epistemic turbulence' of contentious sociopolitical research spaces. But qualitative researchers have strengthened efforts to represent and work through such tensions in our research reports, as we strive for greater transparency and honesty by resisting the urge to produce "neatly packaged (and deliberately sanitized) publications" (Prior, 2017, p. 173). We recognize that "[a]pplied linguistics and educational researchers also often deal with people, which can be the messiest part of real-world research" (McKinley & Rose, 2017, p. 6). It is in this efflorescent space of reflection and reflexivity that this volume is poised to contribute new insights. Individually and collectively, the contributors highlight the power of self-aware, serious, motivated qualitative inquiry to not just study human life through a critical lens but to turn that same analytic gaze upon itself and to see, listen to, and speak back to the real world within and surrounding the stories and spaces of our research.

Four dialogic approaches

The four research approaches represented across this volume are *autoethnography, duoethnography, currere,* and *narrative inquiry.* Despite their respective genealogies, they converge in their dialogic modes of inquiry and their ethnographic, (auto)biographic, and narrative perspectives. Contributions by Bilgen (Chapter 2), Bocanegra-Valle (Chapter 6), and Nik (Chapter 10) showcase the self-reflective capacity of autoethnography by analyzing the researcher's own personal history as a lens to critically evaluate various phenomena and contexts of interest. Currere, as represented by Wang (Chapter 4), Garcia and Masterson (Chapter 8), and Tan and Chang (Chapter 12), is an autoethnographic approach from education that also embodies self-reflection; here, researchers engage in "complicated conversations" with themselves as they reconstruct their past and present educational knowledge and experiences while identifying opportunities for transforming teaching and learning. Extending the tools and perspectives of autoethnography and currere, chapters by Sawyer and Wright (Chapter 3), Lowe (Chapter 7), and Zheng and Lawrence (Chapter 11) describe duoethnography as a distinctive research partnership, where two (or more) researchers engage in collaborative dialogue as they wrestle with the tensions, differences, and contradictions in their respective experiences. Allen, Kim, and Cho (Chapter 5), Okada (Chapter 9), and Jack-Malik and Kuhnke (Chapter 13) round out the volume through their explorations of narrative inquiry, an approach with a long history in Applied Linguistics for investigating practitioner and student identities, experiences, and meaning-making work.

These four approaches are ultimately onto-epistemic projects, as they are concerned with ways of knowing the world and of being known in it. The contributors attend not just to human lived experience, but also to the representation and sense-making of that experience. As both process and product, each approach affords rich insights into individuals' lived and felt experiences and their surrounding social and institutional life-worlds. This dialogic assemblage reminds us that all research, like human life, is storied and re-storied. And each chapter contributes a version of that research story through its selected approach, helping to bring greater clarity to self as both a topic and a site of research. Understanding these approaches as powerful modes of inquiry and writing allows us to appreciate their disruptive, emancipatory, and transformative potential. The contributors invite a renewed exploration of more holistic approaches to investigating and representing experiences, while also promoting an honest and humble engagement with inherent tensions and contradictions. By engaging with these chapters, individually and collectively, other researchers can gain a deeper appreciation of this dialogic work, moving beyond the perception of it as mere autobiographical writing or confessional exercises.

Reflections on reflexivity

Qualitative researchers commonly refer to "reflective" and "reflexive" practice, but the conceptual and practical distinctions between these two terms are often unclear, especially because they are used in overlapping ways. For present purposes, I will collapse their respective genealogies and frame my discussion as *first-order reflexivity* and *second-order reflexivity*.[3] Davies et al.'s (2004) "hall of mirrors" metaphor offers a constructive starting place to contemplate some of the salient characteristics of this dynamic work:

> Standing in front of one mirror, our reflection is caught in another, and that other reflects yet another image in a ceaseless infinite regression….Yet the act of reflexivity creates new thoughts and ideas at the same time as going back over old thoughts and ideas. And is not going back in fact a new process in itself? If reflexivity is a process, a back and forth process, then the act of catching the moment,

3. Here I take inspiration from Kester (2022). For other reviews and treatments of reflective and reflexive practice, I refer readers to various helpful guides (e.g., Consoli & Ganassin, 2023; Etherington, 2004; May & Perry, 2017; McKinley & Rose, 2017; Roulston, 2022; Warriner & Bigelow, 2019).

the doing of the reflexive gaze and of listening with the reflexive ear, must change
the thinking that is being thought. That reflexive process is elusive and exhaust-
ing and often threatens to disrupt the very thing it sets out to observe. Yet it is
necessary for finding both how that constitutive work is done and how it might
(on occasion and perhaps temporarily) be done otherwise.   (p.386)

Davies et al.'s description illustrates many of the possibilities and tensions discussed
throughout this volume: reflection and reflexivity as recursive and multimodal
processes — forward-looking and backward-looking, centering and decentering,
disruptive and generative, cognitive and embodied, simultaneously self- and other-
aware. My aim here is not to provide a definitive understanding of these matters, an
impossible task due to their contingent and emergent nature. However, I hope to
offer some clarity for applied linguists who desire to engage more purposefully with
reflection and reflexivity in their research, publications, and professional training. I
will begin by discussing the various characteristics of first- and second-order reflexivity and how they have been theorized and practiced in qualitative inquiry, giving
special attention to how the contributors to this volume help illuminate and
advance those efforts.

First-order reflexivity

In a good qualitative study, you should write about the biases, values, and experiences you bring to a study as well as how the study may affect participants and
readers.   (Creswell, 2016, p.223)

Reflective research can be understood as a "first-order reflexivity," where researchers
critically examine — or at least acknowledge — how they influence the research and
how the research influences them. Here "reflective" functions as a synonym for
"self-aware," "introspective," and "transparent": a centripetal impetus that pulls the
focus toward the individual researcher, holding them accountable as an active
(co)participant in the research.

Reflection can take many forms, but perhaps the most prominent is the positionality statement,[4] in which researchers disclose their biases, stances, emotions,
beliefs, affiliations, commitments, goals, subjectivities, actions, and other aspects
of their personal and professional identities (e.g., ethnicity, gender, sexuality,
class, (dis)ability, insider/outsider status) and histories that locate them in relation
to their research topics, participants, settings, analyses, and so on. Complicating
such acknowledgements is that our various identities or roles (e.g., researcher,

---

4. Land acknowledgements, preferred pronouns, and DEI (Diversity, Equity, and Inclusion)
statements can also function as de facto positionality statements.

friend, interviewer, confidant, observer, participant, subject, analyst) may shift and blur over the course of the research (see also Allen et al., Chapter 5). What may be relevant at the outset of the study may no longer be as relevant at the end. Our own self-understandings and levels of awareness are always partial and never stable, further complicating self-assessment and self-consistency. I have at times experienced discomfort in reading an author's confessional statement (including my own) and seeing little trace of that professed self-awareness in the rest of the publication. Criticizing shallow forms of reflection, Kenway and McCleod (2004) assert, "many accounts do no more than notice (and often self-indulgently — vanity reflexivity) the autobiography of the researcher" (p. 528). Without consistent, self-critical reflection, we risk falling into "hermeneutic narcissism" (Maton, 2003) and making the positionality statement a pro forma gesture or a "generic conceit" (Prior & Talmy, 2021, p. 3).

But it is a mistake to think of reflection as neutral or "safe." Personal reflection can be an uncomfortable and even "violent act" (Merleau-Ponty, 2002, p. 30). With our positionality statements, for instance, there are inevitably personal and professional risks (e.g., being misunderstood, opening ourselves to criticism and injury to reputation, failing to recognize our own power and privilege, and experiencing discomfort from revisiting painful experiences; see also Bilgen, Chapter 2; Tan & Chang, Chapter 12). Addressing the challenges of autoethnographic research, Edwards (2021) advocates for an "ethic of the self" (p. 3). Because reflection demands self-awareness, it also makes us vulnerable and open to harm. Researchers must therefore navigate the uncomfortable tensions between the *right to speak* and the *right to be heard* — and the various kinds of erasure and silencing that occur (Bilgen, Chapter 2; Bocanegra-Valle, Chapter 6). These risks are especially significant for women and minoritized groups and individuals. With our self-disclosures, there is also the possibility we may unwittingly reveal sensitive aspects of our participants' or colleagues' lives. The decision on how much of ourselves to reveal and account for in our research is challenging, given the limits of self-awareness as well as the foreknowledge that such disclosures will become part of the published, public record. In an earlier publication on narrative research (Prior, 2016), I described these turbulent aspects of reflexivity as "personally uncomfortable and even 'unnatural'...due to a desire to carefully craft a veneer of objectivity and analytical rigor as well as to avoid being accused of emotionalism and overinvolvement" (p. ix). The contributors to the present volume also grapple with these tensions in their reflective practices, while reminding themselves (and us) that qualitative research, especially ethnographic, (auto)biographic, and narrative approaches, requires a rigorous and often uncomfortable process of self-analysis and transparency.

My description of first-order reflexivity has highlighted researchers' self-awareness and transparency concerning their potential influences *on* the research.

It is also productive to consider other factors *reflected by* or *reflected through* our research. For instance, as we become more critically conscious of our various positionalities, we may also do well to consider how our research is *self-reflective* in terms of our personal or professional values: Is this research congruent with who I am or how I wish to be in the world? Does it align with my personal, intellectual, ethical, and sociopolitical commitments? Does this research help advance a more just society? (For other reflective questions, see also Haynes, 2012; Weis & Fine, 2000).

Reflection as first-order reflexivity can also extend beyond the researcher. For instance, we can think of research as *participant reflective*, as we ask how faithfully it represents the voices, realities, and interests of those whom (and alongside whom) we study. Whom do we include in our research and whom do we exclude? Who potentially benefits from this inquiry — and who does not? Does it also strive to represent the individuals, communities, institutions, and other persons and contexts with whom we engage? We should also consider how our research is *reader reflective*. Many of the contributors to this volume emphasize the reader's "active transactional role" (Sawyer & Wright, Chapter 3). How is our research designed to be relevant to the interests, knowledge, and expertise of our audience? Although we cannot fully anticipate how our research will be used (or even misused), Creswell (2016) urges us to remember that "writing has an impact on the reader, who also makes an interpretation of the account and may form an entirely different interpretation than the author or the participants" (p. 224). Can readers see themselves in our research, and how might that support opportunities for naturalistic generalization? Hammersley and Atkinson (2007, p. 202), similarly emphasize the importance of the *text* in the "general process of reflexivity, in that it helps to construct the social phenomena it accounts for" and the need of the researcher to "recognize and understand what textual conventions he or she is using, and what receptions they invite on the part of readers." As this volume's contributors also remind us, researchers have an obligation to pursue ways to make our publications and findings more public-facing, accessible, and relevant to diverse academic *and* non-academic audiences.

Another consideration is how our research is *institutionally reflective*. Does it align with the institutional requirements and best practices (e.g., ethical review board, financial and conflict of interest disclosures), public laws, and the accepted ethics of care of our field/discipline? On a more "macro" level, we may consider the *societally reflective* aspects of our research: Does it represent the society in which we live — or wish to live? That is, if we are to take seriously the social utility of our research, we must ask whether (and how) it engages with and holds up a mirror to the larger sociopolitical environment in which we and our research are embedded. I will expand on this topic later in this chapter.

Second-order reflexivity

So far, I have described reflective research, a first-order reflexivity, as a mode of critical consciousness: a way of seeing and knowing, of positioning oneself and others in relation to the research, and of holding oneself accountable to research participants, to readers, and to the field. In this space of self-interpretation, the researcher is located at the epistemic center. In contrast, *second-order reflexivity* expands the analytic gaze outward, operating as a centrifugal force that decenters the individual researcher (or research team), while it simultaneously embraces and interrogates the various tensions of research and the multilayered contexts (e.g., interpersonal, institutional, societal) that give rise to such tensions. As Kester (2022) writes, "Second-order reflexivity involves reflexivity on the norms of the field more broadly and common taken-for-granted practices" (p. 52). This turns reflexivity back on itself: *reflexivity on reflexivity.* Expanding on this point, Talmy (2014) suggests reflexivity offers a means of evaluating the diverse asymmetries and alternativities of our research: "These *interpretations of the interpretation* can then be considered for their epistemological and ontological assumptions, for what they offer, for what they do not offer, and for points of contact and commonalities as well as divergences and disjunctures between alternative interpretive frames (p. 387, emphasis added). This is perhaps especially salient for research in a constructionist vein, as represented by the chapters of this volume, where reflexivity embodies a hermeneutic (i.e., interpretive) circle — not tracing a single, linear story but weaving back and forth between the individual parts and emerging patterns that form the larger narrative whole (see also Sawyer & Wright, Chapter 3; Wang, Chapter 4).

What I gloss here as "reflexivity," especially "second-order reflexivity," is an exceedingly multidimensional project — potentially circular as it is potently transformative. It finds various points of resonance and tension with other scholarly descriptions of reflexivity and thus deserves a more competent treatment than I can offer here. As a destabilizing force, reflexive practice challenges the epistemic, ontological, and methodological grounds of research. Haynes suggests "reflexivities" may be a more accurate label, and his own taxonomy includes *theoretical reflexivity; methodological reflexivity; ontological reflexivity; emotional reflexivity; cultural, social and political reflexivity*; and *subjective reflexivity*. Bourdieu and Wacquant (1992) refer to "epistemic reflexivity" (p. 46), and Lynch (2000), in his critical review, includes an inventory of no fewer than twenty reflexivities![5] There is certainly no shortage of reflexivities to adopt or to critique.

---

5. In contrast to moral-political versions of reflexivity, another important form is associated with ethnomethodology and conversation analysis, which Lynch espouses, where "*reflexivity* refers to the self-explicating property of ordinary actions" (ten Have, 2004, p. 20). Due to space limitations, I will not address that perspective here.

Second-order reflexivity bears resemblance to Bourdieu's notion of *sociological reflexivity*, which has as "its primary target...not the individual analyst but the social and intellectual unconscious embedded in analytic tools and operations" (Bourdieu & Wacquant, 1992, p. 36). Consequently, "it must be a collective enterprise rather than the burden of the lone academic...and it seeks not to assault but to *buttress the epistemological security* of *sociology*." (p. 36, emphasis in original). Although Bourdieu was concerned at the time with reflexivity as a "sociology of sociology," we can glimpse how this perspective can potentially benefit Applied Linguistics — not by dismantling the field or replacing *objectivities* with *subjectivities*, but with a similar aim to "buttress the epistemological security" of our field while raising the status of the knowledge we generate and ensuring a "domain of linguistic activity that matters in its own right" (Pennycook, 2021, p. 58). For some scholars, this form of reflexivity may be too tame; thus, versions of "radical reflexivity" with more explicit interventionist and restructuring agendas may offer more immediate promise.

Second-order reflexivity also has obvious resonances with the concept of *conscientization* (Freire, 2007), which is more than *individual* consciousness raising or *self*-awareness (i.e., reflection or first-order reflexivity) — or even replacing objectivities with subjectivities. Freire writes,

> [Conscientization] is not and never can be an intellectual or an individualistic effort. Conscientization cannot be arrived at by a psychological, idealist subjectivist road, nor through objectivism....but through the relations of transformation they establish between themselves and the world....in a person's coming face to face with the world and with concrete reality, which is presented as a process of objectification. Any objectification implies a perception which is conditioned by the elements of its own reality.   (pp. 131–132)

Conscientization, like second-order reflexivity, forces us to examine the processes of knowledge creation. It also echoes Bourdieu's perspective that such efforts must be collective rather than individual. In a similar vein, Clegg (1999) draws analogies between "reflection-in-action," a professional and pedagogical tool (see also Schön, 1991; Walsh & Mann, 2017) and feminist "consciousness raising," which employs reflexivity as acts of self-discovery and self-empowerment.

Reflexivity for...what?

As we can see, discovery and transformation are both integral to the reflexive research process. A belief evinced by all the research approaches represented in this volume is that expressing one's own experiences through writing has transformative effects on the individual, their relationships, and, in turn, society. Based on the preceding discussion, we can recognize the emerging landmarks across the terrain of second-order reflexivity: a collective rather than individual project, an effort to make visible the unseen or unconscious, an interrogation of research practices (e.g., modes and means of inquiry and knowledge formation, researcher praxis), a critique of educational institutions (i.e., research as an institution and institutions as objects and subjects of research), and a critique of and transformative engagement with society (i.e., a recognition that reflexivity must be for something beyond itself). It is around their reflexive examinations of *research practices, educational institutions*, and *society* that the contributors to this volume offer some of their most penetrating analyses and methodological contributions. I will consider each of these domains in turn before offering suggestions on how we may further advance this work.

Reflexivity and research practices

As all the contributors to this volume emphasize, reflexivity can help make accountable the typically unseen dimensions of our research approaches, especially the unexamined and unconscious assumptions, the modes of knowledge formation that both shape and are shaped by what have been referred to as *habitus* (Bourdieu & Wacquant, 1992) and *habits of mind* (Young, 2018). An obvious question is whether it is possible to be "reflexive from within," especially in the case of autobiographic and autoethnographic research; however, as Agar (1982) asserts, there is always some potential for reflective (i.e., reflexive) examination — especially in response to our experiences with disruptions:

> Being enmeshed in a tradition does not mean that a portion of it cannot be brought into consciousness and reflectively examined. Conscious reflection occurs when a problem arises, when something goes wrong. The routine flow of traditionally guided daily life is disrupted and consciousness is focused on it. A problem in understanding, in short, occurs with disrupted expectations, an inability of the tradition to make sense of an event.   (p. 781)

But reflexivity need not be motivated only by disruption or discomfort. Wang (Chapter 4) argues that our *everyday experiences* offer us abundant opportunities for self-awareness and transformation as we reflect upon, reconstruct, and learn from those experiences. Indeed, all the volume contributors remind us that our lives — and the stories we tell about them — respond to and embody joy and sadness, encouragement and loss, pleasure and pain. Together, these insights suggest reflexivity applies to a wider, multilayered spectrum of emotional life and must be viewed as an ordinary rather than a special activity (see Sharma, 2021, for an exemplary study).

The contributors also offer their responses to the frequently asked question of *what* and *whose* lived experiences count as "legitimate" topics and sites of research. The (auto)biographic, ethnographic, and narrative approaches represented here unapologetically validate the lived (i.e., spoken, written, and embodied) experiences and stories of all research participants and stakeholders — including the researcher — as authentic data and texts. All four approaches bring into focus people, experiences, ideas, and cultural contexts and artifacts that may otherwise go ignored by other research approaches and left out of our academic publications. These data often take shape not just as narratives or texts but as *counter-narratives* and *counter-texts* that challenge and bend our "commonsense" or taken-for-granted values, beliefs, and practices (see Allen et al., Chapter 5). This expansion of what counts as scholarly data also unlocks a rich multimodal and multisemiotic landscape for various kinds of representation and interpretation, including personal narratives, memories, photos, art, media, images, sounds, and performance (cf. Jack-Malik & Kuhnke, Chapter 13).

This volume thus contributes to a greater reflexive consciousness of our research practices and the preconceived and received views which are part of our professional socialization. All the contributors grapple with the tensions between objectivity and subjectivity and post-positivism and constructionism, especially concerning how they, as researchers and academics, struggle to defend the credibility and rigor of their research. Some readers may find it disconcerting that few of the chapters offer prescribed steps to follow for their selected approach (with the exceptions of 4, 8, and 12 on currere). Instead, the authors offer guidelines or "evolving tenets" (Sawyer & Wright, Chapter 3) to navigate the necessarily emergent processes of biographic and ethnographic inquiry and to analyze and synthesize the stories and insights they generate. In the absence of linear procedures, these chapters invite readers to embrace discomfort and uncertainty, reminding us that malleability is a shared strength of all these approaches. Rather than viewing such tensions and struggles as antagonistic to research, we are encouraged to recognize their power to inspire creativity, reflexivity, resilience, and transformation.

Several of the volume contributors also highlight the power of their dialogic approach to help the researcher uncover and work through emotional, traumatic, and painful events. Bocanegra-Valle (Chapter 6) reports autoethnographic writing can be therapeutic, something that has long been observed by qualitative researchers (e.g., Bochner & Ellis, 2016). Although Jack-Malik and Kuhnke (Chapter 13) did not explicitly address therapeutic benefits of narrative, they noted they found it "scaffolding" for the children and themselves, which facilitated closeness and relational knowing. The links between these four approaches and psychotherapy are unmistakable, especially Jungian psychotherapy in currere (Wang, Chapter 4) and narrative psychology in narrative inquiry (Allen et al., Chapter 5). Narrative and (auto)biographic research and feminist inquiry have long been entwined with psychoanalytic perspectives (Prior, 2016, 2019). However, it is vital to note that most researchers are not professionally trained counselors or psychotherapists. As such, they bear a profound ethical responsibility to avoid any potential confusion between acknowledging "therapeutic" language or outcomes and actually engaging in the practice of "therapy."

Reflexivity and educational institutions

Another target of reflexive practice is our educational institutions. For most of the contributors to this volume, this includes the global behemoth that is English Language Teaching (ELT). Three of the original studies in Section 3 show the powerful potential of their research approaches to make visible the structural realities and inequalities in our classrooms and educational institutions from the perspectives of *all* stakeholders. Duoethnography provided critical tools for Zheng and Lawrence (Chapter 11) to examine how monolingualist and native-speakerist ideologies shaped their professional identities and practices in subtle, but profound ways. Similarly, currere enabled Tan and Chang (Chapter 12) to interrogate their educational histories, allowing them to transform their teaching practices toward critical pedagogy. Jack-Malik and Kuhnke's study (Chapter 13), offers a rare glimpse into ways to mobilize narrative inquiry to support culturally relevant reading intervention for Indigenous children in Canada. Each chapter, through its distinct lens, illustrates the capacity of reflexivity to open up exciting opportunities for learning from teachers' and students' personal histories and lived experiences. However, as Sawyer and Wright (Chapter 3) point out, these pedagogical possibilities are not just relevant in the classroom but in everyday life — in the silences and in speech, writing, and other communicative texts and interactions. A poignant example of these broader applications is evident in Nik's (Chapter 10) autoethnographic study, where her analysis of her experiences as a migrant in Australia exposes the hegemonic power of English and the societal systems of immigrant othering. This exploration lays bare the often "unseen but felt" mechanisms driving cultural assimilation and shaping identity and language practices.

Even attempts at institutional critique often devolve into blaming individual students and teachers, pressuring them to "be better" or "try harder" through more effective implementation of educational strategies and tools, rather than examining the systemic structures and constraints that shape their actions. Consequently, "success" and "failure" are attributed to individuals' self-awareness and self-efficacy, particularly their beliefs, attitudes, motivations, and practices. While the research approaches represented in this volume can contribute to fostering opportunities for individual awareness and professional development, the contributors demonstrate such narrow efforts — regardless how well intended — are no longer tenable. Benesch and Prior (2023), in their critique of contemporary research on emotion labor in Applied Linguistics and ELT, reject an individualist approach and call for institutional analysis and transformation:

> We argue that emotion labor research would be more meaningful if it avoided universalizing tendencies and instead attended to contexts, identities, and power. Doing so would offer hope to teachers who are often subject to unreasonable curricular mandates and behavioral demands that provoke strong reactions. Taming these does nothing to improve educational institutions and outcomes. We therefore call for researchers to attend to emotion labor as a signal not that teachers are emotionally illiterate, but that conditions might need to be reformed in the name of better teaching and learning experiences and improved emotional health of educational institutions.   (p. 8)

Though focused on emotion labor, the critical reflexive and activist agenda advocated by these authors (both of whom employ narrative and ethnographic approaches in their work) aligns well with the second-order reflexivities the contributors to this volume embody in their research.

Reflexivity and society

Another immediate, and often contentious, area of reflexive practice concerns the critique and transformation of society — especially through understanding and improving the human condition (Allen et al., Chapter 5). Applied Linguistics is a multidisciplinary field with diverse interests and commitments, but its practitioners converge around its central project of addressing language-related issues in the real world. Consoli and Ganassin (2023) thoughtfully articulate this project as fundamentally a "moral commitment" to society:

> Given the engagement of applied linguistics with social needs, changes and issues, we have always been a community of researchers implicated with people irrespective of our onto-epistemological affiliations and methodological preferences. It is perhaps the moral commitment to generate knowledge exchange and

> translate our investigations into "social impact" that in the end serves our society
> beyond academia.   (p. 1)

In line with this moral commitment and accompanying aim to achieve social impact, the contributors to the present volume leverage their scholarly efforts to advance social justice and systemic change through documenting and disseminating the experiences and ideas of individuals and communities that might otherwise remain *un*researched, *un*heard, *un*read, *un*felt, and *un*valued. Ideological critique must also be part of these efforts. Lowe (Chapter 7) calls attention to the fact that some ideologies hinder progressive social change by validating the existing social structure and thus hiding the abuses happening within it. Efforts to bring attention to various kinds of social injustices and inequities help rehumanize our professional practices through the legitimization and representation of real people and analyses of their experiences (cf. Consoli, 2022, on reflexivity and *life capital*). They also help us recognize that ethical, socially embedded research requires collaboration and respect, rather than just focusing on extracting information or consuming personal experience for academic profit.

There is little doubt that, individually and collectively, applied linguists have made great strides toward public engagement and advocacy. And the present volume attests to those advances. However, as with first-order reflexivity, documenting and disseminating the stories and texts of marginalized persons must not be viewed as an end in itself. Li Wei (2023) commends reflexive inquiry but challenges researchers to make their sociopolitical positions "even clearer" and to help "make the voices of the disadvantaged and discriminated heard, to turn our society into a more equitable and more just one" (p. 210). Avineri and Martinez (2021) in their special issue on social justice in Applied Linguistics argue, "acknowledgement of social inequities (through observation, analysis, and critique)" (p. 1043) must eventually be itself transformed toward "cultivating relationships for justice (CRJ)" (p. 1043). Aligning with the contributions to the present volume, Avineri and Martinez call attention to "how our 'go to' philosophies, tools, and approaches may reify racist and colonial ideologies and practices" (p. 1051). As I have described above, research practices and institutions are both important domains to apply reflexive practice. Dialogic approaches are particularly well suited for engaging with experience, for supporting critical listening and sitting with silence, for cultivating solidarity and empathy, for employing participatory and emancipatory approaches, and for recognizing the limitations of traditional academic modes of knowledge-making and knowledge-valuing (Avineri & Martinez, 2021; Consoli & Ganassin, 2023). If Applied Linguistics is to ensure it is more than a "descriptive discipline" (cf. Bygate, 2005), and the commitment to social equity and transformation is indeed part of our commitment to the "real world," then cultivating relationships for justice must be a direct outgrowth of that commitment.

The contributors to this volume impel applied linguists to question the entrenched dogma of scientism and objectivism. Even as they call into question our accepted and often unexamined modes and tools of inquiry, they encourage researchers to take advantage of both conventional and alternative ways of knowing and being known: in the "micro" contexts of our research, in the "meso" contexts of our institutions, and in the "macro" contexts of broader society (cf. Douglas Fir Group, 2016). As we can see from the multilayered, even eclectic, conceptual and applied work represented throughout these chapters, autoethnography, duoethnography, currere, and narrative inquiry offer powerful tools to pursue those ends. But reflexivity is not a panacea for the ills of the world or for the world of research. May and Perry (2017) remind us:

> There may be liberation from self-misunderstanding, but there is a need to combine the politics of personal relations with those of the institutions and systems that rule over us. We may then move from the trance of those forces that exist over and through us, to a place of struggle and ultimately judgement and determination of those forces for the future. We do not move towards absolute truth, but we do move towards better ways of coming to understand ourselves through our relations with others and the social contexts we inhabit.   (p. 193)

Concluding reflections

I conclude this chapter with some further comments on researcher reflection and reflexivity. First, as we recognize the limits of our scholarly knowledge and wisdom, a subtle thread woven throughout the chapters of this volume is the need for humility. Our academic field, like others, continues to emphasize researcher rigor, integrity, and ethical obligations; however, humility has received comparatively little attention. As I have argued elsewhere (Prior, 2017), as a "human science," Applied Linguistics has an obligation to "cultivate a discipline of humility that fosters reflexivity and transparency and is receptive to critique" (p. 179). We urgently need more "unsettling dialogues with humility" (Back, 2007, p. 262). And, as the contributors to this volume point out, we also need more unsettling meetings with silence. Avineri and Martinez (2021) advocate "enacting humility alongside offering expertise — thereby reimagining the critical roles, meaningful relationships, and aspirational relevance of applied linguistics now and into the future" (p. 1052).

A second observation stems from the increasingly celebrated status of narrative, ethnographic, and (auto)biographic approaches, such as those represented in the present volume and elsewhere across the social sciences and the humanities. In a cutting critique of "versions of reflexivity associated with 'radical' epistemologies" (p. 46), Lynch (2000) raises concerns with treating reflexivity as "an epistemological achievement that empowers or critically disables its object of (self-)reference" (p. 46). He reminds us that — as with *narrative, affect, discourse, ideology*, or whatever other concept, topic, or approach we promote — there is a kind of intellectual arrogance in attaching a special virtue to reflexivity. Such an attitude is at odds with the reflexive approaches and practices the contributors and others across the field seek to advance. This is not to say that we should not embrace reflexivity as empowering or transformative; rather, it is to argue against elevating it as a "methodological idol" with a kind of unique status or inherent power of its own.

A related concern is with the wider application of reflexivity. Often curiously absent from our contemporary conversations is how reflexivity may contribute to the broader spectrum of research approaches in Applied Linguistics, especially those representing oftentimes incommensurable paradigmatic perspectives. As I have described in this chapter, reflexive practices are endemic to (or at least compatible with) qualitative research. However, how might reflexivity be incorporated effectively into various quantitative and mixed-methods studies? Does reflexivity have a place in *all* research, or must it remain within the purview of only a handful of approaches? Talmy (2014) expresses optimism, as he suggests an interpretivist turn (or at least a reflexive turn) "grounded in…a thoroughgoing reflexivity is one way…that a generative, shared understanding across paradigms…might be attempted" (p. 388). There are also some encouraging signs of efforts to bring reflexivity into quantitative research in the social sciences (e.g., Jamieson, Govaart, Pownall, 2023), and the field of Applied Linguistics is long overdue for such attention.

In conclusion, this volume serves as a testament to the power of reflexivity to enrich our research practices and contribute to positive social change, ultimately fostering a more inclusive and equitable world. These contributions remind us that ours is a responsive, collaborative, creative, ethical, accountable, and values-driven field: an Applied Linguistics *in* and *for* the real world. Therefore, it is imperative that we, as members of this community, continue to explore and apply reflexivity in our research endeavors, ensuring that our efforts remain aligned with addressing the evolving linguistic realities and needs of society.

References

Adams, T. E., Holman Jones, S. L., & Ellis, C. (2015). *Autoethnography*. Oxford University Press.

 Agar, M. (1982). Toward an ethnographic language. *American Anthropologist, 84*(4), 779–795.

Ashmore, M. (1989). *The reflexive thesis: Wrighting sociology of scientific knowledge.* The University of Chicago Press.

doi Avineri, N., & Martinez, D.C. (2021). Applied linguists cultivating relationships for justice: An aspirational call to action. *Applied Linguistics, 42*(6), 1043–1054.

Back, L. (2007). Politics, research and understanding. In C. Seale, G. Gobo, J.F. Gubrium, & D. Silverman (Eds.), *Qualitative research practice* (pp. 249–264). Sage.

doi Basturkmen, H., & Elder, C. (2004). The practice of LSP. In A. Davies & C. Elder (Eds.). *The handbook of applied linguistics* (pp. 672–694). Blackwell.

doi Benesch, S., & Prior, M.T. (2023). Rescuing "emotion labor" from (and for) language teacher emotion research. *System, 113,* 1–10.

doi Block, D. (2007). The rise of identity in SLA research, post Firth and Wagner (1997). *The Modern Language Journal, 91* [Focus issue], 863–876.

doi Bochner, A.P., & Ellis, C. (2016). *Evocative autoethnography: Writing lives and telling stories.* Routledge.

Bourdieu, P., & Wacquant, L.J.D. (1992). *An invitation to reflexive sociology.* Polity Press.

doi Bygate, M. (2005). Applied linguistics: A pragmatic discipline, a generic discipline? *Applied Linguistics, 26*(4), 568–581.

doi Byrnes, H. (2013). Notes from the editor. *Modern Language Journal, 97,* 825–827.

doi Clegg, S. (1999). Professional education, reflective practice and feminism. *International Journal of Inclusive Education, 3*(2), 167–179.

doi Consoli, S. (2022). Life capital: An epistemic and methodological lens for TESOL research. *TESOL Quarterly, 56*(4), 1397–1409.

Consoli, S., & Ganassin, S. (2023). *Reflexivity in applied linguistics: Opportunities, challenges, and suggestions.* Routledge.

Coupland, N., Sarangi, S., & Candlin, C. (Eds.). (2001). *Sociolinguistics and social theory.* Pearson.

Creswell, J.W. (2016). *30 essential skills for the qualitative researcher.* Sage.

doi Davies, B., Browne, G., Honan, E., Laws, C., Mueller-Rochstroh, Bendix Petersen, E. (2004). The ambivalent practices of reflexivity. *Qualitative Inquiry, 10*(3), 360–389.

doi de Bot, K. (2015). *A history of applied linguistics: From 1980 to the present.* Routledge.

De Costa, P.I. (Ed.). (2016). *Ethics in applied linguistics research: Language researcher narratives.* Routledge.

doi De Costa, P.I., & Norton, B. (2017). Introduction: Identity, transdisciplinarity, and the good language teacher. *The Modern Language Journal, 101*(Supplement), 3–14.

doi Douglas Fir Group. (2016). A transdisciplinary framework for SLA in a multilingual world. *Modern Language Journal, 100* (Supplement), 19–47.

doi Edwards, J. (2021). Ethical autoethnography: Is it possible? *International Journal of Qualitative Methods, 20,* 1–7.

Etherington, K. (2004). *Becoming a reflexive researcher.* Jessica Kingsley.

Freire, P. (2007). *Education for critical consciousness.* Continuum.

Friedrich, P. (Ed.). (2023). *The anti-racism linguist: A book of readings.* Multilingual Matters.

doi García, O., Wei, L. (2014). *Translanguaging: Language, bilingualism and education.* Palgrave Pivot.

Hammersley, M., & Atkinson, P. (2007). *Ethnography: Principles in practice* (3rd ed.). Routledge.

Have, P. ten. (2004). *Understanding qualitative research and ethnomethodology.* Sage.

Haynes, K. (2012). Reflexivity in qualitative research. In C. Cassell, & G. Symon (Eds.), *The practice of qualitative organizational research: Core methods and current challenges* (pp. 72–89). Sage.

Jamieson, M. K., Govaart, G. H., & Pownall, M. (2023). Reflexivity in quantitative research: A rationale and beginner's guide. *Social and Personality Psychology Compass, 17*(4).

Kenway, J., & McLeod, J. (2004). Bourdieu's reflexive sociology and 'spaces of points of view': whose reflexivity, which perspective? *British Journal of Sociology of Education, 25*(4), 525–544.

Kester, K. (2022). Global citizenship education and peace education: Toward a postcritical praxis. *Educational philosophy and theory, 55*(1), 45–56.

Kubota, R. (2019). Confronting epistemological racism, decolonizing scholarly knowledge: Race and gender in applied linguistics. *Applied Linguistics, 41*(5), 712–732.

Leung, C., Harris, R., & Rampton, B. (2004). Living with inelegance in qualitative research, in B. Norton & K. Toohey (Eds.), *Critical pedagogies and language learning* (pp. 242–267). Cambridge University Press.

Li, S., & Prior, M. T. (2022). Research methods in applied linguistics: A methodological imperative. *Research Methods in Applied Linguistics, 1*(1), 1–6.

Lynch, M. (2000). Against reflexivity as an academic virtue and source of privileged knowledge. *Theory, Culture & Society, 17*(3), 26–54.

Maton, K. (2003). Reflexivity, relationism & research: Pierre Bourdieu and the epistemic conditions of social scientific knowledge, *Space & Culture, 6,* 52–65.

May, T., & Perry, B. (2017). *Reflexivity: The essential guide.* Sage.

McKinley, J. & Rose, H. (Eds.) (2017). *Doing research in applied linguistics: Realities, dilemmas, and solutions.* Routledge.

Merleau-Ponty, M. (2002). *Phenomenology of perception.* Routledge.

Motha, S. (2020). Is an antiracist and decolonizing applied linguistics possible? *Annual Review of Applied Linguistics, 40,* 128–133.

Ortega, L. (2005). For what and for whom is our research? The ethical as transformative lens in instructed SLA. *Modern Language Journal, 89,* 427–443.

Ortega, L. (2017). New CALL-SLA research interfaces for the 21st century: Towards equitable multilingualism. *Calico Journal, 34*(3), 285–316.

Pavlenko, A. (2007). Autobiographic narratives as data in applied linguistics. *Applied Linguistics, 28*(2), 163–188.

Pavlenko, A. (2013). The affective turn in SLA: From 'affective factors' to 'language desire' and 'commodification of affect.' In D. Gabrys-Barker & J. Bielska (Eds.), *The affective dimension in second language acquisition* (pp. 3–28). Multilingual Matters.

Pennycook, A. (2017). *The cultural politics of English as an international language.* Taylor & Francis.

Pennycook, A. (2021). *Critical applied linguistics: A critical re-introduction* (2nd ed.). Routledge.

Prior, M. T. (2019). Elephants in the room: An "affective turn," or just feeling our way? *The Modern Language Journal, 103*, 517–527.

Prior, M. T. (2017). Managing researcher dilemmas in narrative interview data and analysis. In J. McKinley & H. Rose (Eds.), *Doing research in applied linguistics: Realities, dilemmas, and solutions* (pp. 172–181). Routledge.

Prior, M. T. (2016). *Emotion and discourse in L2 narrative research.* Multilingual Matters.

Prior, M. T., & Talmy, S. (2021). A discursive constructionist approach to narrative in language teaching and learning research. *System, 102*, 1–11.

Rosa, J., & Flores, N. (2017). Unsettling race and language: Toward a raciolinguistic perspective. *Language in Society, 46*, 621–647.

Roulston, K. (2022). *Interviewing: A guide to theory and practice.* Sage.

Schön, D. A. (1991). *The reflective practitioner: How professionals think in action.* Ashgate.

Sharma, B. K. (2021). Reflexivity in applied linguistics research in the tourism workplace. *Applied Linguistics, 42*(2), 230–251.

Talmy, S. (2014). Toward an interpretivist turn in L2 Studies: Reflexivity, the cognitive/social divide, and beyond. *Studies in Second Language Acquisition, 36*, 36–43.

Ushioda, E. (2020). *Language learning motivation: An ethical agenda for research.* Oxford University Press.

Walsh, S., & Mann, S. (2017). *Reflective practice in English language teaching: Research-based principles and practices.* Taylor & Francis.

Walsh, W. D., & Mignolo, C. E. (2018). *On decoloniality: Concepts, analytics, and praxis.* Duke University Press.

Warriner, D., & Bigelow, M. (2019). *Critical reflections on research methods: Power and equity in complex multilingual contexts.* Multilingual Matters.

Wei, L. (2023). Afterword. Journey into applied linguistics: Reflecting on reflexivity and positionality. In S. Consoli & S. Ganassin (Eds.), *Reflexivity in applied linguistics: Opportunities, challenges, and suggestions* (pp. 207–210). Routledge.

Weis, L., & Fine, M. (2000). *Speed bumps: A student-friendly guide to qualitative research.* Teachers College Press.

Young, R. (2018). Habits of mind: How do we know what we know? In A. Phakiti, P. De Costa, L. Plonsky, & S. Starfield (Eds.), *The Palgrave handbook of applied linguistics research methodology* (pp. 31–53). Palgrave Macmillan.

Author index

Subject index

Additionally, the study explores the participants' eye movements at two different points during the treatment, aiming to identify potential changes in attention among participants in the two conditions.

The next two chapters involve teenagers as participants. In Chapter 4, "Attention allocation in (L1) subtitled and (L2) captioned video viewing: Effects of prior vocabulary instruction on input processing and comprehension", by Geòrgia Pujadas and Eva Puimège, eye-tracking data were used to investigate the attention allocation of elementary-level participants during video viewing with subtitles and captions. Specifically, the study examines variations in attention allocation based on the instructional condition (with or without pre-viewing instruction on target vocabulary) and the language displayed on the screen (L2-English or L1-Spanish). Another equally significant aspect of the study is whether the presence of a pre-viewing vocabulary-focused task influences participants' comprehension, leading to trade-off effects.

Chapter 5, entitled "Maximizing L2 learning from captioned TV viewing: Repeated viewing and Language Reactor", authored by Margarita Popova and Imma Miralpeix, compares two viewing methods aimed at enhancing target language learning: repeated viewing and the use of the Language Reactor extension (with individually regulated tools). Employing a mixed-method design, the researchers analyzed the comprehension of video content and vocabulary learning among upper-intermediate teenagers with Russian as their first language and English as the target language. The qualitative analysis of participants' post-viewing questionnaire responses uncovers differences in participants' perceptions of the viewing experience and the learning potential of each viewing method.

In the last four chapters, the participants are young adults. Chapter 6, titled "Multimodal input and L2 pragmatics: An eye-tracking study", by Júlia Barón, M. Luz Celaya and Alicia Martínez-Flor, investigates the potential effectiveness of using captioned videos to help learners acquire target language pragmatics, specifically English requests. The study employed a multiple-choice discourse completion test at both pre-test and post-test stages to examine the effects of the viewing experience on their pragmatic knowledge. Participants' eye movements were observed using eye-tracking technology to explore the elements that attracted their attention in both captioned and uncaptioned videos. Another methodological contribution of the study is the use of retrospective interviews to capture participants' perceptions of the viewing experience in relation to the target pragmatic elements.

Chapter 7, entitled "Contrastive input enhancement in captioned video for L2 pronunciation learning", by Joan C. Mora and Jonás Fouz-González, investigates how novel types of input enhancement on captions draw learners' attention to a difficult vowel contrast in the target language. The participants were university students with Spanish and Catalan as their first languages and English as the target language. The researchers employed two different methods: using two different colors for each sound in one method and using phonetic symbols instead of standard orthography to highlight the contrasted sounds in the other. This study is one of the few focusing on pronunciation learning, specifically perceptual sensitivity to L2 sounds, through audiovisual input, and it opens new ground in this line of research.

In Chapter 8, titled "The role of language aptitude in learning L2 constructions from captioned and uncaptioned audiovisual input", Anastasia Pattemore, M. del Mar Suárez, Maribel Montero Perez and Carmen Muñoz delve into two studies exploring the influence of language learning aptitude, specifically grammatical sensitivity and inference ability as measured by LLAMA F, on L2 grammar acquisition. These studies vary in participants' native languages (Spanish and Catalan in one, Flemish in the other) and target languages (English in one, Spanish in the other), as well as in target grammatical constructions. In this context, the researchers aimed to find out whether language learning aptitude consistently plays a significant role in relation to captioned and uncaptioned viewing.

In Chapter 9, entitled "Vocabulary learning from audiovisual input at first exposure in young adult novice learners", Imma Miralpeix, Ferran Gesa and M. del Mar Suárez explore the extent to which completely novice learners can acquire vocabulary when encountering a new language through multimodal input. The research involved presenting participants with a brief advertisement featuring audio in a language they were familiar with (English) and subtitles in an entirely unfamiliar language they were encountering for the first time (Polish). Furthermore, the study investigates the learning strategies employed by viewers in their attempt to absorb as much as possible from the new language. The study is one of the only available assessing how we try to break into a new language from subtitled audiovisual material.

Finally, in Chapter 10, with the title of "More pieces in the puzzle about language learning through audiovisual input" Carmen Muñoz and Imma Miralpeix bring together findings from the studies presented in this volume and place them within the context of prior research on audiovisual input, particularly within the broader framework of the SUBTiLL project. Selected relevant findings are discussed under three general themes: captioned viewing, learning outcomes across various language dimensions, and individual differences. The chapter ends with a discussion that proposes future research directions.

The book is intended for researchers, graduate students, foreign language teachers, curriculum developers, technology-oriented educators, and anyone excited about the learning potential of audiovisual input and the new horizons that it brings to language teaching and learning.

Language learning from watching cartoons in the primary EFL classroom

Montserrat Casulleras & Imma Miralpeix
Universitat de Barcelona

This chapter presents the results of a study in which two groups of primary school English as a Foreign Language (EFL) learners watched one episode a week of the animated TV series *Curious George* – with L1 subtitles or L2 subtitles – over a period of five months. These beginner students were tested on comprehension and vocabulary recognition immediately after watching each episode and in two special episodes without subtitles (middle and end of treatment). Although significant differences were not always present, the L1-subtitles group tended to score higher in comprehension, and the L2-subtitles group in L2 word recognition. The findings also emphasize the central role of language aptitude and vocabulary size for L2 learning through audiovisual materials in instructional settings.

1. Introduction

The growing availability of subtitled TV programs and films through various platforms such as online streaming and video-on-demand has led to their increased use in second language (L2) acquisition. Using videos in educational settings can foster a dynamic environment, facilitating L2 learning in a manner akin to informal settings (Matielo et al., 2015; Sherman, 2003). Moreover, multimedia resources can enhance vocabulary learning in classrooms (as suggested in, for instance, Danan, 2004; Vanderplank, 2010 or Montero Perez et al., 2013), and encourage students to continue engaging with L2 video content at home (Kuppens, 2010).

While audiovisual materials may sometimes pose challenges for learners with low proficiency, the inclusion of subtitles can serve as a valuable aid in supporting their comprehension of the video narrative. Subtitles serve to complement auditory input (sound), thereby enhancing L2 reading and listening comprehension abilities (Montero Perez, 2022). They can also help L2 learners in acquiring vocabulary (e.g., Sydorenko, 2010; Winke et al., 2010).

https://doi.org/10.1075/lllt.61.01cas

Despite the potential benefits of audiovisual input, there has been limited focus on young learners (up to the age of 12) within this research domain. Studies examining young, low-proficiency L2 learners who engage with multiple episodes of the same television series are rare (with a few exceptions, e.g., Alexiou, 2015; Avello & Muñoz, 2023; Gesa & Miralpeix, 2023), and the existing research typically features one-off studies (e.g., Galimberti & Miralpeix, 2018) rather than comprehensive longitudinal investigations. Consequently, there is an urgent need for research on extensive viewing experiences for young learners to determine the impact of consistent exposure to multimodal input on their L2 acquisition (see also Matielo et al., 2015). Additionally, it is important to understand how individual differences and proficiency level may be related to young learners' language development.

2.   Literature review

Receiving information through multiple modes seems to be advantageous for language learning. Paivio's Dual Coding Theory (1986) posits that combining verbal information with images boosts learning more effectively than verbal information alone. Mayer's Multimedia Learning Theory (2005) underscores the importance of integrating diverse media elements – such as text, images, audio, or video – to enhance learning effectiveness, advocating for their cohesive presentation rather than separate deployment. Sweller's Cognitive Load Theory (1994) maintains that effective learning can be facilitated by instructional designs that maximize the efficiency of cognitive resources.

These insights are especially relevant in exploring the role of multimodal input in L2 acquisition among young learners. Children often enjoy watching TV, which offers both visual and verbal stimuli concurrently. Conversely, TV content in its original language (children's L2) may present too great a challenge for them, leading to inquiries about how subtitles in either the first language (L1) or in the L2 might aid in improving understanding and L2 learning.

2.1   L1/L2 subtitles for content comprehension

Studies indicate that the most beneficial type of subtitles for L2 learners may depend on their proficiency levels (Danan, 2004; d'Ydewalle & Pavakanun, 1995; Vanderplank, 2010, 2016b). According to Danan (2004), for example, L1 subtitles can act as an effective educational tool. It has been established that reading subtitles in the L1 does not interfere with the processing of the spoken language in the soundtrack, irrespective of the viewers' proficiency in the spoken language or their experience with subtitling (d'Ydewalle & Gielen, 1992; Pavakanun &

d'Ydewalle, 1992). Markham and Peter (2003) suggest that L1 subtitles might be more beneficial for beginners, while L2 subtitles (also called 'captions') could be more effective for learners at higher levels of language proficiency.

Research involving beginner or intermediate learners often concentrates on adults or teenagers, especially the former. Most studies have shown benefits of using subtitles (either in L1 or L2) for comprehension compared to not using sub-titles at all: for instance, Baltova (1999) and Vulchanova et al. (2015) found this to be true for teenagers, while Birulés-Muntané and Soto-Faraco (2016) observed similar benefits in adult learners. Typically, L1 subtitles are more conducive to understanding than L2 subtitles, as seen in the work of Bravo (2008) and Pujadas and Muñoz (2020) with teenagers, and Markham et al. (2001) with adults. Never-theless, there have been reports favouring L2 subtitles among adult intermediate learners, such as Hayati & Mohmedi (2011) and Frumuselu et al. (2015). Other studies have reported non-significant differences in comprehension between con-ditions. For instance, Basaran and Köse (2012) found no significant differences in 14-year-old intermediate learners when watching a 19-minute episode of 'Harry Potter' with L1 subtitles, L2 subtitles, or without subtitles. Similarly, the study by Galimberti and Miralpeix (2018) did not reveal significant differences either among three groups of Grade 6 EFL learners (12-year-olds) who viewed an episode of 'The Suite Life of Zack and Cody' with either L1 subtitles, L2 subtitles, or no subtitles at all. So far, to our knowledge, this is the only study comparing subtitle types in primary school learners.

Although authentic videos may be considered overly challenging for this pop-ulation due to their poor proficiency (e.g., Zanon, 2007), cartoons may offer a viable alternative. Typically aimed at younger audiences, cartoons demand less cognitive effort compared to other television genres and can be particularly appropriate for children beginning to learn a foreign language (FL) (Bahrani & Sim, 2012; Bahrani & Soltani, 2011). While it has been posited that comprehen-sion of children's programs requires knowledge of at least 2,000 words (Nation, 2006), Webb and Rodgers (2009) contend that cartoons may require a lower lexi-cal threshold. Nonetheless, there have been scant longitudinal studies focusing on young low-proficiency learners watching cartoons (e.g., Avello & Muñoz, 2023), and there is a lack of research comparing the effects of L1 versus L2 subtitle use.

2.2   L1/L2 subtitles for vocabulary learning

Numerous studies indicate that L1 subtitles can be effective for vocabulary acqui-sition (e.g., Koolstra & Beentjes, 1999; d'Ydewalle & Van de Poel, 1999). The effectiveness of L1 subtitles may be partly attributed to the cognitive engagement involved in translation: as translation facilitates the link of two verbal systems (L1 and L2), students establish more paths for retrieval and can benefit from visual traces as well as from two distinct sets of verbal traces (Danan, 1992; according to Paivio's bilingual Dual Coding Theory, 1986). L2 subtitles, on the other hand, have been found to assist learners in parsing the speech stream and identifying individual words (e.g., Charles & Trenkic, 2015; Danan, 2004). Furthermore, eye-tracking studies provide evidence that L2 subtitles draw learners' attention to the on-screen text more effectively (Montero Perez et al., 2015; Winke et al., 2013), aiding in word recognition.

In studies comparing the effectiveness of L1 versus L2 subtitles for vocabulary acquisition in adults, Stewart and Pertusa (2004) observed no notable disparities in word-form recognition tests between the two conditions among intermediate learners. Frumuselu et al. (2015) reported that learners watching TV series with L2 subtitles scored significantly higher in word-form recognition tests compared to those with L1 subtitles, spanning various proficiency levels from beginner to advanced. Peters et al. (2016) examined intermediate secondary school learners and proposed that L2 subtitles might be more advantageous for learning the formal aspects of word knowledge. However, this advantage depended on the learners' existing vocabulary size. Among lower proficiency learners, they reported no significant distinctions in written form recognition and recall or in meaning recall between those using L1 and L2 subtitles.

Instances of studies with children are rare and the few that exist are one-off studies. Neuman and Koskinen (1992) examined word-form and meaning recognition in beginner learners after viewing segments of a science program, finding that L2 subtitles were more beneficial compared to three other conditions that did not include L1 subtitles (specifically: without subtitles, listening combined with reading, and reading only). In the research by Koolstra and Beentjes (1999) and Lekkai (2014), beginner children exposed to videos with L1 subtitles achieved significantly higher vocabulary scores than their counterparts who viewed the videos without subtitles; however, these studies did not include an L2 subtitles condition for comparison. Moreover, the study by Galimberti and Miralpeix (2018) concluded that L2 subtitles contributed to notably better overall vocabulary recall than L1 subtitles, though the advantage of L2 subtitles over no subtitles was not significant. They also noted no differences among the three conditions in terms of meaning recognition.

2.3   Learner factors in learning from viewing

Apart from input factors, such as the type of subtitles used, learner factors should also be considered when learning an L2. Learners possess unique characteristics, traits, abilities, and preferences, which can influence their language acquisition process and outcomes. For example, a learner's linguistic aptitude has been acknowledged as a variable that can affect learning through audiovisual input. Additionally, differences in learners' L2 proficiency (such as the size of L2 vocabularies) are particularly relevant in studies involving young EFL learners, who typically have a limited command of the L2.

Language aptitude has been defined as a set of cognitive abilities that are "predictive of how well, relative to other individuals, an individual can learn a foreign language in a given amount of time and under given conditions" (Carroll & Sapon, 2002, p. 23). While aptitude has been recognized as a significant influence in L2 acquisition (e.g., Muñoz, 2010; Skehan, 1989), with correlations to the pace of learning for beginners (e.g., Doughty, 2019), investigations into its impact on learning from genuine multimodal input are scarce (see Chapter 8, this volume). Suárez and Gesa (2019), in their longitudinal study on vocabulary learning from viewing, observed an effect of aptitude on meaning recall in intermediate-level high school learners, yet this was not the case for adult university students. Teng (2022), however, reported aptitude effects in incidental vocabulary acquisition from viewing in adult intermediate-level university learners. Therefore, the potential role of aptitude in extensive viewing among young learners is an area that warrants further exploration.

Vocabulary size has been shown to be a good indicator of L2 proficiency (Miralpeix & Muñoz, 2018; Staehr, 2008) and it has also been found to predict learning gains through multimodal input (e.g., Montero Perez et al., 2014; Peters et al., 2016). For example, Peters and Webb (2018) observed that prior vocabulary knowledge had an influence on the vocabulary test results of university EFL learners after watching an hour-long documentary. This effect was found irrespective of the aspect of knowledge tested (meaning recall or meaning recognition). Moreover, Pujadas and Muñoz (2020), comparing L1 vs. L2 subtitles in extensive viewing, found that the L2 vocabulary size of the participants (13–14-year-olds with low proficiency levels) influenced comprehension in the L2 condition.

Finally, a proficiency variable warranting exploration is reading speed (Vanderplank, 2016a). Several experiments conducted with subtitled audiovisual materials have suggested that reading on-screen text is an automatic behaviour (d'Ydewalle & Gielen, 1992; Pavakanun & d'Ydewalle, 1992), and eye-tracking studies have demonstrated that the presence of images alongside text does not necessarily distract young learners from reading (d'Ydewalle & Bruycker, 2007; Tragant & Pellicer-Sánchez, 2019). However, beginner learners often lack reading fluency and may read in a slower and less automatic manner, limiting their ability to fully use L2 subtitles, apart from other limitations stemming from insufficient vocabulary knowledge (Muñoz, 2017). While Muñoz et al. (2022) found no significant effects of reading speed on vocabulary acquisition in adult learners from captioned TV viewing, it remains plausible that such effects may manifest more prominently in beginner younger learners.

In summary, engaging in L2 video viewing can pose challenges for young learners with low L2 proficiency levels, and cartoons may offer an entry point for them, but further research with this young population is needed (see Chapters 2 and 3, this volume). Numerous empirical questions merit further exploration, such as the impact of L1 or L2 subtitles on comprehension and vocabulary acquisition, as well as the potential influence of variables like aptitude, L2 vocabulary size, or reading speed on their learning outcomes. Given that results from one-off studies may not be generalizable, as results may be contingent on the chosen L2 video, there is also a pressing need for longitudinal research including multiple videos to provide deeper insights into the efficacy of this approach for young beginner EFL learners.

3.   Research questions

The present study aims at answering the following research questions in relation to young low-proficiency EFL learners:

RQ1.   Is there any difference between extensive viewing of animated TV series subtitled either in the L1 or in the L2 over time
   1a.   in content comprehension?
   1b.   in written word-form recognition of known and new vocabulary?

RQ2.   Are content comprehension and written word-form recognition scores related to linguistic aptitude and/or proficiency variables (i.e., L2 vocabulary size and L1/L2 reading speed)?

4.   Methodology

4.1   Participants

Participants in the study were 92 Spanish/Catalan bilingual young EFL learners, aged between 11 and 12 years ($M = 11.55$), enrolled in Grades 5 (G5) and 6 (G6) at a semi-private primary school in Catalonia, Spain. None of the participants had previously attended extracurricular English classes. For the study's purposes, the students were divided into two groups, each including a G5 class and a G6 class (no significant differences were observed between these two grades in terms of L2 vocabulary size, as measured by the Vocabulary Size Test – Nation & Beglar,

2007): Grade 5 (M=11.93, SD=5.13); Grade 6 (M=12.51, SD=3.93); $t(90)$=.608, p=.545. One group watched the TV series *Curious George* with Spanish subtitles (L1S, n=47), while the other group watched it with English subtitles (L2S, n=45). The gender distribution was balanced, with 23 females and 24 males in the L1S group and 25 females and 20 males in the L2S group. Although the initial sample consisted of 99 students, only those who had attended at least 18 out of the 20 sessions were included in the final sample.

4.2   Instruments

4.2.1   *TV series*

The TV series chosen for this study was *Curious George*, a North American animated show centered around a curious monkey who navigates various challenges either independently or with the assistance of 'The Man with the Yellow Hat', also known as 'Ted'. *Curious George* was selected for its suitability for young learners, offering richer dialogue compared to other cartoons, and because it was necessary for the students watching the series to comprehend the dialogue to follow the storyline (images alone were insufficient). The episodes feature recurring characters and similar scenarios, facilitating student engagement and comprehension. Participants confirmed that they had not previously watched the series.

The 20 episodes chosen for the treatment, with an average duration of 12 minutes and 26 seconds, were deemed appropriate for the participants' age and proficiency level. The lexical complexity of the episodes was evaluated using VocabProfile v.2 (Cobb, n.d), and approximately 95% coverage was achieved at the 2k level, which was considered suitable for the study's participants.

4.2.2   *Comprehension tests*

There were 20 comprehension tests included in the treatment, one per episode, which consisted of three exercises each: a True/False (T/F) exercise comprising five statements, a Multiple Choice (MC) exercise with five questions, and an item sequencing task involving four events to be ordered according to their occurrence in the episode (see Appendix). These tests were administered immediately after the viewing to assess the participants' understanding of the video content. To ensure that language proficiency did not impede participants' comprehension of the questions, the tests were administered in Spanish to both groups. Content comprehension was evaluated following Rodgers (2013), encompassing general, detailed, and inferential comprehension. One point was awarded for each item, and the maximum achievable score on each test was 14 (see Appendix).

4.2.3 *Vocabulary tests*

The 20 vocabulary tests (one per episode) aimed at assessing participants' ability to recognize written word forms of vocabulary encountered in the videos. Participants were provided with a list of words (as in the Appendix) and were instructed to circle only those appearing in the video they had just watched. They were explicitly informed that not all listed words necessarily appeared in the video, and the exact number of words to be circled was not specified. Each vocabulary test consisted of 12 lexical items, including both single words and multi-word units. Eight out of the 12 items were Target Words (TWs) while the other four served as distractors (not appearing in the video).

All TWs were classified as either 'known' or 'new', depending on whether they had been taught in regular classes. The teacher-researcher, who had been the participants' sole EFL teacher since they started learning the language, selected the appropriate items for this purpose. Including four 'new' and four 'known' words in each vocabulary test served two purposes: firstly, it assessed whether learners recognized 'known words' more frequently than newly encountered words, and secondly, it provided reassurance to students who were unable to identify any new TWs. Distractor words also included known and new vocabulary.

Participants received one point for each correctly circled word or expression, with a maximum score of 8. Hence, there was a total of 160 different TWs (8 per episode), including 80 new lexical items (four per episode), and to 80 known items (distributed in the same way).

4.2.4 *Aptitude test: LLAMA B*

LLAMA B (Meara, 2005) assesses rote learning and associative memory for vocabulary acquisition. Students are given two minutes to learn the names of 20 unfamiliar objects. Subsequently, they are tasked with matching each name to the corresponding object. One point is awarded for each correctly identified object, with a maximum achievable score of 20 on the test.

4.2.5 *Vocabulary Size Test: VST*

All participants were tested using the *Vocabulary Size Test* (VST), version A (Nation & Beglar, 2007). Given their low proficiency level, only bands 1k-3k were administered to these students, each containing ten words. The test uses a multiple-choice format, presenting each word within a brief non-defining context. Learners were required to select the correct meaning from one of the four options provided. Each correctly answered question was awarded one point, resulting in a maximum score of 30 for this test.

4.2.6   Reading speed tests

Two Reading Speed (RS) tests were employed in the study. The Spanish RS test, accessible at https://vip.lecturaagil.com/test-lectura-rapida/, featured an excerpt from *The Little Prince,* comprising 414 words. Participants were instructed to read the text and press a stop button upon completion. Subsequently, they were presented with four multiple-choice comprehension questions, displayed one at a time on the screen. Final scores were provided at the end of the test. For the study, Words per Minute (WPM) were used, and participants scoring less than 75% in comprehension were excluded from the analysis. Similarly, the English RS test followed a parallel format and was sourced from *Free Reader Digest* http://www.freereadingtest.com/ (Fun Facts, Level 1, Story 1).

4.3   Procedure

The materials and TV series were first piloted with a population similar to the sample (from a nearby semi-private primary school) to assess their appropriateness in terms of difficulty and lexical demands. The students encountered no difficulties in completing the tests, and no ceiling effects were observed. They reported enjoying the series and confirmed they had not seen any episodes before.

Prior to the intervention, the participants took the VST on paper, as well as LLAMA B and L1/L2 Reading Speed (RS) tests, which were administered online using the tablets provided by the school to each student. Instructions were given in the students' L1 to avoid misunderstandings.

Before watching the first episode, the teacher-researcher took special care to inform students that subtitles would also appear in the cartoons (which they could read at their discretion). Throughout the five-month treatment period, participants watched a total of 20 episodes on a weekly basis. Eighteen episodes were viewed with either L1 or L2 subtitles, while two episodes (E10 – in the middle, and E20 – at the end of the treatment) were viewed without subtitles, with the soundtrack always in English. Following each viewing session, participants immediately completed both the comprehension and vocabulary tests.

4.4   Data analysis

For our first RQ, to examine the possible influence of time and subtitling language on comprehension and vocabulary, Repeated Measures (RM) ANOVAs were conducted with L2 comprehension and vocabulary scores as dependent variables, and time and group as independent factors. *T*-tests were also employed to explore whether L1 or L2 subtitled input yielded superior benefits for comprehension and written word-form recognition in the episodes. Notably, E10 and E20, lacking subtitles, were given special attention. Finally, due to the violation of the assumption of normality of the known and new words variables (following Kolmogorov-Smirnov test), Mann-Whitney U tests were conducted to assess differences between groups in terms of known and new vocabulary, while Wilcoxon Signed Ranks tests were employed to ascertain if either group significantly recognized more known or new words.

For our second RQ, concerning the potential relationship between comprehension and vocabulary scores with learner-related variables, Spearman *rho* product-moment correlation analyses were conducted between learner-related variables and comprehension and vocabulary scores. As no collinearity effects were found and normality of the residuals was observed, the regression analyses performed helped to determine the extent to which individual variables could explain the variance in comprehension and vocabulary scores.

5. Results

5.1 RQ1a: Effects of watching L1/L2 subtitled TV series on content comprehension

The results of the ANOVA revealed no statistically significant effect for time. However, there was a statistically significant main effect for group, indicating a significant difference between participants who watched the videos with L1S or L2S: ($F_{(1,343)} = 7.85$, $p = .007$, partial eta squared = .102), in favour of the L1S group.

The results of the Independent Samples t-tests indicated that L1S learners achieved significantly higher scores in 13 of the episodes. However, comparisons between groups for episodes E10 and E20 revealed no significant differences in comprehension. Figure 1 illustrates the mean scores attained by both groups across the 20 comprehension tests administered during the treatment, with episodes where L1S students achieved significant comprehension differences highlighted (ovals indicate significant between-group differences).

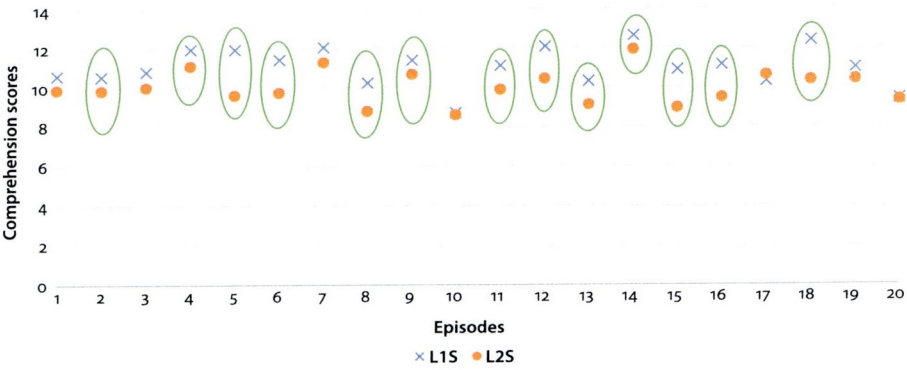

Figure 1. Mean comprehension scores for all episodes in the two groups

5.2   RQ1b: Effects of watching L1/L2 subtitled TV series on L2 vocabulary learning

In relation to vocabulary scores, the results of the ANOVA revealed no statistically significant effect for time. However, there was a statistically significant main effect for group, indicating a significant difference between participants who watched the videos with L1S or L2S: $(F_{(1, 133)} = 12.17$, $p = .001$, partial eta squared $= .152)$, in favour of the L2S group. Additionally, the interaction between time and group exhibited a significant effect $(F_{(11.90, 809.06)} = 2.81$, $p = .001$, partial eta squared $= .040)$.

The Independent Samples t-tests showed significant differences favouring the L2S group in eight episodes, four of which towards the end of the treatment. Despite higher mean scores for L1S students in three episodes (E4, E5, and E8), no significant differences were observed between the groups in these cases. Figure 2 depicts the mean scores achieved by both groups across the 20 vocabulary tests administered during the treatment, with the eight episodes where L2S students achieved significant differences in word-form recognition highlighted (ovals indicate significant differences between groups).

Table 1 presents the vocabulary results in terms of known and new words recognized in the tests. Please note that only the results for the 18 subtitled episodes have been included (but not those from E10 and E20, as the viewing conditions were different). Regarding the total number of known and new words, the results revealed that the L2S group significantly recognized more known and new words than the L1S group. Finally, the Wilcoxon Signed Ranks test demonstrated that both groups significantly recognized more known than new words.

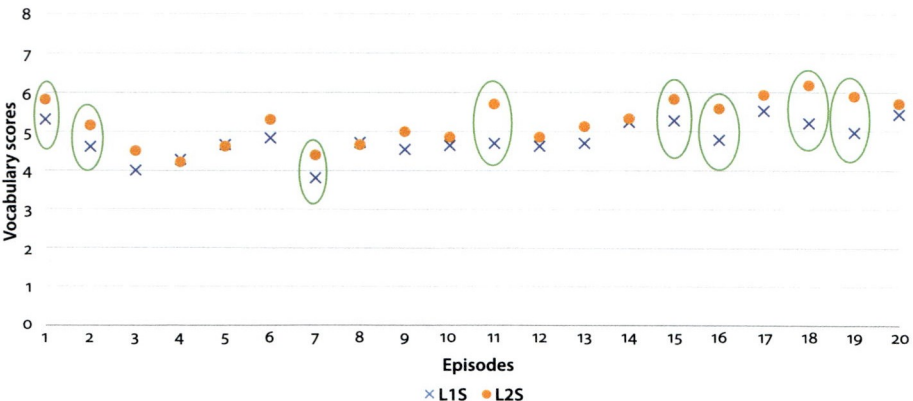

Figure 2. Mean vocabulary scores for all episodes in the two groups

Table 1. L2 word recognition scores for known and new vocabulary in each group

Group	M(SD)		Wilcoxon signed Ranks test results
	Known (max. 72)	New (max. 72)	
L₁S	57.0 (6.95)	27.28 (9.48)	z = 5.97, p = .001
L₂S	60.0 (5.72)	33.53 (8.43)	z = 5.84, p = .001
Mann-Whitney test results	U (92) = 788.500, z = −2.104, p = .035	U (92) = 683, z = −2.928, p = .003	

5.3   RQ2: Aptitude and proficiency effects on content comprehension and vocabulary learning from extensive viewing

Table 2 presents the descriptive results in each group for the variables under study: aptitude, L1/L2 RS (expressed in Words per Minute), and VS. The results of the correlations performed between the mean comprehension and vocabulary scores with aptitude and proficiency variables are reported in Tables 3 and 4.

Language aptitude was found to be significantly associated with comprehension and exhibited the most substantial effects on the comprehension results of both groups. Moreover, it was correlated with vocabulary scores for the L1S group, but not for the L2S group. Regression analyses (Table 5) confirmed that aptitude strongly influenced the comprehension scores in both groups, accounting for up

Table 2. Descriptive statistics for aptitude, L1/L2 RS, and VS

	L1S			L2S		
	M	*SD*	CI	*M*	*SD*	CI
Aptitude	4.98	3.09	5.06–8.35	5.10	2.70	4.40–6.41
Reading Speed (RS)	146.94	57.85	121.80–173.10	95.03	40.44	79.93–110.13
Vocabulary Size (VS)	12.69	4.08	13.02–15.56	11.76	4.98	10.45–14.49

Table 3. Spearman Rho correlations between comprehension scores and aptitude, L1/L2 RS, and VS in each group

	L1S	L2S
Aptitude	$r=.510^{**}, n=47$	$r=.523^{**}, n=44$
Reading Speed (RS)	$r=.371^{*}, n=47$	$r=-.091, n=30$
Vocabulary Size (VS)	$r=.570^{**}, n=47$	$r=.474^{**}, n=45$

** $p<.01$ * $p<.05$

Table 4. Spearman Rho correlations between written-word form recognition scores and aptitude, L1/L2 RS, and VS in each group

	L1S	L2S
Aptitude	$r=.330^{*}, n=47$	$r=.076, n=44$
Reading Speed (RS)	$r=.207, n=32$	$r=-.132, n=30$
Vocabulary Size (VS)	$r=.445^{**}, n=47$	$r=.035, n=45$

** $p<.01$ * $p<.05$

to 24.4% for L1S ($p=.000$) and 24.9% for L2S ($p=.000$). Additionally, it accounted for vocabulary scores by up to 10%, albeit solely in the L1S group ($p=.017$).

VS was also found to be correlated with learners' results in both groups, with a significant effect on comprehension scores for the L1S group (explaining up to 24.2% of the variance, $p=.000$) and for the L2S group (with a 10.8%, $p=.016$). Additionally, VS was positively correlated with vocabulary learning in the L1S group, explaining 8.41% of the word recognition scores ($p=.027$), whereas no correlation was found between VS and vocabulary scores in the L2S group.

Regarding participants' L1/L2 RS, comprehension was found to be minimally associated with the L1 RS, with a very modest correlation. However, L1RS did not reach significance in the regression analysis. Additionally, no effects of L2 RS were observed on the tests' results of the L2S group.

Table 5. Standard regression analyses for L1S and L2S groups

L1S

Dependent variable	Predictor variable	R Square	Adjusted R Square	Std. error of the estimate
Comprehension	Aptitude	.260	.244 ***	1.42
	Reading Speed (L1)	.060	.028	1.61
	Vocabulary Size	.258	.242 ***	1.42
Vocabulary	Aptitude	.120	.100 *	.828
	Reading Speed (L1)	.028	−.004	.875
	Vocabulary Size	.103	.084 *	.836

L2S

Dependent variable	Predictor variable	R Square	Adjusted R Square	Std. error of the estimate
Comprehension	Aptitude	.266	.249 ***	1.22
	Reading Speed (L2)	.003	−.033	1.43
	Vocabulary Size	.128	.108 *	1.33
Vocabulary	Aptitude	.024	.001	.710
	Reading Speed (L2)	.015	−.021	.720
	Vocabulary Size	.000	−.023	.716

*** $p < .001$ * $p < .05$

6. Discussion

Regarding our initial RQ, the data indicate that none of the groups exhibited consistent improvement in comprehension over time, but that the L1S learners generally outperformed their peers, with significantly higher comprehension scores in 13 of the 18 video episodes. This suggests that the inclusion of L1 subtitles likely facilitated comprehension, particularly given the students' lower proficiency in the L2. Due to their superior reading skills in the L1, the L1S group might have been quicker reading the L1 subtitles. In contrast, the learners provided with L2 subtitled videos showed poorer performance on comprehension tests, which could be attributed to the challenging nature of L2 subtitles for students with both low L2 proficiency and weak L2 reading skills. These observations are congruent with Muñoz's (2017) findings that learners with low proficiency levels present more visual fixations on L2 subtitles than on L1 subtitles. However, existing research comparing L1 and L2 subtitles for young L2 learners, such as Başaran & Köse (2012) and Galimberti & Miralpeix (2018), did not report significant differences in comprehension, including studies with control groups viewing non-subtitled videos. It is important to note that these were one-off studies, and as shown in this research, outcomes may vary between episodes (L1S obtained higher means in 17 out of the 18 subtitled episodes and those differences reached statistical significance in 13 episodes). Therefore, future studies should encompass multiple episodes to yield more reliable findings and account for potential episode-specific variability.

While L1 subtitles notably improved comprehension, the availability of subtitles – regardless of the language – aided comprehension in both groups, attesting to the suitability of the materials used. This is evidenced by the drop in scores for both groups for E10, without subtitles, marking the lowest comprehension performance across the study to that point. However, the outcomes in E20, where the L1S group still obtains a low score compared to the rest of the episodes and the L2S group's score is similar to that of E8, E13 or E16, may suggest that the L1 subtitled group was more adversely affected by the absence of subtitles, indicating a possible over-reliance on textual support, unlike the L2 subtitled group.

The L2 subtitles may have facilitated a better 'tuning in' to the spoken language, potentially enhancing the listeners' skills over time, as proposed by Vanderplank (1988, 2019). The results from the non-subtitled episodes imply that the L2 subtitled group's comprehension was less dependent on the presence of on-screen text compared to their L1 subtitled counterparts. Additionally, the slight improvement in scores for both groups in E20 relative to E10 could be attributed to either a cumulative familiarity with the content and task format by the series end or a general enhancement in skills from extended practice, or perhaps a combination of both factors.

The study revealed that exposure to the television show *Curious George* aided participants in recognizing both familiar and novel word-forms. Notably, the L2S group demonstrated higher average scores in word recognition, and performed significantly better than the L1S group in 8 of the 18 episodes. This implies that L2 subtitles might facilitate the segmentation of spoken language into distinct words (Danan, 2004; Winke et al., 2010), which in turn could enhance the recognition of L2 word-forms. Conversely, L1 subtitles may hinder the connection between phonological and written L2 forms, obstructing simultaneous processing with the L2 audio track (Mitterer & McQueen, 2009).

Peters et al. (2016) did not establish a link between subtitle type (L1/L2) and form recognition in a single TV episode among vocational school students with low proficiency, but a different trend appears when younger learners are observed over multiple episodes. Additionally, it is important to highlight that more substantial differences in word-form recognition were observed closer to the end of the study period. In contrast to comprehension – where differences were consistent throughout the treatment – this pattern suggests that learners may require a period of adjustment to TV viewing with L2 subtitles before they can effectively recognize vocabulary from such content.

The data further indicates a distinction in the recognition of known versus new words, with the L2S group recognizing significantly more words in each category than the L1S group. Furthermore, recognition scores for known words were significantly higher, which was also the case, albeit to a lesser degree, for the L1S group. The study suggests that multimodal input, integrating text and auditory stimuli, can enhance the recognition of new vocabulary and particularly reactivate previously learned lexical items. The engagement with both visual and auditory channels likely assisted participants in reinforcing their L2 vocabulary. It is important to notice that prior studies on vocabulary acquisition through viewing did not make this known-new word distinction, highlighting an area ripe for further investigation to validate these findings.

Our results align with d'Ydewalle & Van Poel (1999), demonstrating that FL acquisition in young beginner learners is modest and does not surpass that observed in adults from prior studies. However, our data reveals that participants could recognize approximately 80% of previously known target words and about 40% of new words presented in the videos. Considering the total exposure to subtitled input was just three hours, and despite the absence of a consistent improvement pattern across time, the value of this method in facilitating vocabulary recognition for children with low proficiency should not be underestimated.

The findings related to the second RQ indicate that aptitude positively impacts the FL acquisition of young, beginner learners. Previous studies, such as those by Lambelet (2021) and Muñoz (2014), have established significant positive correlations between aptitude assessments focused on vocabulary and lexical diversity in young learners. Our study further corroborates that higher aptitude is beneficial for comprehension, regardless of subtitle language, accounting for 24% of the variance in comprehension scores across both groups. It should be reminded that our aptitude test (LLAMA B) assesses rote learning of vocabulary, which can help learners recognize and recall words in isolation. Results show that this can contribute to comprehension to some extent. In contrast, a moderate correlation between aptitude and L2 word-form recognition was only observed in the L1S group, implying that aptitude may be more advantageous in demanding tasks – that is, aurally recognizing a word without the aid of the L2-text. This was not as evident for the L2S group, possibly because these learners could readily recognize word forms in the L2 presented in the input. Considering Teng's (2022) and Suárez and Gesa's (2019) findings with older learners, our results affirm the necessity of including aptitude as a key variable in future research on audiovisual input comprehension among young learners as well.

Our findings are also in accordance with the concept of the 'beginners' paradox' (Coady, 1997), originally applied to reading but relevant to audiovisual media consumption as well: learners need to be exposed to multimodal input to learn, but if they do not know enough words, learning will be harder. In line with Vanderplank's 'Threshold Hypothesis' (1988), a core vocabulary baseline will enhance comprehension of the episodes and lexical acquisition from multimodal input, also in the early stages of L2 language learning.

It might come as a surprise that L2 vocabulary size can predict comprehension in the L1S group by as much as 24.2%, while its impact is less pronounced in the L2S group, accounting for only 10.8%. In Pujadas and Muñoz (2020), vocabulary size only predicted comprehension in the captioned condition. Also, Montero Perez et al. (2014) found vocabulary size to be correlated with comprehension scores for L2 subtitled TV viewing. Our findings suggest L2 vocabulary size does influence comprehension, with a slightly more significant effect observed in the L1S group. This could be because our younger, less proficient learners may need more their existing L2 lexical knowledge when no written cues in the L2 are provided, as was the case with the L1S group. The L2S group, on the other hand, had the support of written L2 word forms, perhaps diminishing the necessity to rely as much on their vocabulary breadth.

Additionally, while vocabulary size has been linked to word learning from L2 subtitled TV viewing in older, more proficient learners (e.g., Montero Perez et al., 2014; Peters et al., 2016; Peters & Webb, 2018), our study found it predicted only 8.4% of the vocabulary recognition scores in the L1S group. This discrepancy might be due to the smaller vocabulary sizes and lower proficiency levels compared to those in previous studies. Probably only those with more extensive vocabulary knowledge, viewing the videos with L1 subtitles, were better able to recall certain word forms from the episodes. For the L2S group, even if having L2 written word forms available, reading and learning from L2 subtitles may have been excessively challenging. Supporting this, results relating to reading speed showed that even though there was a moderate correlation with comprehension outcomes in the L1S group, L2 reading speeds might have been too low to influence comprehension or learning.

7. Conclusion, limitations, and further research

This study suggests that L1 and L2 subtitled cartoons can enhance L2 comprehension and vocabulary recognition in young, beginner learners. Yet, it also illustrates that progress does not consistently show a straightforward increase with more exposure. The research underscores the significant influence of language aptitude and L2 vocabulary size, particularly in understanding content from subtitled videos. These insights can inform educators and practitioners involved in language teaching for young audiences. For instance, when content coverage is well-matched to learners' levels, they can follow storylines and recognize new vocabulary in written form. Nevertheless, since vocabulary acquisition can be challenging, integrating some explicit instruction may optimize the learning process (e.g., Gesa & Miralpeix, 2023). In addition to direct teaching methods, repeated viewings could further enhance learning (Alexiou, 2015; see Chapter 5, this volume). Young learners typically enjoy and benefit from watching episodes more than once, especially with L2 subtitles, without perceiving it as repetitive. Encouraging this practice in the classroom could lead students to continue such activities at home. Therefore, fostering strong partnerships between families and educational institutions is recommended to enrich the language learning journey of young students.

While the current study provides valuable insights, certain limitations must be acknowledged to contextualize the findings. Firstly, the participant sample size was relatively modest, highlighting the need for replication with a broader cohort. Secondly, the lack of a control group (where learners watched videos without any subtitles) limits the ability to contrast with non-subtitled viewing conditions fully. This condition was not included because, considering the learners' low proficiency level, it would have posed too great a challenge and risked demotivating them. Thirdly, while the extended duration of the study yielded detailed information on learning over time, it also presents potential side-effects: the participants' growing accustomed to the post-viewing tests could have influenced their performance, thereby affecting the results. The study did not address the long-term retention of the newly acquired vocabulary either; focusing on immediate learning meant that no delayed posttest was employed to measure long-term retention.

This research also encounters limitations concerning the scope of vocabulary knowledge evaluated. Our examination was confined to word-form recognition; the ability to connect these forms to their meanings was not explored. Consequently, future research should investigate whether L1 subtitles facilitate the integration of form and meaning more effectively than L2 subtitles in vocabulary acquisition. Regarding the chosen known and new words, the selection was based on the judgment of the participants' teacher, which introduces a subjective bias.

The study has substantiated the role of aptitude in learning from multimodal input at low proficiency levels, independently of subtitle type. However, it only used one measure of aptitude, the LLAMA B test, which evaluates associative memory and rote learning capacities. Investigating a range of aptitude subcomponents in young learners would provide a more nuanced understanding of how different facets of aptitude influence language acquisition. Additionally, while reading speed was included as a predictive variable, future research could measure this skill both pre- and post-study to confirm if extensive viewing impacts the development of reading speed over time (as shown by the study in Chapter 2). Finally, the choice of cartoons as the medium for this study, following pilot tests with similar age groups, was purposeful. However, genres such as child-friendly sitcoms may also be valuable educational resources, provided they offer suitable lexical coverage (as observed by Galimberti & Miralpeix, 2018, or Gesa & Miralpeix, 2023). Incorporating a diverse range of materials in future studies could broaden our understanding of how different types of multimodal input contribute to language learning.

Acknowledgements

This work was supported by grants PID2019-110594GB-100 from the Spanish Ministry of Science and Innovation and 2023SGR00303 from the Catalan Agency for Management of University and Research Grants (AGAUR) to the second author. We are also thankful to the reviewers for helping us improve the manuscript with their valuable comments.

Ethical Considerations

The study protocol adhered to the good practices of data collection, data anonymization, data processing, and data storage of the Institutional Review Board of the University of Barcelona (IRB00003099).

References

Alexiou, T. (2015). Vocabulary uptake from Peppa Pig: A case study of preschool EFL learners in Greece. In C. Gitsaki & T. Alexiou (Eds.), *Current issues in second/foreign language teaching and teacher development: Research and practice* (pp. 285–301). Cambridge Scholars.

Avello, D., & Muñoz, C. (2023). The development of receptive language skills from captioned-video viewing in primary school EFL learners. *Education Sciences, 13*(5), 479.

Bahrani, T., & Sim, T. S. (2012). Audiovisual news, cartoons and films as sources of authentic input. *The Turkish Online Journal of Educational Technology (TOJET)*, *11*(4), 56–64. Retrieved on 28 May 2024 from http://www.tojet.net/articles/v11i4/1145.pdf

Bahrani, T., & Soltani, R. (2011). The pedagogical values of cartoons. *Research on Humanities and Social Sciences*, *1*(4), 19–23. Retrieved on 28 May 2024 from https://core.ac.uk/download/pdf/234672893.pdf

Baltova, I. (1999). The effect of subtitled and staged video input on the learning and retention of content and vocabulary in a second language (Unpublished doctoral dissertation) University of Toronto. Retrieved on 28 May 2024 from https://tspace.library.utoronto.ca/bitstream/1807/13234/1/nq41096.pdf

Başaran, H., & Köse, G. (2012). The effects of captioning on EFL listening comprehension. *Procedia – Social and Behavioural Sciences*, *70*, 702–708.

Birulés-Muntané, J., & Soto-Faraco, S. (2016). Watching subtitled films can help learning foreign languages. *PLoS ONE 11*(6), 1–10.

Bravo, M. (2008). Putting the reader in the picture: Screen translation and foreign-language learning (Unpublished doctoral dissertation). Universitat Rovira i Virgili. Retrieved on 28 May 2024 from http://hdl.handle.net/10803/8771

Carroll, J. B., & Sapon, S. M. (2002). *Manual for Modern Language Aptitude Test (MLAT)*. Second Language Testing, Inc.

Charles, T. J., & Trenkic, D. (2015). Speech segmentation in a second language: The role of bimodal input. In Y. Gambier, A. Caimi, & C. Mariotti (Eds.), *Subtitles and language learning: Principles, strategies and practical experiences* (pp. 173–198). Peter Lang. https://www.peterlang.com/document/1053134

Coady, J. (1997). L2 vocabulary acquisition through extensive reading. In J. Coady & T. Huckin (Eds.), *Second language vocabulary acquisition* (pp. 225–237). Cambridge University Press.

Cobb, T. (n.d.). VocabProfile (Version 2) [computer software]. Retrieved on 15 February 2022 from https://www.lextutor.ca/vp/comp

Danan, M. (1992). Reversed subtitling and Dual Coding Theory: New directions for foreign language instruction. *Language Learning*, *42*(4), 497–527.

Danan, M. (2004). Captioning and subtitling: Undervalued language learning strategies. *Meta: Translators' Journal*, *49*(1), 67–77.

Doughty, C. (2019). Cognitive language aptitude. *Language Learning*, *69*(1), 101–126.

d'Ydewalle, G., & De Bruycker, W. (2007). Eye movements of children and adults while reading television subtitles. *European Psychologist*, *12*(3), 196–205.

d'Ydewalle, G., & Gielen, I. (1992). Attention allocation with overlapping sound, image, and text. In K. Rayner (Ed.), *Eye movements and visual cognition* (pp. 415–427). Springer.

d'Ydewalle, G., & Pavakanun, U. (1995). Acquisition of a second/foreign language by viewing a television program. In P. Winterhoff-Spurk (Ed.). *Psychology of media in Europe: The state of the art, perspectives for the future* (pp. 51–64). Westdeutscher Verlag.

d'Ydewalle, G., & Van De Poel, M. (1999). Incidental foreign-language acquisition by children watching subtitled television programs. *Journal of Psycholinguistic Research*, *28*(3), 227–245.

Frumuselu, A.D., De Maeyer, S., Donche, V., & Gutiérrez-Colon, M. del M. (2015). Television series inside the EFL classroom: Bridging the gap between teaching and learning informal language through subtitles. *Linguistics and Education, 32*(B), 107–117.

Galimberti, V., & Miralpeix, I. (2018). Multimodal input for Italian beginner learners of English. A study on comprehension and vocabulary learning from undubbed TV series. In C.M. Coonan, & A. Bier, & E. Ballarin (Eds.), *La didattica delle lingue nel nuovo millennio. Le sfide dell'internazionalizzazione* (pp. 615–626). Edizioni Ca'Foscari. Retrieved on 28 May 2024 from https://edizionicafoscari.unive.it/it/edizioni4/libri/978-88-6969-228-4/multimodal-input-for-italian-beginner-learners-of/.

Gesa, F., & Miralpeix, I. (2023). Extensive viewing and L2 vocabulary learning: Two studies in EFL classes with children and adolescents. *ITL – International Journal of Applied Linguistics.*

Hayati, A., & Mohmedi, F. (2011). The effect of films with and without subtitles on listening comprehension of EFL learners. *British Journal of Educational Technology, 42*(1), 181–192.

Koolstra, C.M., & Beentjes, J.W.J. (1999). Children's vocabulary acquisition in a foreign language through watching subtitled television programs at home. *Educational Technology Research and Development, 47*(1), 51–60.

Kuppens, A.H. (2010). Incidental foreign language acquisition from media exposure. *Learning, Media and Technology, 35*(1), 65–85.

Lambelet, A. (2021). Lexical diversity development in newly arrived parent-child immigrant pairs: Aptitude, age, exposure, and anxiety. *Annual Review of Applied Linguistics, 41*, 76–94.

Lekkai, I. (2014). Incidental foreign language acquisition by children watching subtitled television programs. *The Turkish Online Journal of Educational Technology (TOJET), 13*(4), 81–87. Retrieved on 28 May 2024 from https://files.eric.ed.gov/fulltext/EJ1043240.pdf

Markham, P., & Peter, L.A. (2003). The influence of English language and Spanish language on foreign language listening/reading comprehension. *Journal of Educational Technology Systems, 31*(3), 331–341.

Markham, P., Peter, L.A., & McCarthy, T.J. (2001). The effects of native language vs target language captions on foreign language students' dvd video comprehension. *Foreign Language Annals, 34*(5), 439–445.

Matielo, R., D'Ely, R.C.S.F., & Baretta, L. (2015). The effects of interlingual and intralingual subtitles on second language learning/acquisition: A state-of-the-art review. *Trabalhos Em Linguística Aplicada, 54*(1), 161–182.

Mayer, R.E. (2005). *The Cambridge handbook of multimedia learning.* Cambridge University Press.

Meara, P. (2005). *LLAMA language aptitude tests.* Lognostics.

Miralpeix, I., & Muñoz, C. (2018). Receptive vocabulary size and its relationship to EFL language skills. *International Review of Applied Linguistics in Language Teaching, 56*(1), 1–24.

Mitterer, H., & McQueen, J.M. (2009). Processing reduced word-forms in speech perception using probabilistic knowledge about speech production. *Journal of Experimental Psychology: Human Perception and Performance, 35*(1), 244–263.

doi Montero Perez, M. (2022). Second or foreign language learning through watching audio-visual input and the role of onscreen text. *Language Teaching* 55(2), 163–192.

doi Montero Perez, M., Desmet, P., & Peters, E. (2015). Enhancing vocabulary learning through captioned video: An eye-tracking study. *The Modern Language Journal*, 99(2), 308–328.

doi Montero Perez, M., Peters, E., Clarebout, G., & Desmet, P. (2014). Effects of captioning on video comprehension and incidental vocabulary learning. *Language Learning & Technology*, 18(1), 118–141.

doi Montero Perez, M., Van Den Noortgate, W., & Desmet, P. (2013). Captioned video for L2 listening and vocabulary learning: A meta-analysis. *System*, 41(3), 720–739.

doi Muñoz, C. (2010). Staying abroad with the family: A case study of two siblings' second language development during a year's immersion. *ITL – International Journal of Applied Linguistics*, 160, 24–48.

doi Muñoz, C. (2014). The association between aptitude components and language skills in young learners. In M. Pawlak & L. Aronin (Eds.), *Essential topics in applied linguistics and multilingualism, second language learning and teaching* (pp. 51–68). Springer.

doi Muñoz, C. (2017). The role of age and proficiency in subtitle reading. An eye-tracking study, *System*, 67, 77–86.

doi Muñoz, C., Pattemore, A., & Avello, D. (2022). Exploring repeated captioning viewing as a way to promote vocabulary learning: Time lag between repetitions and learner factors. *Computer Assisted Language Learning*.

doi Nation, I. S. P. (2006). How large a vocabulary is needed for reading and listening? *The Canadian Modern Language Review*, 63(1), 59–82.

Nation, I. S. P., & Beglar, D. (2007). A vocabulary size test. *The Language Teacher*, 31(7), 9–13. Retrieved on 28 May 2024 from https://openaccess.wgtn.ac.nz/articles/journal_con tribution/A_vocabulary_size_test/12552197

doi Neuman, S. B., & Koskinen, P. (1992). Captioned television as comprehensible input: Effects of incidental word learning from context for language minority students. *Reading Research Quarterly*, 27(1), 94–106.

Paivio, A. (1986). *Mental representations: A dual coding approach*. Oxford University Press.

Pavakanun, U., & d'Ydewalle, G. (1992). Watching foreign television programs and language learning. In F. L. Engel, D. G. Bouwhuis, T. Bosser, & G. d'Ydewalle (Eds.), *Cognitive modelling and interactive environments in language learning* (pp. 193–198). Springer.

doi Peters, E., Heynen, E., & Puimège, E. (2016). Learning vocabulary through audiovisual input: The differential effect of L1 subtitles and captions. *System*, 63, 134–148.

doi Peters, E., & Webb, S. (2018). Incidental vocabulary acquisition through viewing L2 television and factors that affect learning. *Studies in Second Language Acquisition*, 40(3), 551–577.

doi Pujadas, G., & Muñoz, C. (2020). Examining adolescent EFL learners' TV viewing comprehension through captions and subtitles. *Studies in Second Language Acquisition*, 42(3), 551–575.

doi Rodgers, M. P. H. (2013). English language learning through viewing television, an investigation of comprehension, incidental vocabulary acquisition, lexical coverage, attitudes, and captions (Unpublished doctoral dissertation). Victoria University of Wellington.

Sherman, J. (2003). *Using authentic video in the language classroom*. Cambridge University Press.

Skehan, P. (1989). *Individual differences in second language learning.* Edward Arnold.

Stæhr, L. S. (2008). Vocabulary size and the skills of listening, reading and writing. *The Language Learning Journal*, 36(2), 139–152.

Stewart, M. A., & Pertusa, I. (2004). Gains to language learners from viewing target language closed-captioned films. *Foreign Language Annals*, 37(3), 438–442.

Suárez, M. D., & Gesa, F. (2019). Learning vocabulary with the support of sustained exposure to captioned video: Do proficiency and aptitude make a difference? *The Language Learning Journal*, 47(4), 497 – 517.

Sweller, J. (1994). Cognitive load theory, learning difficulty, and instructional design. *Learning and Instruction*, 4(4), 295–312.

Sydorenko, T. (2010). Modality of input and vocabulary acquisition. *Language Learning & Technology*, 14(2), 50–73.

Teng, M. F. (2022). Incidental L2 vocabulary learning from viewing captioned videos: Effects of learner-related factors. *System*, 105, 1–12.

Tragant, E., & Pellicer-Sánchez, A. (2019). Young EFL learners' processing of multimodal input: An eyetracking study. *System*, 80, 212–223.

Vanderplank, R. (1988). The value of teletext sub-titles in language learning. *ELT Journal*, 42, 272–281.

Vanderplank, R. (2010). Déjà vu? A decade of research on language laboratories, television and video in language learning. *Language Teaching*, 43(1), 1–37.

Vanderplank, R. (2016a). 'Effects of' and 'effects with' captions: How exactly does watching a TV programme with same-language subtitles make a difference to language learners? *Language Teaching*, 49(2), 235–250.

Vanderplank, R. (2016b). *Captioned media in foreign language learning and teaching: Subtitles for the deaf and hard-of-hearing as tools for language learning.* Palgrave Macmillan.

Vanderplank, R. (2019). 'Gist watching can only take you so far': Attitudes, strategies and changes in behaviour in watching films with captions. *The Language Learning Journal*, 47, 407–423.

Vulchanova, M., Aurstad, L. M. G., Kvitnes, I. E. N., & Eshuis, H. (2015). As naturalistic as it gets: Subtitles in the English classroom in Norway. *Frontiers in Psychology*, 5(1), 1–10.

Webb, S., & Rodgers, M. P. H. (2009). Vocabulary demands of television programs. *Language Learning*, 59(2), 335–366.

Winke, P., Gass, S., & Sydorenko, T. (2010). The effects of captioning videos used for foreign language listening activities. *Language Learning & Technology*, 14(1), 65–86.

Winke, P., Hall, B. W., Road, R. C., & Gass, S. (2013). Factors influencing the use of captions by foreign language learners: An eye – tracking study. *The Modern Language Journal*, 97(1), 254–275.

Zanon, N. T. (2007). Learning vocabulary through authentic video and subtitles. *TESOL-SPAIN*, 31, 5–8. Retrieved on 28 May 2024 from https://www.tesol-spain.org/uploaded_files/files/TESOL-SPAIN-newsletter-sample2.pdf

Appendix.   Comprehension and vocabulary tests (Episode 9)

Comprehension (one question in each part is provided as example)

"Un Mono Esquiador"

1. Marca si estos enunciados son verdaderos (V) o falsos (F):
   - Bill tiene unos esquís nuevos para Jorge.   V / F

2. Escoge la respuesta correcta (A, B o C):
   - Para Ted, la primera regla para jugar en la nieve es...
     A. Saber esquiar.
     B. No tener miedo al frío.
     C. Poder salir de casa.

3. Ordena cronológicamente (del 1 al 5) estos hechos que pasan en el capítulo que acabas de ver. El número 3 te puede servir de guía para ordenar los demás.
   ____ Bill le dice a Jorge que, para subir una pendiente, haga zigzag.
   ____ Jorge se pregunta cómo el cerdo Mike ha llegado hasta allí.
   _3_ Jorge puede ver casas y granjas desde la cima de la montaña.
   ____ Con esquís, Jorge cree poder ir allá donde haya nieve.
   ____Para las niñas, la bajada de Jorge es impresionante.

Vocabulary

Marca con un círculo las palabras y expresiones que han aparecido en este vídeo:

hot cocoa	ice	sled	snowshoes
shovel	leave	hill	all the way
skiing	vessels	boots	water cycle

The development of L1 and L2 reading skills from captioned video viewing in primary school EFL learners

Daniela Avello[1,2] & Carmen Muñoz[1]
[1] Universitat de Barcelona | [2] Universidad de O'Higgins

This investigation explored the extent to which captioned video viewing (11 episodes) fostered the development of L2 reading skills in a group of 92 L1-Spanish primary school learners of English (years 4 and 5). It also assessed the influence of L1- and L2-related factors on students' reading performance over time. The analyses revealed learners' significant improvement in L2 reading skills as a result of the treatment and that L2-related factors were stronger predictors than L1-related factors. One interesting finding was that the treatment also enhanced the development of L1 reading skills, particularly in the case of fifth graders. This outcome lent support to the idea that in early L2 learning stages, students rely on their L1 linguistic infrastructure to deal with L2 print.

1. Introduction

Second language (L2) reading may be challenging for primary school learners due to their still-developing first language (L1) literacy skills and their typically lower L2 proficiency level (Birch & Fulop, 2021; Holmes & Myles, 2019). Likewise, L2 readers appear to be at a disadvantage compared to L1 readers due to their limited exposure to L2 print, which is key to enhancing their familiarity with L2 orthographic patterns and attaining high levels of automaticity in lower-level reading skills (e.g., text decoding; Grabe, 2009; Grabe & Stoller, 2020). Possibly, the complexity of reading may explain why this activity is less popular among learners in comparison with other leisure activities, such as viewing or gaming (Muñoz, 2020; Wouters et al., 2024).

As a result, a small but increasing number of studies have explored the extent to which learners' exposure to multimodal input may support L2 reading instruction. Overall, the evidence suggests that the simultaneous processing of aural and written input (with and without imagery), as in reading-while-listening, may

https://doi.org/10.1075/lllt.61.02ave

facilitate the reading process (Pellicer-Sánchez, 2022) and increase young learners' motivation to do this activity (e.g., Tragant et al., 2019). However, the effects of reading captions (i.e., subtitles in the same language of the audio) may be different due to the dynamic nature of onscreen text. Likewise, it remains unknown whether the findings of the few studies conducted in L1 settings on the effects of captions on the development of L1 reading skills (e.g., Linebarger et al., 2010) may also be translated to foreign language learning contexts.

The literature suggests that to compensate for their limited knowledge of the target language in the initial stages, L2 readers rely on interlanguage reading, that is, the integration of learners' L1 and L2 knowledge (Birch & Fulop, 2021; Jiang et al., 2019). Thus, at lower L2 proficiency levels, L1 reading and its underlying cognitive mechanisms may play a role in L2 reading. Still, there is evidence that L2-related factors (e.g., vocabulary knowledge) are stronger predictors of L2 reading in comparison with L1 reading skills (Alderson et al., 2016; Jeon & Yamashita, 2014; Sparks, 2021). Hence, the aim of the present study is threefold. Firstly, it seeks to determine whether students' processing of captions fosters the development of L2 reading skills. Secondly, it intends to disentangle whether primary school learners' reading performance over time may be predicted by L1- and/or L2- related factors. Thirdly, considering the potential role of learners' L1 reading skills in the processing of L2 print, this study explores the extent to which the treatment also enhances the development of L1 reading skills.

2.   Literature review

2.1   The beneficial effects of captions

The evidence has shown that the presence of bimodal verbal input (i.e. audio and text) is not usually redundant for L2 learners as it is for L1 learners (Mayer & Fiorella, 2022). On the contrary, the presence of audio support may allow learners to decode the text with greater ease (Kormos et al., 2019; Pellicer-Sánchez, 2022; Toscano-Fuentes & Julián de Vega, 2018), while the processing of written text may also facilitate aural word recognition and speech segmentation (Charles & Trenkic, 2015). In fact, the addition of written input is strongly recommended for L2 learners since it may be revisited while available on screen (Mayer et al., 2020). Equally important, the lower effort devoted to the processing of bimodal verbal input may allow viewers to devote more attention to images to enhance comprehension (Pellicer-Sánchez, 2022).

The scant evidence on the use of captioned videos in the target language with late primary school learners (years 5 and 6) indicates that they are capable of processing and integrating verbal and non-verbal visual input, though they devote greater attention to captions than images (Tragant & Pellicer-Sánchez, 2019). Likewise, the literature suggests that primary school learners need to make a greater cognitive effort and rely more on onscreen text in comparison with adolescents and adults (Casulleras & Miralpeix, this volume; Muñoz, 2017). This higher reliance on captions may be related to young learners' typically lower proficiency level, and their still- developing cognitive and reading skills (Holmes & Myles, 2019; Muñoz, 2017).

A handful of studies on the development of L1 reading skills from captioned video viewing with primary school learners have shown captions to develop lower-level reading skills, such as word recognition and non-word reading (e.g., Kothari et al., 2002; Linebarger, 2001; Linebarger et al., 2010). Although it is uncertain whether the positive outcomes obtained in L1 contexts may be replicated with young L2 learners, research on out-of-school exposure has shown a positive relationship between viewing and the development of L2 reading skills (Lindgren & Muñoz, 2013; Wouters et al., 2024). Yet, as Wouters et al. (2024) explained, the positive correlation between viewing and L2 reading skills might be stronger if the input involved more L2 print. It may thus be hypothesized that the use of captions might counteract L2 learners' lack of exposure to written texts to complement L2 reading programs (Webb, 2015) and reach the thousands of hours of practice required for the automatization of lower-level reading skills (Grabe & Stoller, 2020).

Although the ultimate aim of reading instruction is to reach high levels of comprehension, the development of lower-level reading skills seems to be a requirement to fulfil this objective (Nassaji, 2014). When readers struggle with lower-level reading processes (e.g. text decoding and word recognition), they have lower attentional resources available to achieve appropriate levels of comprehension (Nassaji, 2014; Sadoski & Paivio, 2013). In other words, learners' extensive exposure to captioned videos may eventually improve learners' lower-level reading skills to lead to the building of coherent mental representations of the written input (Alderson et al., 2015; Grabe & Stoller, 2020; Nassaji, 2014).

2.2   The relationship between L1 and L2 reading skills

L2 learners do not need to learn to read in the L2 from scratch when they have already been instructed to read in the L1. Thus, in early L2 learning stages, students are thought to rely on their L1 reading skills to process L2 print (i.e., interlanguage reading; Birch & Fulop, 2021; Jiang et al., 2019). Specifically, learners progressively assimilate and accommodate their linguistic infrastructure to the characteristics of the L2 (Birch & Fulop, 2021; Jiang et al., 2019; Perfetti et al.,

2007), a process that evolves as a function of L2 proficiency and familiarity with the patterns of the target language (Jiang et al., 2019). In the case of L1-Spanish learners of English, interlanguage reading may be facilitated by the common alphabetic writing system of the two languages, despite their differences in orthographic transparency (Birch & Fulop, 2021).

If L1 reading skills were also at play in young learners' processing of L2 captions, we should not rule out the possibility of obtaining significant gains in both L1 and L2 reading skills due to learners' increase in the amount of time devoted to interlanguage reading. Nonetheless, the extent to which primary school learners may rely on their L1 reading skills and benefit from this activity in either language is uncertain since their L1 literacy skills are not fully developed (Holmes & Myles, 2019), and they may need to make a great effort to cope with the speed of captions (Muñoz, 2017).

2.3   The influence of L1- and L2-related factors on L2 reading performance

There is strong evidence that L2 reading cannot be fully detached as a language or reading problem given that learners' reading performance has been shown to be influenced by multiple factors, such as L2 knowledge and L1 reading skills (Grabe & Jiang, 2018; Nassaji, 2014; Perfetti et al., 2007; Sparks, 2021). Yet, learners' L1 reading skills seem to compensate only partially for their L2 knowledge gaps while reading (Yamashita, 2002). In different age groups, the evidence has demonstrated that L2-related factors are stronger predictors of L2 reading in comparison with L1-reading skills and the underlying cognitive mechanisms (Alderson et al., 2016; Sparks, 2021; Yamashita, 2002). In fact, the superior performance shown by L1 readers may be mainly attributed to their significantly larger vocabulary size (Kormos, 2017; Miralpeix & Muñoz, 2018) and grammatical knowledge compared with L2 readers (Grabe & Stoller, 2020).

As for bimodal texts, the scant evidence has shown that upper primary school students' L1 reading skills may either predict to a certain extent L2 reading fluency (Tragant et al., 2019) or show non-significant influence on their L2 reading performance (Kormos et al., 2019). Thus, it may be hypothesized that the lower cognitive demands involved in the processing of bimodal texts (Pellicer-Sánchez, 2022) might enhance the role of L2-related factors over L1 reading skills. Accordingly, the literature only appears to be consistent in that L2-related factors are stronger predictors of L2 reading under unimodal and bimodal input conditions (Alderson et al., 2016; Jeon & Yamashita; 2014; Sparks, 2021).

2.4   Reading efficacy

The concept of reading efficacy refers to comprehension-based reading rate (Llanes, 2018) given that this is a measure that integrates students' reading speed (number of words read per minute) and comprehension. As Sadoski and Paivio (2013) highlight, word recognition differs from lexical access in that L2 readers may well be able to decode a word whose meaning is unknown, resulting in poor levels of comprehension. Thus, together, lower- and higher-level reading processes appear to be more effective at discriminating between high- and low-achievers (Grabe, 2009). In short, an efficient reader is capable of decoding a text with ease in order to ensure the availability of enough cognitive resources to attain high levels of comprehension.

3.   Rationale and research questions

Most research on audiovisual input has focused on vocabulary learning and young adults, and far less attention has been paid to the development of reading skills (Montero Perez, 2022; Muñoz, 2022) and primary school learners (Montero Perez & Rodgers, 2019). The present study attempted to fill these gaps by assessing the extent to which the use of captioned videos enhanced the development of L1 and L2 reading skills in this under-researched age group.

The research questions on English reading efficacy that guided our study are:

1.   To what extent does the use of captioned videos in the target language foster the development of L2-English reading efficacy (L2 efficacy)?
2.   To what extent are learners' gains in L2 efficacy influenced by age, and L1- and L2-related factors (i.e. L2 vocabulary knowledge, L1 efficacy, L1 reading habits and attitude towards reading)?
3.   To what extent do L1- and L2-related factors influence learners' performance in L2 efficacy at pretest and posttest?

The following research questions focused on Spanish reading efficacy:

4.   To what extent does the use of captioned videos in the target language foster the development of L1-Spanish reading efficacy (L1 efficacy)?
5.   To what extent are learners' gains in L1 efficacy influenced by age, and L1- and L2-related factors (i.e. L2 efficacy, L1 text segmentation, L1 reading habits and attitude towards reading)?
6.   To what extent do L1- and L2-related factors influence learners' performance in L1 efficacy at pretest and posttest?

4.   Methodology

We implemented a pretest-posttest research design to assess learners' gains in L1 and L2 reading efficacy by integrating measures of lower- and higher-level reading processes through silent reading speed (words read per minute = WPM) and reading comprehension, respectively (see Llanes, 2018).

4.1   Participants

We used convenience sampling (seven intact classes) to conduct this study with 129 L1-Spanish primary school learners of English (girls = 62; boys = 67) in fourth (aged 9–10; $n=64$) and fifth grade (aged 10–11; $n=65$) from a non-elitist private school in Chile. The participants from the experimental groups ($n=96$; year 4 [EG-Y4] = 47; year 5 [EG-Y5] = 49) fulfilled the following requirements: watching all the episodes, completing the pre and posttests, and not requiring special support from the teachers to participate in this intervention. The participants had a low L2 proficiency level (pre-A1-A1, according to the Common European Framework of Reference). In addition, learners reported either limited or non-existent out-of-school exposure, including little experience with captioned videos and extensive reading (see Avello, 2023).

The comparison groups consisted of fourth and fifth graders from the same school, which attended their regular English lessons. Due to time constraints associated to Covid-19 pandemic, these groups only completed either the L2 or the L1 efficacy test. Comparison group 1 (CG-Y5 henceforth; year 5; $n=16$) was assessed in terms of L1 efficacy, while comparison group 2 (CG-Y4 onwards; year 4; $n=17$) was tested in L2 efficacy.

4.2   Treatment and procedures

Before the treatment, the participants took four tests in order to measure receptive L2 vocabulary knowledge, and L1 and L2 reading skills (see Figure 1). Prior to their administration, we formally requested parents' consent, which was complemented by children's oral confirmation of their willingness to participate in this study.

The participants in the experimental group watched 11 episodes[1] of the animated cartoon Charlie and Lola (Carrington & Child, 2005–2008). To this aim

---

1. The 11 viewing sessions (110 minutes) were distributed from two to four episodes a week. Given that the analyses failed to detect significant differences between the groups as a function

we used the data show projector and the speakers available in each classroom. The length of the episodes (10 minutes) was found to be suitable for young learners since they are still developing their literacy and cognitive skills. Short episodes may be particularly useful for students with shorter attention spans and those less-skilled readers who need to make a greater cognitive effort to process the text under time pressure (Marzá & Torralba, 2015; Zabalbeascoa et al., 2015). In addition, the analyses of the scripts calculated with VocabProfiler on Lextutor (BNC and COCA) (Cobb, 2019) indicated that, on average, the episodes reached 91.3% vocabulary coverage at the K1 level, surpassing the 80% suggested to comprehend audiovisual input (Durbahn et al., 2022). These results are in line with the findings of the eye-tracking study by Tragant and Pellicer-Sánchez (2019) with fifth graders from Spain, who, despite their higher levels of attention to captions, were able to process both text and images. The appropriacy of the TV program was also confirmed by a pilot group of fourth graders from Chile, whose responses indicated that this animated cartoon was motivating and matched their characteristics (see Avello, 2023).

After the treatment, the participants were administered the L1 and L2 efficacy tests (see Figure 1). Finally, after four weeks, they were asked to complete a questionnaire on L1 reading habits and attitude towards reading (L1 reading habits, henceforth).

4.3   Instruments

4.3.1   *Spanish and English reading efficacy tests*

We assessed silent reading speed and text comprehension, which were integrated to obtain students' reading efficacy measures (Llanes, 2018). We decided to measure silent reading speed over oral reading fluency because of its higher reliability (Alderson et al., 2015, p.71) and its proximity to the processing of captions. Two forms (A and B) were created for each language, which were administered in counterbalanced order.

---

of the distance between episodes (see Avello, 2023), the participants in this study were simply grouped in terms of year level.

Pretests	Treatment	Immediate posttests
– L2 vocabulary knowledge test – L1 efficacy test – L2 efficacy test – Spanish text segmentation test	– 11 viewing sessions (11 episodes)	– L1 efficacy test[*] – L2 efficacy test[*] – Questionnaire on L1 reading habits and attitude towards reading[**]

[*] Administered during the following three days after the treatment [**] Administered four weeks later.

Figure 1. Research design

The results from these instruments were reading speed (WPM = [n° of words in the text/number of seconds used to read the whole passage] * 60) and comprehension (one point was awarded to each correct answer). The total number of correct answers was used to calculate the percentage of comprehension (number of correct answers * 100/N° of questions). Hence, the formula used to calculate reading efficacy was ([WPM * % comprehension]/100). Because reading speed (WPM) was participant-dependent, there was no maximum score for this test.

The two fiction texts used to test L1 reading efficacy were adapted from a set of sample materials aligned with the curriculum for fourth graders in the Chilean context (Santillana, 2014). The ATOS readability formula was used to measure text complexity (average sentence and word length, and word difficulty level), and confirm that the texts were comparable and suitable for the sample groups (see Appendix B). As for text comprehension, we formulated six multiple-choice comprehension questions that focused on textually explicit/literal (four questions) and implicit information (two questions). The alternatives for each question consisted of a correct answer, three distractors, and the 'I don't know' option to prevent learners from guessing.

We adapted two non-fiction texts from the pre-A1 starters' sample papers (Cambridge Assessment English, 2018) to assess L2 efficacy. The Flesch-Kincaid reading ease and grade level were calculated to assess text readability. The values obtained showed that the two texts were comparable and suitable for the target groups (see Appendix A). By following the same structure used in the L1 efficacy tests, we formulated four questions that elicited textually explicit information while one question tested textually implicit information.

These instruments were pilot-tested with 14 Chilean primary school learners of similar characteristics to identify the conflictive items and improve them prior to the intervention. With the experimental and comparison groups, the reading efficacy tests were administered in small groups (four students maximum) to guarantee students' comprehension of the instructions, and also ensure an accurate measure of reading speed by means of a stopwatch per child. The students were explicitly asked to read the texts only once at their own pace to reach appropriate levels of comprehension. Based on the challenges involved in the measurement of silent reading speed, the texts contained red circles to remind the students to signal the beginning and the end of their silent reading process. They were not allowed to revisit the text to answer the comprehension questions.

4.3.2 EFL picture vocabulary test

This instrument assessed young learners' receptive L2 vocabulary knowledge at the level of meaning recognition. Given the positive relationship found between L2 vocabulary knowledge and L2 proficiency (Miralpeix, 2020), we administered this test to discriminate between high and low achievers. We adopted the format of the Picture Vocabulary Size test (PVST) developed by Anthony and Nation (2017), as well as the adaptations made by Puimège and Peters (2019). The 50 target words (K1 and K2 frequency bands) selected for this test were taken from the Cambridge A2 Key for Schools vocabulary list (Lanes et al., 2019). Each target word was first uttered in isolation and then used in a non-defining sentence. We created a video with the prompts (presented in written and aural form by a native speaker) to ensure the same testing conditions in all groups. The students had to select the picture that represented the meaning of the target word (four options: A, B, C, or D and the 'I don't know' option). This measure was pilot-tested with six groups of L2-English learners ($N=188$) of similar characteristics to identify and improve the conflicting items. One point was awarded to each correct answer (maximum score = 50 points).

4.3.3 Spanish text segmentation test

The Spanish text segmentation test (L1 segmentation test henceforth) was administered to measure silent reading fluency (Toscano-Fuentes & Julián de Vega, 2018) in L1-Spanish focusing on the assessment of lower-level reading skills such as phonological decoding and visual word recognition (Torres-Díaz et al., 2020), as well as the role of vocabulary and grammatical knowledge in text comprehension (Alderson et al., 2015). On a text that lacked spaces and punctuation marks, the students had one minute to draw vertical lines between the words by following a linear order (i.e., they were not allowed to skip lines). To this end, we adapted one of the texts from the EGRA test (Early Grade Reading Assessment) used with primary school learners in Spain (Fernández Corbacho, 2016). The resulting instrument was pilot-tested with students from the same school that did not participate in the intervention in order to improve the instructions and the administration process. The words that were accurately segmented were awarded one point (maximum score = 72 points).

4.3.4 *Questionnaire on L1-reading habits and attitude towards reading*

A questionnaire was administered to explore learners' L1 reading habits and attitude towards reading. It was an adaptation of the questionnaire developed by Granena and colleagues (2015) in Spain. This questionnaire consisted of 8 questions (2 Likert-scale and 6 multiple-choice questions) that were assessed by an expert researcher and a local EFL teacher prior to their administration in pen-and-paper format (maximum score = 25 points). The Cronbach alpha coefficient ($\alpha = .791$) indicated that the instrument was reliable (Pallant, 2016). On the whole, the data confirmed that L1 reading is mostly seen as an obligation in the Chilean context (Rivas, 2019), and only a limited number of students read for pleasure (see Avello, 2023).

4.4   Data analyses

Data analyses were performed in SPSS v.29. First, we assessed normality of distribution and collinearity between variables (Tolerance > .3; VIF < 3.33). After running the preliminary analyses that tested group comparability, we ran a series of generalized linear mixed models (GLMMs; linear models) and general linear models (GLMs) in order to explore EG-Y4 and EG-Y5's gains in L1 efficacy and L2 efficacy as a result of the treatment. In addition, we calculated multiple linear regressions to assess the influence of L1- and L2-related factors on students' performance over time. The GLMMs included Satterthwaite approximation and robust covariances, suggested for small sample groups and unbalanced data.

5.   Results

5.1   Preliminary analyses

A series of ANOVAs and t-tests were run in order to assess the initial differences between the experimental groups (EG-Y4 and EG-Y5) and the comparison groups (CG-Y4 and CG-Y5) in L2 efficacy, L1 efficacy, L2 vocabulary knowledge, L1 segmentation, and L1 reading habits (see Table 1). The variables that were not normally distributed were square root (SQRT) transformed to reach appropriate normality values ($p > .05$); this was the case for L1 efficacy and L2 efficacy.

In terms of L2 efficacy, an ANOVA test indicated that the groups differed significantly ($F(2) = 8.934$, $p < .001$, $\eta^2 = .144$). However, the Tukey post-hoc comparisons showed that the significant differences were not found between EG-Y4 and CG-Y4 ($p=.842$) but between EG-Y4 and EG-Y5. As for L1 efficacy, the ANOVA test indicated that the comparisons between groups only approached significance ($F(2)=2.814$, $p=.064$, $\eta^2=.051$), confirming that EG-Y5 and CG-Y5 did not differ significantly ($p>.05$). In sum, the experimental and comparison groups from the same year levels were comparable.

Table 1. Descriptive statistics

Group	L2 efficacy (pretest)	L1 efficacy (pretest)	L2 vocabulary knowledge	L1 segmentation	L1 reading habits
	M (SD)	*M (SD)*	*M (SD)*	*M (SD)*	*M (SD)*
EG-Y4	44.91 (30.35)	79.15 (40.17)	14.47 (6.28)	24 (8.93)	12.64 (5.43)
EG-Y5	72.67 (34.83)	99.70 (50.68)	20.5 (10.81)	36.72 (15.46)	12.45 (5.04)
CG-Y4	44.91 (30.35)				
CG-Y5		80.94 (27.29)			

Independent-samples t-tests between EG-Y4 and EG-Y5 indicated that EG-Y5 scored significantly higher in L2 vocabulary knowledge ($t(86)=3.227$, $p<.001$, $r=.32$) and L1 segmentation ($t(88)=4.749$, $p<.001$, $r=.44$), but not in L1 reading habits ($t(92)=0,181$, $p=.857$, $r=.018$).

5.2   English reading efficacy

5.2.1   *The development of L2 efficacy*

To assess the performance of the experimental groups (EG-Y4 and EG-Y5) and the comparison group (CG-Y4) over time (see Table 2), we ran a compound symmetry structure GLMM (linear model) with student identification as subjects, and time as repeated measures. The analysis was calculated with learners' L2 efficacy scores as the target variable, while group, time, and their interaction were entered as fixed factors.

The results yielded significant main effects for time ($F(1,120)=29.693$, $p<.001$) and group ($F(2,130)=16.853$, $p<.001$), and a significant interaction between time and group ($F(2,116)=11.889$, $p<.001$). The Bonferroni pairwise contrasts indicated that only EG-Y4 and EG-Y5 showed significant improvement from pretest to posttest (see Table 3). In addition, the contrast estimates suggested that EG-Y5 obtained slightly higher gains in comparison with EG-Y4 at descriptive level.

Each group's performance was also compared in relation to their silent L2 reading speed, and their levels of comprehension. With respect to the former,

Table 2. L2 efficacy: Descriptive statistics

	L2 efficacy			L2 reading speed (WPM)		L2 comprehension %	
	Pretest score	Posttest score	Mean gains	Pretest	Posttest	Pretest	Posttest
	M	M	M	M	M	M	M
	(SD)	(SD)	(SD)	(SD)	(SD)	(SD)	(SD)
EG-Y4	44.91	68.98	24.17	96.17	108.39	44.26	62.17
	(30.35)	(46.17)	(33.56)	(32.89)	(44.50)	(20.82)	(22.80)
EG-Y5	72.67	109.62	36.49	123.70	142.16	57.39	75.11
	(34.83)	(52.14)	(36.28)	(37.85)	(47.40)	(20.05)	(21.39)
CG-Y4	50.06	42.53	−7.53	92.76	96.65	51.76	44.71
	(31.24)	(21.18)	(25.66)	(29.41)	(26.59)	(21.28)	(20.65)

Table 3. L2 efficacy: Time pairwise contrasts

Group	Time pairwise contrasts	Contrast estimate	SE	t	df	Adj. Sig.	95% CI Lower	95% CI Upper
EG-Y4	Pretest – Posttest	−1.584	0.256	−6.199	122	<.001	−2.090	−1.078
EG-Y5	Pretest – Posttest	−1.892	0.275	−6.877	95	<.001	−2.438	−1.346
CG-Y4	Pretest – Posttest	0.443	0.411	1.079	134	0.282	−0.369	1.256

The sequential Bonferroni adjusted significance level is .05.
Confidence interval bounds are approximate.

we calculated a compound symmetry structure GLMM (linear model) with student identification as subjects, and time as repeated measures. We entered learners' silent reading speed scores as the target variable (WPM; see Table 2 above), including group, time, and their interaction as fixed factors. The results revealed significant effects for time ($F(1, 146) = 13.863, p < .001$) and group ($F(2, 133) = 12.150, p < .001$), but not for their interaction ($F(2, 133) = 1.752, p = .177$). However, the Bonferroni pairwise contrasts (see Table 4) indicated that only EG-Y4 and EG-Y5 showed significant improvement over time, especially in the case of EG-Y5.

With respect to L2 comprehension (see Table 2 above), the results of the GLMM (linear model) showed significant effects for time ($F(1, 98) = 13.472, p < .001$), group ($F(2, 120) = 10.263, p < .001$), and their interaction ($F(2, 102) = 7.326, p = .001$). The Bonferroni pairwise contrasts revealed that EG-Y4 and EG-Y5 showed similar significant improvement from pretest to posttest, while CG-Y4 scored non-significantly lower at posttest (see Table 5). This outcome explains the non-significantly lower L2 efficacy score obtained by CG-Y4 at posttest, at descriptive level (Table 2).

Table 4. Silent L2 speed: Time pairwise contrasts

Group	Time pairwise contrasts	Contrast estimate	SE	t	df	Adj. sig.	95% CI	
							Lower	Upper
EG-Y4	Pretest – Posttest	−12.217	5.211	−2.344	82	.021	−22.584	−1.850
EG-Y5	Pretest – Posttest	−17.923	4.962	−3.612	104	<.001	−27.762	−8.083
CG-Y4	Pretest – Posttest	−3.882	5.632	−.689	211	.491	−14.985	7.220

The least significant difference adjusted significance level is .05.

Table 5. L2 text comprehension: Time pairwise contrasts

Group	Time pairwise contrasts	Contrast estimate	SE	t	df	Adj. sig.	95% CI	
							Lower	Upper
EG-Y4	Pretest – Posttest	−17.554	3.401	−5.162	116	<.001	−24.290	−10.818
EG-Y5	Pretest – Posttest	−17.742	3.434	−5.166	116	<.001	−24.544	−10.940
CG-Y4	Pretest – Posttest	7.059	5.985	1.179	88	.241	−4.835	18.952

The least significant difference adjusted significance level is .05.

5.2.2   *The influence of age and L1- and L2-related factors on learners' gains*

With the aim of exploring the differences in L2 efficacy gains between EG-Y4 and EG-Y5 (see Table 2), we ran a General Linear Model (GLM; gains = L2 efficacy posttest score – L2 efficacy pretest score) with year level as fixed factor, and the following covariates: students' L1 efficacy and L2 efficacy pretest scores, L2 vocabulary knowledge, and L1 reading habits. The results did not show a significant difference between EG-Y4 and EG-Y5 ($F(1) = .752$, $p = .388$, $\eta^2 = .009$), but they revealed significant effects for L2 efficacy at pretest ($F(1) = 6.903$, $p = .010$, $\eta^2 = .079$) and L2 vocabulary knowledge ($F(1) = 25.590$, $p < .001$, $\eta^2 = .242$); this was not the case for L1 reading habits ($F(1) = .825$, $p = .367$, $\eta^2 = .010$) and L1 efficacy pretest ($F(1) = .348$, $p = .557$, $\eta^2 = .004$). The eta squared values showed that L2 efficacy pretest had a moderate effect size, while L2 vocabulary knowledge had a large effect size. In other words, L2 vocabulary knowledge appeared to be the strongest predictor of learners' L2 efficacy gains over time.

5.2.3   *The influence of L1- and L2-related factors on learners' performance at pretest and posttest: L1 efficacy and L2 vocabulary*

To assess the influence of L1- and L2-related factors on learners' performance in L2 efficacy at each testing time, we performed a multiple linear regression for each testing time by including L2 vocabulary knowledge and L1 efficacy pretest as predictor variables. At pretest, the results revealed that L2 vocabulary knowledge and L1 efficacy pretest predicted 44% of the variance ($F(2,85) = 35.540$, $p < .001$, $R^2 = .443$). The standard coefficients indicated that L2 vocabulary knowledge was a stronger predictor ($\beta = 47\%$, $p < .001$) than L1 efficacy pretest ($\beta = 30\%$, $p = .001$). At posttest, the analyses showed that these factors increased their predictive value: L2 vocabulary knowledge and L1 efficacy pretest explained 52% of the variance ($F(2,85) = 48.371$, $p < .001$, $R^2 = .52$). The standard coefficients confirmed that students' performance at posttest was explained by L2 vocabulary knowledge to a greater extent ($\beta = 62\%$, $p < .001$) than L1 efficacy pretest ($\beta = 18\%$, $p = .028$). Therefore, L1 efficacy pretest predicted their performance at L2 efficacy pretest and posttest but not their L2 efficacy gains.

5.3   Spanish reading efficacy

5.3.1   The development of L1 efficacy

To determine whether the treatment resulted in significant learning benefits in L1 efficacy (see Table 6), we ran a compound symmetry structure GLMM (linear model) with student identification as subjects, and time as repeated measures. We entered L1 efficacy at pretest and posttest as the target variable, and the following independent variables: group (EG-Y4, EG-Y5 and CG-Y5), time (pretest and posttest), and their interaction.

Table 6. L1 efficacy: Descriptive statistics

	L1 efficacy			L1 reading speed (WPM)		L1 comprehension %	
	Pretest score M (SD)	Posttest score M (SD)	Mean gains M (SD)	Pretest M (SD)	Posttest M (SD)	Pretest M (SD)	Posttest M (SD)
EG-Y4	79.15 (40.17)	96.20 (50.16)	17.04 (29.56)	114.78 (36.00)	128.50 (47.02)	68.11 (23.23)	73.57 (23.13)
EG-Y5	99.70 (50.68)	147.13 (58.34)	46.18 (40.73)	148.41 (44.25)	167.02 (48.84)	65.20 (20.09)	86.64 (17.96)
CG-Y5	80.94 (27.29)	87.13 (43.66)	6.19 (27.82)	92.44 (22.43)	104.63 (44.14)	86.46 (15.18)	82.29 (15.48)

The results revealed significant effects for time ($F(1,136) = 42.040$, $p < .001$), group ($F(2,134) = 8.350$ $p < .001$), and the interaction between time and group ($F(2,125) = 10.878$, $p < .001$). The Bonferroni pairwise contrasts indicated that only the experimental groups showed significant improvement (see Table 7). The contrast estimates indicated that EG-Y5 obtained higher gains than EG-Y4 at descriptive level.

Table 7. L1 efficacy: Time pairwise contrasts

Group	Time pairwise contrasts	Contrast estimate	SE	t	df	Adj. sig.	95% CI	
							Lower	Upper
EG-Y4	Pretest – Posttest	−0.866	0.232	−3.733	140	<0.001	−1.325	−0.407
EG-Y5	Pretest – Posttest	−2.157	0.275	−7.842	74	<0.001	−2.706	−1.609
CG-Y5	Pretest – Posttest	−0.233	0.350	−0.664	209	0.507	−0.923	0.458

The sequential Bonferroni adjusted significance level is .05.
Confidence interval bounds are approximate.

Each groups' performance was also compared in relation to their silent L1 reading speed and their levels of comprehension (see Table 6 above). As for silent reading speed, we calculated a compound symmetry structure GLMM (linear model) with student identification as subjects, and time as repeated measures. We entered learners' silent reading speed scores as the target variable (see Table 4), including group, time, and their interaction as fixed factors. The results revealed significant effects for time ($F(1,72) = 25.084$, $p < .001$) and group ($F(2,108) = 18.512$, $p < .001$), but not for their interaction ($F(2,82) = .249$, $p = .780$). However, the Bonferroni pairwise contrasts (see Table 8) indicated that only the experimental groups showed significant improvement over time, and EG-Y5 scored slightly higher than EG-Y4 at descriptive level.

Concerning L1 text comprehension (see Table 6), the results revealed significant effects for time ($F(1,132) = 11.789$, $p < .001$), group ($F(2,133) = 5.608$, $p = .005$), and their interaction ($F(2,123) = 11.334$, $p < .001$). The Bonferroni pairwise contrasts indicated that only EG-Y5 scored significantly higher at posttest, while EG-Y4 and CG-Y5 did not show significant progress over time (see Table 9).

Table 8. Silent L1 speed: Time pairwise contrasts

Group	Time pairwise contrasts	Contrast estimate	SE	t	df	Adj. sig.	95% CI	
							Lower	Upper
EG-Y4	Pretest – Posttest	−.582	.149	−3.911	105	<0.001	−.877	−.287
EG-Y5	Pretest – Posttest	−.690	.139	−4.980	148	<0.001	−.964	−.416
CG-Y5	Pretest – Posttest	−.498	.289	−1.722	57	.090	−1.076	.081

The sequential Bonferroni adjusted significance level is .05.
Confidence interval bounds are approximate.

Table 9. L1 text comprehension: Time pairwise contrasts

Group	Time pairwise contrasts	Contrast estimate	SE	t	df	Adj. sig.	95% CI	
							Lower	Upper
EG-Y4	Pretest – Posttest	−5.457	3.102	−1.759	115	.081	−11.601	.688
EG-Y5	Pretest – Posttest	−21.298	3.299	−6.456	94	<0.001	−27.849	−14.748
CG-Y5	Pretest – Posttest	4.165	4.773	.873	170	.384	−5.257	13.587

The sequential Bonferroni adjusted significance level is .05.
Confidence interval bounds are approximate.

5.3.2 *The influence of age and L1- and L2-related factors on learners' gains*

To explore the differences in gains between EG-Y4 and EG-Y5 (see Table 6 for descriptive statistics), we ran a General Linear Model (GLM) with year level as fixed factor and students' L1 efficacy and L2 efficacy pretest scores, L2 vocabulary knowledge, and L1 reading habits as covariates. The results showed significant effects for year level ($F(1) = 6.248$, $p = .014$, $\eta^2 = .069$), L1 efficacy pretest ($F(1) = 12.373$, $p < .001$, $\eta^2 = .128$), L2 efficacy pretest ($F(1) = 20.079$, $p < .001$, $\eta^2 = .193$), and L1 reading habits ($F(1) = 5.158$, $p = .026$, $\eta^2 = .058$). The eta squared values indicated that L1 and L2 efficacy pretest scores had a large effect size, while year level, and L1 reading habits had a moderate effect size (in this order). Thus, L2 efficacy pretest was found to be the strongest predictor of learners' gains in L1 efficacy over time.

5.3.3 *The influence of L1- and L2-related factors on learners' performance at pretest and posttest: L2 efficacy, L1 segmentation and L1 reading habits*

To calculate the influence of L1- and L2-related factors on learners' L1 efficacy scores at pretest and posttest, we ran a multiple linear regression for each testing time by including L2 efficacy pretest, L1 segmentation, and L1 reading habits as predictor variables. L1 reading habits did not explain students' performance at any of the testing times and it was removed from these analyses. At pretest, the results indicated that L2 efficacy pretest and Spanish segmentation predicted 40% of the variance ($F(2, 86) = 29.726$, $p < .001$, $R^2 = .395$). The standard coefficients revealed that L1 segmentation showed a slightly higher predictive value ($\beta = 40\%$, $p < .001$) than L2 efficacy pretest ($\beta = 38\%$, $p < .001$). At posttest, these two variables predicted 62% of the variance ($F(2, 85) = 71.004$, $p < .001$, $R^2 = .617$), indicating that both factors increased their predictive value, particularly L2 efficacy pretest ($\beta = 51\%$ vs. 46%).

6.   Discussion

This study was designed to determine the extent to which the viewing of 11 captioned episodes of an animated cartoon in the English class contributed to the development of L1 efficacy and L2 efficacy. In addition, it assessed the influence of age (year level), and L1- and L2-related factors on students' outcomes over time.

6.1   L2 efficacy

In answer to the first research question, the results indicated that the treatment was significantly beneficial for the experimental groups, but not for the comparison groups. This finding extends those of studies conducted in L1 contexts (e.g., Kothari et al., 2002; Linebarger, 2001; Linebarger et al., 2010) in that the use of captioned videos fosters the development of L2 reading skills in primary school EFL learners, contributing to the reading practice required to decode texts efficiently and attain higher levels of comprehension (Grabe, 2009; Grabe & Jiang, 2018; Grabe & Stoller, 2020). However, this finding may be associated with primary school learners' strong reliance on written support (Casulleras & Miralpeix, this volume; Muñoz, 2017; Tragant & Pellicer-Sánchez, 2019), therefore further research should determine whether this positive outcome is replicated with adolescents and adults.

The second research question was concerned, first, with the influence of age on the results. EG-Y5 obtained slightly higher gains than EG-Y4, but their difference did not reach significance when controlling for L1 and L2 efficacy pretest scores, L2 vocabulary knowledge, and L1 reading habits. Rather, the results suggested that the extent to which learners benefitted from the treatment depended on their L2 efficacy at pretest, and L2 vocabulary knowledge to a greater degree. Therefore, the more proficient participants may have been better equipped to cope with the high cognitive demands involved in the processing of captions. Less-skilled readers might have struggled to sustain their attention on the onscreen text while viewing a 10-minute episode (Marzá & Torralba, 2015; Zabalbeascoa et al., 2015). Therefore, the extent to which learners processed L2 print may have been key to boosting their gains (Wouters et al., 2024).

As for the third research question, the analyses of the influence of L1- and L2-related factors on the results confirmed that L2 vocabulary knowledge also explained learners' performance at each testing time. Although L1 efficacy pretest score was not found to predict learners' L2 efficacy gains, it contributed to learners' performance at pretest and posttest significantly. In line with previous studies with young L2 learners (Tragant et al., 2019), the significant role played by L1 efficacy at each testing time further supports the idea that learners use their L1 linguistic infrastructure to somewhat compensate for their L2 knowledge gaps in early L2 reading stages (Birch & Fulop, 2021; Jiang et al., 2019; Perfetti et al., 2007). The results also confirmed that L2-related factors are stronger predictors of L2 reading than L1-related factors (Alderson et al., 2016; Sparks, 2021; Yamashita, 2002). The non-significant contribution of L1 reading habits to learners' gains in L2 efficacy may be associated with the fact that only few students reported being frequent readers outside school, and even fewer considered reading as a leisure activity. Therefore, the amount of practice devoted to this activity on students' own initiative may have been insufficient to influence their performance in L2 efficacy over time.

6.2   L1 efficacy

In answer to the fourth research question, the results revealed that in contrast with the comparison group (CG-Y5), EG-Y4 and EG-Y5 showed significant improvement in L1 efficacy as a result of the treatment. This finding is somewhat surprising given that learners were only exposed to captions in L2-English. This outcome corroborates that in early stages, students rely on their L1 reading skills to process L2 print (Yamashita, 2002). Therefore, reading in one language seems to foster the improvement of their reading skills in both languages.

The fifth research question addressed the influence of age, and L1- and L2-related factors on learners' gains. As for age, in comparison with L2 efficacy, the treatment appeared to be more beneficial for EG-Y5 than EG-Y4 as seen in EG-Y5's slightly higher improvement in silent reading speed, and mostly in their significant gains in comprehension. However, it is hard to disentangle whether the results may be mainly attributed to fifth graders' significantly higher L2 vocabulary size, stronger L1 literacy skills, or their stage of cognitive development. As mentioned above, it also seems possible that fifth graders used captions more effectively than fourth graders, and managed to stay on task for an extended period of time. Additionally, fourth graders may require longer exposure to captioned videos to show a noticeable improvement in L1 efficacy. On the whole, the results suggest that fifth graders were better equipped to profit from their captioned viewing experience to obtain significant gains in both languages. Hence, in this study, fifth graders seem to be at the stage where the processing of captions is neither too challenging nor too easy to attain high levels of comprehension and enhance the development of literacy skills (Linebarger et al., 2010).

As for the influence of L1 and L2-related factors on learners' gains (fifth research question), and on their performance in L1 efficacy at each testing time (sixth research question), the findings once again lent support to interlanguage reading and the underlying linguistic infrastructure employed to process texts in both languages (Birch & Fulop, 2021; Jiang et al., 2019). Likewise, L2 efficacy pretest score was not only found to be a prominent predictor of learners' L1 efficacy gains, but also of their performance in L1 efficacy at posttest, confirming that the participants who were more proficient in the target language processed the written support with greater ease to benefit from it. As for the potential influence of L1 reading habits on the outcomes, the results indicated that the students who read more frequently and showed a more positive attitude towards reading obtained higher gains at posttest. To put it another way, learners' progress was accounted by the synergy of their L1 reading habits and exposure to captions throughout the intervention.

7. Conclusion

Overall, the findings of the present study revealed that captioned videos are effective at enhancing primary school learners' L1 and L2 reading skills. This outcome may be particularly relevant for contexts where students do not seem to enjoy reading either in the L1 due to cultural and educational issues (Rivas, 2019), or in the L2 due to the complexity of the task (Muñoz, 2020; Wouters et al., 2024). It goes without saying that captioned videos do not replace extensive reading programs, however, they might become an effective tool to break the vicious circle of less-skilled readers' reluctance to read (Birch & Fulop, 2021). Accordingly, captioned videos could have an important place inside and outside the L2 classroom. Specifically, the implementation of a principled viewing approach in the L2 classroom may be required to encourage primary school learners to take ownership of their viewing process and do this activity at home (Webb, 2015).

This study is not without limitations. Firstly, because of the Covid-19 pandemic restrictions, we could only recruit participants from a specific year level (either year 4 or year 5) as comparison groups for the administration of each of reading efficacy measures (in English and Spanish). Another limitation was associated to the length of the treatment and the characteristics of the context. Overall, the participants of this study had a low L2 proficiency level and reported little or non-existent exposure to the target language outside the classroom. It may be hypothesized that the positive results obtained in the present study after a relatively short treatment were due to children's first intensive captioned viewing experience. In consequence, these outcomes might not be replicated with participants who have already developed the habit of reading outside school (L1 and L2), or with those who are already familiar with the reading of onscreen text. Further investigations should shed light in this regard by implementing captioned viewing experiences of varying lengths, and assessing primary school students from different contexts, proficiency levels, and age ranges.

Acknowledgments

This study was supported by the APIF scholarship granted by the University of Barcelona to the first author, and the grant PID2019-110594GB-100 awarded by the Spanish Ministry of Science, Innovation and Universities, and 2023SGR00303 by the Catalan Agency for Management of University and Research Grants (AGAUR) to the second author. We would like to thank the reviewers for their critical evaluation and helpful recommendations.

Ethical considerations

The protocols of data collection, data anonymization, data processing, and data storage of the current study were approved by the Institutional Review Board of the University of Barcelona (IRB0003099).

References

Alderson, J.C., Haapakangas, E.L., Huhta, A., Nieminen, L., & Ullakonoja, R. (2015). *The diagnosis of reading in a second or foreign language.* Routledge.

Alderson, J.C., Huhta, A., Nieminen, L. (2016). Characteristics of weak and strong readers in a foreign language. *The Modern Language Journal, 100*(4), 1–28.

Anthony, L., & Nation, I.S.P. (2017). *Picture Vocabulary Size Test (version 1.2.0) [Computer software and measurement instrument].* Waseda University. Retrieved on 28 May 2024 from http://www.laurenceanthony.net/software/pvst

Avello, D. (2023). L2 learning from captioned-video viewing in primary school students. (Unpublished doctoral dissertation). University of Barcelona. Retrieved on 28 May 2024 http://hdl.handle.net/2445/196164

Birch, B., & Fulop, S. (2021). *English L2 reading: Getting to the bottom* (4th ed.). Routledge.

Cambridge Assessment English. (2018). *Pre A1 starters, A1 movers and A2 flyers sample papers. For exams from 2018.* Retrieved on 28 May 2024 from https://www.cambridgeenglish.org/exams-and-tests/movers/preparation/

Carrington, M., & Child, L. (Executive producers). (2005–2008). *Charlie and Lola* [Animated TV series]. Tiger Aspects Productions.

Charles, T., & Trenkic, D. (2015). Speech segmentation in a second language: The role of bimodal input. In Y. Gambier, A. Caimi & C. Mariotti (Eds.), *Subtitles and language learning. Principles, strategies and practical experiences* (pp. 173–197). Peter Lang.

Cobb, T. VocabProfilers [computer program]. Retrieved on 30 October 2019 from https://www.lextutor.ca/vp/eng/

Durbahn, M., Macís, M., Rodgers, M., & Peters, E. (2022). *Lexical coverage in L2 viewing comprehension: An extension of van Zeeland and Schmitt (2012)* [Conference presentation]. EuroSLA 31st conference, University of Fribourg, Switzerland.

Fernández Corbacho, A. (2016). Desarrollo de habilidades tempranas de la destreza lectora en inglés como lengua extranjera (Unpublished doctoral dissertation). Universidad de Huelva.

Grabe, W. (2009). *Reading in a second language. Moving from theory to practice.* Cambridge University Press.

Grabe, W., & Jiang, X. (2018). First and second language reading. In J.I. Liontas (Ed.), *The TESOL encyclopedia of English language teaching* (pp. 1–7). John Wiley & Sons.

Grabe, W., & Stoller, F. (2020). *Teaching and researching reading* (3rd ed.). Routledge.

Granena, G., Muñoz, C., & Tragant, E. (2015). L1 reading factors in extensive L2 reading-while-listening instruction. *System, 55,* 86–89.

Holmes, B., & Myles, F. (2019). *White Paper: Primary languages policy in England. The way forward.* Retrieved on 28 May 2024 from www.ripl.uk/policy/

Jeon, E., & Yamashita, J. (2014). L2 reading comprehension and its correlates: A meta-analysis. *Language Learning, 64,* 160–212.

Jiang, J., Ouyang, J., & Liu, H. (2019). Interlanguage: A perspective of quantitative linguistic typology. *Language Sciences, 74,* 85–97.

Kormos, J. (2017). *The second language learning processes of students with specific learning difficulties.* Routledge.

Kormos, J., Kosak, M., & Pizorn, K. (2019). The role of low-level first language skills in second language reading, reading-while-listening and listening performance: A study of young dyslexic and non-dyslexic language learners. *Applied Linguistics, 40*(5), 834–858.

Kothari, B., Takeda, J., Joshi, A., & Pandey, A. (2002). Same language subtitling: A butterfly for literacy? *International Journal of Lifelong Education, 21*(1), 55–66.

Lanes, A., Love, R., Kalman, B., Brenchley, M., & Pickles, M. (2019). Updating the A2 key and B1 preliminary vocabulary lists. *Cambridge Research English Research Notes,* 1–9.

Lindgren, E., & Muñoz, C. (2013). The influence of exposure, parents, and linguistic distance on young European learners' foreign language comprehension. *International Journal of Multilingualism, 10,* 105–129.

Linebarger, D. (2001). Learning to read from television: The effects of using captions and narration. *Journal of Educational Psychology, 93*(2), 288–298.

Linebarger, D., Taylor Piotrowski, J., & Greenwood, C. (2010). On-screen print: The role of captions as a supplemental literacy tool. *Journal of Research in Reading, 33*(2), 148–167.

Llanes, A. (2018). Reading in English as a foreign language: Examining differences in reading speed, comprehension, efficacy and L1 cross-linguistic influence across grades. *Investigaciones Sobre Lectura, 9,* 1–49.

Marzá, A., & Torralba, G. (2015). Incidental language learning through subtitled cartoons: Is it possible in a dubbing country? In Y. Gambier, A. Caimi & C. Mariotti (Eds.), *Subtitles and language learning. Principles, strategies and practical experiences* (pp. 199–219). Peter Lang.

Mayer, R., & Fiorella, L. (2022). Introduction to multimedia learning. In R. Mayer & L. Fiorella (Eds.), *The Cambridge handbook of multimedia learning* (3rd ed., pp. 3–16). Cambridge University Press.

Mayer, R., Fiorella, L., & Stull, A. (2020). Five ways to increase the effectiveness of instructional videos. *Education Tech Research Dev, 68*, 837–852.

Miralpeix, I. (2020). *L1 and L2 vocabulary size and growth*. In S. Webb (Ed.), *The Routledge handbook of vocabulary studies* (pp. 189–206). Routledge.

Miralpeix, I., & Muñoz, C. (2018). Receptive vocabulary size and its relationship to EFL language skills. *IRAL – International Review of Applied Linguistics in Language Teaching, 56*(1), 1–24.

Montero Perez, M. (2022). Second or foreign language learning through watching audio-visual input and the role of on-screen text. *Language Teaching, 55*(2),163–192.

Montero Perez, M., & Rodgers, M. (2019). Video and language learning. *The Language Learning Journal, 47*(4), 403–406.

Muñoz, C. (2017). The role of age and proficiency in subtitle reading: An eye tracking study. *System, 67*, 77–86.

Muñoz, C. (2020). Boys like games and girls like movies. Age and gender differences in out-of-school contact with English. *Revista Española de Lingüística Aplicada, 33*(1).

Muñoz, C. (2022). Audiovisual input in L2 learning. *Language, Interaction and Acquisition, 13*(1), 125–143.

Nassaji, H. (2014). The role and importance of lower-level processes in second language reading. *Language Teaching, 47*(1), 1–37.

Pallant, J. (2016). *SPSS survival manual. A step by step guide to data analysis using IBM SPSS* (6th ed.). McGraw Hill Education.

Pellicer-Sánchez, A. (2022). Multimodal reading and second language learning. *ITL-International Journal of Applied Linguistics, 172*(1), 2–17.

Perfetti, C.A., Liu, Y., Fiez, J., Nelson, J., Bolger, D.J., & Tan, L. (2007). Reading in two writing systems: Accommodation and assimilation of the brain's reading network. *Bilingualism: Language and Cognition, 10*(2), 131–146.

Puimège, E., & Peters, E. (2019). Learners' English vocabulary knowledge prior to formal instruction: The effect of learner-related and word-related factors. *Language Learning, 69*, 943–977.

Rivas, F. (2019, February 21). ¿Por qué los chilenos leen poco? Jóvenes autores creen que el problema puede empezar en los colegios. *Bio Bio Chile*. Retrieved on 28 May 2024 from https://www.biobiochile.cl/noticias/artes-y-cultura/libros/2019/02/21/por-que-los-chilenos-leen-poco-jovenes-autores-creen-que-el-problema-puede-empezar-en-los-colegios.shtml

Sadoski, M., & Paivio, A. (2013). A dual theoretical model of reading. In D.E. Alvermann, N.J. Unrau, & R.B. Ruddell (Eds.), *Theoretical models and processes of reading* (pp. 886–922). International Reading Association.

Santillana. (2014). *Lenguaje y comunicación para cuarto básico serie Bicentenario*. Santillana.

Sparks, R.L. (2021). Identification and characteristics of strong, average, and weak foreign language readers: The simple view of reading model. *Modern Language Journal, 105*, 507–525.

Torres-Díaz, R., Mosquera, R., Ontivero, M., Romero, Y., González, E., Alvarez-Rivero, A., Ojeda, J., Peón, B., Recio, & B., Valdés-Sosa, M. (2020). Text segmentation ability predicts future reading efficiency in Spanish-speaking children. *System*, *204*, 1–6.

Toscano-Fuentes, C. M., & Julián de Vega, C. (2018). Videos musicales en el aula de inglés de primaria para la mejora de la fluidez lectora. *Tejuelo*, *28*, 43–66.

Tragant, E., Llanes, À., & Pinyana, À. (2019). Linguistic and non-linguistic outcomes of a reading-while-listening program for young learners of English. *Reading and Writing*, *32*, 819–838.

Tragant, E., & Pellicer-Sánchez, A. (2019). Young EFL learners' processing of multimodal input: Examining learners' eye movements. *System*, *80*, 212–223.

Webb, S. (2015). Extensive viewing: Language learning through watching television. In D. Nunan & J. Richards (Eds.), *Language learning beyond the classroom* (pp. 159–168). Routledge.

Wouters, M., Bollansée, L., Prophete, E., & Peters, E. (2024). The relationship between extramural English and learners' listening comprehension, reading comprehension, motivation, and anxiety. *Vigo International Journal of Applied Linguistics*, 165–193.

Yamashita, J. (2002). Mutual compensation between L1 reading ability and L2 language proficiency in L2 reading comprehension. *Journal of Research in Reading*, *25*, 81–95.

Zabalbeascoa, P., González-Casillas, S., & Pascual-Herce, R. (2015). Bringing the SLL project to life: Engaging Spanish teenagers in learning while watching Foreign language audiovisuals. In Y. Gambier, A. Caimi & C. Mariotti (Eds.), *Subtitles and language learning. Principles, strategies and practical experiences* (pp. 105–126). Peter Lang.

Appendix A.   English reading efficacy. Text characteristics

Text	Flesch kincaid reading ease	Flesch kincaid grade level	Number of sentences	Number of words	Average Nº of words per sentence	Average syllables per word
Text A	91.9	2.9	11	108	9.82	1.24
Text B	92.7	2.8	11	108	9.82	1.23

Appendix B.   Spanish reading efficacy. Text characteristics

Text	ATOS level (readability formula)	Word count	Average word length	Average sentence length
Text A	8.6	200	4.5	20
Text B	8.1	200	4.5	20

The effects of textual enhancement on young learners' attention and vocabulary acquisition through captioned cartoons

Rebeca Finger-Bou & Carmen Muñoz
Universitat de Barcelona

This study aimed to analyze the effects of textual enhancement of captions on vocabulary acquisition by 17 L1-Spanish/Catalan primary school learners of English in fifth grade. Participants watched 11 episodes of a children's television series. They were divided into two groups: one watched the videos with regular captions, and one with enhanced captions, where target words were bolded and highlighted in yellow. Vocabulary gains were assessed through pre- and post-tests that tapped into form recall and form recognition. Results showed higher learning in the enhanced captions group, particularly in terms of form recognition. Additionally, an eye-tracking analysis showed that the enhanced-captions group had longer fixation durations initially, but the difference disappeared by the end of the intervention.

1. Introduction

Researchers agree that the quantity, quality, and intensity of exposure to a second language (L2) have a significant impact on language learning. The increasing access to audiovisual resources, including television, streaming services, and social media, has transformed the way we consume information, communicate with others, and ultimately, the way we learn languages. In that sense, language learners are certainly motivated to watch television programs in the L2, as has been documented in surveys on language learners' engagement with the L2 outside of the educational setting (Peters & Muñoz, 2020).

Multimodal input, as a fusion of visual elements, auditory verbal input, and written verbal information (such as captions in the language of the audio [L2] or subtitles in the viewer's language [L1]), has the potential to enhance language learning (Muñoz, 2022). This occurs when both visual and verbal channels are activated simultaneously. According to Mayer's (2009) Cognitive Theory of Mul-

https://doi.org/10.1075/lllt.61.03fin

timedia Learning, the simultaneous reception of information through separate channels can increase our limited attentional capacities. This has been attributed to the complementary nature of the three input sources (audio, visual, and caption text), which collectively support the learning process from audiovisual input by effectively disseminating information (Vanderplank, 2016). The auditory component allows learners to associate spoken words with their correct pronunciation, the visual element aids in recognizing contextual clues and facial expressions, while the written captions provide additional reinforcement and a textual representation of the spoken language.

On this basis, researchers have delved into the intrinsic advantages of using audiovisual material, and in particular captioned videos to boost comprehension and the learning of L2 vocabulary, collocations, grammar, and pronunciation learning (Montero Perez, 2022). The inclusion of captions enables learners to visually recognize and comprehend the written words associated with the spoken language, thereby enhancing the overall learning experience. Some studies have gone a step further in trying to optimize this process by strategically directing learners' attention to specific segments within the captions, hence increasing the saliency of target items (e.g., Puimège et al., 2022). However, results have been mixed and the question remains as to whether textually enhanced captions offer a substantial advantage over regular or unenhanced captions (Montero Perez, 2022). Moreover, due to the scarcity of studies with primary school learners, the impact of textual enhancement on their viewing and learning experiences remains largely unexplored. The present study, therefore, examines the effects of textual enhancement of captions on young learners' acquisition of L2 vocabulary. Additionally, it explores potential changes over time in young learners' attention to textually enhanced and unenhanced captions by means of their eye movements.

2. Literature review

2.1 Vocabulary acquisition through multimodal input

Most studies in this line of research have focused on vocabulary learning and have demonstrated that video can serve as a valuable means for acquiring L2 vocabulary, as noted in Montero Perez (2022). Some of those studies have looked at incidental word learning from non-captioned/subtitled videos, finding modest, yet significant gains (e.g., Feng & Web, 2020; Puimège & Peters, 2019, 2020). For example, Peters and Webb (2018) observed that exposure to a one-hour English documentary had a significant impact on the incidental vocabulary learning of 63 Flemish EFL learners through a meaning recognition and meaning recall test. Montero

Perez's (2020) study involved the manipulation of a French video to incorporate 15 pseudowords as targets for incidental learning of 63 Dutch learners of French. Results indicated learning at both the form and meaning recognition levels. A strong connection was also observed between previous vocabulary knowledge and the ability to acquire new words from video content. Other studies have investigated learning of formulaic sequences from audiovisual input, as in Puimège and Peters (2019, 2020). Following the viewing of an English documentary, significant incidental learning was observed for both form (Puimège & Peters, 2019) and meaning (Puimège & Peters, 2020) of formulaic sequences, for 20 Dutch EFL and 77 Flemish EFL learners, respectively. Another study by Feng and Webb (2020) investigated the impact of written, audio, and audiovisual L2 input on incidental vocabulary learning of 76 Chinese university EFL learners. Tests conducted at one-week intervals showed that vocabulary learning occurred in all modes, and it was retained. In fact, there were no significant differences between the modes, with similar vocabulary gains. The study also found a significant relationship between prior vocabulary knowledge and learning outcomes, while no such correlation was observed between frequency of occurrence and learning.

Other studies have focused on the effects of viewing audiovisual material with (L2) captions or (L1) subtitles, generally finding a positive impact on L2 vocabulary learning, as simultaneous on-screen written representations of the soundtrack prove advantageous for language learners (Muñoz, 2022). The potential improvement of L2 vocabulary learning from video through the addition of captions has been reported by two meta-analyses. In an early meta-analysis, Montero Perez and colleagues (2013) synthesized data from ten studies, identifying a substantial overall effect of captions on vocabulary acquisition, both single words and multiword units, regardless of the specific type of vocabulary test used for the proficiency level of the learners. The analysis revealed that captioned videos consistently led to significantly greater vocabulary gains compared to uncaptioned videos, which was attributed to the assistance provided by captions in segmenting and decoding auditory input. Another more recent meta-analysis and scoping review conducted by Reynolds et al. (2022) examined 139 studies, 34 of which met inclusion criteria. The scoping review revealed a predominant focus on assessing receptive knowledge over productive knowledge, and form and meaning knowledge over knowledge of use. As for the meta-analysis, it demonstrated a positive impact on vocabulary acquisition from viewing any form of captioned or subtitled videos, with captions showing the most substantial effects.

The studies so far reviewed have usually taken place in just one session. Arguably, research examining effects of viewing over time may yield findings with more direct pedagogical applications and more ecologically valid. A study by Rodgers and Webb (2020) examined the impact of watching over seven hours of television on incidental vocabulary learning among 187 Japanese university students. Participants watched ten 42-minute episodes of an American drama, and their receptive knowledge of 60 word-families was assessed before and after viewing using two vocabulary tests of varying sensitivities. The findings revealed significant vocabulary learning from television viewing, with a positive correlation between frequency of word occurrence and learning. This study's results contributed valuable insights for future longitudinal studies investigating L2 vocabulary acquisition through extensive television viewing.

Not until recently have studies included younger age students. Gesa and Miralpeix (2023) reported a longitudinal teaching intervention aimed at enhancing the learning of target words among secondary school EFL learners over an academic year. Two groups of tenth graders (a total of 64) were exposed to new words weekly through language exercises. The experimental group also watched a captioned TV series featuring these target words. The results of pre- and post-tests on form and meaning recall indicated that intentional learning played a primary role, but additional exposure to the captioned TV series significantly increased vocabulary gains at various testing times.

Another study, by Pujadas and Muñoz (2019), also investigated the impact of extensive television viewing considering factors such as the language of on-screen text (subtitles in the L1 or captions in the L2), type of instruction (pre-teaching target items or not), and learners' proficiency. The study involved 106 eighth graders in a year-long intervention with 24 episodes of a TV series. Each class was assigned to one of four treatments: captions and pre-teaching, captions and non-pre-teaching, subtitles and pre-teaching, and subtitles and non-pre-teaching. Results indicated that participants learned vocabulary in all four conditions, with greater gains in recalling form than in recalling meaning. Pre-teaching the target items positively influenced performance, regardless of on-screen text language. Moreover, learners' proficiency before the intervention was found to correlate with higher gains.

Two recent extensive studies have used captioned viewing with primary school learners, challenging the view that young learners can only cope with L1 subtitles. One was conducted by Casulleras (2023) and spanned five months, involving two groups of Spanish/Catalan primary school students learning English as a foreign language (EFL) (see also Chapter 1 in this volume). They were a total of 92 students (grades 5 and 6; 11–12 years old), exposed to an animated TV series with English audio and either Spanish (L1) or English (L2) subtitles. While both groups demonstrated understanding and vocabulary acquisition, the L1 group exhibited higher comprehension scores, whereas the L2 group appeared to be superior in recognizing L2 word-forms, confirming previous results by

Pujadas and Muñoz (2019, 2020). Proficiency effects were noted, with L2 vocabulary size significantly impacting comprehension in both groups.

Finally, and of special interest for the present study (see below), Avello (2023) investigated the benefits of extensive captioned-video viewing on English vocabulary learning (form recall and form recognition) in 136 fourth and fifth graders (9–11 years old) in Chile. The intervention included after-viewing activities that focused either on meaning or on forms. The results indicated significant improvement in vocabulary learning, with fifth graders showing an increase of 4 words (approx. 11%) in form recall and of almost 8 words (approx. 22%) in form recognition.

2.2   Textual enhancement in captions and the role of attention

It has been suggested that paying attention to captions can facilitate the recognition of unfamiliar or unknown words, implying that awareness of captions ideally brings learners closer to L2 acquisition. Thus, caption enhancement is a form of external input enhancement, originally defined by Sharwood Smith (1993) as any deliberate attempt to emphasize specific aspects of L2 input to capture learners' attention towards these enhanced and salient features.

Only a few studies have redirected learners' attention to captions through the enhancement of specific target items. In one such study by Montero Perez and colleagues (2014) a group of 133 Flemish undergraduate students watched French video clips with various captioning conditions. The findings indicated that captioning, particularly keyword captions and textually enhanced captions, significantly improved form and meaning recognition, though not overall comprehension or meaning recall, compared to a control group without captions. As in other studies, participants' vocabulary size showed significant correlations with both comprehension and vocabulary test scores.

Another extensive study that investigated the effects of enhanced captions was conducted by Pattemore and Muñoz (2022). The study explored different captioning modes (regular captions, textually enhanced captions, and no captions) on learning various L2 grammatical constructions. A total of 112 undergraduate students watched ten full-length TV series episodes over five weeks, targeting 27 frequently occurring grammatical constructions. Results showed mixed effects of captioning: textually enhanced captions led to immediate learning outcomes, while unenhanced captions resulted in higher long-term effects.

The operationalization of learners' attention is a critical step in investigating their processing of textually enhanced captions. Eye-tracking methodology has been used to quantify the amount of time that participants' eyes focus on the target enhanced items. For example, Winke's (2013) focus was on the response of 55 English language learners to enhanced English passive constructions. The study showed that, while textual enhancement promoted attention, as learners spent more time rereading the passive forms, the effects were not strong enough for immediate, measurable learning to take place. In contrast, Lee and Révész (2018) found textual enhancement successful in effectively guiding the attention of 48 Korean learners of English to pronominal anaphoric reference. In this case, textual enhancement also led to higher gains in receptive knowledge of English anaphora. Likewise, employing multimodal input-based tasks, Lee & Révész (2020) found that 72 Korean learners of English were successfully guided toward the target grammatical constructions through captioning and textual enhance-ment. Additionally, positive correlations were identified between attention to cap-tions and learners' gains.

In an L2 vocabulary study, Montero Perez et al. (2015) explored the impact of two attention-enhancing techniques on the learning and processing of new French words by 34 L2 learners using a captioned video. The research gathered eye-movement data and conducted vocabulary tests to examine the effects of type of captioning (full or keyword captioning) and test announcement (intentional or incidental, that is, informing or not about upcoming tests). Eye-tracking analysis showed a significant interaction between type of captioning and test announce-ment. Additionally, eye-tracking measures showed a positive correlation with word learning for learners in the full captioning, intentional group.

To explore whether the potential advantage of textually enhanced captions boosted L2 acquisition of multiword units, a study by Puimège et al. (2022) inves-tigated a group of 28 EFL learners who watched a captioned video featuring both enhanced and unenhanced multiword units. The analyses revealed that enhanced items gathered increased visual attention, characterized by longer reading times, reduced single word skipping, and more instances of re-reading. A positive cor-relation was observed between the duration of visual attention and the likelihood of recall in an immediate post-test. However, the results showed that item diffi-culty and attention duration were more influential than textual enhancement in predicting learning outcomes.

Also exploring the impact of visual input enhancement on caption-reading behavior, Choi (2023) investigated English collocation acquisition by 53 Korean undergraduate students with high-intermediate proficiency. Participants watched a 6-minute video either with unenhanced captions or with enhanced captions. While caption-reading behaviors did not differ between the groups, the enhance-ment group excelled in collocation acquisition and recalled more target colloca-tions in the caption recall test compared to the control group. Notably, attention to target collocations did not significantly correlate with collocation test scores in either group.

In sum, studies that have used enhanced captions, regardless of enhancement type (highlighting, bolding or keywords), have yielded mixed results (see Montero Perez, 2022), which might imply that increased attention to form does not automatically lead to retention of semantic knowledge (Leow & Martin, 2017). More research is needed to assess the interplay of attention and L2 learning through eye-tracking technology.

2.3   Young learners and enhanced attention

Eye-tracking studies with young L2 learners are very scant (Pellicer-Sánchez et al., 2020). Two recent exceptions focused on different types of multimodal input. The study by Serrano and Pellicer-Sánchez (2019) using graded readers with primary school learners compared reading-only vs reading-while-listening conditions. The researchers found that, in the reading-only condition, readers spent more time processing the text, while in the reading-while-listening mode, more time was allocated to processing images, but comprehension scores were similar in both conditions. Interestingly, a significant negative relationship emerged between the time spent processing text and comprehension scores in both modes, highlighting the complex interactions involved in multimodal processing among young learners.

Drawing on information processing theories, Tragant and Pellicer-Sánchez (2019) employed an eye-tracker to analyze how two groups of students interacted with two types of multimodal materials: an illustrated storybook with audio support and a video with captions. Results revealed that, regardless of the format, learners spent more time processing the text than the visual input. The study suggests that storybooks and captioned videos are effective in engaging students with reading, as the visual information does not distract attention from the text. Notably, the book format displayed consistent reading behavior, while the video format exhibited greater variability in learners' processing patterns.

These studies offer valuable insights into the viewing behavior of young learners, but much is still unknown. To advance our knowledge of the potential benefits of using enhanced captions with young L2 learners, the present exploratory study will, firstly, analyze whether there is observable evidence of incidental vocabulary acquisition among primary school EFL learners from extensive viewing. To that aim, it will employ the same materials used in Avello's (2023) study looking for confirmation of those positive results with same-age students (fifth graders). Secondly, the present study aims to examine whether there is a differential impact on vocabulary gains between textually enhanced and regular captions. Thirdly, the study aims to investigate children's viewing behaviors when watching with enhanced or unenhanced captions and potential changes over the course of the intervention. To our knowledge, no previous viewing study has focused on young learners' viewing behavior over an extended experience with enhanced captions. Comparing the effects of this textual enhancement at the beginning and end of the intervention may shed some more light on young learners' viewing behavior. More specifically, this study pursues to answer the following research questions:

1. Is there evidence of incidental vocabulary acquisition in fifth graders as measured by form recall and form recognition tests after watching 11 episodes of a captioned cartoon series?
2. Does caption enhancement lead to higher vocabulary gains than regular captions?
3. Is there a change in children's viewing behavior from the beginning to the end of the intervention? If so, is the change similar for regular and enhanced captions?

3. Methodology

3.1 Participants

The participants were 17 L1-Spanish/Catalan fifth grade learners of English who were enrolled at a language school (11 males and 6 females). Their ages varied from 10 to 11 years old ($M = 10.24$, $SD = 0.59$). Two groups were formed from intact classes. One group was provided with regular captions (RC), and the other with enhanced captions (EC). The two groups had the same teacher, who was the first author of this study. A background information questionnaire was handed out to assemble personal information and information about external sources of input, such as out-of-school exposure to L2 media. Our participants reported watching TV series, movies, or cartoons in English with L1-Spanish/Catalan subtitles around once a week, and with L2-English captions nearly with the same frequency. Parental consent forms were gathered from all students.

3.2 Audiovisual material: *Charlie and Lola*

Eleven episodes of the animated series *Charlie and Lola* (Carrington & Child, 2005–2008) were chosen for this study due to the suitability of this series for the intended participants in terms of age and content. This same series was used in the study by Avello (2023) with same-age children. One episode of this cartoon series was also successfully used in the study (above) by Tragant and Pellicer-Sánchez (2019).

3.3   Target words

The target items were 36 words, including nouns and adjectives (see Table 1). Enhanced versions of the regular captions were created with the application *SubtitleEdit* (v3.5.18) and embedded on the video with *HandBrake* (v1.3.0-v1.3.3), where target words were presented in yellow and bold. These were the same target words used in the study by Avello's (2023), which will facilitate the comparison of vocabulary learning in the two studies.

3.4   Instruments

3.4.1   *EFL picture vocabulary test*

This test evaluated the learners' general L2 vocabulary knowledge by assessing their ability to recognize the meaning of 50 words. It was designed by Avello (2023) following the format of the Picture Vocabulary Size test (PVST) developed by Anthony and Nation (2017), and was satisfactorily used in Avello's study; see also Puimège and Peters (2019).

3.4.2   *Pre- and post-tests*

Vocabulary learning was assessed through pre- and post-tests that tapped into form recall and form recognition. Both tests were adapted from Avello's study (2023) (e.g., the recognition test used Spanish in Avello's study and Catalan in the present study). First, a dictation test was used to assess the recall of written-word forms, with the assumption that learners would acquire this knowledge through simultaneous processing of both aural and written input, specifically through captions. Each target word was presented within a sentence. After listening to each sentence twice, students were asked to fill in the blanks, i.e.: This animal has _____ (answer: wings). These sentences were recorded by a native English speaker and presented in a video to ensure uniform test conditions such as time constraints and the number of repetitions for all participant groups. One point was awarded for correct answers and half a point for partial knowledge (see Avello 2023).

Second, a multiple-choice test assessed form recognition (see Figure 1). Target words were removed from each sentence, and students were provided with a translation in L1-Catalan. The task required them to deduce the missing target word by selecting the appropriate alternative from the provided choices; that is, by mapping the form with its L1 meaning, which also implied meaning knowledge. To discourage guessing and ensure accuracy, students were given the option to select "I don't know" if they were uncertain about the correct answer.

Table 1. Target words

Target word	Frequency	Part of speech
Bandage	5	Noun
Busy	9	Adjective
Cabbage	3	Noun
Careful	6	Adjective
Clever	7	Adjective
Costume	3	Noun
Creaky	5	Adjective
Drop	6	Noun
Fairy	18	Noun
Fluffy	19	Adjective
Forest	3	Noun
Hairy	7	Adjective
Handbag	7	Noun
Kitten	3	Noun
Lead	3	Noun
Leaf	20	Noun
Mermaid	6	Noun
Mud	3	Noun
Pea	8	Noun
Pillow	3	Noun
Pleased	6	Adjective
Puddle	9	Noun
Sausage	4	Noun
Shell	6	Noun
Slipper	3	Noun
Sticky	4	Adjective
Stripy	3	Adjective
Suitcase	4	Noun
Track	7	Noun
Trolley	4	Noun
Useful	4	Adjective
Wand	5	Noun
Web	8	Noun
Wide	7	Adjective
Wing	3	Noun
Wobbly	18	Adjective

8. Birds have _____ (ales).
   a. Winds
   b. Feathers
   c. Beaks
   d. Noods
   e. I don't know (no ho sé)

Figure 1. Multiple-choice test: Sample item

3.4 Procedure

The experimental sessions were organized during the regular class time. The nature of the experiment remained undisclosed to all participants, and the teacher refrained from offering any supplementary practice on vocabulary. Prior to treatment, a training/pilot session with the eye-tracker was conducted in class, so that young learners could be familiarized with the innovative technology. A short musical video from the *Charlie and Lola* franchise was selected, namely "Bat Cat." The eye-tracker was calibrated using a 5-point calibration. Participants' eye-movements were recorded using Tobii T120 (Tobii, www.tobii.com), which is a desktop eye-tracker with the camera and infrared light integrated in the monitor, with a sampling rate of 120 Hz. Visual and auditory input was displayed using Tobii Studio (v3.2.3).

After piloting the eye-tracker, the participants completed a background questionnaire and took the vocabulary pre-test and the EFL picture vocabulary test (see Table 2). Afterwards, participants watched one episode (which lasted approx. 10 minutes) per class, twice a week, with either regular or enhanced captions. After episode 11, participants took the post-test.

Table 2. Experimental procedure

Session 1	Session 2	Session 3	Session 4	Session 5 & 6	Session 7	Session 8 to 14	Session 15	Session 16
Eye-tracker pilot	Background information questionnaire	Form recall and form recognition pre-tests	EFL Picture Vocabulary Test	Episodes 1 to 2	Episode 3 with eye-tracker	Episodes 4 to 10	Episode 11 with eye-tracker	Form recall and form recognition post-tests

Episodes 3 and 11 were viewed individually through the eye-tracker. Episode 3 was selected under the assumption that the children would have become somehow acquainted with the viewing experience by that point, and episode 11 was chosen as the final episode for assessing any potential changes resulting from the intervention. Episodes 3 and 11 were analyzed on *Lextutor* (Cobb, 2019) for coverage, tokens, word types, type-token ratio, and lexical density (see Table 3). Both episodes had at least a 90% coverage at K1, compared to the 80% threshold suggested for audiovisual input by Durbahn et al. (2020, 2022), which indicates suitability for low proficiency learners and comparability in terms of vocabulary profile.

Table 3. Vocabulary profile for episodes 3 and 11

Episode	Coverage	Tokens and types	Type-token ratio	Lexical density
E3: "I must take absolutely everything"	K1: 91.1% K2: 93.9%	Tokens: 952 Types: 285	0.30	0.51
E11: "I will be especially, very careful"	K1: 90.6% K2: 93.8%	Tokens: 1.084 Types: 272	0.25	0.50

3.5   Data analysis

The software IBM SPPS Statistics 27 version was used for the analyses. First, the normal distribution of scores was assessed and confirmed. Then, an independent samples t-test was conducted to assess the comparability between experimental groups (enhanced and regular captions). Previous vocabulary size as measured by the EFL picture vocabulary test was non-significantly different across both groups ($p = .135$); see descriptive statistics in Table 4.

Table 4. Descriptive statistics: Vocabulary size

	Vocabulary size (max: 50)			
	M	*SD*	Min.	Max.
Regular ($n = 8$)	26.63	9.54	16	32
Enhanced ($n = 9$)	20.33	4.50	9	24
All participants ($N = 17$)	23.29	7.96	9	32

3.5.1   *Vocabulary tests*

In the form recall pre- and post-tests, one point was given to each 100% accurate response while half a point was awarded to those responses that approached the target form. Form recognition pre- and post-tests, however, were scored dichotomously (0 or 1).

3.5.2 *Eye-tracking data*

Every target word, either enhanced or unenhanced, was selected as AOI (i.e.: Area of Interest). The AOIs were manually drawn, making sure the space around each word remained the same for all AOIs. The eye-movement measure under analysis was *average fixation duration* (the mean of the duration for each individual fixation within an AOI, that is, the sum of the duration for all fixations divided by the total fixation count). The percentage of eye-tracking samples correctly identified for participants was set at 70%, and the rest was discarded.

4. Results

The descriptive statistics of the pre-test and post-test scores appear in Table 5, results for each test range from 0 to 1.

Table 5. Descriptive statistics: Pre-test, post-test and absolute gains

	Form recall					
	Pre-test		Post-test		Absolute gains	
	M	*SD*	*M*	*SD*	*M*	*SD*
Regular (*n* = 8)	0.29	0.39	0.39	0.43	0.10	0.14
Enhanced (*n* = 9)	0.26	0.36	0.47	0.43	0.21	0.40
All participants (*N* = 17)	0.28	0.37	0.44	0.43	0.16	0.39
	Form recognition					
	Pre-test		Post-test		Absolute gains	
	M	*SD*	*M*	*SD*	*M*	*SD*
Regular (*n* = 8)	0.48	0.50	0.53	0.50	0.05	0.43
Enhanced (*n* = 9)	0.46	0.49	0.67	0.47	0.21	0.58
All participants (*N* = 17)	0.47	0.50	0.61	0.49	0.14	0.52

Analyses were conducted separately for form recall and for form recognition using GLMMs with participants as subjects and item and time as repeated measures.

4.1   Vocabulary acquisition through multimodal input

The first research question addressed the effects of viewing the captioned series regardless of experimental condition. For form recall, *L2 Vocabulary Knowledge* ($F(1, 998) = 10.648$, $p = .001$) and *Time* ($F(1, 998) = 59.766$, $p < .001$) emerged as significant main effects in the model (see Table 6).

Table 6. Results from GLMM: Fixed coefficients for form recall regardless of experimental group

Model term	Coefficient	Std. error	t	Sig.	Exp (coeff.)	95% CI for Exp (coeff.)	
						Lower	Upper
Intercept	−2.467	.7228	−3.414	.001	.085	.021	.350
Vocabulary	.092	.0282	3.263	.001	1.097	1.037	1.159
Time = 1	−1.109	.1434	−7.731	< .001	.330	.249	.437
Time = 2	0[b]	.	.	.	.	.	.

All participants showed an improvement of 8.4 words (23.3%) from pre-test to post-test in form recall ($p < .001$) (see Figure 2).

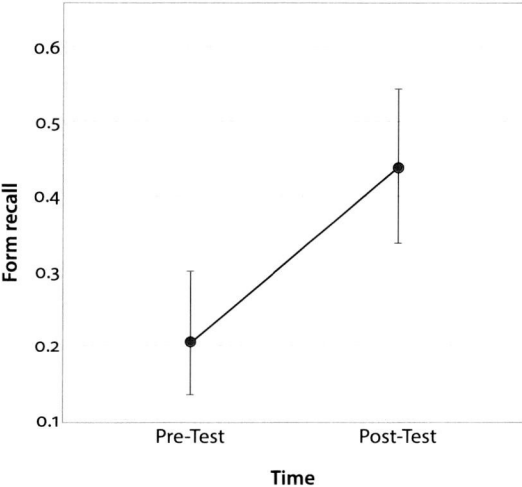

Figure 2. Form recall by time

In terms of form recognition, *L2 Vocabulary Knowledge* $(F(1, 1289) = 6.973,$ $p = .008)$ and *Time* $(F(1, 1289) = 27.660, p < .001)$ also had significant main effects (see Table 7).

Table 7. Results from GLMM: Fixed coefficients for form recognition regardless of experimental group

Model term	Coefficient	Std. error	*t*	Sig.	Exp (coeff.)	95% CI for Exp (coeff.)	
						Lower	Upper
Intercept	−.986	.5672	−1.738	.082	.373	.123	1.135
Vocabulary	.061	.0232	2.641	.008	1.063	1.016	1.113
Time = 1	−.579	.1100	−5.259	< .001	.561	.452	.696
Time = 2	0[b]	.	.	.	.	.	.

The pairwise comparison (see Figure 3) showed a significant increase of 5.1 words (14.2%) from pre-test to post-test $(p < .001)$.

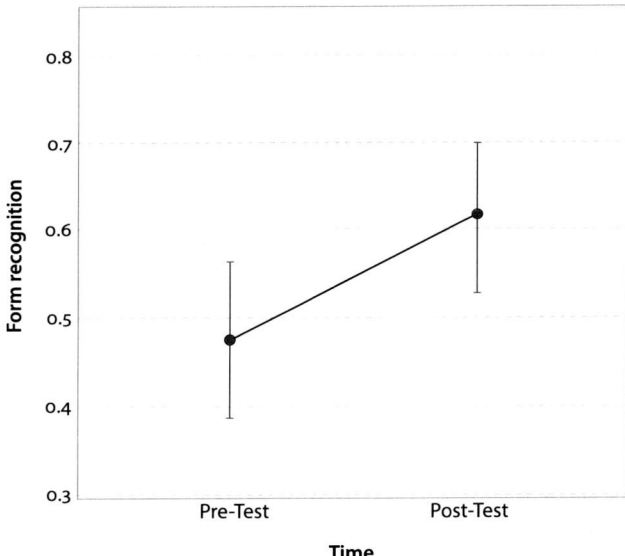

Figure 3. Form recognition by time

4.2   The effects of textual enhancement

The second research question aimed to investigate the impact of enhanced captions, in comparison to regular captions, on the acquisition of L2 vocabulary. In terms of form recall, significant main effects of *L2 Vocabulary Knowledge* ($F(1,996) = 10.704$, $p = .001$), and *Time* ($F(1, 996) = 54.909$, $p < .001$) and a significant interaction between *Experimental Group* and *Time* ($F(1,996) = 6.050$, $p = .014$) were found in the analyses, as well as a non-significant main effect of *Experimental Group* ($F(1,996) = 1.213$ $p = .271$) (see Table 8).

Table 8. Results from GLMM: Fixed coefficients for form recall

Model term	Coefficient	Std. error	*t*	Sig.	Exp (coeff.)	95% CI for Exp (coeff.)	
						Lower	Upper
Intercept	−2.338	.7300	−3.202	.001	.097	.023	.405
Vocabulary	.100	.0305	3.272	.001	1.105	1.041	1.173
Time = 1	−1.421	.1957	−7.261	< .001	.242	.165	.355
Time = 2	0[b]	.	.	.	.	.	.
Exp_Group = 1	−.895	.4774	−1.875	.061	.409	.160	1.043
Exp_Group = 2	0[b]	.	.	.	.	.	.
[Exp_Group = 1]*[Time = 1]	.694	.2823	2.460	.014	2.003	1.151	3.485
[Exp_Group = 2]*[Time = 1]	0[b]	.	.	.	.	.	.
[Exp_Group = 1]*[Time = 2]	0[b]	.	.	.	.	.	.
[Exp_Group = 2]*[Time = 2]	0[b]	.	.	.	.	.	.

There was a significant increase from pre-test to post-test for both groups: for RC ($p = .001$) of 4.7 words (12.9%), and for EC ($p < .001$) of 11.2 words, (31.1%). Even though comparisons at pre-test were non-significant between the two groups ($p = .715$), the pairwise contrasts showed significant differences between both groups at post-test, where knowledge in the post-test was significantly higher for the EC group ($p = .050$) (see Figure 4).

For form recognition, we found significant main effects of *L2 Vocabulary Knowledge* ($F(1,1287) = 9.572$, $p = .002$), and *Time* ($F(1,1287) = 22.710$, $p < .001$) and a significant interaction between *Experimental Group* and *Time* ($F(1,1287) = 7.630$, $p = .006$), as well as a non-significant main effect of *Experimental Group* ($F(1,1287) = 3.015$ $p = .083$) (see Table 9).

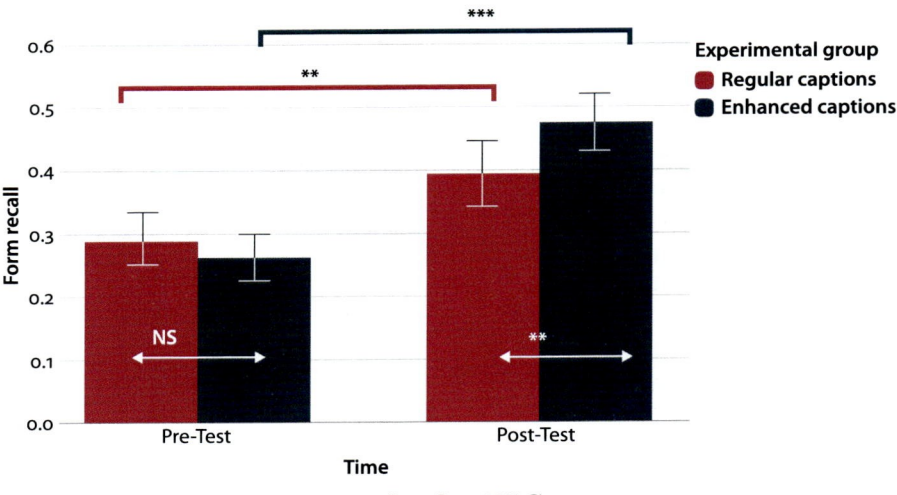

Figure 4. Form recall by time by experimental group
NS = not significant, ** $p < .05$, *** $p < .001$

Table 9. Results from GLMM: Fixed coefficients for form recognition

Model term	Coefficient	Std. error	t	Sig.	Exp (coeff.)	95% CI for Exp (coeff.)	
						Lower	Upper
Intercept	−.837	.5527	−1.514	.130	.433	.146	1.281
Vocabulary	.072	.0234	3.094	.002	1.075	1.027	1.125
Time = 1	−.852	.1511	−5.639	< .001	.426	.317	.574
Time = 2	0[b]	.	.	.	.	.	.
Exp_Group = 1	−.936	.3813	−2.454	.014	.392	.186	.829
Exp_Group = 2	0[b]	.	.	.	.	.	.
[Exp_Group = 1]*[Time = 1]	.624	.2259	2.762	.006	1.866	1.198	2.907
[Exp_Group = 2]*[Time = 1]	0[b]	.	.	.	.	.	.
[Exp_Group = 1]*[Time = 2]	0[b]	.	.	.	.	.	.
[Exp_Group = 2]*[Time = 2]	0[b]	.	.	.	.	.	.

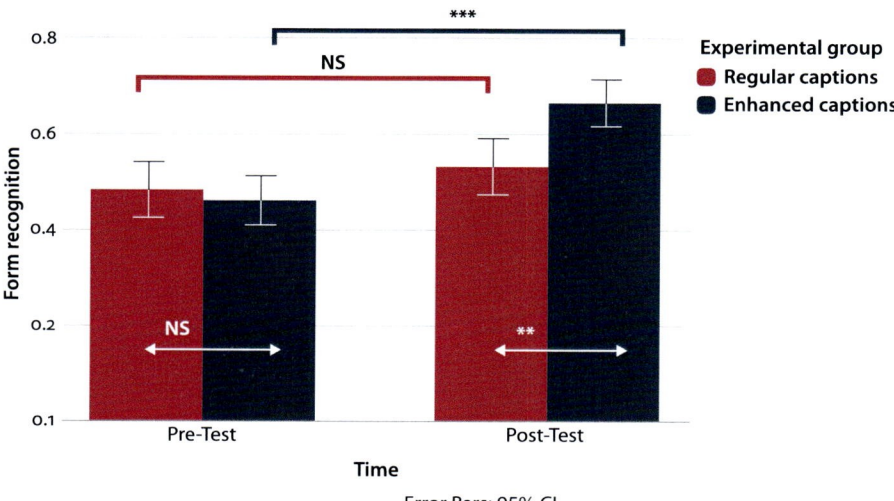

Figure 5. Form recognition by time by experimental group
NS = not significant, ** $p<.05$, *** $p<.001$

Between-group differences were not significant at pre-test ($p=.399$), whereas they were significant at post-test ($p=.012$) (see Figure 5). Pairwise comparisons between groups displayed significant differences between testing times exclusively for the EC group ($p<.001$), with an increase of 7.1 words (19.9%) from pre-test to post-test. Whereas RC's increase of 2.1 words (5.7%) resulted not significant ($p=.175$).[1]

4.3   Attention behavior at two times

The third research question asked whether there was a change in viewing behavior in terms of attention from episode 3 to episode 11 and whether input enhancement drew learners' visual attention to the target words differently. The analysis was exploratory due to the limited number of target words in each episode and the presence of words previously encountered in earlier episodes (see Table 10).[2]

The descriptive data for the eye-tracking metrics is displayed in Table 11. We decided to exclude the target word "fluffy" from our analyses given its outlier

---

1. A complementary analysis based on relative gains (see Horst et al., 1988) confirmed these findings. Two independent samples t-tests showed that EC's relative gains were higher than RC's in both form recall ($p=.002$) and form recognition ($p<.001$).

2. When conducting a separate analysis controlling target words that were previously seen (by maintaining only those that appear in each episode), results show similar viewing behaviors.

Table 10. Frequency of target words per episode

Episode 3			Episode 11		
Target word	**Before**	**In the episode**	**Target word**	**Before**	**In the episode**
Fairy	14	4	Careful	3	3
Mermaid	2	1	Fluffy	0	18
Slipper	0	3	Handbag	0	7
Stripy	0	3	Kitten	2	1
Suitcase	0	4	Mud	2	1
Track	2	5	Pleased	5	1
Wand	0	5	Shell	0	6
Wings	0	1	Sticky	1	3
			Trolley	0	4

occurrence in episode 11 (18 repetitions). We also excluded the word "fairy" due to its very frequent occurrence prior to episode 3 (14 repetitions), with the aim of mitigating any potential influence of word familiarity on participants' viewing behavior. After their removal, the range of occurrence of target words in these two episodes was 1 to 7 ($M = 3.25$; $SD = 1.88$).

Table 11. Descriptives for the eye-tracking metrics (ms)

	Average fixation duration							
	Episode 3				Episode 11			
	M	*SD*	Min.	Max.	*M*	*SD*	Min.	Max.
All participants ($N=17$)	267.5	186.2	0	1149.2	247.6	112.7	0	618.0
Regular Captions ($n=8$)	224.0	191.6	0	1149.0	237.7	67.7	83.0	298.0
Enhanced Captions ($n=9$)	311.0	171.0	0	1032.0	255.1	137.2	0	618.0

As the data for average fixation duration was not normally distributed, the variable was log transformed. To analyze the eye movements in both episodes, we conducted a GLMM with the eye-tracking metrics as outcome variable. The analysis showed that there was no significant main effect of *Frequency* on average fixation duration ($p=.249$). There was a significant effect of *Episode* (3 vs 11) ($F_{(1, 223)}=11.933$ $p<.001$) but the interaction between *Experimental Group* and *Episode* did not reach significance ($F_{(1, 223)}=1.514$ $p=.072$). Moreover, *Experimental Group* did not show a significant main effect ($F_{(1, 223)}=.960$ $p=.328$) (see Table 12).

A pairwise comparison (see Figure 6) shows that average fixation is significantly higher in episode 3 for the EC group ($p=.049$), and this difference dis-

Table 12. Results from GLMM: Fixed coefficients for average fixation

Model Term	Coefficient	Std. error	t	Sig.	95% Confidence interval	
					Lower	Upper
Intercept	−1.526	.0951	−16.052	< .001	−1.713	−1.339
Frequency	.017	.0143	1.157	.249	−.012	.045
Episode = 3	.268	.0808	3.313	< .001	.108	.427
Episode = 11	0[b]	.	.	.	.	.
Exp_Group = 1	−.032	.1239	−.259	.796	−.276	.212
Exp_Group = 2	0[b]	.	.	.	.	.
[Exp_Group = 1]* [Episode = 3]	−.141	.1143	−1.231	.072	−.366	.085
[Exp_Group = 2]* [Episode = 3]	0[b]	.	.	.	.	.
[Exp_Group = 1]* [Episode = 11]	0[b]	.	.	.	.	.
[Exp_Group = 2]* [Episode = 11]	0[b]	.	.	.	.	.

appears by episode 11 (p = .796). Moreover, the EC group decreases their average fixation time significantly (p < .001). In the case of RC, however, their average fixation does not change significantly (p = .117) between the two episodes.

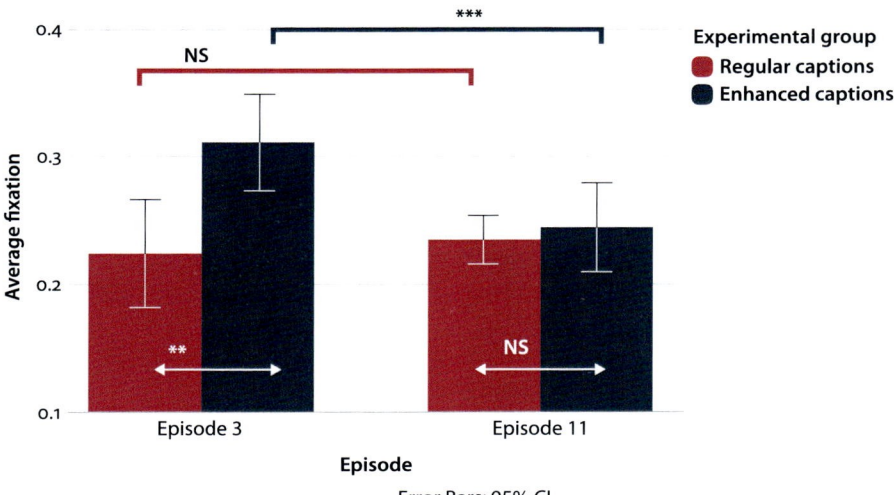

Figure 6. Average fixation by episode
NS = not significant, ** p < .05, *** p < .001

5. Discussion

The present study is, to our knowledge, the first extensive viewing intervention with young learners to explore the extent to which audiovisual materials with textually enhanced or regular captions promote incidental vocabulary learning. The study also explores the changes in children's viewing behavior over the intervention period, providing further insights into the dynamics of young learners' attention to textually enhanced and regular captions.

The first research question asked whether the viewing of 11 episodes of a captioned cartoon series would result in incidental vocabulary acquisition among fifth graders, as assessed through form recall and form recognition tests. The results showed that the viewing of these episodes led to a significant increase in vocabulary knowledge across all participants, impacting both form recall and form recognition. The number of learned words was modest, as has been previously observed in situations where learning occurs in incidental conditions, but higher than the 7% average found in viewing studies of older and more proficient participants (see Webb et al., 2023). Moreover, other words that were not target items may also have been learned to some degree, as argued by Webb and colleagues (2023). Additionally, the results revealed a significant main effect of previous vocabulary knowledge for both tests, which is in accord with many previous studies (e.g., Feng & Webb, 2020; Montero Perez, 2020; Pattemore & Muñoz, 2022; Peters & Webb, 2018; Pujadas & Muñoz, 2019); see Chapter 1 in this volume as well. This common finding highlights the importance of considering individual differences in vocabulary proficiency when evaluating the impact of audiovisual materials on language learning outcomes. Our results align with previous research that underscores the advantages of incorporating captioned videos in language learning contexts (e.g., Gesa & Miralpeix, 2023; Montero Perez et al., 2013; Reynolds et al., 2022) and confirms the extension of these benefits to younger learners in incidental conditions (Avello & Muñoz, 2023).

Regarding the second research question, we examined differences between the two conditions, enhanced and regular captions. Between-group differences were found to be not significant in both pre-tests. For both, form recall and form recognition, in addition to the significant effect of previous vocabulary knowledge, there arose a significant interaction between group and time. This indicated that the impact of using textually enhanced captions or regular captions was different in the post-tests. Regarding the regular captions group, results showed a statistically significant increase only for form recall, which was slightly lower than in Avello's study (8.3% vs 11.1%), but not for form recognition. This result partly differs from Avello's (2023) result, in that the fifth graders in her study showed a significant advantage with regular captions also in form recognition. An explanation for their higher gains, even though their prior receptive vocabulary knowledge was slightly lower ($M = 20.5$ vs. $M = 26.4$), could be related to the inclusion of after-viewing tasks in the intervention, which may have increased learners' attention to the videos. Also, in the present study, both form recall and form recognition tests were administered on the same day, which may have affected participants' capacity on the second test. On the other hand, the enhanced captions group in our study showed a significant increase in both form recall and form recognition, similar to Avello's participants. It is possible that post-viewing tasks in one study and caption enhancement in the other had analogous effects, increasing learners' attention to unknown words. In sum, in the current study, the use of enhanced captions proved to be more efficient than the use of regular captions, as evidenced by the significant improvements in both recall and recognition compared to regular captions. This is in line with research that suggests that textual enhancement might have a positive impact on L2 learning (Choi, 2023; Lee & Révész, 2018; 2020; Puimège et al., 2022).

Finally, to address the third, exploratory, research question, we examined whether there was a change in viewing behavior from soon after the beginning (episode 3) to the end of the intervention (episode 11), and whether this behavior was different in the two groups. Although the findings are preliminary because the effect of the different target words in the two episodes could not be totally controlled, the analysis of the eye-tracking data indicated significantly longer fixations at the beginning than at the end. However, looking at the two participant groups separately revealed that in episode 3 the EC group exhibited a significantly higher average fixation duration than the RC group, and that in episode 11 this difference had disappeared. The higher average fixation observed when participants engaged with enhanced captions is in general accordance with previous results (e.g., Montero Perez et al., 2015; Puimège et al., 2022). On the other hand, the result that the effect of enhancement diminished over time has not been previously observed in this line of research, the likely reason being that eye-tracking studies have generally taken place in one session and could not examine the effect of habituation on participants' viewing behavior. An exception could have been the study by Lee and Révész (2018), in which eye-tracking data was collected in two days over the span of one week, but the researchers did not compare between the groups, enhanced or regular captions, and two short sessions might not have been long enough for potential differences to emerge. Interestingly, in a study addressing the effects of frequency and enhancement in university students' learning of formulaic sequences through reading, Northbrook et al. (2022) found a short-lived effect of textual enhancement, but the multiple exposures to the target sequences seemingly cancelled out the effect of enhancement. The researchers went on to suggest that enhancement primarily influences the formation of initial memory traces, whereas repetition may affect long-term retention. While more research that occurs over a span of several sessions/weeks is needed to confirm the hypothesis that the effect of enhancement on reading behavior may be transitory, the finding by Northbrook and colleagues with university students suggests that the phenomenon may not be exclusively associated to young age.

6.   Conclusion

In this study, enhanced captions exhibited greater effectiveness in promoting incidental vocabulary acquisition than regular captions. Thus, the use of enhanced captions emerges as a valuable strategy for enhancing the incidental learning of new L2 vocabulary among primary school learners as well, a population that is still understudied in incidental vocabulary learning (Webb et al., 2023) and in viewing studies specifically. Moreover, by means of an eye-tracking analysis, this study suggested that the learners' attention levels to enhanced captions were higher towards the beginning of the intervention to diminish by the end, eventually approaching the attention levels observed with regular captions. This preliminary finding opens new avenues for research in the areas of captioned viewing and reading.

Nonetheless, this study should be considered in light of some limitations. First, the relatively small sample size may impact the generalizability of our findings and the results should be interpreted with caution. This small sample prevented us from counterbalancing episodes so that half of the participants watched episode 3 first and the other half watched episode 11 first to avoid having confounding episode-related variables across the comparison, as suggested by a reviewer. Another shortcoming is the limited quality of the eye-tracking data from young learners, leading to a 70% threshold and subsequent data loss. Future research is needed that confirms the decline of attention to enhanced captions, as measured by the eye-tracking methodology as well as by participants' own accounts. Similarly, future studies could investigate how attention patterns relate to language acquisition outcomes by comparing groups watching episodes with and without captions. On another note, the lack of a no-treatment control group limited understanding of potential testing effects, as performance might be influenced by factors beyond exposure to television. Moreover, administering both recall and recognition tests in one session raises concerns about testing effects; a split-testing approach could address this. To finish, although target item frequency did not emerge as significant, this could be due to their low exposure in the non-manipulated TV series or their varied distribution across episodes. However, the interplay between item frequency and textual enhancement appears as a potentially worthwhile enquiry (see Northbrook et al., 2022) for future viewing studies. Pedagogically, our findings imply that incorporating textual enhancements in captions can be a beneficial strategy for improving L2 vocabulary learning in primary school students. In this sense, primary school educators may find value in integrating enhanced captions in the videos used in language learning activities.

Acknowledgements

This study has been made possible thanks to the support of the Joan Oró Predoctoral Program from the Secretaria d'Universitats i Recerca del Departament de Recerca i Universitats of the Government of Catalonia (2023 FI-1 00629), which is co-funded by the European Union, to the first author. This study has also had the support of the research project PID2019-110594GB-100 from the Spanish Ministry of Science and Innovation and 2023SGR00303 from the Catalan Agency for Management of University and Research Grants (AGAUR) to the second author. We wish to express our sincere gratitude to Dr Daniela Avello for her invaluable assistance and provision of experimental materials. We would also like to thank the reviewers for their constructive feedback.

Ethical considerations

The protocols of data collection, data anonymization, data processing, and data storage of the current study were approved by the Institutional Review Board of the University of Barcelona (IRB0003099).

References

Anthony, L., & Nation, I. S. P. (2017). Picture Vocabulary Size Test (version 1.2.0) [Computer software and measurement instrument]. Waseda University. Retrieved on 28 May 2024 from http://www.laurenceanthony.net/software/pvst

Avello, D. (2023). L2 learning from captioned-video viewing in primary school students [Unpublished doctoral dissertation]. University of Barcelona.

Avello, D., & Muñoz, C. (2023). The development of receptive language skills from captioned video viewing in primary school EFL learners. *Education Sciences*, *13*(5), 479.

Carrington, M., & Child, L. (Executive producers). (2005–2008). *Charlie and Lola* [Animated TV series]. Tiger Aspects Productions.

Choi, S. (2023). Visual saliency in captioned digital videos and learning of English collocations: An eye-tracking study. *Language Learning & Technology*, *27*(1), 1–21.

Cobb, T. (2019). VocabProfilers [computer program]. Accessed 30 Oct 2019 at https://www.lextutor.ca/vp/eng/

Durbahn, M., Macís, M., Rodgers, M., & Peters, E. (2022). Lexical coverage in L2 viewing comprehension: An extension of van Zeeland and Schmitt (2012) [Conference presentation]. EuroSLA 31st conference, University of Fribourg, Switzerland.

Durbahn, M., Rodgers, M., & Peters, E. (2020). The relationship between vocabulary and viewing comprehension. *System, 88*, 1–13.

Feng, Y., & Webb, S. (2020). Learning vocabulary through reading, listening, and viewing: Which mode of input is most effective? *Studies in Second Language Acquisition, 42*(3), 499–523.

Gesa, F., & Miralpeix, I. (2023). Extensive viewing as additional input for foreign language vocabulary learning: A longitudinal study in secondary school. *Language Teaching Research*.

Horst, M., Cobb, T., & Meara, P. (1998). Beyond a Clockwork Orange: Acquiring second language vocabulary through reading. *Reading in a Foreign Language, 11*, 207–223.

Lee, M., & Révész, A. (2018). Promoting grammatical development through textually enhanced captions: An eye-tracking study. *The Modern Language Journal, 102*(3), 557–577.

Lee, M., & Révész, A. (2020). Promoting grammatical development through captions and textual enhancement in multimodal input-based tasks. *Studies in Second Language Acquisition, 42*(3), 1–27.

Leow, R. P., & Martin, A. (2017). *Enhancing the input to promote salience of the L2. A critical overview*. Routledge.

Mayer, R. E. (2009). *Multimedia Learning* (2nd ed.). Cambridge: Cambridge University Press.

Montero Perez, M. (2020). Incidental vocabulary learning through viewing video. The role of vocabulary knowledge and working memory. *Studies in Second Language Acquisition, 42*(4), 749–773.

Montero Perez, M. (2022). Second or foreign language learning through watching audio-visual input and the role of on-screen text. *Language Teaching, 55*(2), 163–192.

Montero Perez, M., Peters, E., & Desmet, P. (2015). Enhancing vocabulary learning through captioned video: An eye-tracking study. *The Modern Language Journal, 99*, 308–328.

Montero Perez, M., Van Den Noortgate, W., & Desmet, P. (2013). Captioned video for L2 listening and vocabulary learning: A meta-analysis. *System, 41*(3), 720–739.

Muñoz, C. (2022). Audiovisual input in L2 learning. *Language, Interaction and Acquisition, 13*(1), 125–143.

Northbrook, J., Allen, D., & Conklin, K. (2022). 'Did you see that?' – The role of repetition and enhancement on lexical bundle processing in English learning materials. *Applied Linguistics, 43*(3), 453–472.

Pattemore, A., & Muñoz, C. (2022). Captions and learnability factors in learning grammar from audio-visual input. *The JALT CALL Journal, 18*(1), 83–109.

Pellicer-Sánchez, A., Tragant, E., Conklin, K., Rodgers, M., Serrano, R., & Llanes, À. (2020). Young learners' processing of multimodal input and its impact on reading comprehension: An eye-tracking study. *Studies in Second Language Acquisition, 42*(3), 577–598.

Peters, E., & Muñoz, C. (2020). Introduction to the special issue. Language learning from multimodal input. *Studies in Second Language Acquisition, 42*, 489–497.

doi Peters, E., & Webb, S. (2018). Incidental vocabulary acquisition through viewing L2 television and factors that affect learning. *Studies in Second Language Acquisition*, *40*(3), 551–577.

doi Puimège, E., Montero Perez, M., & Peters, E. (2022). Promoting L2 acquisition of multiword units through textually enhanced audiovisual input: An eye-tracking study. *Second Language Research*, *39*(2), 471–492.

doi Puimège, E., & Peters, E. (2019). Learning L2 vocabulary from audiovisual input: An exploratory study into incidental learning of single words and formulaic sequences. *Language Learning*, *69*, 424–438.

doi Puimège, E., & Peters, E. (2020). Learning formulaic sequences through viewing L2 television and factors that affect learning. *Studies in Second Language Acquisition*, *42*(3), 525–549.

doi Pujadas, G., & Muñoz, C. (2019). Extensive viewing of captioned and subtitled TV series: a study of L2 vocabulary learning by adolescents, *The Language Learning Journal*, *47*(4), 479–496.

doi Pujadas, G., & Muñoz, C. (2020). Examining adolescent EFL learners' TV viewing comprehension through captions and subtitles. *Studies in Second Language Acquisition*, *42*(3), 1–25.

doi Reynolds, B. L., Cui, Y., Kao, C.-W., & Thomas, N. (2022). Vocabulary acquisition through viewing captioned and subtitled video: A scoping review and meta-analysis. *Systems*, *10*(133).

doi Rodgers, M. P. H., & Webb, S. (2020). Incidental vocabulary learning through viewing television. *ITL – International Journal of Applied Linguistics*, *171*(2), 191–220.

doi Serrano, R., & Pellicer-Sánchez, A. (2019). Young L2 learners' online processing of information in a graded reader during reading-only and reading-while-listening conditions: A study of eye-movements. *Applied Linguistics Review*, *13*(1), 49–70.

doi Sharwood Smith, M. (1993). Input enhancement in instructed SLA: Theoretical bases. *Studies in Second Language Acquisition*, *15*, 165–179.

doi Tragant, E., & Pellicer-Sánchez, A. (2019). Young EFL learners' processing of multimodal input: Examining learners' eye movements. *System*, *80*, 212–223.

doi Vanderplank, R. (2016). Captioned media in foreign language learning and teaching: Subtitles for the deaf and hard-of-hearing as tools for language learning. *Palgrave Macmillan*.

doi Webb, S., Uchihara, T., & Yanagisawa, A. (2023). How effective is second language incidental vocabulary learning? A meta-analysis. *Language Teaching*, *56*(2), 161–180.

doi Winke, P. M. (2013). The effects of input enhancement on grammar learning and comprehension: A modified replication of Lee (2007) with eye-movement data. *Studies in Second Language Acquisition*, *35*(2), 323–352.

Attention allocation in (L1) subtitled and (L2) captioned video viewing

Effects of prior vocabulary instruction on input processing and comprehension

Geòrgia Pujadas[1] & Eva Puimège[2,3]
[1] Universitat de Barcelona | [2] KU Leuven | [3] Fonds Wetenschappelijk Onderzoek – Vlaanderen (FWO)

Pre-directing learners' attention to novel words facilitates learning through meaning-focused input, but little is known about the effect that vocabulary-focused activities may have on video processing and comprehension. This study investigates attention allocation in (L1) subtitled and (L2) captioned video viewing and explores potential trade-offs between pre-viewing instruction and comprehension. Eighty-seven Catalan/Spanish L2-English beginner learners watched an eight-minute video with either captions or subtitles while their eye-movements were recorded. Half of the participants in each language condition were pre-taught vocabulary. Results showed that pre-viewing instruction affected attention allocation only in the captions group, with participants tending to spend less time on target captions and comprehension-relevant captions. Allocating attention to vocabulary, however, did not seem to hinder comprehension in a significant manner.

1. Introduction

Learning vocabulary is an essential aspect of language learning (e.g., Schmitt, 2010), and a challenge for learners who find themselves in a context with limited contact with the second language (L2). L2 television[1] has become a popular choice for foreign language (FL) teachers and learners alike to increase contact with the target language, especially among children and teenagers who prefer watching television to reading (Lindgren & Muñoz, 2013; Peters, 2019). L2 television offers

---

1. The term *L2 television* is used throughout the chapter as an umbrella term for television programs, films, TV series or documentaries, independently of whether these are watched on a traditional TV set, a computer, or hand-held devices.

https://doi.org/10.1075/lllt.61.04puj

learners the chance to encounter (novel) words in context accompanied by visual support (Peters, 2019; Pujadas & Muñoz, 2023; Rodgers, 2018). Further, the possibility of adding captions (in the same language as the audio) or subtitles (in the first language [L1]) can compensate for a (perceived) gap between learners' L2 proficiency and the difficulty level of this type of non-adapted input.

In an instructed context, vocabulary learning can be additionally boosted by deliberately pre-directing learners' attention to novel words (e.g., through textual enhancement, glossed captions, or pre-viewing vocabulary-focused activities), which has been shown to significantly increase the odds of learning those words (e.g., Gesa & Miralpeix, 2023; Majuddin et al., 2021; Montero Perez, 2019; Montero Perez et al., 2018; Pujadas & Muñoz, 2019). However, as attentional capacity is limited (Robinson, 2003; VanPatten, 2004), allocating attention to specific words might divert attentional resources from other aspects in the video, such as the global understanding of the content (Choi, 2017). Still, little is known about these potential trade-offs in the context of video-viewing, especially for young beginner FL learners.

The present study follows up on Pujadas and Muñoz's (2019, 2020) longitudinal classroom-based pedagogical intervention investigating vocabulary learning and comprehension through TV viewing with beginner adolescent L2-English learners in Spain. Pujadas and Muñoz (2019) found that including a short vocabulary pre-viewing activity had a significant positive effect on word learning. The analysis of learners' comprehension rates, however, showed that students who received instruction prior to viewing tended to have lower comprehension than those who were not pre-taught target vocabulary (Pujadas & Muñoz, 2020), hinting at a possible trade-off between a focus on vocabulary and comprehension of the video content. The present one-off study seeks to investigate if prior instruction on video-related vocabulary affects students' attention allocation and comprehension of the video content when viewing a subtitled or captioned TV series by collecting eye-tracking data from the same sample of EFL beginner learners.

2.   Literature review

2.1   Vocabulary learning through L2 television

L2 television is a valuable source of meaning-focused input to help FL learners increase their exposure to authentic L2 input, which is fundamental for vocabulary development and increasing L2 proficiency (Webb, 2015). L2 television exposes learners to repeated encounters with low-frequency words (Rodgers & Webb, 2011), and the images in the video provide online meaning support that benefits word learning (Peters, 2018; Pujadas & Muñoz, 2023; Rodgers, 2018). Numerous studies have shown that vocabulary can be learnt incidentally through audiovisual materials (e.g., Peters & Webb, 2018; Rodgers & Webb, 2020), even though there is considerable variation in gains across studies (Webb et al., 2023). Recent research has shown that even young beginner-level learners who are less familiar with viewing the original version can benefit from viewing L2 television (e.g., Avello & Muñoz, 2023; Pujadas & Muñoz, 2019, 2020).

The extent to which FL learners can benefit from video input is likely to depend on the degree to which it is understood. When the language of the videos falls beyond the viewers' perceived L2 proficiency level, adding captions in the target language can make content more accessible. The bulk of research suggests that captioned viewing leads to higher gains in vocabulary than uncaptioned viewing (see Montero Perez et al., 2013; Webb et al., 2023). Captions aid speech segmentation, aural and written form recognition, and initial form-meaning mapping (Montero Perez et al., 2013). However, when L2 proficiency is too low, learners may not be able to cope with the fast speech rate and lexical difficulty of the content. As a result, some learners might simply not make the effort to process the L2 text, as evidenced by their eye movements during L2 TV viewing (Muñoz, 2017). Adding subtitles in the native language can be a viable alternative to enhance comprehension and maintain their attention, particularly in the case of young FL learners, whose L2 reading skills might not be as developed as their L1 reading skills.

2.2   The importance of attention allocation

Successful vocabulary learning depends to some extent on learners' degree of attention to the novel L2 forms (e.g., Laufer & Hulstijn, 2001; Schmitt, 2008). Eye-tracking studies on vocabulary learning through reading and viewing have provided evidence that the degree of attention to and engagement with novel words predicts word learning (e.g., Montero Perez et al. 2015; Pellicer-Sánchez et al., 2021a; Puimège et al., 2023), with higher number of fixations and longer dwell times leading to higher vocabulary gains. These results can be linked to the Noticing Hypothesis (Godfroid et al., 2010; Schmidt, 1990), which underscores the importance of conscious attention to L2 forms to enable learning, and indirectly to the Involvement Load Hypothesis (Laufer & Hulstijn, 2001), which postulates that the learning and retention of novel or unfamiliar words is contingent on the degree of involvement in processing those words. TV series and films are generally characterized by fast-paced dialogues and the need to simultaneously process audio, image, and text (when captions/subtitles are added). In this context, noticing of and involvement with new vocabulary items may more strongly depend on variables such as working memory capacity and L2 proficiency level (e.g., Gass et al., 2019). Beginning learners may, for example, have greater difficulty directing their attention to relevant elements of the input, due to cognitive overload (e.g., Ayres & Sweller, 2005). Therefore, explicitly directing learners' attention to target L2 words may be a valuable strategy to promote learning.

2.3 Pre-viewing instruction as an attention enhancing technique

In reading-based research, many studies have provided evidence for the benefits of vocabulary-focused attention-enhancing techniques, such as textual enhancement (e.g., Elgort et al., 2023; Pellicer-Sánchez et al., 2021a; 2021b; Puimège et al., 2023). Similarly, research investigating the effectiveness of attention-enhancing techniques during video viewing has consistently shown that the use of these strategies has a positive effect on vocabulary learning and word processing. Such techniques include keyword captioning (e.g., Montero Perez et al. 2015; Teng, 2022), glossed captions (e.g., Montero Perez et al. 2018; Teng, 2022), advanced organizers (e.g., Teng, 2022), test announcement (e.g., Montero Perez et al., 2015) or typographic enhancement of novel word(s) in a captioned video (e.g., Finger-Bou & Muñoz in this volume; Majuddin et al., 2021).

While these strategies have been shown to draw attention to target vocabulary, their effectiveness relies in part on the learners' ability to process them appropriately. When viewing a film or TV episode there is little time to establish a form-meaning link or guess the meaning from context, even if attention has been directed to the L2 form (Puimège et al., 2023). This might pose a challenge for beginner (and younger) FL learners, who may need extra support, such as word-focused instruction prior to encountering novel words in the video. Language-focused tasks allow learners to effectively link form and meaning, and this helps them to quickly develop a lexical foundation that can later facilitate learning through meaning-focused input (Webb & Nation, 2017). Research on the role of language-based activities prior to viewing is still scarce, but evidence from studies in reading (e.g., Pellicer-Sánchez et al., 2018, 2021a; Webb, 2009) and listening (e.g., Chang & Read, 2006; Chung, 2002) supports the value of pre-viewing instruction for vocabulary learning, reporting higher gains when learners are exposed to target words (or pseudowords) prior to reading or listening to a text.

In the context of viewing, few studies have investigated the effects of teaching words appearing in the video prior to viewing it. Montero-Perez (2019) was the first study to explore the effect of pre-viewing instruction on vocabulary gains as well as attention allocation. Participants (30 intermediate L2-French learners) watched a captioned video containing ten pseudowords, five of which were taught prior to viewing the video (i.e., participants were given time to study the pseudowords' form-meaning link, their translations and example sentences). Results showed that the pseudowords that were pre-learnt had higher form and meaning recognition scores compared to the ones that were not, and eye-tracking data revealed that pre-viewing instruction did not seem to affect learners' attention to learnt pseudowords.

Pujadas and Muñoz (2019) investigated the effects of pre-viewing instruction on vocabulary learning with four groups of Grade 8 EFL beginner learners. Participants ($N=106$) viewed 24 full episodes of a TV series. A total of 120 target words appearing in the episodes were taught prior to viewing in two experimental groups (one with L2 captions, one with L1 subtitles) while the other two groups only viewed the episodes. Results revealed that pre-viewing instruction groups had significantly higher gains in both form transcription and meaning recall, while the language of the on-screen text had no significant main effect on learning. Interestingly, when combined with instruction, captions led to higher gains than subtitles, while subtitles were more beneficial when there was no instruction. The authors suggest that learners might have established the form-meaning connection during the vocabulary-focused activity and reinforced the aural and written form connection with the captioned video, which in turn helped meaning recall. When instruction was not available, subtitles could provide the word meanings and connect them to the aural L2 form. Gesa and Miralpeix (2023) also conducted a 21-episode longitudinal study with two groups of Grade 10 EFL learners ($N=64$) to investigate the effectiveness of intentional language-focused activities when combined with video viewing and found that, although most gains derived from the language-focused activities, the addition of video viewing significantly contributed to learning.

2.4   Trade-off effects

The aforementioned studies indicate that allocating attention to specific words during video viewing can increase the odds of learning those words. However, if attentional resources are limited (Robinson, 2003; VanPatten, 2004) directing attention to L2 forms in the captions/subtitles may deplete attention and negatively affect the processing of other aspects in the video, such as the audio, the images, or the general understanding of the story. A case in point is Pujadas and Muñoz's (2020) study, which explored differences in comprehension across the same four experimental conditions and the same participants as their 2019 study. The authors found, unsurprisingly, a significant advantage of L1-subtitled viewing over L2-captioned viewing across the 24 episodes, but also reported that the two groups with vocabulary-focused instruction tended to score lower in the comprehension tests compared to those who did not receive instruction prior to viewing. Although the difference did not reach statistical significance, it hinted at a possible trade-off between attention to vocabulary and general comprehension of the video.

Similar attentional trade-off effects have been reported in other studies with adult learners, both in reading (e.g., Choi, 2017; Lee, 2007), and TV viewing (Majuddin et al., 2021). For example, in a study exploring the effects of textual enhancement on grammar learning and comprehension, Lee (2007) found that textual enhancement assisted learning of the grammatical elements, but hindered comprehension of the content of the text. Choi (2017) investigated the effect of textual enhancement on collocation learning and content recall from a text and found that while textual enhancement had a positive impact on collocation learning, participants recalled significantly less unenhanced text. Analysis of eye-tracking data further showed that participants spent longer processing time on unfamiliar collocations compared to the group who read the text unenhanced, suggesting that additional cognitive resources were allocated to the unknown enhanced collocations at the expense of content comprehension. Majuddin et al. (2021) investigated the efficacy of captioned L2 television for the acquisition of multiword expressions, alongside the effects of enhancement and repetition. While repeated viewing had a positive effect on both comprehension and the acquisition of multiword expressions, they found that typographic enhancement reduced the benefits of captions for comprehension.

Although different in methodology, these studies indicate that allocating attentional resources to specific linguistic aspects (such as novel words, multiword expressions, or grammar forms) may detract attention from the text or video content. Little is known, however, regarding the effect that instruction may have on attention allocation during reading or viewing. Pellicer-Sánchez et al. (2021a) investigated the effect of pre-reading vocabulary instruction on learners' attention and vocabulary learning through eye-movement data. The study found that having instruction prior to reading (i.e., having access to the pseudowords' definitions, completing a matching activity, and having the chance to correct mistakes) led to larger vocabulary gains and faster processing of target words compared to reading-only and instruction-only conditions. While cumulative reading times were a predictor of meaning recognition, Pellicer-Sánchez et al. reported no significant difference in reading times between the pre-instructed condition and the reading-only condition. In a later study, Pellicer-Sánchez et al. (2021b) found that reading times on target words were longer in the pre-teaching condition, when frequency of exposure was controlled. Elgort et al. (2023) also explored the effect of pre-viewing definitions of unfamiliar vocabulary (i.e., pseudowords) with L1 and L2 readers. Eye-tracking data showed that pre-viewing led to fewer and shorter fixations on novel vocabulary compared to reading-only. Thus, unlike

Pellicer-Sánchez et al.'s (2021b) findings, pre-viewing led to decreased attention on novel words, which the authors explained in terms of increased processing ease. Finally, Montero Perez (2019) is the only study to have gathered eye-tracking data on the effects of instruction before viewing a video. As stated above, pre-viewing instruction had a positive effect on word learning but did not affect attention to those words. More specifically, pre-learning words did not affect participants' number of fixations or time spent on the pseudowords in the captions, the whole caption area, or the images, although pre-learnt pseudowords were skipped more often. However, pre-learning did affect viewing behavior during post-test completion, with greater fixation times spent on unknown pseudowords in the pre-viewing instruction condition compared to viewing-only.

2.5   Rationale and research aims

To date, findings regarding the effects of pre-viewing instruction on attention allocation remain inconclusive, with some studies reporting attention-enhancing effects through longer reading times (Pellicer-Sánchez et al., 2021b), and others reporting enhanced processing fluency through shorter and fewer fixations (Elgort et al., 2023). Further, little is known about attentional trade-off effects on input comprehension, particularly when attentional resources are limited and cognitive pressure is high (e.g., Pujadas & Muñoz, 2020). These trade-off effects may be especially relevant in the context of L2 viewing, where learners may only benefit from attention enhancement if they are able to successfully distribute and shift their attention between L2 form and other elements of the input (e.g., Gass et al., 2019). Both from a theoretical and a more practical, L2-teaching perspective, it is important to find out how the effects of pre-teaching on L2 video processing play out in beginning EFL learners, who have had limited experience with L2 viewing and with L2 input in general.

The present study seeks to investigate the effects of vocabulary instruction on beginner adolescent EFL learners' attention allocation when viewing a TV series. It examines the extent to which attention allocation varies depending on the instructional condition (with vs. without pre-viewing instruction on target vocabulary) and on-screen text language (L2 [English] captions vs. L1 [Spanish] subtitles), and whether the presence of vocabulary-focused activities affects comprehension of the video content. Specifically, the study addresses the following research questions:

1. To what extent does pre-viewing instruction on target vocabulary affect attention allocation on captions/subtitles containing those items? Is the effect the same for L2 and L1 text?
2. To what extent does pre-viewing instruction on target vocabulary affect comprehension rates? Is the effect the same for L2 and L1 text?
3. To what extent does pre-viewing instruction on target vocabulary affect attention allocation on captions/subtitles containing information relevant to comprehension of the video content? Is the effect the same for L2 and L1 text?

3. Methodology

3.1 Participants

The initial pool of participants were 95 secondary school students in Grade 8 (aged 13), who at the time of the experiment had recently completed a larger pedagogical intervention on the use of TV series for language learning at school (see Pujadas & Muñoz, 2019, 2020, 2023). Participants were Catalan-Spanish balanced bilinguals, and they were beginner L2 English learners; they were at the A1 level in the Common European Framework of Reference, as measured by Oxford Placement Test (OPT), and had a mean receptive vocabulary knowledge of 1,977 words, as measured by the X_Lex test[2] (Meara & Milton, 2003).

Participants were assigned to the same experimental condition they had been assigned in Pujadas and Muñoz's (2019, 2020) studies, which placed them in one of the following four experimental conditions: Instruction + English Captions (IC), Instruction + Spanish Subtitles (IS), No Instruction + English Captions (NIC), and No Instruction + Spanish Subtitles (NIS). After data collection, seven participants with a tracking ratio lower than 85% were excluded from analysis, and another participant was excluded due to a calibration problem. The final sample included 87 participants (57 female, 30 male).

3.2 Audiovisual materials

Nine clips were extracted from episode 16 (season 2) of the TV series *Fresh off the Boat* (Khan et al., 2015) and were put together using a video editing tool. At the time of the experiment, participants had watched 24 episodes of this same TV series and were familiar with the characters and the context of the story, but none

---

2. The X_Lex test measures receptive vocabulary knowledge up to 5,000 words. It presents 120 items in a check-list format, plus nonwords to control for guessing.

of them had seen this episode before. The selected clips belonged to a single sub-plot, and created a logical sequence of events that could be understood without watching the rest of the 20-minute episode. The total length of the resulting video was 7 minutes and 52 seconds. The script's lexical profile was analyzed using the Range software (Nation & Heatley, 2002), and results showed that the fragment reached 96.2% coverage at the 2,000-word level, making it suitable for this sample of participants.

Two versions of the video were created: one with English captions and one with Spanish subtitles. The video contained a total of 209 captions/subtitles, most of which were displayed in a single line ($n = 154$). Captions/subtitles were revised and modified to ensure that both versions (i.e., both languages) were comparable. Table 1 displays the average number of words, characters, and time on screen of English captions and Spanish subtitles.

Table 1. Descriptives (means) for captions/subtitles length and time on screen

	N words	N characters without spaces	N characters with spaces	Time on screen (milliseconds)
English captions	6.03	25.33	30.44	1818 ($SD = .670$)
Spanish subtitles	5.38	25.83	30.28	1823 ($SD = .670$)

3.3   Target words

Five target words were selected from the input (frequency of occurrence in brackets): *diner* (2), *tip* (6), *order* (12), *huge* (3), *alone* (2). These were selected based on frequency of occurrence (i.e., appeared at least twice), and the likelihood of being unknown by participants, (which was confirmed by the schoolteachers). The five target items appeared in 21 out of the 209 captions/subtitles.

3.4   Pre- and post-viewing tasks

Before viewing the video, participants in the instructed conditions (i.e., IC, IS) completed a pre-viewing task, which aimed at teaching the five target items. The task consisted of a word-search and matching exercise: participants had to find the five words in the word search and match them with their definition in Spanish (see Appendix A). The first letter and the total number of letters of the target words were provided. Once finished, the first author checked that the answers were correct, and corrected them if they were not. This procedure ensured that all participants were familiar with the meanings of the target words prior to viewing the L2 video.

After viewing the video, all participants completed a vocabulary task,[3] immediately followed by a short 5-item comprehension test. The comprehension text included 2 multiple-choice items and 3 true-false items (see Appendix B) and combined textually explicit items (the answer was stated explicitly) and inferential items (learners had to find and integrate different pieces of information). The test was administered in Spanish to avoid errors attributable to poor comprehension of the questions, and the images alone did not provide enough information to answer them.

3.5   Procedure

Data were collected individually in a single session (which lasted approximately 20–30 minutes) in an office at the secondary school. Participants were assigned to the same experimental condition as in the longitudinal study and were familiar with the procedure of the viewing session and they expected the pre- and post-viewing tasks.

Participants' eye movements were recorded using a desktop-mounted Tobii Pro Lab eye-tracker (sampling rate = 120 Hz; accuracy = 0.5°; drift = .01°). Recording was binocular. Participants sat in front of the monitor at a distance of 60–65 cm, and the video was displayed with a 1280×1024 screen resolution. They wore headphones to isolate themselves from any background noise and were asked to remain as still as possible while watching the eight-minute-long video after completing a five-point calibration. Participants in the instructed conditions started the session by completing the pre-viewing task, and then proceeded to viewing the video with either English captions (IC) or Spanish subtitles (IS). Participants in the other two conditions started directly by watching the video, either with English captions (NIC) or Spanish subtitles (NIS). The vocabulary post-viewing task and the comprehension test were administered immediately after the video in a pencil-and-paper format.

---

3. In the post-viewing task, participants had to listen to five words and write them down (word-form transcription), and then select the correct translation out of five options provided (meaning recognition). An 'I don't know' option was also included. To avoid priming effects, a retrospective report was used to assess prior knowledge of the target words, but results were found to be unreliable as several participants provided (incorrect) translations that were identical to the distractors in the vocabulary post-test, indicating that they were reporting knowledge obtained after viewing the video and completing the tasks. Consequently, data from the vocabulary post-viewing task was not analyzed, as the lack of a reliable measure of prior knowledge of the target words made it impossible to calculate vocabulary gains.

3.6   Scoring and data analysis

Comprehension items were scored as either correct (1) or incorrect (0), with a maximum score of 5. For the eye-tracking data, dynamic areas of interest (AOIs) were created for the target and non-target captions/subtitles (176 x 1280 pixels),[4] and the image area (527 x 1280 pixels). A 5-pixel gap was left between the text and image AOIs, to account for small inaccuracies (Bisson et al., 2014). Text areas containing target vocabulary were coded as 'target-vocabulary AOIs', and text areas containing relevant information to answer comprehension questions were coded 'question-relevant AOIs'. Interrater reliability for question-relevant AOIs was of 94%, and conflicting cases were discussed until an agreement was reached.

All statistical analyses were conducted in JASP (JASP Team, 2024). To address the first research question, which investigated attention allocation on target-vocabulary AOIs (i.e., captions/subtitles containing pre-taught vocabulary), we ran two separate linear mixed effects models: one focusing on participants' dwell times and another focusing on the number of fixations. Both dwell time and number of fixations can be considered aggregate measures reflecting the total amount of attention to the on-screen text (Godfroid, 2019). Dwell time captures the total amount of time spent reading the captions/subtitles, whereas fixation count captures the number of times participants fixate on the on-screen text. Both variables were normalized for duration (total fixation duration / AOI presentation duration) and number of words (total number of fixations / number of words in the AOI) (Godfroid, 2019). The mixed models included random intercepts for participants, as well as fixed effects for language of on-screen text (English or Spanish), instruction (yes or no), their two-way interaction, and the number of characters in the target-vocabulary AOI (a continuous variable). Pairwise comparisons were performed using a Bonferroni adjustment. To address the second research question, which focused on comprehension rates, we conducted a Chi-square test to analyze the distribution of comprehension scores (maximum score = 5) across the four groups. To address the third research question, which explored attention allocation on question-relevant AOIs (i.e., captions/subtitles that contained information relevant to answering the five comprehension questions), we ran linear mixed effects models focusing on those AOIs. This variable was coded by assigning a score of 0 (not relevant) or 1 (relevant) to each of the captions in the video. The resulting distribution of relevant/irrelevant captions/subtitles for each of the comprehension questions is depicted in Table 2. The models included the same fixed and random effects as those for the first research question.

---

4. The text area for one-line captions/subtitles was 100 pixels, but a larger area was set (i.e., 176 pixels) to include two-line captions/subtitles.

Table 2. Number of question-relevant AOIs for each comprehension questions

Comprehension question	Type	N question-relevant AOIs
1. Why do Mitch and Nancy ignore Jessica?	multiple-choice	16
2. Why does Louis refuse to be alone with his children?	multiple-choice	9
3. Louis goes to the diner because the children ask him to get them coffee.	true-false	14
4. Louis usually spends just a little time with his children when he comes back from work.	true-false	16
5. Jessica convinces the baseball coach to leave a tip for Mitch and Nancy.	true-false	17

Note. The total number of captions in the video was 209.

4.   Results

Table 3 presents descriptive information on participants' initial proficiency and vocabulary knowledge. There were no significant differences amongst experimental groups in terms of proficiency ($F(3,74) = 0.184$, $p = .907$) or vocabulary knowledge ($F(3,74) = 0.802$, $p = .497$). Results of the eye-tracking measures are presented in Table 4.

Table 3. Descriptive statistics for L2 knowledge: Means and *SD* (in parentheses) by group

	N	Oxford Placement Test (max. 200)	X_Lex (max. 5000)
Instruction + Captions (IC)	21	97.26 (11.65)	1958.82 (521.79)
Instruction + Subtitles (IS)	23	92.82 (13.21)	2112.50 (404.21)
No Instruction + Captions (NIC)	21	93.16 (15.21)	1958.33 (555.26)
No Instruction + Subtitles (NIS)	22	94.00 (14.73)	1878.57 (554.20)
All	87	94.26 (13.55)	1976.97 (508.95)

Table 4. Descriptive eye-tracking results for all on-screen text AOIs: Means and *SD* (in parentheses) by group

	N	N fixations	Dwell time (milliseconds)
Instruction + Captions (IC)	21	3.48 (1.58)	714 (332)
Instruction + Subtitles (IS)	23	5.31 (1.04)	998 (237)
No Instruction + Captions (NIC)	21	4.73 (1.18)	901 (231)
No Instruction + Subtitles (NIS)	22	4.88 (1.69)	886 (345)
All	87	4.62 (1.53)	878 (301)

4.1 Effect of instruction on dwell times and number of fixations on target-vocabulary AOIs

Visual inspection of the residual plots indicated that the linear mixed effects models met the assumptions of linearity, homoscedasticity, and normal distribution of residuals. The results of both models are summarized in Tables 5 and 6 and predicted outcomes are plotted in Figures 1 and 2. AOIs length in number of characters was a significant predictor of both normalized dwell times and number of fixations. None of the other predictors significantly predicted normalized dwell times, and there was no significant interaction between Language of on-screen text and Instruction. However, the plot presented in Figure 1 indicates that normalized dwell times on target-vocabulary AOIs were somewhat shorter in the IC group compared to the other groups.

For the normalized number of fixations, fixed effects for both the Language of on-screen text and Instruction were statistically significant. There was also a significant interaction between these two variables. Pairwise comparisons showed that the NIC condition had a higher number of fixations on the target-vocabulary AOIs than the IC condition (B = 0.17, Z = 3.42, p = .002). Further, Spanish subtitles were associated with a higher normalized number of fixations compared to the English captions, both in the IS (B = 0.401, Z = 8.346, p < .001) and NIS (B = 0.217, Z = 4.334, p < .001) groups. However, there was no significant difference in normalized number of fixations between the groups with access to Spanish subtitles (B = −0.014, Z = −0.287, p = 1.000).

Table 5. Summary of the linear mixed effects model for normalized dwell time on target-vocabulary AOIs

	B	SE	t	p
Fixed effects				
Intercept	0.457	0.020	22.344	< .001
N characters	0.003	4.505×10^{-4}	5.770	< .001
Language of on-screen text	−0.019	0.014	−1.374	0.173
Instruction	0.011	0.014	0.838	0.405
Language of on-screen text * Instruction	0.024	0.014	1.734	0.087
Random effects	**Variance**	**SD**		
(1|Participant)	0.121	0.015		
Residual	0.178	0.032		
AIC	−802.919			

Note. The reference level for Language of on-screen text is "English", the reference level for Instruction is "No instruction"

Table 6. Linear mixed effects model summary for normalized number of fixations on target-vocabulary AOIs

	B	SE	t	p
Fixed effects				
Intercept	1.133	0.032	35.247	< .001
N characters	−0.010	7.994×10^{-4}	−12.548	< .001
Language of on-screen text	−0.155	0.017	−8.901	< .001
Instruction	0.039	0.017	2.246	0.028
Language of on-screen text * Instruction	0.046	0.017	2.647	0.010
Random effects	**Variance**	**SD**		
(1|Participant)	0.145	0.021		
Residual	0.316	0.100		
AIC	1104.511			

Note. The reference level for Language of on-screen text is "English", the reference level for Instruction is "No instruction"

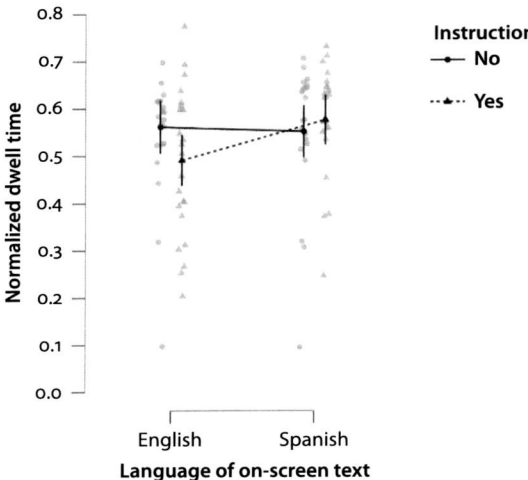

Figure 1. Predicted values of normalized dwell time by Language of on-screen text and Instruction on target-vocabulary AOIs

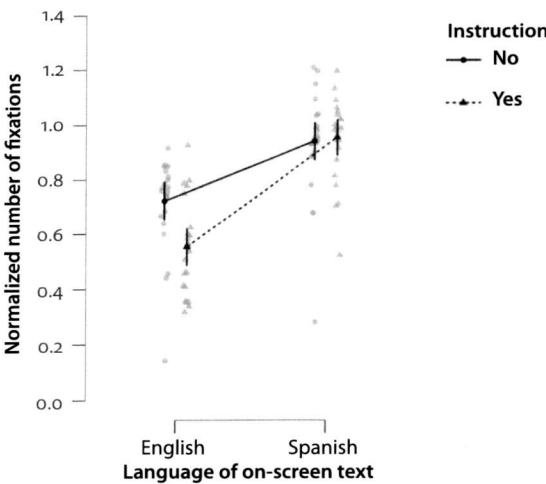

Figure 2. Predicted values of normalized number of fixations by Language of on-screen text and Instruction on target-vocabulary AOIs

4.2   Effect of instruction on comprehension rates

Scores on the comprehension test ranged between three and five out of five correct responses. Two participants who scored lower than 3 were excluded from the analyses, because the Chi square test does not work well when a large proportion of expected counts are below 5 (Cochran, 1954). The distribution of scores across experimental conditions is presented in Table 7. As can be gleaned, scores were higher in the two groups who viewed the video with Spanish subtitles compared to the two English captions groups. Results of the Chi square test indicated that comprehension scores differed significantly between the four experimental groups ($X^2 = 43.37$, $p < .001$). Comprehension scores were also numerically higher in the NIC group compared to the IC group. However, in a separate Chi square test focusing on the results of the English captions groups, this difference did not reach statistical significance ($X^2 = 5.63$, $p = .060$).

Table 7. Distribution of comprehension scores across the experimental groups

			Comprehension			
		N	3	4	5	M (SD)
Captions	Instruction (IC)	21	12	8	1	3.476 (.602)
	No Instruction (NIC)	21	6	9	6	4.000 (.775)
Subtitles	Instruction (IS)	23	0	7	16	4.696 (.470)
	No Instruction (NIS)	22	0	4	18	4.818 (.395)
	All	87	18	28	41	4.264 (.784)

4.3   Effect of instruction on dwell times and number of fixations on question-relevant AOIs

The results of the models focusing on the question-relevant AOIs are presented in Tables 8 and 9. The predicted outcomes of both models are visualized in Figures 3 and 4.

For the normalized dwell time, there was no effect of Language of the on-screen text nor Instruction, and no interactions emerged. For the normalized number of fixations, the fixed effect of Language of the on-screen text was significant, but the effect of Instruction was not significant. The two-way interaction between Language and Instruction was also statistically significant. The pairwise comparisons partly reflect those found for target-vocabulary AOIs. The NIC group had a significantly higher number of fixations on question-relevant AOIs than the IC (B = 0.16, Z = 2.81, $p = .015$). The Spanish subtitles condition led

to a significantly higher normalized number of fixations than the English captions condition in the IS group (B = 0.33, Z = 5.89, *p* < .001), and in the NIS group
(B = 0.14, Z = 2.41, *p* = .032). Further, there was no significant difference in normalized number of fixations on relevant captions between the two Spanish subtitles groups (B = −0.03, Z = −0.50, *p* = .620).

Table 8. Linear mixed effects model summary for normalized dwell time
on question-relevant AOIs

	B	SE	*t*	*p*
Fixed effects				
Intercept	0.47	0.02	30.76	< .001
N characters	0.00	0.00	10.45	< .001
Language of on-screen text	−0.02	0.01	−1.25	.215
Instruction	0.01	0.01	0.40	.687
Language of on-screen text * Instruction	0.02	0.01	1.66	.101
Random effects	Variance	SD		
(1|Participant)	0.02	0.13		
Residual	0.04	0.19		
AIC	−2637.87			

Note. The reference level for Language of on-screen text is "English", the reference level for Instruction is "No instruction".

Table 9. Linear mixed effects model summary for normalized number
of fixations on question-relevant AOIs

	B	SE	*t*	*p*
Fixed effects				
Intercept	1.34	0.03	52.90	< .001
N characters	−0.013	0.00	−23.70	< .001
Language of on-screen text	−0.12	0.02	−5.82	< .001
Instruction	0.03	0.02	1.65	.102
Language of on-screen text * Instruction	0.05	0.02	2.35	.021
Random effects	Variance	SD		
(1|Participant)	0.03	0.18		
Residual	0.23	0.48		
AIC	8245.05			

Note. The reference level for Language of on-screen text is "English", the reference level for Instruction is "No instruction".

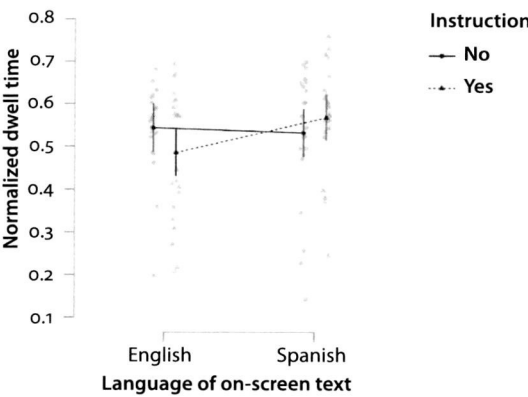

Figure 3. Predicted values of normalized dwell time by Language of on-screen text and Instruction on question-relevant AOIs

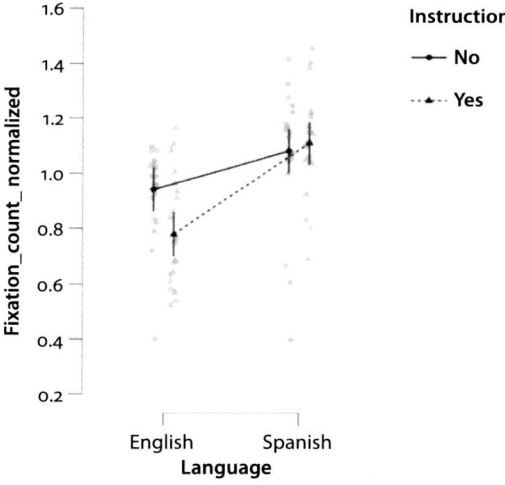

Figure 4. Predicted values of normalized number of fixations by Language of on-screen text and Instruction on question-relevant AOIs

5.   Discussion

This study followed up on Pujadas and Muñoz's (2019, 2020) longitudinal studies by investigating the effect of pre-viewing vocabulary instruction on participants' attention allocation when viewing L2-captioned and L1-subtitled video. The study aimed to provide greater insight into the effects of deliberate focus on vocabulary on input processing and comprehension through eye-tracking data. Overall, results from the present study mirrored those of the longitudinal intervention, showing an advantage of L1 subtitles for content comprehension (Pujadas & Muñoz, 2020). Eye-tracking data also showed, overall, that participants who watched the video with Spanish subtitles fixated on the text containing target words and question-relevant information significantly more often than participants who watched the same video with English captions. This suggests that they made greater use of L1 text to support comprehension of the L2 video, which is also reflected in the higher number of correct responses on comprehension questions by IS and NIS groups. In line with previous findings (Muñoz, 2017), this provides further evidence that beginner learners may prefer TV viewing with L1 subtitles. It should be noted, nonetheless, that comparing online processing measures (i.e., dwell times, number of fixations) between two different languages is tricky, even after controlling for duration and length of the on-screen text. Therefore, generalizations should be made with caution. It should also be noted that participants were L2 beginners, and thus variations in their reading speed might have played a more prominent role in the present study than in studies involving more advanced learners.

Our first research question investigated the extent to which instruction affects dwell times and number of fixations on target-vocabulary AOIs, and whether the effect was the same for L1 and L2 text. Mixed effects models revealed a main effect of language on the normalized number of fixations, indicating that learners with access to Spanish subtitles fixated on target-vocabulary AOIs a significantly higher number of times compared to learners in the English caption groups. Furthermore, a significant interaction between language and instruction on the number of fixations indicates that instruction affected visual attention in learners who watched the video with captions, but not in learners who viewed the video with subtitles. For learners in the IC group, instruction may have had a facilitative effect on word processing: learners had just seen the target words or had already learnt them, and this might have speeded up processing of captions containing those words in context. This finding is in line with the results of Elgort et al. (2023), who found that pre-viewing words and their definitions led to shorter fixation times on pre-viewed words during reading. However, the finding does not match results found by Pellicer-Sánchez et al. (2021b), who reported longer reading times in their pre-teaching condition. Like Pellicer-Sánchez et al., the current study controlled the participants' pre-learning success by ensuring that participants made the form-meaning link through explicit feedback. However, in the present study, the time pressure associated with the viewing activity may have led to more superficial processing of the target vocabulary. As participants were already familiar with the target words and their meanings, this may have facilitated their processing of the word forms, without necessarily leading to more elaborate semantic processing. As Pellicer-Sánchez et al.'s (2021b) reading treatment did not involve any time pressure, their participants might have made greater efforts to reinforce the form-meaning mappings of the target words during reading. However, more evidence is needed to validate this interpretation. Following Elgort et al. (2023), we suggest that a future study might directly compare different pre-exposure activities (e.g., pre-viewing words and pre-teaching words), while controlling for time on task.

In contrast, there was no apparent effect of pre-teaching in the IS group. Learners in this group might not have noticed the target words in the subtitles (as they were written in Spanish, and would only *hear* them in English), and they might have processed them like the NIS group, that is, regardless of whether they had been pre-taught the target words or not. It is interesting to note that the large variability within the IC group suggests that the effect of instruction on caption use varied considerably across participants. For some learners, recognizing the English words in the captions may have triggered their curiosity or made them try to see how the words were used in context, leading to greater attention to the captions in general, whereas for others, the initial recognition of the English words may not have led to greater caption use.

Our second research question explored whether a focus on vocabulary would affect comprehension of the video content. In line with prior research, subtitled viewing had a significant advantage over captioned viewing, regardless of the instruction condition (Pujadas & Muñoz, 2020). Results also showed that the presence of pre-viewing instruction did not have a significant effect on comprehension rates, although the difference between instructed and non-instructed groups approached significance ($p = .06$) in the English captions condition. With L2 captions – a viewing condition more challenging than L1 subtitles – the IC group tended to have lower comprehension scores than the NIC group. Although this effect was not statistically significant, it would suggest a trade-off effect between focus on vocabulary and comprehension, in line with previous findings (Choi, 2017; Lee, 2007; Majuddin et al., 2021; Pujadas & Muñoz, 2020). When participants had access to L1 subtitles, on the other hand, instruction did not have any impact on comprehension rates. As L1 text could be processed more automatically than L2 text, the IS group might have been able to follow the subtitles with little effort, even if participants were paying more attention to the target-vocabulary AOIs. It is also possible that differences could not be observed because scores were at ceiling level for IS and NIS groups, which might have been due to the low number of comprehension questions and the participants' familiarity with the series, allowing them to rely on their top-down listening skills. Further, participants only had to learn five novel words, which might not have been enough to significantly overwhelm their limited attentional capacity.

Our third research question investigated the effect of instruction on attention allocation to AOIs that were relevant to answer comprehension questions. Results showed a pattern that resembled what was found for target-vocabulary AOIs, with the IC group spending significantly less time on question-relevant AOIs than the other three conditions. Participants in the IC group may have benefited from a facilitative processing effect on vocabulary, which might have caused them to skip or skim captions, including question-relevant captions. The NIC group, in contrast, did not have this processing advantage in terms of vocabulary. This may have led to greater attention to the L2 captions throughout the video. Access to L1 text, on the other hand, seemed to be unaffected by the pre-teaching of L2 vocabulary. The presence of L1 text may have facilitated comprehension to the point that it neutralized any effects of pre-viewing instruction on attention allocation during viewing.

The present results appear to align with findings demonstrating that attentional trade-offs may occur when enhancing learners' focus on vocabulary in L2 input processing (e.g., Choi, 2017). Whereas previous studies have found that attention enhancement may lead to shorter fixations on comprehension-relevant information (e.g., Choi, 2017), the present study found that pre-teaching words led to shorter fixations on L2 on-screen text overall, in the presence of simultaneous spoken L2 input. This finding suggests that teaching words prior to viewing can affect beginner L2 learners' online processing during TV viewing with captions (see also Pujadas & Muñoz, 2020), but further research is needed to confirm this trend.

6.   Conclusion and further research

This study was the first to explore the effect of pre-viewing instruction on young, beginner EFL learners' attention allocation during video viewing. The study also investigated whether attention to vocabulary affected learners' comprehension of the video content. We found that pre-viewing instruction affected participants' attention allocation only when viewing the video with English captions, with participants tending to spend less time on captions containing target vocabulary and comprehension-relevant captions if they had been pre-taught target vocabulary. Attention to a small number of vocabulary items, however, did not seem to hinder comprehension in a significant manner.

From a pedagogical point of view, findings support the inclusion of short language-focused activities prior to viewing a video for young EFL beginner learners (which have been shown to be beneficial for vocabulary learning, e.g., Pujadas & Muñoz, 2019), as attention to a reduced number of lexical items does not seem to overwhelm learners' attention capacity. When viewing the video with L1 subtitles, the presence of pre-viewing instruction did not have any effect on attention allocation. L1 text is processed more automatically than L2 text, making comprehension easier and freeing up cognitive resources that could be used on the processing of other linguistic aspects. However, the similar viewing patterns in the instructed and non-instructed groups in the L1 subtitles condition suggest that participants did not process novel words any differently when encountering their L1 translations in the subtitles. This might be because the learners did not have time to establish the link between the L2 aural form and the L1 written word.

This study of exploratory nature has several limitations that should be acknowledged. First, we only included a small number of comprehension items, which may have caused a ceiling effect in learners' comprehension scores, particularly in the L1 subtitles groups. Further, the number of target words was also relatively small, which may have reduced any trade-off effects between attention to L2 words and input comprehension. A replication with a different type of video (e.g., a documentary, which is typically richer in terms of lexis and content) might allow for the inclusion of a higher number of vocabulary items and comprehension questions. Similarly, due to the eye-tracker resolution limitations, it was not fully possible to assess whether participants were looking at the target words specifically or at the full text area. A replication study analyzing fixations in each novel word (i.e., word-based AOIs) would shed more light on this matter. Future research should also include a reliable measure of prior vocabulary knowledge to assess whether increased attention to novel words is conducive to learning. Finally, the eye-tracking data may have been affected by the location of data collection (secondary school vs. laboratory) and the participants' age (e.g., shorter attention span, less able to sit still). Though any generalization of the findings of this experimental study should be made with care, they contribute to research on language learning through L2 television, and provide valuable data on young, beginner learners' online processing of captions and subtitles. The results are also relevant for the EFL classroom context, in which students are often asked to split their attention on different aspects of learning, and can inform teachers about the various processing demands learners cope with during video viewing.

Acknowledgements

This work has been supported by the FI-DGR 2016, grant 2020FI_B2 00179 from the Catalan Agency for Management of University and Research Grants (AGAUR), and the Margarita Salas grants to the first author. We would like to thank the school and all participants that took part in this study for their interest and time, and C. Muñoz and the reviewers for their valuable insights on this chapter.

Ethical considerations

The protocols of data collection, data anonymization, data processing, and data storage of the current study were approved by the Institutional Review Board of the University of Barcelona (IRB00003099).

References

Avello, D., & Muñoz, C. (2023). The development of receptive language skills from captioned video viewing in primary school EFL learners. *Education Sciences*, 13(5), 479.

Ayres, P., & Sweller, J. (2005). The split-attention principle in multimedia learning. In R. E. Mayer (Ed.), *The Cambridge handbook of multimedia learning* (pp. 135–146). Cambridge University Press.

Bisson, M. J., Van Heuven, W. J., Conklin, K., & Tunney, R. J. (2014). Processing of native and foreign language subtitles in films: An eye tracking study. *Applied Psycholinguistics*, 35(2), 399–418.

Chang, A. C. S., & Read, J. (2006). The effects of listening support on the listening performance of EFL learners. *TESOL Quarterly*, 40(2), 375–397.

Choi, S. (2017). Processing and learning of enhanced English collocations: An eye movement study. *Language Teaching Research*, 21(3), 403–426.

Chung, J. M. (2002). The effects of using two advance organizers with video texts for the teaching of listening in English. *Foreign Language Annals*, 35(2), 231–241.

Cochran, W. G. (1954). Some methods for strengthening the common χ^2 tests. *Biometrics*, 10(4), 417–451.

Elgort, I., Wetering, R. V. D., Arrow, T., & Beyersmann, E. (2023). Previewing novel words before reading affects their processing during reading: An eye-movement study with first and second language readers. *Language Learning*.

Gass, S., Winke, P., Isbell, D. R., & Ahn, J. (2019). How captions help people learn languages: A working-memory, eye-tracking study. *Language Learning & Technology*, 23(2), 84–104.

Gesa, F., & Miralpeix, I. (2023). Extensive viewing as additional input for foreign language vocabulary learning: A longitudinal study in secondary school. *Language Teaching Research*.

Godfroid, A. (2019). *Eye tracking in second language acquisition and bilingualism: A research synthesis and methodological guide*. Taylor and Francis.

Godfroid, A., Housen, A., & Boers, F. (2010). A procedure for testing the Noticing Hypothesis in the context of vocabulary acquisition. In M. Pütz & L. Sicola (Eds.), *Cognitive processing in second language acquisition: Inside the learner's mind* (pp. 169–197). John Benjamins.

Khan, N., Kasdar, J., Melvin, M., Blomquist, R., Huang, E., & McEwen, J. (2015). *Fresh off the Boat [TV series].* ABC.

Laufer, B., & Hulstijn, J. (2001). Incidental vocabulary acquisition in a second language: The construct of task-induced involvement. *Applied linguistics, 22*(1), 1–26.

Lee, S. K. (2007). Effects of textual enhancement and topic familiarity on Korean EFL students' reading comprehension and learning of passive form. *Language Learning, 57*(1), 87–118.

Lindgren, E., & Muñoz, C. (2013). The influence of exposure, parents, and linguistic distance on young European learners' foreign language comprehension. *International Journal of Multilingualism, 10*(1), 105–129.

Majuddin, E., Siyanova-Chanturia, A., & Boers, F. (2021). Incidental acquisition of multiword expressions through audiovisual materials: The role of repetition and typographic enhancement. *Studies in Second Language Acquisition, 43*(5), 985–1008.

Montero Perez, M. (2019). Pre-learning vocabulary before viewing captioned video: An eye-tracking study. *The Language Learning Journal, 47*(4), 460–478.

Montero Perez, M., Peters, E., & Desmet, P. (2015). Enhancing vocabulary learning through captioned video: An eye-tracking study. *Modern Language Journal, 99*(2), 308–328.

Montero Perez, M., Peters, E., & Desmet, P. (2018). Vocabulary learning through viewing video: The effect of two enhancement techniques. *Computer Assisted Language Learning, 31*(1–2), 1–26.

Montero Perez, M., Van Den Noortgate, W., & Desmet, P. (2013). Captioned video for L2 listening and vocabulary learning: A meta-analysis. *System, 41*(3), 720–739.

Muñoz, C. (2017). The role of age and proficiency in subtitle reading. An eye-tracking study. *System, 67,* 77–86.

Nation, P., & Heatley, A. (2002). Range: A program for the analysis of vocabulary in texts [software].

Pellicer-Sánchez, A., Conklin, K., & Vilkaitė-Lozdienė, L. (2021a). The effect of pre-reading instruction on vocabulary learning: An investigation of L1 and L2 readers' eye movements. *Language Learning, 71*(1), 162–203.

Pellicer-Sánchez, A., Conklin, K., & Vilkaitė-Lozdienė, L. (2021b). (Re) Examining the benefits of pre-reading instruction for vocabulary learning. *TESOL Quarterly, 56*(1), 363–375.

Peters, E. (2019). The effect of imagery and on-screen text on foreign language vocabulary learning from audiovisual input. *TESOL Quarterly, 53*(4), 1008–1032.

Peters, E., & Webb, S. (2018). Incidental vocabulary acquisition through watching a single episode of L2 television. *Studies in Second Language Acquisition, 40*(3), 551–577.

Puimège, E., Montero Perez, M., & Peters, E. (2023). The effects of typographic enhancement on L2 collocation processing and learning from reading: An eye-tracking study. *Applied Linguistics, 45*(1), 88–110.

Pujadas, G., & Muñoz, C. (2019). Extensive viewing of captioned and subtitled TV series: A study of L2 vocabulary learning by adolescents. *The Language Learning Journal, 47*(4), 479–496.

Pujadas, G., & Muñoz, C. (2020). Examining adolescent EFL learners' TV viewing comprehension through captions and subtitles. *Studies in Second Language Acquisition, 42*(3), 551–575.

doi Pujadas, G., & Muñoz, C. (2023). Measuring the visual in audio-visual input: The effects of imagery in vocabulary learning through TV viewing. *ITL-International Journal of Applied Linguistics 174*(2), 263–290.

doi Robinson, P. (2003). Attention and memory during SLA. In C. Doughty & M. Long (Eds.), *Handbook of research in second language acquisition* (pp. 631–678). Blackwell.

doi Rodgers, M. P. (2018). The images in television programs and the potential for learning unknown words: The relationship between on-screen imagery and vocabulary. *ITL-International Journal of Applied Linguistics, 169*(1), 191–211.

doi Rodgers, M. P. H., & Webb, S. (2011). Narrow viewing: The vocabulary in related television programs. *TESOL Quarterly, 45*(4), 689–717.

doi Rodgers, M. P. H., & Webb, S. (2020). Incidental vocabulary learning through watching television. *ITL – International Journal of Applied Linguistics, 171*(2), 191–220.

doi Schmidt, R. W. (1990). The role of consciousness in second language learning. *Applied Linguistics, 11*(2), 129–158.

doi Schmitt, N. (2008). Instructed second language vocabulary learning. *Language Teaching Research, 12*(3), 329–363.

doi Schmitt, N. (2010). *Researching vocabulary: A vocabulary research manual.* Palgrave MacMillan.

doi Teng, F. (2022). Vocabulary learning through videos: Captions, advance-organizer strategy, and their combination. *Computer Assisted Language Learning, 35*(3), 518–550.

doi VanPatten, B. (2004). *Processing instruction: Theory, research, and commentary.* Routledge.

Webb, S. (2015). Extensive viewing: Language learning through watching television. In D. Nunan & J.C. Richards (Eds.), *Language learning beyond the classroom* (pp. 159–168). Routledge.

doi Webb, S. A. (2009). The effects of pre-learning vocabulary on reading comprehension and writing. *Canadian Modern Language Review, 65*(3), 441–470.

Webb, S., & Nation, P. (2017). *How vocabulary is learned.* Oxford University Press.

doi Webb, S., Uchihara, T., & Yanagisawa, A. (2023). How effective is second language incidental vocabulary learning? A meta-analysis. *Language Teaching, 56*(2), 161–180.

Appendix A.   Pre-viewing activity

Read the definitions and look for the English words in the wordsearch. The first letter of
the words is marked with a circle. Good luck!

```
E  T  A  H  J  L  P  J  Y  P  E  L (A) X
A  H  H  H  C  G  K  L  J  O  I  L  J  D
(D) F  I  P  O  M  Q  U  D  T  O (T) B  C
U  I  K  V  J  B  K  T  E  N  I  S  P  J
H  K  N  P  L  Y  O  E  E  Y  D  J  S  R
W  R  O  E  J  V  J  Z  U  Z  F  B  X  M
N  X  X  A  R  H  T  Y  J  Z  Y  Z  R  Y
I  M  D  B  F  U (H) C  R  W  K  R  V  B
D  L  N  D  A  U  K  Y  K  C  O  J  N  X
A  L  O  W  G  E  I  T  V (O) W  Q  H  I
Y  I  L  E  Q  M  M  E  N  R  X  K  Y  W
Y  V  X  I  Z  H  A  R  E  D  L  T  D  V
S  N  C  P  X  K  J  E  D  E  W  V  O  W
K  Z  H  A  Z  A  L  G  P  R  L  T  V  G
```

1. Small, informal and inexpensive establishment where you can have coffee or small
    snacks. (5 letters) D_____
2. Small extra amount of money that you give to the waiters who perform a service for
    you. (3 letters) T_____
3. Very big. (4 letters) H_____
4. Food or drinks that someone has requested at a restaurant. (5 letters) O_____
5. Without anyone or anything. (5 letters) A_____

Note: The original task was in Spanish (i.e., instructions, definitions); it has been translated to
English for comprehensibility.

Appendix B.   Comprehension test

A. **Select the correct answer:**
  1. Why do Mitch and Nancy ignore Jessica?
      a. Because they never listen to her.
      b. Because she cannot fire them now.
      c. Because Louis tells them to listen to her.
  2. Why does Louis refuse to be alone with his children?
      a. Because he doesn't like to spend time with them.
      b. Because he's afraid they'll stop admiring him.
      c. Because the children prefer their mother.
B. **Indicate if the following statements are true (T) or false (F):**
  T / F Louis goes to the diner because the children ask him to get them coffee.
  T / F Louis usually spends just a little time with his children when he comes back from work.
  T / F Jessica convinces the baseball couch to leave a tip for Mitch and Nancy.

Note: The original task was in Spanish; it has been translated to English for comprehensibility.

Maximizing L2 learning from captioned TV viewing

Repeated viewing and Language Reactor

Margarita Popova & Imma Miralpeix
Universitat de Barcelona

This study compares comprehension and vocabulary gains in L1 Russian (upper)-intermediate adolescents who watched two episodes of a Netflix series in L2 English for the same amount of time under two conditions: Repeated Viewing (RV) with captions; and Viewing with the Chrome extension *Language Reactor* (LR), with individually regulated tools to enhance learning. Both conditions were equally helpful for comprehension and vocabulary learning (relative gains up to 51%), suggesting the comparability of effects of repeated viewing and watching with LR if the watching time is the same. A qualitative analysis of learners' viewing behaviour revealed differences between the conditions: while the RV group focused more on the episodes' content, the LR group paid closer attention to language.

1. Introduction

Although the effectiveness of language learning from multimodal input has been demonstrated for most students (e.g., Reynolds et al., 2022), incidental learning from TV viewing (occurring unintentionally) has proven to be challenging. This remains true even with the inclusion of on-screen text or pre-teaching target vocabulary to encourage intentional learning (e.g., Gesa & Miralpeix, 2023). Acquiring a word involves numerous encounters with it in different contexts (Rodgers & Webb, 2020) and large amounts of input are usually needed. Apart from relatively rare studies involving, for example, repeated viewing (e.g., Muñoz et al., 2022) or computer-assisted technology applied to video-watching, such as highlighted keywords on captions (L2 subtitles), glossed captioning, etc. (e.g., Fievez et al., 2023; Wu & Yang, 2022), other options to maximize learning through viewing have not been extensively explored. It should also be noted that techno-logically-enhanced exposure has normally been used *additionally* and not *instead*

https://doi.org/10.1075/lllt.61.05pop

of other forms of treatment (formal instruction, etc.), providing experimental groups with an uneven amount of exposure time, which might distort results. Furthermore, studies have often involved short videos and primarily university student samples. The current mixed-methods study has addressed these gaps, investigating whether L2 learning from captioned TV series can be maximized with teenagers when they use an edutainment application in comparison with the more "conventional" repeated viewing.

2.   Literature review

2.1   Audiovisual input and new edutainment tools in L2 learning

Audiovisual input implies the combination of verbal and non-verbal information via sound, video/image and written on-screen text. Whether and how this kind of input can be beneficial for L2 students has been studied since the early 1980s, starting with the work by Price (1983), among others.

The two major theories on multimedia input, Paivio's Dual Coding Theory (1986) and Mayer's Cognitive Theory of Multimedia Learning (2014) agree that presenting information in several formats (visual and audial, words and images) is likely to be more profitable for learners than using one-channel means of input (reading or listening), as it activates two cognitive subsystems and ensures more effective data processing. However, Sweller's Cognitive Load Theory (1994) indicates that multimodal input may be regarded as more challenging, overloading cognitive capacities and hindering L2 learning.

Recent research has found positive effects of multimodal input on different aspects of language learning, including comprehension (Pujadas & Muñoz, 2020) and vocabulary gains (Gesa, 2019; Rodgers, 2013). The rapid development of digital video technologies has led to the appearance of edutainment, the *"convergence of entertainment and learning resources"* (Bird, 2005, p. 311), facilitating engagement with the language through multiple channels.

Watching films and series with streaming services has become a popular tool for L2 acquisition nowadays. To support the process, a toolbox called *Language Reactor* (LR), formerly known as *Language Learning with Netflix*, was developed in 2019. It provides fast user-friendly access to simultaneous bilingual (dual) subtitles (in L1 and L2), instant word translations, detailed word definitions, full script of the video with flexible navigation and words marked in different colours depending on the frequency bands they belong to, as well as control buttons allowing viewers to pause or rewatch specific segments and apply different speed regulations.

Compatible with Netflix and YouTube, it is claimed that LR provides an engaging instrument for more effective L2 learning through video watching. The concept behind this app is that it may help to change viewers' attitudes towards L2 learning, as it combines the comfort of naturalistic TV watching with tools that may facilitate vocabulary acquisition, enabling students to become independent subjects of the learning process and motivating more people to learn languages extensively. LR may also help to optimize the viewing experience due to an increased sense of agency (Alm, 2021b).

To our knowledge, there have been few studies published on LR. Of those published to date, Gouleti et al.'s (2020) eye-tracking study revealed differences in learner strategies with subtitles in different languages, and showed that dual subtitles with L1 first were the most beneficial. Alm (2021a, 2021b) described learner strategies and attitudes towards LR functions, encouraging more reflective and extensive at-home viewing, than conventional entertaining watching. In Fievez et al. (2023), at-home watching of six episodes of a French series led to high incidental vocabulary acquisition (28% form and 35% meaning recall) among Dutch university students. However, the study compared these gains to those of a no-treatment control group, rather than to those from viewing the videos without the app.

2.2   Comprehension and vocabulary learning through captioned and repeated video viewing

Several studies have assessed the effects of on-screen text when watching videos, often demonstrating the advantages of having this written information (see, e.g., Montero Perez et al., 2013 or Montero Perez, 2022). Captions are perceived as additional orthographic, phonological, and semantic scaffolding, increasing students' opportunities to learn more vocabulary. Subtitles (L1 on-screen text) can favour cognitive processing and content comprehension (e.g., Frumuselu et al., 2015 in adults; Chapter 1 in this volume, in young learners). It has also been observed that, in low-level students (e.g., with vocabulary size -VS- below 3,000 word families), L1 subtitles are often more beneficial (e.g., Webb & Rodgers, 2009). However, the shortcomings of L1/L2 subtitles cannot be ignored, as overusing them can impede learning and lead to developing just reading skills instead of listening skills (Winke et al., 2010).

There is also research that has sought the most adequate combination of audio and on-screen text for L2 learning (e.g., L1 audio plus L2 subtitles or vice versa) or to add extra features to traditional full captioning, such as highlighted keywords or glossed captions (e.g., Fievez et al., 2023; Montero Perez et al., 2013). Dual subtitles and personalised control over subtitle selection can increase a focus on form, raising awareness of languages (Vanderplank, 2016a), although the research to date on the topic is scarce.

Vandergrift and Goh (2012) and Webb (2015) emphasized the benefits of repeated viewing of the same episode and encouraged watching series rather than films to provide vocabulary recirculation. However, very few studies have investigated repeated viewing. For example, Muñoz et al. (2022) compared immediate (in the same session) and spaced (with a week interval) repetition of the same captioned videos, revealing the latter to be a slightly more favourable condition for vocabulary acquisition. Researchers have also experimented with the order of captioned/non-captioned viewings. For instance, Winke et al. (2010) found that captioning during the first showing of the videos was more effective for performance on aural vocabulary tests.

Nevertheless, whether video viewing alone can lead to considerable gains in acquisition remains a subject of discussion. Incidental learning (i.e., unintentional learning via L2 input without a focus on form; Long, 2017) mostly fosters very little progress, as demonstrated, for example, by Webb et al. (2023). This is one reason why studies that check vocabulary progress through (captioned/subtitled) viewing often combine it with explicit instruction or training (e.g., Gesa & Miralpeix, 2023; Pujadas & Muñoz, 2019) to promote intentional learning.

2.3   Viewing behaviour when learning from viewing

Although at-home L2 series-viewing is becoming increasingly popular, not much research has been published on extensive out-of-the-classroom TV watching, apart from, for example, that on the EURECAP Project – European Research on Captioning – (Vanderplank, 2016a), in which adult L2 learners watched captioned materials in informal settings over a period of 5–6 weeks. Many researchers point out the benefits of increasing the amount of input for L2 learning, particularly for listening comprehension, which tends to be undertrained in formal instruction settings (Nation & Newton, 2009; Vandergrift, 2007). Extensive viewing can be a good option for learners in limited L2 input contexts, especially in dubbing countries, as there are fewer possibilities to benefit from original version TV. Repeated viewing with app support can become a first step towards encouraging independent technology-enhanced activities, which may improve students' engagement in the learning process (in line with Mills et al., 2004; Vanderplank, 2010).

Learners' viewing behaviour remains relatively understudied, despite the acknowledgment that student strategies and skills during listening and reading can significantly influence information intake (Vanderplank, 2016b). There has also been limited research comparing learners' perceptions of the viewing experience with actual comprehension or learning outcomes, with some studies suggesting a correlation (e.g., BavaHarji et al., 2014, in adults) and others finding a less consistent pattern (e.g., Casulleras, 2023, in young learners).

In edutainment, Bird (2005) distinguishes two user types: those making active use of all inbuilt functions; and those choosing to enjoy watching and postponing learning. Bird insists that effective edutainment must address both learner strategies: learning while watching and learning after watching. Among the studies conducted on learners' behaviour and Netflix's tools, Dizon's (2018) participants appreciated the freedom to choose from the many options offered by the platform, which raised their interest in L2 learning and increased pragmatics awareness. Alm (2021b) investigated learner strategies in extensive watching of self-selected films, pointing out that subtitles and the replay function embedded in Netflix favour focusing on language. Some participants also admitted greater reliance on subtitles in the first viewing compared to the second. However, many students in the same study felt overwhelmed with the detailed translations provided.

As can be observed, most of the existing research has concentrated on non-repeated captioned/subtitled viewing by advanced young adult participants exposed to short videos, with few exceptions involving several episodes of the same series or repeated viewing, as well as additional edutainment tools for a per-sonalised video experience.

The present study seeks to assess the effectiveness of Repeated Viewing (RV) of captioned episodes (with no control over the pace of viewing) versus self-regulated watching with *Language Reactor* (LR) among teenagers learning English as a foreign language (EFL). With this aim, the study poses the following research questions:

1. Is Repeated Viewing (RV) with captions or Language Reactor use (LR) more effective for content comprehension and vocabulary learning when watching TV series?
2. What are the learners' viewing behaviour and learning perceptions in each case?

3. Methodology

3.1 Participants

The participants in this study were Russian L1 teenagers, all being volunteers recruited either through the first author's personal network or through posts on social media. The initial sample included 46 students, of whom two students par-ticipated only in the pre-test and could not continue for personal reasons. Four students did not meet the study's entry criteria in terms of L2 proficiency level, operationalised with a VS test, demonstrating extremely low scores (below 2,200 words). Hence, the final sample comprised 40 students, with a mean age of 15.5 years old ($SD = .258$), 65% females, 35% males. In line with the Russian school curriculum, they were expected to have reached at least the B1 (intermediate) level of L2 English, according to the Common European Framework of Reference for Languages. The participants were randomly divided into two groups before the pre-test (Table 1). According to Kolmogorov-Smirnov tests of normality, the data on age and receptive VS were normally distributed ($p > .05$). Independent-samples *t*-tests revealed that the groups were comparable in terms of age and VS.

Table 1. Participants' N, mean age, VS and gender, by group

	N	Mean age (SD)	Mean VS (SD)	Males (%)	Females (%)
Repeated Viewing (RV)	19	15.26 (.40)	4422.37 (341.16)	47.4	52.6
Language Reactor (LR)	21	15.71 (.33)	5276 (285.46)	23.8	76.2

The groups were also equal in terms of socioeconomic status, operationalised as parents' education; in most of the families, both parents had higher education (RV 89.5%, LR 90.5%). Most of the participants in both groups were living in Russia at the time of testing (with the rest living in non-English-speaking European countries): 89.5% of the RV and 85.7% of the LR group have lived most of their lives in Russia. The groups had comparable language backgrounds and proficiency, as indicated by similar average school grades in English, the age at which they began learning English, and the amount of additional English instruction they received.

3.2   Instruments

3.2.1   TV series

The first two consecutive episodes of the Netflix series *Greenhouse Academy* (Chamizer, 2017) were chosen, based on the participants' age and English level. These episodes offered comprehensible neutral content (e.g., school theme, absence of violence), and their length (approximately 25 minutes) made it possible to watch it twice in one hour. Participants had not seen this series before the intervention. To check the coverage the participants would have of each episode, a corpus analysis was conducted with VocabProfile v.2.6 (Cobb, n.d.) (see Table 2). Since the participants' mean VS was 4,870.52 ($SD = 228.288$), the coverage of the series was adequate ($\approx 98\%$).

Table 2. Cumulative coverage for the five first frequency bands, by episode

Frequency band		1K (1,000)	2K (2,000)	3K (3,000)	4K (4,000)	5K (5,000)
Cumulative coverage (%)	Episode 1	91	94.7	96.3	97.9	98.5
	Episode 2	91.8	95.4	96.3	97.6	98.2

3.2.2 *Vocabulary size test*

To operationalise L2 proficiency level, the receptive vocabulary size test V_YesNo (Meara & Miralpeix, 2015) was chosen due to its easy administration and successful use in similar studies. In this test, students are provided with a list of words (one at a time) and are asked to answer whether they know their meaning, with guessing controlled through pseudowords. The maximum score is 10,000.

3.2.3 *Vocabulary pre-test and post-tests*

Word meaning recall was checked by asking learners to provide L1 translations of the Target Words (TWs). The words appeared in different random order in pre- and post-tests, with 15 seconds to write the translation (to prevent deception), programmed on Testportal.net due to its free access and very flexible timing settings.

For each episode, 20 TWs that the participants were not expected to know were selected. The 40 words were first pre-tested, with the addition of 10 distractors from 1K frequency band (50 pre-test items in total). TWs appeared in different frequencies in the videos (30 occurred between 2 and 12 times, and 10 appeared once). Cognates and words in high-frequency bands (1K and 2K) were avoided whenever possible, and word categories and word lengths were balanced. One point was awarded for each correct translation, so the minimum raw score was 0 and the maximum was 20 for each episode.

3.2.4 *Comprehension tests*

Based on Rodgers (2013), comprehension tests after each episode included 5 true/false questions, 5 multiple-choice questions and an ordering task with six items (see Appendix A), combining general, detailed, and inferential questions divided equally between the episode units. In each episode, the maximum score was 16 and results are given in percentages. Comprehension tests were administered in the students' L1 (Russian) through the platform Quizizz.com, as it allowed for the preparation of timed questions of different types with good visualization and easy access.

3.2.5 *Questionnaires*

The background questionnaire contained 15 questions. The post-viewing questionnaires (Appendix B) included multiple-choice questions and Likert-scale questions (14 in total), as well as one open question to share impressions after viewing. Although two post-viewing questionnaires were administered (with variations tailored to each group), six questions remained consistent across both groups. These questions pertained to viewing behaviour (such as reading subtitles or listening), reasons for subtitle reading (if applicable), perceived usefulness of the language exposure in the series for future application, perceived difficulty of the language and plot, as well as impressions following viewing. The LR questionnaire also included questions on tool usage, whereas the RV questionnaire asked about the attention paid to several aspects in each viewing. All the questionnaires were hosted on Google Forms.

3.3   Procedure

The current study was an online intervention, with all the sessions taking place on Zoom (either individually or in small groups), lasting 60–70 minutes each. The data collection process took approximately one month, adapting to the participants' timetables. All the forms, questionnaires, comprehension tests, and instructions were provided in the participants' L1.

The background questionnaire was filled in online several days before Session 1. Session 1 took place at least 1 week before Session 2 (to minimize any priming effect of the vocabulary tests) and included the VS test, the vocabulary pre-test, training on all the platforms used in the study, and watching trial videos to familiarise themselves with Netflix and LR (for the LR group). Sessions 2 and 3, conducted with a 1–2-day pause between them, each included one episode viewing, comprehension and vocabulary tests and post-viewing questionnaires. The RV group watched the episode twice (50 min. in total) and the LR group were given 50 minutes to watch the episode using the app.

Two episodes were included in this study for two reasons: (1) previous research has shown that results from TV viewing may be episode dependent (e.g., Gesa, 2019; Rodgers, 2013) and that findings from one-off studies with just one video may not be reliable; (2) viewing behaviour might be different in the first and second episodes, and the researchers wanted to account for this if it was the case. The series was viewed on Netflix from the first author's screen with the RV group, and on Netflix with the embedded LR from individual participants' screens with the LR group.

3.4   Scoring and analyses

The vocabulary pre- and post-tests were scored consistently in the same way. To provide valid scoring, a second rater (an L1 Russian linguist, experienced EFL teacher) was asked to rate 10% of the data (vocabulary pre-tests and post-tests); 98.6% agreement was reached.

As some TWs may already be known in the pre-test, the study used relative vocabulary gains as a fine-grained measure of vocabulary progress (Horst et al., 1998). Relative gains were calculated according to the formula:

$$\text{Relative vocabulary gains} = \frac{\text{N of TWs learnt}}{\text{N of items tested} - \text{N of TWs known}} \times 100$$

where "TWs learnt" refers to the number of items answered correctly only in the post-test, but incorrectly in the pre-test; "TWs known" refers to the number of items with correct answers in both the pre-test and post-test; and "N of items tested" equals 20 per episode.

Statistical analyses were conducted using SPSS (v. 27). Vocabulary scores followed a normal distribution, so parametric tests were used. However, comprehension scores deviated from normality, requiring non-parametric tests. Cronbach's Alpha was used to check the internal consistency reliability of the comprehension and vocabulary tests (raw scores), indicating good reliability: .944 for vocabulary pre- and post-tests and .719 for comprehension tests.

To ensure there were no significant differences between episodes in each group, preliminary paired-samples t-tests were conducted between Episode 1 and 2 to assess L2 vocabulary results, and its non-parametric analogue Wilcoxon signed-ranks tests for non-normally distributed comprehension scores.

To answer RQ1, independent-samples t-tests were run to compare the groups' vocabulary gains and non-parametric Mann-Whitney U tests to compare the groups' comprehension. To answer RQ2, a qualitative analysis of the answers to the post-viewing questionnaires was performed, focusing on the frequencies of the answers in each group and the patterns emerged from the most repeated responses.

4. Results

4.1 RQ1: Comprehension and vocabulary learning in RV and LR groups

The related-samples Wilcoxon signed-ranks test, comparing comprehension between the episodes for the same group, revealed no significant differences between the comprehension of the two episodes: ($Z=.798$, $p=.425$) for RV and ($Z=.498$, $p=.618$) for LR. Regarding vocabulary gains, the paired-samples t-tests revealed no significant differences between the episodes for either group ($t(18)=-.905$, $p=.377$) for RV and ($t(20)=-927$, $p=.365$) for LR. Therefore, the results are not episode dependent.

The descriptive statistics for comprehension scores are shown in Table 3. Figure 1 shows comprehension outcomes in the two groups. Mann-Whitney U test comparing comprehension between the conditions failed to reveal statistically significant differences: ($U=213.00$, $p=.728$) in Episode 1 and ($U=200.50$, $p=.979$) in Episode 2, which suggests that comprehension under the two conditions was equally effective.

Table 3. Comprehension (in percentages) in Episodes 1 and 2, by group

		M	SD	Min.	Max.	95% CI	Median	IQR
Episode 1	RV ($n=19$)	76.58	23.47	20	100	[65.27, 87.89]	87	26
	LR ($n=21$)	80.90	16.85	47	100	[73.24, 88.57]	87	17
Episode 2	RV ($n=19$)	79.74	22.28	20	100	[69.00, 90.47]	93	26
	LR ($n=21$)	84.19	13	60	100	[78.27, 90.11]	87	22

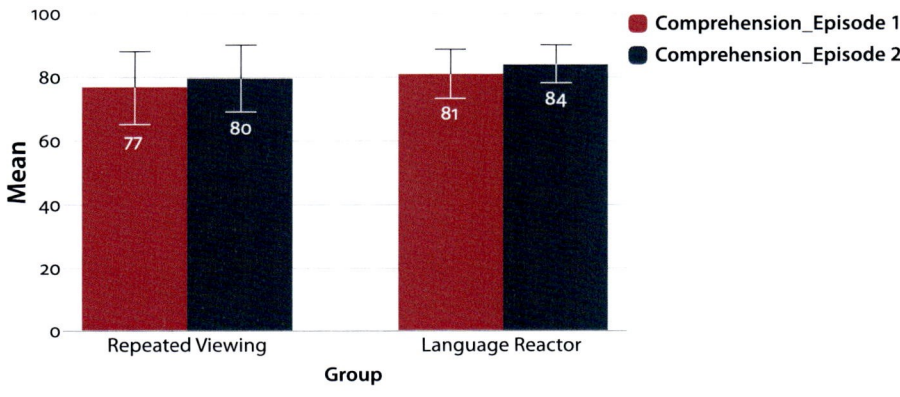

Figure 1. Comprehension (in percentages) in Episodes 1 and 2, by group

The descriptive statistics for vocabulary gains are shown in Table 4. Independent-samples *t*-tests failed to yield significant differences between the groups: $(t\,(38)=-1.228,\ p=.227)$ for Episode 1 and $(t(38)=-1.328,\ p=.192)$ for Episode 2.

Relative vocabulary gains, presented in Figure 2, show that, in both episodes, participants using LR gained more than those watching the series without it. However, this difference did not reach significance for relative vocabulary gains.

Table 4. Relative vocabulary gains in Episodes 1 and 2, by group

		M	*SD*	Min.	Max.	95% CI
Episode 1	RV ($n=19$)	34.97	26.23	0	84.62	[22.32, 47.60]
	LR ($n=21$)	44.62	23.5	12.5	100	[33.92, 55.32]
Episode 2	RV ($n=19$)	38.68	25.25	0	100	[26.51, 50.85]
	LR ($n=21$)	50.7	31.31	0	100	[36.45, 64.95]

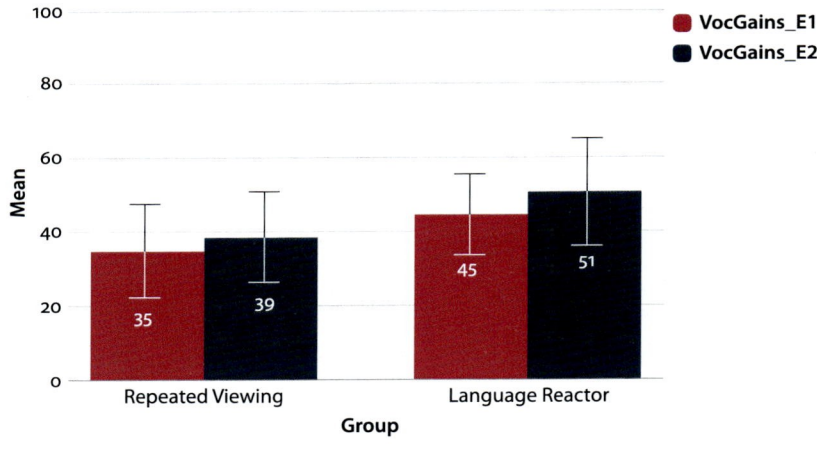

Figure 2. Relative vocabulary gains (in percentages) in Episodes 1 and 2, by group

4.2   RQ2: Learners' viewing behaviour and learning perceptions

Learner choices were analysed based on the answers to the post-viewing question-naires (see Appendix B): six questions (five multiple-choice and one open) were the same for each group, while the rest were different, as the exposure conditions were different for each group.

The answers to the five multiple-choice questions common to both groups revealed their different dynamics in terms of relying on the on-screen text. About a half of the LR students chose "mostly listening and sometimes reading" in each episode (47% in Episode 1 and 52% in Episode 2), with the rest of the students either always "only listening" or "listening and reading at the same time". The RV group, in contrast, seem to have changed their tactics. In Episode 1, the majority of the RV group (57.9%) opted for "mostly listening and sometimes reading" but, in Episode 2, the same number of students switched to "listening and reading at the same time". Only one RV participant stopped using captions in Episode 2 and "only listened" and, in the LR group, there were two participants choosing "listening only" after Episode 1 and three after Episode 2.

The two groups rated the plot interest equally, whereas language difficulty was perceived differently: in the RV group, 15.8% (Episode 1) and 31.6% (Episode 2) evaluated it as "rather difficult", compared to 0% (Episode 1) and 4.8% (Episode 2) in the LR group. In contrast, the usefulness of the language they were exposed to while watching was rated more highly by the LR group, with up to 28.6% seeing it as "very useful" (compared to only 5.3% in the RV group). In Episode 2, the number of LR participants explicitly paying attention to the language was particularly high, with 71.4% perceiving it as "(rather) useful" (compared to 42.1% in the RV group).

In response to the question "Why did you use captions?" (with the option of choosing more than one answer), ≈70% of RV participants (compared to less than 30% in the LR group) chose multiple reasons, with over 20% selecting more than three reasons. 63.2% of the RV group used captions "to learn new words" (compared to 9.5% in the LR group).

The answers to the rest of the questions, unique for each group, demonstrated that, in the RV group, repeated viewing contributed to better plot comprehension: at least 5.3% (viewing 1) versus 31.6% (viewing 2) reported 100% understanding, but not always improved vocabulary understanding (5.3% after both viewings of Episode 1). With respect to the potential usage of LR tools, which were not available to them, more than 40% of the RV participants would consistently want to use not only captions, but also L1 subtitles simultaneously with captions, and more than 60% to have detailed translations available, perceiving them as potentially "(rather) useful", with speed regulation considered the least useful function.

Even though the LR group had the possibility of controlling the playback speed, speed regulation was the least popular option, with the rest of LR functions actively used in both episodes and positively evaluated by most viewers. All participants considered on-screen text crucial and used it often (mostly opting for dual subtitles).

Pause was used for multiple reasons by up to one-third of the LR participants. Table 5 shows the percentage of participants that considered each option "very useful" or "rather useful" and the percentages of actual use for each option.

Table 5. LR tools perceived usefulness and actual use by LR group ($n = 21$)

	"Rather /very useful" (%)		Actively used (%)	
	Episode 1	Episode 2	Episode 1	Episode 2
Dual subtitles	100	100	95.2	95.2
Pausing	66.6	81.0	60.1	66.7
Rewind	90.5	81.0	*	*
Repeating phrase	95.2	85.7	71.4	66.7
Speed regulation	42.8	57.2	0	4.8
Detailed translation	95.2	95.2	57.1	52.4

* No separate question presented in the questionnaires

Qualitative analysis of the open question highlighted the groups' different foci. The RV group paid very close attention to the plot, with one-third of the comments related to separate scenes and plot lines: "*I was very sorry for Hayley. She took care of Alex, and he was so rude to her*".

After watching Episode 1 twice, about 20% perceived the difference between the two viewings. "*At some moments, I could not understand at once what was meant but, with the second viewing, all of these problems were solved*", or "*the second viewing allowed me to pay attention to some words, phrases and moments that I did not hear with the first viewing*". This is in line with the participants' evaluation of their explicit attention to the input (e.g., "attention to words you want to learn"). While 9–10 participants paid 'high' or 'very high' attention to words during the first viewing of each episode, 14–15 participants did so during the second viewing, indicating increased language awareness.

Few students (10.5%) enjoyed guessing word meanings from the context ("*It is cool to understand the meanings of the words from the context*"), with about 40% highlighting the lack of scaffolding: "*Sometimes it was difficult to be fast enough to read the captions, while trying to understand the words*", or "*some words were really unknown. I had never encountered them before, and I could not translate them*". Captions alone were not enough to ensure complete language understanding: "*I felt a desire to get some explanations about some expressions*". Several participants mentioned that they would appreciate tools such as pausing, speed regulations and detailed translation.

One participant got bored with the repeated viewing: "*It was rather difficult to watch the film twice because the plot was fairly clear from the first viewing*". However, 15% expressed an overall positive impression of the process: "*It is always good to watch a film in the original language. This was a good experience for sure*".

Different findings were obtained for the LR group. Over one-third mentioned their explicit focus on active vocabulary learning with special attention to unusual words and chunks: "*I had to analyse phrases and enrich my vocabulary*", or "*I have learnt several new words and interesting expressions, which will be useful for further language studying*".

The perception of some aspects changed between the episodes. After watching Episode 1, one of the participants wrote:

> The most difficult thing was to combine understanding the plot, analysing the phrases and their translation, listening and comprehension, and reading the on-screen text.

The same person commented about Episode 2:

> This time, it was much easier to use several types of comprehension of the information simultaneously. I mostly listened, and quite seldom looked at the text. Therefore, I understood the text more easily, because I did not multitask between listening and reading at the same time. [...] My abilities have improved, and it has become easier for me to watch.

Their attitude towards dual subtitles also changed, with many participants relying on them more in Episode 1 and combining them with other tools in Episode 2. The participant who wrote after Episode 1, "*Simultaneous subtitles in two languages helped a lot*", noticed that in Episode 2, "*I really loved the function of translating separate words*".

The function of detailed translation was appreciated by one-fifth of participants in Episode 1 and one-third in Episode 2, "*It was interesting [...] to click on new words. It was useful to use the detailed translation and to hear the word pronunciation again*". Many trained analytical skills, comparing a word meaning in context and isolation,

> The function of translation of separate words is very good. But sometimes, because of the context, the words are translated differently. But, in these situations, Russian subtitles helped, so everything was clear.

Three participants raised issues related to the application interface, e.g., "*dual subtitles took up too much space on the screen, I would like to make them smaller*".

About one-fifth of the participants explicitly acknowledged a positive attitude towards the LR application, e.g., "*a good programme for learning English and maintaining it, for improving your level and learning new words and the detailed translation. Very handy"*, and *"it was certainly more interesting than traditional texts in coursebooks"*. Many particularly pointed out the usefulness of such practices (e.g., *"training listening and comprehension was useful"*) and the desire to continue using LR after the experiment: e.g., *"overall, I liked working with this platform because it allows me to find the meanings of new words fast and easily, and it is convenient to use in general"*, and *"I learnt how to use this application and I am going to use it to learn languages that I am studying, not only English"*.

5.   Discussion

5.1   Comprehension and vocabulary learning in RV and LR groups

The current study was set up to compare the effect of two conditions (Repeated Viewing with captions and using the LR application) on content comprehension and vocabulary learning by L1 Russian teenagers while watching TV series. Both conditions demonstrated language gains, and the absence of significant differences between the conditions suggests that, if students are allowed to have the same amount of exposure to the videos – either with repeated viewing or with LR –, the outcomes can be comparable. Results would support Vandergrift & Goh's (2012) and Webb's (2015) ideas about the effectiveness of repeated viewing to provide vocabulary recirculation and enhance learning.

Both groups showed very high comprehension scores with high means of above 76% (e.g., 72.70% for less proficient teenagers in Pujadas & Muñoz, 2020; and 81.47% for university students in Gesa, 2019). The absence of significant differences between the conditions might be explained by a possible ceiling effect, as the vocabulary coverage of the series was high (≈98%), which might have made them easy to follow. However, it should be borne in mind that comprehension entails far more than just coverage, especially if learners are not usually exposed to this type of input, and that range of comprehension scores varied from 20% to 100%. It should also be noted that the standard deviations for the LR group are narrower than those in the RV group, and that the minimum values for comprehension are much higher in the LR group. These figures suggest that the level of understanding could be higher within this group.

Relative vocabulary gains showed that participants could learn up to half of the TWs (mean between 35% and 51% per episode), in line with Fievez et al.'s (2023) participants, showing 36.47% relative gains in meaning recall while using LR. In the present study, learners using LR got slightly higher vocabulary scores in both episodes than the RV group, but differences were not significant. A longitudinal intervention with more exposure would help to see whether these differences progressively become bigger as students get used to these practices, or if the amount of learning remains stable in both groups. It should be noted that higher results may have been obtained in both conditions had form or meaning recognition been assessed, as recalling word meaning is more challenging for students than word or meaning recognition.

5.2   Learners' viewing behaviour and learning perceptions

When comparing learners' watching behaviour, the RV group showed attention to plot details and a high degree of understanding the content of the series, which was perceived and explicitly formulated by many participants. Successful focus on content, combined with the lack of consistent attention towards language due to the partial insufficiency of scaffolding, may be seen as the major trait for the RV condition.

The RV group had to rely mainly on captions, with most participants using captions for several reasons (i.e., "to understand the dialogues" and "to learn new words"), rather than for a single purpose. This highlights the importance of captions as the main source of scaffolding in this condition. In Episode 2, already familiar with the format of the tests, the participants increased their reliance on reading captions (the majority chose "listening and reading" in Episode 2 instead of "mostly listening" in Episode 1). This suggests that listening alone could be sufficient for conventional viewing, but not when tests are expected, especially once they have been tested after the previous episode. This is consistent with Muñoz's (2017) eye-tracking experiment revealing teenagers' active reliance on subtitles, and with Winke et al.'s (2010) participants using subtitles not only to learn the exposed language, but also to understand the content (a *crutch*, according to Winke et al.).

Moreover, the LR group had a variety of tools to choose from, which explains why only less than 30% of participants used the on-screen text for multiple reasons. Instead of relying solely on dual subtitles, the LR group benefitted, for example, from the option of pausing, which was used for several reasons by 19% of participants in Episode 1 and 33.33% in Episode 2. This suggests gradually learning to apply different LR tools and developing learner strategies, whereas the RV group used captions as the primary means of reference due to the absence of other assistance. Both groups showed little interest in speed regulations, with all the other tools perceived very positively and used actively by the LR group. Therefore, the qualitative findings suggest that the availability of viewing control by the participants changes the nature of the viewing: the control afforded by LR seems to be important for many learners, echoing findings in Vanderplank (2019).

Language learning was seen to work differently in the two groups. The RV group used captions "to learn new words" 6.65 times as often as the LR group, which had other instruments for word learning. This range of tools could be the reason why perceived language difficulty for those who used the application was low (a maximum of 4.8% considered language as "rather difficult", compared to 31.6% in the RV group). However, none of the participants in either group considered the language "very difficult", implying that the presence of captions (and the other resources available for the LR group) was useful. Having multiple tools at their disposal, the LR participants must have felt less pressure than their RV peers, which allowed them to see the language as an object of active studying, with almost 30% perceiving the language they were exposed to as "very useful" (5.4 times as many as in the RV group). This is in line with Frumuselu et al. (2015) and Winke et al. (2010), who pointed out that additional scaffolding provided by multimedia can foster cognitive processing. It may also suggest that LR tools can be used as a more flexible alternative to traditional formal training, which is often provided to supplement L2 viewing (e.g., Gesa & Miralpeix, 2023; Pujadas & Muñoz, 2019).

Analysis of the answers to the open question on the impressions after watching the episodes highlighted more differences between the groups' priorities. The RV group stated that their focus was on the episode plot and, in line with Alm's (2021b) participants, demonstrated a different attitude towards the two viewings, with the second often perceived as additional linguistic scaffolding. Some students remarked that they already got the grasp of the content from the first viewing, which is why they could pay more attention to understanding the language in the second viewing. However, some students admitted that even the two viewings were not enough for them to understand the language at the desired level. When asked about scaffolding, the RV group expressed a desire to have access to options such as pausing or translations.

The LR group's answers revealed a focus on active vocabulary learning, combining dual subtitles with other tools, namely pausing and detailed translation (the latter is in line with Fievez et al., 2023). Nevertheless, even though the LR's vocabulary gains tended to be higher, significant differences between groups were not found and there was a mismatch between learners' perceptions of learning and actual learning. It is also worth noting that many participants did not use some of the LR functions much, and still preferred to watch largely for entertainment – as did many participants in the EURECAP project (Vanderplank, 2019). The comparison of the two conditions, though, suggests the effectiveness of the tools combined in LR and their conscious demand by learners. The students' positive feedback towards LR usage corroborates ideas expressed by Mills et al. (2004) or Vanderplank (2010) on learners' engagement. Finally, considering the participants' comments, LR seems to be favourable for higher-order cognitive processes (Krathwohl, 2002) such as analysing and evaluating, along with using higher layers of knowledge, namely procedural and meta-cognitive knowledge, which enhances the pedagogical potential of the application.

However comparable the general outcomes may be, the two groups' experiences with the multimedia material were remarkably different. This allows us to hypothesise that a more prolonged series viewing could help to determine how learners get used to each treatment, how L2 learning develops over time in each condition, and which specific aspects of the viewing options are more beneficial than others in the LR group.

6.   Conclusion, limitations, and further research

The present study compared two rather underexplored conditions that can promote L2 learning from viewing. They are both relevant to formal education and extensive out-of-the-classroom TV viewing. The experiment controls for amount of exposure to the videos, which helps in ensuring comparability of the two conditions. The lack of significant differences between the groups in terms of content comprehension and vocabulary learning is combined with distinctions in the learners' behaviour, as it seems evident that the RV group focused more on comprehension, whereas the LR one was language-oriented.

In terms of the pedagogical implications of the study, both content comprehension and vocabulary acquisition from viewing proved effective, consistent with prior research. Additionally, the expressed interest in L2 learning through captioned viewing, coupled with the considerable awareness of tools, and viewing strategies displayed by teenagers in both viewing conditions, should be considered when planning L2 curricular and extracurricular activities for this age group.

Further research should aim to overcome the limitations of the current study. Firstly, low numbers in the groups can lead to a higher risk of Type 2 errors in the statistical tests. Even if two episodes have been used, larger samples should be recruited to enhance the statistical power of the experiment and longer interventions should be carried out, as longer-term longitudinal research over an extended period may help elucidate the weak and strong points of learning from TV viewing in each condition. Secondly, the LR group was not familiar with the application before the study. The lack of practice might have influenced the results, although the participants were introduced to and practised with the app in the training session. Furthermore, L2 proficiency was operationalised using a VS test, instead of a full-scaled proficiency level test. Although VS is a good indicator of learners' overall performance (e.g., Miralpeix & Muñoz, 2018), future studies could consider a more detailed control of L2 proficiency, with listening and reading abilities being taken into account. Finally, given the results obtained in the post-viewing questionnaires, students' engagement with edutainment apps such as LR should be further explored in relation to L2 learning.

Acknowledgements

This work was supported by grants PID2019-110594GB-100 from the Spanish Ministry of Science and Innovation and 2023SGR00303 from the Catalan Agency for Management of University and Research Grants (AGAUR) to the second author. The authors would also like to thank the reviewers for their very interesting comments and suggestions.

Ethical Considerations

The study protocol adhered to the good practices of data collection, data anonymization, data processing, and data storage of the Institutional Review Board of the University of Barcelona (IRB0003099).

References

Alm, A. (2021a). Language learning with Netflix: Extending out-of-class L2 viewing. *2021 International Conference on Advanced Learning Technologies (ICALT), Tartu, Estonia* (pp. 260–263). IEEE.

Alm, A. (2021b). Language learning with Netflix: From extensive to intra-formal learning. *The EuroCALL Review, 29*(1), 81–92.

BavaHarji, M., Alavi, Z., & Letchumanan, K. (2014). Captioned instructional video. Effects in content comprehension. vocabulary acquisition and language proficiency. *English Language Teaching, 7*(5), 1–16.

Bird, S.A. (2005). Language learning edutainment: Mixing motives in digital resources. *RELC Journal, 36*(3), 311–339.

Casulleras, M. (2023). Language learning from subtitled TV series in the primary EFL classroom (Unpublished doctoral dissertation). University of Barcelona. Retrieved on 28 May 2024 from http://hdl.handle.net/2445/201785

Chamizer, G. (Producer). (2017). *Greenhouse Academy*. Season 1. Netflix original series. Retrieved on 1 June 2023 from https://www.netflix.com/watch/80095436?trackId =255824129

Cobb, T. (n.d.). *VocabProfile* (Version 2.6) [computer software]. Retrieved on 1 June 2023 from https://www.lextutor.ca/vp/comp

Dizon, G. (2018). Netflix and L2 learning: A case study. *The EuroCALL Review, 26*(2), 30–40.

Fievez, I., Montero Perez, M., Cornillie, F., & Desmet, P. (2023): Promoting incidental vocabulary learning through watching a French Netflix series with glossed captions. *Computer Assisted Language Learning*, 36(1–2), 26–51.

Frumuselu, A., De Maeyer, S., Donche, V., & Gutiérrez-Colón, M. del M. (2015). Television series inside the EFL classroom: Bridging the gap between teaching and learning informal language through subtitles. *Linguistics and Education*, 32, 107–117.

Gesa, F. (2019). L1/L2 subtitled TV series and EFL learning: A study on vocabulary acquisition and content comprehension at different proficiency levels (Unpublished doctoral dissertation). University of Barcelona. Retrieved on 28 May 2024 from http://hdl.handle .net/10803/668505

Gesa, F., & Miralpeix, I. (2023). Extensive viewing as additional input for foreign language vocabulary learning: A longitudinal study in secondary school. *Language Teaching Research*.

Gouleti, A., Dimitriadis, G., & Kokonis, M. (2020). Exploring the educational potentials of language learning with Netflix tool: An eye-tracking study. *Ex-centric Narratives: Journal of Anglophone Literature, Culture and Media*, 4, 113–136.

Horst, M., Cobb, T., & Meara, P. (1998). Beyond a Clockwork Orange: Acquiring second language vocabulary through reading. *Reading in a Foreign Language*, 11, 207–223. http:// hdl.handle.net/10125/66953

Krathwohl, D. R. (2002). A revision of Bloom's taxonomy: An overview. *Theory Into Practice*, 41(4), 212–218.

Long, M. (2017). Instructed second language acquisition (ISLA): Geopolitics, methodological issues, and some major research questions. *Instructed Second Language Acquisition*, 1(1), 7–44.

Mayer, R. E. (2014). Cognitive theory of multimedia learning. In R. E. Mayer (Ed.). *The Cambridge handbook of multimedia learning* (pp. 43–71). Cambridge University Press.

Meara, P., & Miralpeix, I. (2015). V_YesNo. Lognostics. Retrieved on 28 May 2024 from https:// www.lognostics.co.uk/tools/V_YesNo/V_YesNo.htm

Mills, N., Herron, C., & Cole, S. (2004). Teacher assisted versus individual viewing of foreign language video: Relation to comprehension, self-efficacy, and engagement. *Calico Journal*, 21, 291–316.

Miralpeix, I., & Muñoz, C. (2018). Receptive vocabulary size and its relationship to EFL language skills. *IRAL – International Review of Applied Linguistics in Language Teaching*, 56(1), 1–24.

Montero Perez, M., Van Den Noortgate, W., & Desmet, P. (2013). Captioned video for L2 listening and vocabulary learning: A meta-analysis. *System*, 41(3), 720–739.

Montero Perez, M. (2022). Second or foreign language learning through watching audio-visual input and the role of on-screen text. *Language Teaching*, 55(2), 163–192.

Muñoz, C. (2017). The role of age and proficiency in subtitle reading. An eye-tracking study. *System*, 67, 77–86.

Muñoz, C., Pattemore, A., & Avello, D. (2022). Exploring repeated captioning viewing as a way to promote vocabulary learning: Time lag between repetitions and learner factors. *Computer Assisted Language Learning*.

Nation, P., & Newton, J. (2009). *Teaching ESL/EFL listening and speaking*. Routledge.

Paivio, A. (1986). *Mental representations: A dual coding approach*. Oxford University Press.

Price, K. (1983). Closed-captioned TV: An untapped resource. *Newsletter – Massachusetts Association of Teachers of English to Speakers of Other Languages, 12*(2), 1–8. Retrieved on 28 May 2024 from https://www.matsol.org/assets/documents/Currentsv12n02Fall1983.pdf

Pujadas, G., & Muñoz, C. (2019). Extensive viewing of captioned and subtitled TV series: A study of L2 vocabulary learning by adolescents. *The Language Learning Journal, 47*(4), 479–496.

Pujadas, G., & Muñoz, C. (2020). Examining adolescent EFL learners' TV viewing comprehension through captions and subtitles. *Studies in Second Language Acquisition, 42,* 551–575.

Reynolds, B., Cui, Y., Kao, C., & Thomas, N. (2022). Vocabulary acquisition through viewing captioned and subtitled video: A scoping review and meta-analysis. *Systems, 10,* 133.

Rodgers, M. (2013). English language learning through viewing television: An investigation of comprehension, incidental vocabulary acquisition, lexical coverage, attitudes, and captions (Doctoral dissertation). Victoria University of Wellington.

Rodgers, M., & Webb, S. (2020). Incidental vocabulary learning through viewing television. *ITL – International Journal of Applied Linguistics, 171*(2), 191–220.

Sweller, J. (1994). Cognitive load theory, learning difficulty, and instructional design. *Learning and Instruction, 4*(4), pp. 295–312.

Vandergrift, L. (2007). Recent developments in second and foreign language listening comprehension research. *Language Teaching, 40*(3), 191–210.

Vandergrift, L., & Goh, C. (2012). *Teaching and learning second language listening.* Routledge.

Vanderplank, R. (2010). Déjà vu? A decade of research on language laboratories. television and video in language learning. *Language Teaching, 43*(1), 1–37.

Vanderplank, R. (2016a). *Captioned media in foreign language learning and teaching: Subtitles for the deaf and hard-of-hearing as tools for language learning.* Palgrave Macmillan.

Vanderplank, R. (2016b). 'Effects of' and 'effects with' captions: How exactly does watching a TV programme with same language subtitles make a difference to language learners? *Language Teaching, 49*(2), 235–250.

Vanderplank, R. (2019). 'Gist watching can only take you so far': attitudes, strategies and changes in behaviour in watching films with captions. *The Language Learning Journal, 47*(4), 407–423.

Webb, S. (2015). Extensive viewing: Language learning through watching television. In D. Nunan & J.C. Richards (Eds.) *Language learning beyond the classroom* (pp. 175–184). Routledge.

Webb, S., & Rodgers, M. (2009). Vocabulary demands of television programs. *Language Learning, 59*(2), 335–366.

Webb, S., Uchihara, T., & Yanagisawa, A. (2023). How effective is second language incidental vocabulary learning? A meta-analysis. *Language Teaching, 56*(2), 161–180.

Winke, P., Gass, S., & Sydorenko, T. (2010). The effects of captioning videos used for foreign language listening activities. *Language Learning & Technology, 14*(1), 65–86.

Wu, H. & Yang, X. (2022). Effectiveness of textually-enhanced captions on Chinese High-school EFL learners' incidental vocabulary learning. *Porta Linguarum, 38,* 209–228.

Appendix A.   Comprehension test for Episode 1 (one question in each part is provided as example)

Mark if these statements are true (T) or false (F)

1. Alex and Hayley's mother got interested in studying space while she was at university. (T/F)
    [...]

Choose the correct answer (A, B or C)

1. Why did Hayley change her mind about Alex's basketball practice while talking with her friends?
    A.   She did not want Alex to hang out with her friends.
    B.   She wanted Alex to enter the Greenhouse Academy so that she could use his room.
    C.   She was preparing a surprise for him while he was playing basketball.

    [...]

Put these statements in the correct chronological order – the way they go in the episode. Statements 1 and 5 will serve as a guideline

1	Alex and Hayley's mother died at the launch of the spacecraft.
2	Alex and Hayley quarreled and upset their father.
3	Alex met Daniel in the hall.
4	Alex took the written exam.
5	Alex attacked Daniel while playing basketball.
6	Hayley quarreled with the Greenhouse Academy's managers.
7	Alex and Hayley learnt that they both had been accepted to the Greenhouse Academy.
8	Hayley took the written exam.

Appendix B.   Post-viewing questionnaire

Questions to both RV and LR Groups	Possible answers
While watching this episode, you…	Listened and read subtitles at the same time.
	Mostly listened and sometimes read subtitles.
	Only listened and did NOT read subtitles.
	Only read subtitles and almost did NOT listen.
Evaluate the plot of the episode from 1 to 5. The more interesting, the higher score you should give.	Likert scale from *very boring* (1) to *very interesting* (5).
If you used subtitles, why do you think you did that?	Without the subtitles, I would not understand the heroes' words.
	Subtitles help me understand what is going on.
	When I see subtitles on the screen, I cannot help looking at them just because they are there.
	Subtitles help me learn English and remember new words.
	I did not use subtitles.
Evaluate the difficulty of the English language in the episode from 1 to 5. The more difficult, the higher score you should give.	Likert scale from *very easy* (1) to *very difficult* (5).
Evaluate the potential use of viewing the episode for your English language from 1 to 5. The more useful, the higher score you should give.	Likert scale from *completely useless* (1) to *very useful* (5).
Share your impressions after watching this episode. What was difficult? What was boring? What was the most interesting? What was useful?	Free-form open answer.
Questions to RV group only	
What do you think about the speed of subtitles?	I always had time to read subtitles when I wanted to.
	Sometimes I did not have time to read all the subtitles.
	The subtitles were too fast, I did not have time to read them.

Appendix B. *(continued)*

While watching the episode for the **first** time, indicate to which aspect you paid more attention. For each aspect, choose from 1 to 5. 1 = *did not pay attention at all*, 5 = *paid a lot of attention*.	Events and the plot.
	Relationships between the heroes, their motives and desires.
	Words and expressions that I don't know.
	Words and expressions that I would like to remember and use myself.
While watching the episode for the **second** time, indicate to which aspect you paid more attention. For each aspect, choose from 1 to 5. 1 = *did not pay attention at all*, 5 = *paid a lot of attention*.	Events and the plot.
	Relationships between the heroes, their motives and desires.
	Words and expressions that I don't know.
	Words and expressions that I would like to remember and use myself.
In your opinion, approximately what percentage of the episode's **content** did **you** understand after the **first** watching?	0%, 10%, 20%, 30%, 40%, 50%, 60%, 70%, 80%, 90%, 100%.
In your opinion, approximately what percentage of the episode's **content** did you understand after the **second** watching?	0%, 10%, 20%, 30%, 40%, 50%, 60%, 70%, 80%, 90%, 100%.
In your opinion, approximately what percentage of the episode's **vocabulary** did you understand after the **first** watching?	0%, 10%, 20%, 30%, 40%, 50%, 60%, 70%, 80%, 90%, 100%.
In your opinion, approximately what percentage of the episode's **vocabulary** did **you** understand after the **second** watching?	0%, 10%, 20%, 30%, 40%, 50%, 60%, 70%, 80%, 90%, 100%.
Was the speed of the audio always adequate for understanding?	Yes, I always could follow the heroes' words.
	Sometimes it was too fast, and I did not always manage to follow the heroes' words.
	No, I very often could not follow the heroes' words.
In your opinion, which additional functions would help you understand this episode better while watching? Score each one from 1 to 5. 1 = *would be completely useless*, 2 = *would be almost useless*, 3 = *can't evaluate*, 4 = *would be rather useful*, 5 = *would be very useful*.	Pause.
	Repetition of the previous phrase.
	Forwarding and rewinding.
	Changing the speed of the video.
	Subtitles/captions in different languages.
	Detailed word translation (like in a dictionary).

Appendix B. *(continued)*

Questions to LR group only	
How did you use the captions/subtitles?	I watched the whole episode with the captions/subtitles.
	I watched only part of the episode with the captions/subtitles.
	I did not use captions/subtitles.
Did you use captions in L2 (English) or subtitles in L1 (Russian)?	I used them both simultaneously.
	Only in Russian.
	Only in English.
	Sometimes in Russian, sometimes in English.
	I did not use captions/subtitles.
How many times approximately did you use the Pause?	None
	1–10
	11–20
	21–30
	31–40
	More than 40
If you used the Pause, why do you think you did that?	To read the subtitles more attentively.
	To analyze the previous phrases.
	To analyze events and heroes' relationships.
	To rewind and rewatch complicated scenes.
	I did not use the Pause.
How many times approximately did you use the function of repeating the Previous phrase?	None
	1–10
	11–20
	21–30
	31–40
How many times approximately did you use the function of the Detailed word translation?	None
	1–10
	11–20
	21–30
	31–40

Appendix B. *(continued)*

At which speed did you watch the episode?	Always slow.
	Sometimes slow, sometimes normal.
	Always normal.
	Sometimes fast, sometimes normal.
	Always fast.
	Sometimes fast, sometimes slow, sometimes normal.
How many times approximately did you watch the whole episode?	1
	1.5
	2
Evaluate the usefulness of each of the functions of Language Reactor. Score each one from 1 to 5. 1 = *completely useless*, 2 = *almost useless*, 3 = *can't evaluate*, 4 = *rather useful*, 5 = *very useful*.	Pause.
	Repetition of the previous phrase.
	Forwarding and rewinding.
	Changing the speed of the video.
	Subtitles/captions in different languages.
	Detailed word translation.

Multimodal input and L2 pragmatics
An eye-tracking study

Júlia Barón,¹ M. Luz Celaya¹ & Alicia Martínez-Flor²
¹ Universitat de Barcelona | ² Universitat Jaume I

Analyzing the effects of multimodal input in the acquisition of second/ foreign language (L2) pragmatics is a recent area in research. In this line, the use of eye-tracking to investigate L2 pragmatics remains limited (Godfroid, 2019). This study aimed to explore the effects of multimodal input on L2 requests among English as a Foreign Language (EFL) learners, while monitoring them with a webcam eye-tracker. The study used a multiple-choice discourse completion test at pre and posttest to evaluate the effects of viewing audio-visual material with or without captions. Additionally, a subset of participants was interviewed regarding pragmatic perception. Findings indicate that participants exposed to captioned videos performed better in the posttest and relied on captions when viewing, a result corroborated by retrospective interviews.

1. Introduction

In the last few years, we have witnessed an exponential increase in the use of audio-visual material due to the emergence of online platforms such as Netflix, HBO, Prime, or Disney+, which allow people to watch a variety of movies or TV series, with the option to visualize them in the original language. This has led to a growing interest in investigating the effects of multimodal input on foreign/second (L2) language learning. In the case of the field of L2 pragmatics, the use of multimodal input has been praised for exposing learners to contextualized samples of the target language (see Bruti, 2016) and making them aware of how sociopragmatic aspects may influence pragmalinguistic choices (see Derakhshan & Eslami, 2020). However, more studies are needed to understand what learners focus on when they are exposed to multimodal input and, in relation to this, whether the use of captions and subtitles benefit the acquisition of the L2 pragmatics. In this line, the use of eye-tracking to investigate L2 pragmatics has not received enough attention yet (Godfroid, 2019); this tool might provide further

https://doi.org/10.1075/lllt.61.06bar

information about what learners do while watching audiovisual material. This study, therefore, explores the effects of multimodal input on L2 requests by English as a Foreign Language (EFL) undergraduate learners who were asked to watch four scenes from the Netflix series *Emily in Paris*; one group watched the scenes with captions (CapG) and the other without captions (NCapG) while their eye movements were recorded using eye-tracker. Additionally, four students from each group were randomly selected for an interview to gain an in-depth understanding of their perceptions when watching the scenes.

2.   Review of the literature

The use of audio-visual material to provide multimodal input in the L2 classroom has become increasingly popular thanks to the appealing materials available from the world of pedagogy and to the easy and regular access to online platforms and social networks nowadays. Research studies have analyzed the effects of using such material in the L2 classroom and several benefits for the acquisition of different areas of the L2 have been pointed out, especially in foreign language (FL) contexts where learners have limited opportunities to interact in the FL (see Finger-Bou & Muñoz, 2023, and Gesa & Miralpeix, 2023 on vocabulary; Pattemore & Muñoz, 2022 on grammar; and Pujadas & Muñoz, 2020 on comprehension, to name but a few studies in our research project). Recent research has specifically addressed the effects of multimodal input on the acquisition of the L2 pragmatics as well, although such studies are still fewer in number. Multimodal input presents several features that make it an adequate means to learn pragmatics. It has been claimed that multimodal input provides learners with contextualized samples of the L2 thanks to the similarities between fictional and real conversations (see Bruti, 2016; Qi & Lai, 2017, among others). In this sense, as stated by Celaya et al. (2023), the use of this type of input enhances intercultural learning, especially in the FL classroom where students are not exposed to the L2 outside the classroom context. Furthermore, according to Derakhshan and Eslami (2020), multimodal input helps learners develop sociopragmatic competence (the ability to acknowledge the effect of context on language) and makes them aware of how sociopragmatic aspects may influence pragmalinguistic choices (the use of the appropriate language in specific social contexts).

The bulk of research on multimodal input has compared groups of learners under different conditions of multimodality (see Peters & Muñoz, 2020 for an exhaustive review of types of multimodal input), both in classroom contexts and in experimental settings; this has allowed researchers in the area of pragmatics to point to the most effective modalities for teaching and learning L2 pragmatics.

Regarding experiences in real language classes, at a public university in the US, Abrams (2014) used films to analyze pragmatic awareness in German as a FL in a group of 37 first language (L1) English learners in two intact classes. The two groups did a pre/posttest Written Discourse Completion Test (WDCT). Then, the experimental group, apart from watching films, had seven weeks of teaching that included some instruction on pragmatics and tasks that focused on the relationship between language and the social context in the film; however, the control group only completed tasks on vocabulary and comprehension questions on the film. Findings revealed that learners in the experimental group became more aware of social norms in conversations and could, therefore, provide more appropriately pragmatic answers in the WDCTs.

In a similar context to the one in the present study, Alcón and Pitarch (2010) used excerpts from *Stargate* to measure the effect of a controlled type of instruction based on several techniques, e.g. identification, noticing and explanation, to raise awareness of refusals in EFL in a sample of 99 Spanish-Catalan bilingual university learners. After the analysis of retrospective verbal reports, the researchers concluded that the type of instruction followed in the treatment was beneficial to notice and understand refusals in EFL. Also focusing on refusals, Usó-Juan and Martínez-Flor (2022) designed a research-based instructional method to teach refusals based on the use of audiovisual materials at the discourse level. The researchers followed a "pre-watching / while-watching and post-watching" procedure to offer a large number of activities that may help bridge the gap between research and practice in the acquisition of the L2 pragmatics; additionally, according to the researchers, such activities will empower "learners with agency" (p. 62) or, in other words, will make the learners' own perspectives and beliefs on the communicative act relevant. In a previous study, Usó-Juan and Martínez-Flor (2021) analyzed the way film analysis can enhance (meta)pragmatic awareness in real communicative encounters. Two exhaustively-analyzed examples that focus on request modification devices were offered for use in the FL classroom, namely, a dialogue in the film *The Day after Tomorrow* and another in *My Big Fat Greek Wedding*. The researchers defend the idea that the use of awareness-raising questions that analyze both context and language and lead to reflective thinking will make learners aware of the relationship between sociocultural factors and linguistic choices. It would be necessary to implement this teaching proposal to find out whether the expected benefits would be evident in a classroom.

Also, in a similar context to the one in the present study, Khazdouzian et al. (2021) analyzed 28 university Spanish-Catalan EFL learners with levels B2 to C1 who were randomly assigned to two groups, namely, those who watched one season of the TV sitcom *Modern Family* with captions and those who watched it without captions. Neither of the groups had received explicit instruction on pragmatics in class and this task was part of out-of-class activities. With a pre/posttest design, the acquisition of requests and suggestions were analyzed by means of a WDCT. The statistical analysis yielded few significant differences, so the researchers did not find a clear effect of captions versus the non-captioned condition, although the interviews carried out with some of the participants revealed that those who watched the episodes with captions reported a higher understanding than the non-captioned group, and, hence, a higher level of pragmatic awareness. In general terms, however, the use of audio-visual material seemed to make an impact in both groups, since the participants were able to provide a larger number of request and suggestion strategies in the posttest than in the pretest.

In a study following a similar design with 31 participants at a lower level of proficiency and younger ages (mean age 13 years old), but also L1 Spanish-Catalan EFL learners, Barón and Celaya (2022) analyzed several speech acts, requests among them, with excerpts from TV series (*Big Bang Theory, Stranger Things, Supernatural* and *Friends*) under captioned and non-captioned conditions. The experiment lasted seven sessions and in each of them the participants carried out an open role-play with situations like the video excerpts that they were later exposed to; they were given between two and three minutes to prepare the task and then they recorded themselves. After this, they watched the video excerpt twice while they were allowed to take notes about any expressions or vocabulary that seemed interesting to them, and carried out the same role-play, but no instruction was provided at any time. As above, results showed the benefits of using audio-visual material in each group, as seen in the differences between the first and the second role-plays, but, contrary to Khazdouzian et al. (2021), the group that had watched the excerpts with captions produced a higher number of pragmatic expressions than the other group and the differences were statistically significant. The lower level of proficiency of the participants in Barón and Celaya (2022) may be responsible for the effectiveness of captions, since captions added more information that learners could use. Additionally, the fact that the learners in this study were guided step by step whereas in Khazdouzian et al. (2021) learners watched the material on their own might also be another reason for the different results.

As Derakhshan and Eslami (2020, p.657) have claimed, more research is needed to study the effects of the use of "multimodal input integrating visual, auditory, and textual information" and, as seen above, this is especially so in relation to L2 pragmatics. We believe, therefore, that "eye-tracking" techniques, which have been extensively used in many other areas of Second Language Acquisition (SLA), may yield relevant findings on the acquisition of L2 pragmatics. However, to the best of our knowledge, the analysis of the effects of this type of input for the acquisition of the L2 pragmatics has not made use of such tools so far (see Godfroid, 2020, for a research synthesis in SLA). Considering the findings reviewed above, we aim at investigating the effects of two different conditions (captions and no captions) on the acquisition of EFL requests by L1 Spanish/Catalan university learners. The research questions (RQs) that have guided the present study are:

RQ1. What are the effects of captioned-video viewing on the learning of requests, as compared to non-captioned video viewing?

RQ2. Is there a difference in visual behavior when watching captioned and uncaptioned videos?

RQ3. What are learners' perceptions of their pragmatic learning in relation to the presence of captions (or not) in the videos?

3.   Methodology

3.1   Participants

The study involved 43 Spanish-Catalan undergraduate students (35 female/8 male; mean age = 20.5) who were in the third year of the English Studies Bachelor degree at a Spanish university. The learners had an advanced level of English (or C1 according to the Council of Europe level), as illustrated by the Quick Placement Test (2001) distributed among them prior to the beginning of the study. They also completed a short survey to collect information on i) their L1s, ii) gender, iii) age, iv) whether they had been abroad in an English-speaking country and for how long, v) whether they had contact with English native speakers (NSs) and how frequently, vi) as well as whether they watched TV and films in English, and if so, how often, whether they used subtitles and if that was case, in which language. The learners' L1s was Spanish and/or Catalan (L1 Spanish-Catalan $n=35$, L1 Catalan $n=8$; L1 Spanish $n=6$). All of them had spent some time abroad in an English-speaking country as part of their studies, which varied from 15 days to 3 months. Regarding their contact with English NSs, 34 claimed to have either weekly ($n=18$) or monthly ($n=16$) regular contact. As for their practice of watching TV/films in English, all of them indicated that they had contact with audio-visual material in English, which varied in terms of frequency: daily ($n=22$), weekly ($n=11$) or monthly ($n=5$). Out of them, 26 claimed to watch it without subtitles, whereas 17 indicated that they used captions or subtitles ($n=15$ English captions, $n=2$ L1 subtitles). The students belonged to two intact classes and were asked to watch four scenes from the Netflix series *Emily in Paris*; they were randomly assigned to one group watching the clips with captions

(Captioned group, CapG; $n=17$) and the other group without captions (Non-Captioned group, NCapG; $n=26$).

3.2   Instruments

3.2.1   *Selected scenes from the series Emily in Paris*

Four scenes from the Netflix series *Emily in Paris* were selected. This series involves Emily, an American woman from the Midwest, who is hired by a marketing firm in Paris to provide them with an American perspective on business. The reason to choose this series was that the main character, Emily, was involved in a variety of social and cultural interactions. The selected scenes showed four requesting situations that varied according to the sociopragmatic factors of power/social status, social distance, and degree of imposition (Brown & Levinson, 1987) (see Table 1). Thus, two levels of social status were considered (i.e. low and equal), two levels of power/social distance (i.e. stranger and acquaintance), as well as two levels of degree of imposition (i.e. low and high). Each scene was preceded by a brief contextualization so that participants would know who the characters were, what their relationship was, and rank of imposition implied in the situation (see Appendix A).

Table 1. Contextualization of the four selected scenes from the series Emily in Paris

Scene	Contextual setting	Participants' roles Relationship between the speakers	Power	Social distance	Degree of imposition
1	Interview on the street	Emily asks an actress to answer some questions	Low	Stranger	Low
2	Apartment	Emily asks her neighbor to talk to the plumber	Equal	Acquaintance	Low
3	Phone/ kitchen restaurant	Emily asks her neighbor (who is the chef of a restaurant) to book a table	Equal	Acquaintance	High
4	Phone/ donation for an auction	Emily asks an important client for permission to visit him to discuss an important issue	Low	Stranger	High

3.2.2   *Multiple-choice discourse completion test (MCDCT)*

We opted for a MCDCT because this format allows us to collect large amounts of data in a short period of time to assess participants' pragmatic awareness (Bardovi-Harlig, 2013). The test was submitted to revision by the researchers themselves, who are bilingual speakers of the participants' languages and near NSs of English – one of them also has a high level of proficiency in French. The agreement reached was 100%.

It consisted of 12 questions: three questions for each of the four scenes that were selected in the TV series and that students were asked to watch. Thus, there were two questions that illustrated the same situation that appeared in the selected clip (i.e. including the same type of request form) plus a distractor (i.e. including the same type of lexical form or expression) that also appeared in the same scene. The questions were designed based on the sociopragmatic factors from Brown and Levinson's (1987) politeness theory, namely power, social distance, and degree of imposition (P/D/I) (see Appendix B). Example (1) below shows the first question from the test which illustrates the same type of situation in scene 1 from the TV series (i.e., someone who wants to ask a question to a person they do not know). Participants had to choose the response (i.e., that includes the request) that they considered more suitable for the situation. The MCDCT was used as a pretest (to control for the variability of the participants' pragmatic competence prior to the viewing), and as a posttest to check the effects of the audiovisual material (with/without captions) on their pragmatic knowledge. The items of both the pre- and posttest were presented in the same order because they followed the same presentation as the situations from the series; however, in the posttest the order of the three options in each item was changed.

Example 1.
If you wanted to interview somebody on the street for a study that you must carry out for class, which of the options below would you choose?
a.   Can I ask you a question?
b.   Do you mind if I ask you a question?
c.   Is it ok if I ask you a question?

3.2.3   *RealEye*

To analyze the students' viewing of the selected clips, the RealEye eye-tracker was used. RealEye is an online webcam eye-tracker that allows researchers to collect large data samples through a web-browser. To examine the participants' performance in the eye-tracker, a selection of Areas of Interest (AoI) was created. For the CapG group, the AoIswere the eyes and mouth of the character speaking, since they are considered to provide understanding of pragmatic interactions (Scotto, 2022), as well as the captions. In the case of the NCapG, since they were not exposed to captions, the AoIs selected were only eyes and mouth. The AOIs were dynamic and once the mouth, the eye or the caption disappeared from the screen, the AOI disappeared.

3.2.4 *Retrospective interviews*

To gain an in-depth understanding of learners' perceptions when watching the scenes, semi-structured interviews were conducted with 4 students selected at random from each of the two groups (i.e., CapG and NCapG). Each interview lasted between 40–50 minutes and was carried out in the participants' L1 (i.e. Spanish or/and Catalan) to enable them to share their thoughts more freely and prevent any misunderstanding. Subsequently, all the interviews were transcribed and translated into English. The interviews were conducted by the third author, as she was the lecturer of both groups of learners. The interviews were organized around four parts, namely (1) watching the selected clip, (2) focusing on the contextual aspects from the scene from the clip (i.e., sociopragmatic issues), (3) focusing on the linguistic aspects related to the requests appearing in the scene (i.e., pragmalinguistic issues), and (4) reviewing and comparing the responses chosen in the questions related to that scene from the pre and posttest viewing test. This was repeated for each of the four scenes.

First, the interviews started with the researcher showing again the scene to the learner being interviewed (either with captions or without captions). Second, the researcher asked the learner questions related to the context of the scene (i.e. what he/she pays attention to, what is happening, the nature of the relationship between the characters, the main goal of the conversation, among other issues). The learners of the CapG were also asked if they read and paid attention to the captions. Third, the researcher asked the learner questions about the features of the language used in the scene (i.e., how Emily asks for what she needs or whether there are any expressions or explanations before or after Emily's request). Fourth, the researcher went through the learner's responses in the pre-viewing test questions, asking him/her to reflect about his/her responses (i.e., what happens in this situation, which expressions are used in the three options proposed as a response, what he/she pays attention to in order to select one particular option, or whether Emily has used the same expression in the scene that has just been watched and why). Then, the learner was asked to compare his/her responses with the ones chosen in the posttest and reflect about whether he/she had used the same option. The purpose of the interviews was thus to allow learners to further elaborate and provide explanations for their perceptions when watching the scenes as well as their responses in the pre/post- viewing tests.

3.3   Data collection procedure

The study followed a pre/posttest design to ascertain the effects of viewing audio-visual material with or without captions. Two weeks prior to the testing time the tools (both the MCDCT and the online webcam Eye-tracking program) were piloted with students in the same university degree as the participants ($n=5$) as well as with English NSs ($n=5$). After receiving their feedback, they were modified accordingly. Then, data for this study were collected in two sessions. Each session lasted about 50 minutes. In the first session, learners were assigned a code (to be used in the different parts of the study) to preserve participants' identity, completed the Quick Placement Test, the short survey to get background information and they were explained about the study.

In the second session, learners were given the pre-viewing test (i.e., the MCDCT) and they were allowed 30 minutes to read the situations and to answer them. After that, when all students handed in their tests, the researcher introduced the plot and main characters of the Netflix series *Emily in Paris*, so that they were familiarized with the series and ready for the scenes they were going to watch. They were also introduced to the RealEye eye-tracker program, how it worked and what they had to do. The four clips showing the four different scenes from the series were uploaded on the RealEye experimental platform to record the participants' eye movements while watching the video excerpts. The students used their own laptops and earphones individually, and they accessed RealEye through a link that was shared with them through the virtual course campus. Two different links were created, one for the CapG and one for the NCapG. Before each clip was to be viewed, the eye-tracking system was calibrated using 40 calibration dots. It was used in class, allowing 10 minutes for each participant. Before watching each of the four selected scenes, a screen with the contextualization of the scene was presented to them.

Once everything was clear, they watched the four video excerpts (each group under one condition, either with captions or without captions) and their eye movements were recorded. Immediately after watching the four scenes, learners completed the posttest, which included the same situations employed in the pretest (for comparison purposes) and they were arranged in the same order, since they followed the order of the scenes being watched. Again, students were given 30 minutes to answer the test. Qualitative interviews to students selected at random ($n=4$ for each group; 3 female and 1 male) were conducted two weeks after this session.

3.4   Data analysis

Regarding the analysis of the participants' responses in the MCDCT, the correct and incorrect responses were coded: they were given a 0 for incorrect responses and 1 for correct responses. A Linear Mixed Effects Model was then applied to check differences between pre and posttest, and the effects of the caption condition on the MCDCT. In relation to the participants' performance in the eye-tracker software, visit counts on the AoI (the number of visits a participant makes to an AoI) were examined and a *t*-test to check differences between the CapG and the NCapG group was applied.

To check what the groups were focusing on in their viewing, a repeated measures ANOVA was run to examine possible differences between the AoIs selected for this group. The statistical analysis of the data was conducted using Version 25.0 of the Statistical Package for the Social Science (SPSS). The data was qualitatively complemented with semi-structured interviews with four participants from each group, as explained above, to gain an in-depth understanding of their perceptions when watching the scenes and their responses in the MCDCTs. The data from the interviews was analyzed by the three researchers to ensure reliability.

4.   Results

4.1   RQ1: What are the effects of captioned-video viewing on the learning of requests, as compared to non-captioned video viewing?

The aim of this RQ was to examine whether the caption condition influenced the participants' responses in the MCDCT. Although on average, the learners in the NCapG had more correct items in the pretest ($M=.739$, $SE=.050$, 95% $CI=.630–.825$) than those from the CapG ($M=.670$, $SE=.068$, 95% $CI=.527–.787$), no statistically significant differences were found between the CapG and the NCapG ($p=.446$). In the posttest, more correct responses were only observable in the Caption group (*CapG: M=.894*, *SE=.036*, 95% *CI=.801–.946* vs. *NoCapG: M=.706*, *SE=.053*, 95%*CI=.592–.799*), and this was statistically significant ($p=.000$). A linear mixed model analysis was carried out where Group (Cap/NCap), Test (MCDCT) and their interactions were included as fixed factors, and Subject was used as random intercept (being "Test" testing time [pre and post] and test score the dependent variable). The analysis revealed that there was no significant main effect of Group ($F(1.10)=2.919$, $p<.088$, with a small effect size eta square $=.004$); however, there was a significant main effect of Test ($F(1.10)=6.986$, $p<.008$, with a small effect size eta square $=.011$), and a significant interaction of Group and Test ($F=(1.00)=12.537$, $p<.000$, with a small effect size, eta square .019) (see Table 2 for descriptive statistics).

Table 2. Descriptive statistics

Group	Test	M	SD	N
Captions	Pretest	.66	.476	112
	Posttest	.88	.322	112
	Total	**.77**	**.420**	**224**
No captions	Pretest	.73	.447	216
	Posttest	.69	.462	216
	Total	**.71**	**.454**	**432**
Total	Pretest	.70	.457	328
	Posttest	.76	.428	328
	Total	.73	.443	656

Pairwise comparisons did not show a main effect of the pretest ($F=1.128$, $p<.289$), but it did on the posttest ($F=12.634$, $p<.000$). As for Group, the main effect of the CapG reached statistical significance ($F=13.601$, $p<.000$), but it did not in the case of the NCapG ($F=.581$, $p<.446$). Therefore, as can be seen in Figure 1 below, those from the CapG did better in the MCDCT in the posttest, whereas those from the NCapG performed worse in the posttest than in the pretest, but this drop in scores was not statistically significant.

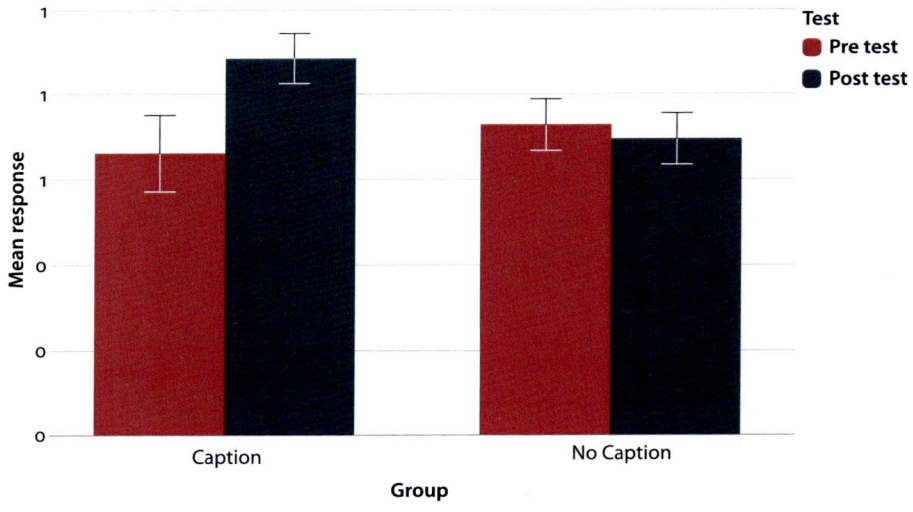

Figure 1. Caption vs. No Caption Group Pre/Post test gains comparison

4.2   RQ2: Is there a difference in visual behavior when watching captioned and uncaptioned videos?

To answer the second RQ, we calculated the number of visits that learners from the two conditions made to the different AoIs created in the four different clips. For comparison purposes, captions are not included as an AoI, since one group watched the scenes with captions and the other one did not; thus, captions were not an AoI comparable in the two groups. Therefore, we first present the results per each group in terms of the viewing of the eyes and mouth of the character talking. Table 3 provides the visit counts by group.

Table 3. Total number of visits to the AoI (Eyes and Mouth) by group

	CapG (*n*=17)				NCapG (*n*=25)			
			95%CI				95%CI	
Clip 1	*M*	*SD*	Lower	Upper	*M*	*SD*	Lower	Upper
Eyes	.12	.332	.00	.29	.44	1.805	.00	1.32
Mouth	.12	.332	.00	.31	.04	.200	.00	.14
Clip 2								
Eyes	1.67	1.879	.82	2.53	1.32	2.462	.50	2.33
Mouth	.83	1.098	.35	1.40	2.20	2.041	1.42	3.00
Clip 3								
Eyes	.12	.332	.00	.29	.84	1.784	.20	1.54
Mouth	.71	1.213	.19	1.38	1.64	2.644	.70	2.78
Clip 4								
Eyes	.47	1.281	.00	1.17	.32	.557	.12	.54
Mouth	.18	.728	.00	.56	.64	.860	.31	1.00

Then, an independent samples *t*-test was carried out to compare the total number of visits to the AoIs (Eyes and Mouth). The results revealed that statistically significant differences could only be found in the second clip ($t(-2.579)=41$, $p=.014$), in which those from the NCapG ($M=2.20$, $SD=2.041$) seemed to watch more the Mouth than those from the CapG ($M=.83$, $SD=1.098$). For the rest of clips, no statistically significant differences were found (see Table 4 for a summary of results).

Table 4. Results from the independent samples t-test on the Eyes and Mouth AoIs

Clip 1	t	df	p
Eyes	−.725	40	.472
Mouth	.946	40	.397
Clip 2			
Eyes	.501	40	.619
Mouth	−2.579	40	*.014
Clip 3			
Eyes	−1.677	40	.101
Mouth	−1.359	40	.182
Clip 4			
Eyes	.522	40	.604
Mouth	−1.821	40	.076

To check whether there were differences between the AoIs selected for the CapG (Eyes, Mouth and Captions) in the first clip, we ran a One-way within subjects ANOVA. Due to the data violating the assumption of sphericity (Mauchly's $p < .05$), a Huynh-Feldt correction was applied. For clip one, the ANOVA revealed there was a significant effect of AoI ($F(1.20) = 4.423$, $p = .043$, multivariate eta squared = .217). Pairwise comparisons revealed that there were significant differences between Captions and Eyes and Mouth ($p = .046$), but not for Eyes and Mouth. As can be seen in the descriptive statistics below, learners watched captions the most (Table 5).

Table 5. Descriptive statistics for Clip 1

	M	SD	N
Eyes	.12	.332	17
Mouth	.12	.332	17
Captions	.65	.862	17

For the second clip, the assumption of sphericity was not violated. The results showed there was a significant effect of AoI ($F(2.34) = 3.988$, $p = .028$, multivariate eta squared = .190). Pairwise comparisons revealed that there were significant differences between Captions and Eyes and Mouth ($p = .028$), but not for Eyes and

Mouth. As can be seen in the descriptive statistics below, in contrast to clip 1, learners watched captions the least (Table 6).

Table 6. Descriptive statistics for Clip 2

	M	SD	N
Eyes	1.67	1.879	18
Mouth	.83	1.098	18
Captions	.61	.608	18

As for the third clip, the assumption of sphericity was not violated either. The results reported no statistically significant effect of AoI ($F(1.16) = 2.346$, $p = .128$, multivariate eta squared = .190). However, pairwise comparisons revealed significant differences between Captions and Eyes ($p = .028$), and for Eyes and Mouth ($p = .037$), but not between Mouth and Captions ($p = 1.000$). As the descriptive statistics in Table 7 show, learners watched Eyes the least as compared to the other two AoIs.

Table 7. Descriptive statistics for Clip 3

	M	SD	N
Eyes	.12	.332	17
Mouth	.71	1.213	17
Captions	.71	.920	17

Finally, the assumption of sphericity was not violated either for clip 4. No statistically significant effect of AoI was shown ($F(1.16) = 2.195$, $p = .121$, multivariate eta squared = .190). However, pairwise comparisons reported statistically significant differences between Captions and Mouth ($p = .038$), and between Eyes and Mouth ($p = .037$), but not between Mouth and Captions ($p = 1.000$). As can be seen in the descriptive statistics Table 8 below, learners allocated their attention to captions the most, followed by the Eyes and Mouth.

Table 8. Descriptive statistics for Clip 4

	M	SD	N
Eyes	.47	1.281	17
Mouth	.18	.728	17
Captions	1.12	1.654	17

4.3   RQ3: What are learners' perceptions of their pragmatic learning in relation to the presence of captions (or not) in the videos?

4.3.1   *Captions group*

When asked about the MCDC, the learners were able to reflect on their own responses. They were shown their answers, and they were also asked to watch the clips again. This helped them explain their choices in the pretest and after watching the videos again, they either discussed their responses or realized that they should have chosen a more appropriate response in the posttest. For instance, Excerpt (1) shows a student's reflection (Participant 1 CapG) on an incorrect answer in the pretest but correct in the posttest:

Excerpt 1.
"In the pretest I used *would you mind* because it sounded correct to me, but after watching the scene, I understood the situation and I saw that I had to use *can you*".

However, in Excerpt (2) below, we have an example of a participant (Participant 2 CapG) who had incorrectly answered both the pre- and the post- test, but after watching the clips again and discussing with the interviewer, she changed her mind:

Excerpt 2.
"I just saw the use of *please*, and immediately thought that it was the correct one, but now I think I should have used *I was just wondering if*".

Going through the MCDCTs and the videos again did not only engage the participants in discussing their responses, but also triggered discussion about what their own thoughts were about the situations and pragmatic exchanges presented in the clips. In addition, they were also able to explain what they would do in those particular situations, showing how agency is an important aspect to consider when pragmatics comes into play when learning an L2. For instance, in Excerpts (3) (Participant 4 CapG) and 4 (Participant 3 CapG), the participants explain their choices and add some personal information about their personality that seemed to influence what they chose.

Excerpt 3.
"In the first clip, it was clearly *do you mind* because Emily doesn't know the person. And I am also very polite, in fact, I think that sometimes I am too polite".

Excerpt 4.
"Yeah, in clip 4 Emily uses *I was wondering if*, which is similar to question 12 in the test, but I wouldn't use this expression to go to a shop, I would use *please* for that situation".

When asked about the captions, all the participants claimed that having captions helped them while watching TV series to understand what was happening as well as made them feel more confident (see students' comments in Excerpts (5) [Participant 2 CapG] and 6 [Participant 4 CapG]).

Excerpt 5.
"I read the subtitles because they are there, so I look at them, and they also help understand".

Excerpt 6.
"I feel more confident with the subtitles because they help me understand".

4.3.2 *No captions group*

The comments that learners from the NCapG condition made were very similar to those from the CapG. The interview helped them reflect on their own responses in the tests as well as to reflect on agency when deciding what to say in different contexts. For instance, in Excerpt (7) (Participant 1 NCapG), it can be seen how the participant justifies his response.

Excerpt 7.
"I chose the longest request, because when you want to get something, you can't just ask for it, you need to explain and justify".

As in the CapG, there were also participants who had incorrectly answered both the pre- and the posttest, but it was while doing the interview that they changed their mind (see Excerpt (8) [Participant 2 NCapG]):

Excerpt 8.
"I chose the ones with *can I ask you* but now I see that those situations are more formal, so I would now go for *would you mind if*".

One participant (Excerpt (9) [Participant 4 NCapG]) also made a very interesting comment which had to do with the tone and intonation that one uses when requesting. This suggests that they also take into account aspects that go beyond linguistic and contextual elements, and that are related to paralanguage elements:

Excerpt 9.
"Well I don't know in the test, in situation 12, maybe I would choose *I was wondering* or *please*, it would depend on the tone".

When talking about the use of captions, their comments were similar to the ones made by the learners from the CapG. They all agreed that when they watched on their own they were useful and helped them understand, but also considered them a way of learning the L2 (see Excerpts (10) [Participant 3NCapG] and 11 [Participant 4 NCapG]):

Excerpt 10.
"We didn't have subtitles here, but at home I use them because it helps me understand".

Excerpt 11.
"I use subtitles at home not because I don't understand but to learn vocabulary, because there is always vocabulary that I don't know".

5. Discussion

The results displayed in section 4 show that when examining the effects of captions on EFL requests, as measured through the MCDCT (RQ1), differences between the pre and posttest were found, since learners who were exposed to input with captions had better results in the posttest than those who were not exposed to them. Regarding the analysis of the AoIs more frequently visited by the learners from the two conditions (RQ2), findings revealed that the CapG watched captions the most, compared to the other AoI included in the analysis (i.e., eyes and mouth), since they were exposed to them as opposed to the other group; however, both groups tended to look at the mouths and eyes of the characters in similar amounts. Finally, when examining the learners' perceptions towards pragmatics and captions (RQ3) as analyzed through EFL requests, the learners interviewed from the two groups agreed on most of the aspects discussed in the interviews, such as, for instance, the fact that watching the videos again during the interviews made them reflect about their own responses, and that, for the CapG, watching the videos with captions was useful and helped them understand the situation better.

The present study seems to be in line with previous research investigating the effects of audio-visual material to enhance L2 learning, not only in pragmatics but in other areas of SLA (as in Finger-Bou & Muñoz, 2023; Gesa & Miralpeix, 2022; Pattemore & Muñoz, 2020, among others). More specifically, it supports previous studies that have reported that captions tend to lead to higher gains in language learning (see Muñoz, 2017). In fact, the current study showed that those learners who viewed the four clips with captions performed better than those who did not, with differences that reached significance between the two groups. As in Barón and Celaya (2022), it could be argued that the presence of captions helps learners identify the different pragmalinguistic devices that are used to perform specific speech acts. However, those who do not have such support may miss such information, especially when no prior instruction has been provided before being exposed to input. However, our findings do not match those in Khazdouzian et al. (2021), since in their case, no changes were found between groups from pre to posttest. It should be considered, though, that in their study learners had to watch a whole season of a TV series on their own, and no instruction was given on pragmatics. In the case of Barón and Celaya (2022) and the current study, participants were exposed to short clips that were especially selected for pragmatic exchanges to be easily noticeable, so they might have been easier to notice. This may suggest that if we want to deal with pragmatic aspects with our students through audio-visual material, some guidance and shorter clips (as opposed to whole TV series or full episodes) may foster pragmatic awareness and learning. Regarding the use of captions, the learners interviewed (regardless of the condition) agreed that captions helped them not only understand the plot but also learn new aspects of language (as in Finger-Bou & Muñoz, 2023). Therefore, if captions lead to gains in pragmalinguistic competence and learners find them useful and make them feel more confident, it would seem advisable to use them when learning L2 pragmatics.

Regarding the results obtained from the eye-tracker, they may suggest that it did not provide sufficient information about what visual aspects help students focus on pragmatic aspects. In terms of attention to on-screen text, the eye-tracker confirmed that those who had captions relied on them when watching the video excerpts and this had a positive effect on the posttest, which meant that they facilitated noticing the pragmalinguistic devices used in the TV series to request in situations with different P/D/I (as in Barón & Celaya, 2022, although no eye-tracker was used in their study). Thanks to the eye-tracker, we could also see that all groups, regardless of the caption condition, watched the mouth and the eyes of the characters. This was also supported by the learners' comments in the interviews, since some of them pointed out that mouths and eyes, as well as gestures, might provide non-verbal information that may help them understand pragmatic exchanges.

In relation to other elements that may be affecting the learners' pragmatic choices, apart from the captions, eyes or mouth, the interviews showed that they also tend to rely on aspects that cannot be viewed, such as tone, intonation, their own personal experiences, their personalities, their awareness of what language is expected in a formal or informal situation, among other factors. In this sense, the interviews provided very valuable information to understand what learners believe about pragmatics. For instance, in clips 1 and 2, learners focused less on the AoI selected, and in the interviews, they claimed that other elements in the video excerpts caught their attention: the views of Paris, the clothes the characters wore or the relationship between the main characters. In addition, a very important aspect which emerged in the interviews was agency, also discussed in Usó-Juan and Martínez-Flor (2022). As the learners pointed out, even if the scenes presented in the video excerpts showed a specific request strategy, this did not mean that they would use such strategy in real-life, since they might not feel comfortable with such a pragmatic move or felt identified with it. Last, but not least, the interview itself showed that helping them and guiding them through the video analysis, as well as going back to their responses helped them reflect on pragmatic aspects. This might suggest that guidance (or instruction) would help learners notice and understand L2 pragmatics faster and more efficiently (as also found in Abrams, 2014; Alcón & Pitarch, 2010; Usó-Juan & Martínez-Flor, 2021).

6. Conclusion

The aim of this study was to contribute to the research on the effects of multimodal input in L2 pragmatic learning with a focus on requests. First, the findings of this study reveal that captions have positive effects on pragmatic awareness of L2 requests, since the learners participating in the current study who belonged to the CapG obtained significantly better results in the posttest MCDCT than those who were not exposed to captions. Second, as the eye-tracker showed, if captions are present, learners pay attention to them. Other elements in the video excerpts presented were also visited by all learners, such as the eyes and mouth of the characters. Finally, the interviews conducted with a sample of students from the two conditions agreed that captions are beneficial for them, not only to understand but also to learn. Additionally, the interviews helped identify other aspects that learners focus on when watching audio-visual material with pragmatically salient scenes.

The present study is not without limitations. The study focused only on requests. Future studies of this type should also include a wider variety of speech acts, to explore whether different speech acts can also be learnt through multimodal input. Moreover, the current study included a limited number of scenarios (only four clips). Future studies should analyze more from different TV series and films, including a variety of genres as well. Also, this study used RealEye eye-tracker which, among other limitations, only allowed recording 10 minutes per participant. Finally, other AoIs, such as gestures, should be included in future studies to further understand what learners focus on when pragmatics is at the core of the scenes presented.

All in all, this study has shed some light on how multimodal input may enhance the learning of L2 pragmatics. This study supports previous research regarding the positive effects of captions on pragmatic learning, both from a pragmalinguistic and a sociopragmatic perspective. The findings also suggest that adding audio-visual material plus metapragmatic explanations as part of the class curriculum to deal with pragmatics in class may help learners contextualize; raise pragmatic awareness on situations with different power, distance, and imposition; and help them notice new pragmalinguistic strategies as well as develop socio-pragmatic competence.

Acknowledgements

The first two authors would like to acknowledge the support of grants PID2019-110594GB-100 from the Spanish Ministry of Science and Innovation (MCIN/AEI/10.13039/501100011033) and 2021SGR00303 from the Commissioner for Universities and Research, Government of Catalonia. The third author would like to acknowledge the support of the research project PID2020-117959GB-I00 from the Spanish Ministry of Science and Innovation (MCIN/AEI/10.13039/501100011033) and additional funding by Projectes d'Innovació Educativa de la Unitat de Suport Educatiu 51020/24 (Universitat Jaume I). The authors are grateful to the participants in the study for their commitment and enthusiasm at all times and to the reviewers for their constructive feedback.

Ethical considerations

The research was conducted in accordance with the ethical guidelines set forth by the Ethics Committee of Universitat Jaume I, where the study was conducted. Approval for the study was obtained on 04.04.2022 (CD/24/2022). All students were required to read and sign a consent form indicating their voluntary participation in the study prior to its inception.

References

Abrams, Z. I. (2014). Using film to provide a context for teaching L2 pragmatics. *System, 46*, 55–64.

Alcón, E., & Pitarch, J. G. (2010). The effect of instruction on learners' pragmatic awareness: A focus on refusals. *International Journal of English Studies, 10*(1), 65–80.

Bardovi-Harlig, K. (2013). Developing L2 pragmatics. *Language Learning, 63*(1), 68–86.

Barón, J., & Celaya, M. L. (2022). "May I do something for you?" The effects of audio-visual material (captioned and non-captioned) on EFL pragmatic learning. Special Issue: Teaching second language pragmatics in the current era of globalization. *Language Teaching Research, 26*(2), 238–255.

Brown, P., & Levinson, S. C. (1987). *Politeness: Some universals in language use.* Cambridge University Press.

Bruti, S. (2016). Audiovisual texts and subtitling in the teaching of pragmatics. *Trans-kom*, 9(2), 186–207.

Celaya, M. L., Amengual, M., Martínez-Flor, A., & Barón, J. (2023). Using audio-visual material in *Second Language Acquisition* courses: An analysis for English Philology/English Studies. In L. J. Conejero Magro, C. Blanco García, L. Méndez Márquez, & J. Ruiz Morgan (Eds.), *Bridging cultures. English and American studies in Spain* (121–127). Universidad de Extremadura.

Derakhshan, A., & Eslami, Z. R. (2020). The effect of metapragmatic awareness, interactive translation, and discussion through video-enhanced input on EFL learners' comprehension of implicature. *Applied Research on English Language*, 9(1), 637–664.

Finger-Bou, R., & Muñoz, C. (2023). The effects of regular and enhanced captions on incidental vocabulary acquisition. ELIA. *Estudios de Lingüística Inglesa Aplicada*,23, 15–50.

Gesa, F., & Miralpeix, I. (2023). Extensive viewing as additional input for foreign language vocabulary learning: A longitudinal study in secondary school. *Language Teaching Research*.

Godfroid, A. (2020). *Eye-tracking in second language acquisition and bilingualism. A research synthesis and methodological guide*. Routledge.

Khazdouzian, Y., Celaya, M.L., & Barón, J. (2021). When watching is not enough: The effects of captions on L2 pragmatics acquisition and awareness. *RAEL, Revista Electrónica de Lingüística Aplicada*, 19(2), 90–107.

Muñoz, C. (2017). The role of age and proficiency in subtitle reading. An eye-tracking study. *System, 67*, 77–86.

Pattemore, A., & Muñoz, C. (2022). Captions and learnability factors in learning grammar from audio-visual input. *JALT CALL*, 18(1), 83–109.

Peters, E., & Muñoz, C. (2020). Introduction to special issue of *Language learning from multimodal input. Studies in Second Language Acquisition*, 42(3), 489–497.

Pujadas, G., & Muñoz, C. (2020). Examining adolescent EFL learners' TV viewing comprehension through captions and subtitles. *Studies in Second Language Acquisition*, 42(3), 551–575.

Qi, X., & Lai, C. (2017). The effects of deductive instruction and inductive instruction on learners' development of pragmatic competence in the teaching of Chinese as a second language. *System, 70*, 26–37.

Quick Placement Test. (2001). *Paper and pen test*. Oxford University Press.

Scotto, S. C. (2022). A pragmatics-first approach to faces. *Topoi, 41*(4), 641–657.

Usó-Juan, E., & Martínez-Flor, A. (2021). Fostering learners' (meta)pragmatic awareness through film analysis. *Language Value*, 14(1), 85–111.

Usó-Juan, E., & Martínez-Flor, A. (2022). Using audiovisual material to teach refusals from a discursive perspective: A research-based proposal. *Complutense Journal of English Studies, 30*, 53–66.

Appendix A.   Selected scenes from *Emily in Paris*

Scene 1 (Season 1. Episode 3) (7:20–8:26)

There is an important shoot about perfume with an actress. She is wearing "the perfume" – walking across the bridge Pont Alexandre III. First, Emily is walking across the bridge with Antoine and Sylvie and talking about the shoot. Then, she stops and approaches the actress to ask her some questions.

Antoine: Has Sylvie told you about the shoot?

Antoine: Has Sylvie told you about the shoot?

Emily: No, she hasn't

Antoine: So, we follow this elegant young woman walking to work, and as she crosses the bridge, she becomes every man's fantasy and desire. Our tagline is "Dream of Beauty"

Emily: Well, I feel like I'm dreaming right now. This view is magical.

Antoine: It's so nice to see Paris through fresh eyes.

Sylvie: [Umm] Let's just make sure we don't see any tourists in cargo pants.

Emily: [she stops and approaches the actress]
Um, I'm just gonna grab some content for social.
Uh, bonjour. Je suis Emily from Savoir.

Actress: I don't speak French.

Emily: Me either.
Um, okay, good.
Do you mind if I ask you a couple of questions? Okay
Where are you from?

Actress: Serbia

Emily: And what is your dream of beauty?

Actress: Private jet

Emily: Okay. Wh-

Man comes: Excuse me. We are ready to shoot. Okay?

Actress: Okay.
[no pictures]

Emily: Oh, merci … beaucoup

Scene 2 (Season 1. Episode 3) (10:58–11:43)

Emily is at her apartment with the plumber. Her shower doesn't work. The plumber is talking in French. Emily does not understand anything. She goes to Gabriel's apartment to ask him for help.

Emily: Hi. Can you come talk to my plumber? It's an emergency.

Gabriel: Good morning, Gabriel. How are you today?

Emily: Good morning, Gabriel. How are you today?

Gabriel: Thank you for asking. I was having a very nice dream, and this American girl banged on my door and woke me up. Or maybe I'm still dreaming?

Emily: You're not dreaming. You're wide awake. **Don't let him leave** until he fixes my shower.

Scene 3 (Season 1. Episode 4) (17:55–20:00)

Emily is with her boss, her workmates, a well-known client, and a potential new client, Mr. Zimmer. They are going to have an important business dinner together to discuss the possibility of having the perfume from their firm in Mr. Zimmer hotels. Emily has made a reservation in a three-star Michelin restaurant, but because of a misunderstanding with the date, there is no table for them, so she phones Gabriel and asks him for help. Gabriel is in the kitchen, working in his restaurant.

Gabriel: [in French] Halo

Emily: [in English] Hi. Gabriel. It's Emily.

Gabriel: Who?

Emily: Emily! Emily Cooper, your neighbor

Gabriel: Oh, Emily, hi! It's hard to hear you.

Emily: Yeah, I've got a massive favor, okay? I have a very important client

Gabriel: Uh. The lingerie ...

Emily: Yeah, yeah and some other clients. **Can you take six?**

Gabriel: Uh, tonight?

Emily: Yes, perfect ...

Gabriel: No, no, no

Emily: I really need your help, Gabriel, okay? My job depends on it.

Gabriel: We're planning to close in 3 min.

Emily: Okay, I'll see you in 15. Merci

Scene 4 (Season 1. Episode 9) (1:29–3:43)

Emily has a conversation with Judith Robertson, representative of the association The American Friends of the Louvre (AFL), in an American restaurant. Mrs. Robertson wants Emily to talk to Pierre Cadault about the possibility of donating a dress to be auctioned for the AFL. After their conversation, Emily is walking across the street and phones Mathieu Cadault.

(Emily wants to talk to Pierre)

Mathieu: Emily from Savoir, how are you?

Emily: I am good, thanks, Mathieu. **I was wondering if I could come by** the atelier to discuss something with you and Pierre.

Mathieu: He's working nonstop with Fashion Week so close. But I can meet you for a drink tonight, if you'd like.

Emily: Oh, I'm going to a gallery opening with some friends.

Mathieu: Text me the address, and I'll see you there.

Appendix B.   Sample questions of the multiple-choice discourse completion test (distractors not included)

1. If you wanted to interview somebody on the street for a study that you have to carry out for class, which of the options below would you choose?
    a. Can I ask you a question?
    b. Do you mind if I ask you a question?
    c. Is it ok if I ask you a question?

4. Your partner has an urgent appointment to take the rabbit you share to the vet. Your partner is in a traffic jam, and he/she won't be in time to go to the vet. You are at home and have nothing to do now, but you didn't know about the appointment. Which of the options below would you expect your partner to say?
    a. Listen, I am in a traffic jam; get the rabbit and go to the vet.
    b. Hi, I am in a traffic jam right now and I have an urgent appointment at the vet for our rabbit. Would you mind taking him to the vet? I will meet you there.
    c. Hi, listen, I am in a traffic jam right now, and I have an urgent appointment at the vet for our rabbit. Can you take him, please? I will meet you at the vet.

7. One of your classmates has bought several tickets for a concert of your parents' favorite singer. You wanted to invite them to the concert, but the tickets are sold out. When your classmate tells you about the tickets, you have an idea. What would you tell your classmate?
    a. Wow! How lucky! I need a huge favor! My parents love this singer and I have been trying to buy tickets but haven't been able to find any. They were sold out from day one! Can you sell me two tickets? It would really mean a lot to me if I could take them to the concert.
    b. Wow! How lucky! Why don't you sell me two tickets? I wanted to invite my parents to the concert.
    c. Wow! How lucky! I need two tickets.

10. Your teacher has set an exam from one day to the other and you have a doctor's appointment that you cannot change. Which of the options below would you choose?
    a. Dr Marín, you have set an exam for tomorrow, and I am afraid I have a doctor's appointment. I was wondering if I could do it on another day since the appointment cannot be changed.
    b. Dr Marín, please postpone the exam. I have a doctor's appointment.
    c. Dr Marín, can you change the date of the exam? I have a doctor's appointment.

Contrastive input enhancement in captioned video for L2 pronunciation learning

Joan C. Mora & Jonás Fouz-González

Universitat de Barcelona | Universidad de Murcia

This study investigated the potential of input enhancement in captioned video to facilitate learners' perceptual sensitivity to a difficult L2 vowel contrast (/æ/-/ʌ/). Participants were randomly assigned to two control and four experimental viewing conditions to explore the effects of audiovisual input (a 30-minute TV episode) on perceptual learning. Textual enhancement on captions highlighted target sounds contrastively (two colors) or non-contrastively (one color) in words transcribed orthographically or in IPA phonetic symbols. Learners' /æ/-/ʌ/ perception gains were assessed through lexical and phonetic identification and discrimination tasks. Eye-gaze measures were used to determine the effectiveness of enhancement in drawing learners' attention to the target contrast across viewing conditions. Perceptual learning was observed, although not always consistently across tasks and conditions.

1. Introduction

Approaches to second language (L2) pronunciation teaching and learning since Munro and Derwing's (1995) seminal article have emphasized the importance of intelligibility as opposed to nativelikeness as the goal of pronunciation instruction (Derwing & Munro, 2015; Levis, 2005, 2020). In line with this shift in objectives, the outcome of recent pronunciation instruction research advocates the integration of pronunciation-focused activities in communicative approaches to language teaching, either through a combination of explicit instruction and pronunciation-based form-focused instruction (Darcy & Rocca, 2022) or through the manipulation of task design variables in task-based pronunciation instruction (Mora & Mora-Plaza, 2023).

However, given the limited time of the typical foreign language (FL) learning classroom (3–4 weekly hours), the development of oral skills – including

https://doi.org/10.1075/lllt.61.07mor

pronunciation – becomes a pedagogical challenge (Muñoz, 2014). In such contexts, the implementation of pedagogical efforts to embed pronunciation instruction into communicative language teaching is important and useful for pronunciation learning. Nevertheless, several pronunciation training techniques may also contribute to providing the extra in and out-of-class focused practice on L2 speech learners need for pronunciation development. Such techniques include, among others, high-variability phonetic training (HVPT) (Thomson, 2018), shadowing (Hamada, 2019), imitation of a foreign (target language) accent in the L1 (Henderson & Rojczyk, 2023), comprehensibility and accentedness peer- and self-assessment training (Strachan et al., 2019), and embodied pronunciation training (Chan, 2018). Except for HVPT, which accumulates decades of research on training conditions, there is still a dearth of research on the effectiveness of pronunciation training methods and techniques. In the current study, we focus on the potential of audiovisual exposure through captioned video as a pronunciation training technique (Wisniewska & Mora, 2020). We extend previous research in this area by testing the effectiveness of two novel textual input enhancement techniques (the use of contrastive enhancement and phonetic symbols) for the development of perceptual sensitivity to a difficult English vowel contrast (/æ/-/ʌ/).

1.1   Audiovisual input and language learning

Films and video materials such as TV series and documentaries constitute a substantial source of rich L2 input to which learners can have regular access outside the language classroom. Additionally, current technology allows media viewers to superimpose text on the screen in the form of intra-language subtitles (captions). This kind of audiovisual exposure provides large amounts of authentic linguistic input in communicative contexts with the speech processing aid of on-screen text and images. Despite the wide range of factors potentially affecting the effectiveness of exposure to audiovisual input via film and TV series (e.g., intra- or inter-language subtitles, learners' L2 proficiency and age, the genre of the viewing materials, individual differences in attention and working memory), solid empirical evidence has now accumulated indicating that audiovisual input can benefit language learning (see Muñoz, 2023, and the chapters in this volume). For example, audiovisual input in the form of subtitled and captioned video has shown its effectiveness in enhancing comprehension (Montero Perez et al., 2013; Pujadas & Muñoz, 2020), vocabulary acquisition (Gesa & Miralpeix, 2023; Rodgers & Webb, 2020), grammatical development (Lee & Révész, 2020; Pattemore & Muñoz, 2020) and speech segmentation skills (Charles & Trenkic, 2015; Mitterer & McQueen, 2009). Such benefits originate in the learning advantage that multimodal input processing provides compared to unimodal input processing. The presence of complementary information across multiple sensory modalities or "multimodal enrichment" (Mathias & von Kriegstein, 2023) appears to benefit learning in an ample variety of tasks.

1.2   Audiovisual input in L2 pronunciation learning

Audiovisual input can benefit L2 speech learning through the simultaneous presentation of cross modal (audiovisual) information related to the phonetic properties of speech sounds. For example, within embodied pronunciation training (Chan, 2018; Baills et al., 2022), combining the auditory presentation of Mandarin Chinese tones with hand gestures illustrating their pitch movement facilitates tone learning (Zhen et al., 2019). Similarly, visuospatial hand gestures describing the acoustic properties of segmental contrasts – such as the use of a fist-to-open-hand burst gesture mimicking the auditory and articulatory features of aspirated stops – have been shown to enhance phonetic learning, leading to more accurate production of aspirated stops (Li et al., 2021; Xi et al., 2020).

Audiovisual input in the form of subtitled video can also potentially benefit L2 pronunciation learning, as it allows learners to decode phono-lexical representations of L2 words with the aid of their written form. Seeing the orthographic representation of a word form in the on-screen text and simultaneously perceiving its auditory form facilitates word recognition (Bird & Williams, 2002), which enhances the comparison between auditory word forms and their phono-lexical representations. Moreover, some research suggests that pronunciation learning might take place implicitly simply by watching others speak the L2. For example, Weber and Geissler (2023) found German learners of English to improve their production of English /æ/ for first formant (F1) frequency after exposing them to one episode of an English-language television show. Similarly, Hutchinson and Dmitrieva (2022) asked American English speakers without previous exposure to French to watch a 45-minute episode of a documentary in French with and without English subtitles and found that both groups could shadow French /y/ words more accurately after the exposure.

A potential limitation of captioned video for L2 pronunciation learning is that it is highly cognitively demanding in terms of information processing, as visual (text + on-screen action) and auditory processing happen simultaneously. In such a complex input-processing situation, it is likely that meaning and comprehension – and therefore attention to lexis – are prioritized over phonological form, which would imply that incidental learning of L2 vocabulary is more likely than incidental pronunciation learning. Therefore, a methodological challenge of using L2 captioned video to enhance L2 pronunciation learning is how to promote attention to pronunciation in such a highly cognitively demanding meaning-focused activity. Wisniewska and Mora (2020) achieved this by asking learners questions related to the pronunciation of specific words appearing in the TV material used in an 8-week treatment (16 L2 videos). In their study, 90 participants were randomly assigned to one of two viewing conditions (with or without captions), and one of two task-focus conditions implemented through questions appearing on the screen during the viewing (directing attention to phonetic form or meaning). Learners improved in their speech segmentation skills irrespective of viewing condition but gains in perceptual sensitivity to contrastive vowels were only found for participants in the meaning-focused condition with captions. Nevertheless, gains in production occurred in the uncaptioned pronunciation-focused condition and in the captioned meaning-focused condition, suggesting that focusing on phonetic form in a captioned video might have been too cognitively overloading.

Another way to facilitate learners' attention to phonetic form is through input enhancement (Sharwood Smith, 1993), such as highlighting text in reading tasks, which has been shown to be effective in promoting grammar and vocabulary learning (Leow et al., 2019). Recent studies have shown that textual enhancement in captioned video promotes the acquisition of grammar (Lee & Révész, 2020) and vocabulary (Finger-Bou & Muñoz, 2023; Chapter 3 in this volume). While research on the efficacy of textual input enhancement in L2 captioned video to promote pronunciation learning is still incipient, the scant studies available on the effectiveness of textual input enhancement for pronunciation learning suggest that it may also have positive effects. For example, Stenton (2013) found it effective at improving accuracy in lexical stress production by French learners of English. Alsadoon and Heift (2015) found that it promoted noticing and improved the recognition of the orthographic form of English vowels in Arabic learners of English. Finally, Galimberti et al. (2023) implemented a novel audio-synchronized textual enhancement technique that highlighted target words typically mispronounced by learners 300 or 500 milliseconds before their auditory onset in the video soundtrack. This was done to direct learners' visual attention to target words and activate their phono-lexical representations as the word was heard in the soundtrack. All synchronized and unsynchronized enhancement conditions led to significantly faster rejection of mispronunciations in a lexical choice task, suggesting that highlighting proved effective in updating learners' phono-lexical representations. These studies suggest that the use of textual enhancement in on-screen text (subtitles and captions) during audiovisual exposure might promote pronunciation learning in the same way it promotes language learning by directing learners' attention to linguistic form (Montero Perez, 2022).

Other ways to exploit textual enhancement for L2 pronunciation may encompass the use of different colors (color-contrastive enhancement) or different types of text. Using different colors to represent different target sounds should be more informative than using a single color. In this way, learners are not only informed of the presence of a target sound, but also which of the target sounds they are hearing. This should, in turn, promote noticing that sounds learners might perceive as similar or identical are actually different. Another possibility is to use phonetic symbols. Given the low correspondence between sounds and orthography in English, phonetic symbols offer a pedagogic advantage in allowing teachers to refer to sounds unambiguously (Mompean & Fouz-González, 2021; Mompean & Lintunen, 2015) and in labelling stimuli in perception tasks (Fouz-González & Mompean, 2021). Using standard orthography to represent target sounds may limit the extent to which learners apply what they learn with exposure to one particular spelling to other spellings (e.g., associating /ɜː/ as <ur> in b*ur*n and t*ur*n might hinder learners' ability to identify /ɜː/ as the same vowel in b*ir*d or w*or*d). Further research is therefore needed on the effectiveness of different types of textual enhancement in L2 captioned video for L2 pronunciation learning.

1.3   The current study

The current study explores the potential of input enhancement in captioned video to facilitate L2 pronunciation learning. We examined the differential effects of two types of textual enhancement in L2 captioned video in the perception of an English vowel contrast (/æ/-/ʌ/) that is difficult to acquire for L1-Spanish learners of English, as they are both mapped onto their single L1 low vowel category /a/ (Cebrian, 2019; Rallo Fabra & Romero, 2012). The two types of enhancement explored were: contrastive (two colors) or non-contrastive (one color) textual enhancement (*Enhancement Type*) in target words and the use of IPA symbols as opposed to standard orthography (*Text Type*). We assessed differential effects between enhanced (highlighted in one color) and unenhanced captions, between contrastive input enhancement (two target sounds in different colors) and non-contrastive enhancement (both sounds in one color), and between standard orthography or IPA symbols in presenting /æ/ and /ʌ/ in target words. Thus, the study addressed two research questions (RQs):

RQ1.   Does color-contrastive textually enhanced input in captioned video facilitate perceptual sensitivity to an L2 sound contrast?

RQ2.   Does the use of IPA symbols in textually enhanced words in captioned video facilitate perceptual sensitivity to an L2 sound contrast?

2.   Methods

2.1   Research design and experimental procedures and materials

This study employed a pre-test>treatment>post-test design (Figure 1). Testing and training took place individually in a single 90-minute session in the GRAL SLA lab at the University of Barcelona. The participants completed four perception tests (Figure 1) consisting of two identification tasks and two discrimination tasks (see 2.5 below). Then they were randomly assigned to one of five viewing conditions (C) to watch a 30-minute episode of the TV series *Ted Lasso* with captions while their eye-gaze was being recorded on an eye-tracker. Selected target words containing the difficult vowel contrast /æ/-/ʌ/ were presented in either standard orthography (C2 and C3) or in IPA symbols (C4 and C5), with (C2, C3, C4, C5) or without (C1) textual enhancement. In the textually enhanced conditions, the target sounds /æ/ and /ʌ/ (or the letters representing them) were highlighted either in yellow (*non-contrastive*) or in two colors, yellow for /æ/ and purple for /ʌ/ (*contrastive*). In addition, control learners (C6) performed the pre- and post-tests without viewing the TV episode (Figure 1). Participants watching the video were instructed to pay attention to the vowel contrast in words like *cup* /kʌp/- *cap* /kæp/ and were told that they would be asked comprehension questions to check their understanding of the episode at the end. Then they completed the same four perception tasks again as post-tests.

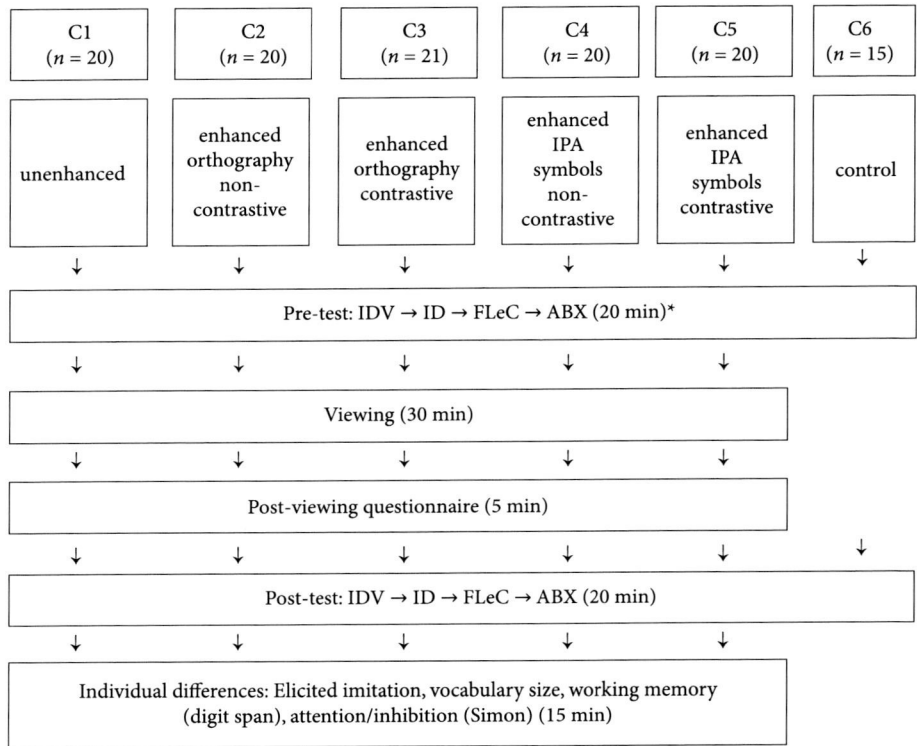

Note: *IDV = Identification test with words from the video; ID = identification test with untrained nonwords; FLeC = forced lexical choice test with words from the video; ABX = discrimination test with untrained nonwords

Figure 1. Experimental design

2.2 Participants

Participants were 116 advanced learners of EFL (27 males, 89 females) enrolled in the second of two courses in English phonetics in an English studies degree at the University of Barcelona, had had extensive practice in English phonetic transcription, and could read IPA symbols fluently (Table 1). Most participants reported being used to watching films/TV shows in English either daily (31.6%) or several times a week (34.7%) and to do so using captions in English either always (30.5%) or often (28.4%). They were randomly assigned to the following conditions:[1]

1.   C1 (*n* = 19): watched the episode with regular orthographic captions (no enhancement).

---

1. Eight participants (2 from C2, C4 and C5, and 1 from C1 and C3; 5 female), were excluded from the study because their rate of eye-gaze recordings did not reach 90%.

2. C2 ($n=18$): watched the episode with orthographic captions and the two target sounds in yellow (enhanced, non-contrastive).
3. C3 ($n=20$): watched the episode with orthographic captions and the two target sounds in yellow and purple (enhanced, contrastive).
4. C4 ($n=18$): watched the episode with the target words in phonemic transcription (IPA symbols) and the two target sounds in yellow (enhanced, non-contrastive).
5. C5 ($n=18$): watched the episode with the target words in phonemic transcription and the two target sounds in yellow and purple (enhanced, contrastive).
6. C6 ($n=15$): did not watch the episode and completed a series of reading and oral narrative tasks instead (Control).

Table 1. Participants' demographics

Variables	*M*	*SD*	95%CI
Age (years)	20.9	3.6	20.2–21.6
AO English (years)	5.8	2.9	5.2–6.4
Spoken L2 Input[*]	3.1	1.5	2.97–3.3
Spoken L2 Output[*]	1.9	1.4	1.8–2.1
Self-estimated Overall Proficiency[**]	7.1	1.1	6.9–7.3
Self-estimated Pronunciation Proficiency[†]	6.9	1.1	6.7–7.1
Yes/No Vocabulary Test (0–10,000 words)[‡]	6519	1308	6259–6778

Note.
[*] Hours/week (h/w) on average: 1 = 1–5 h/w; 2 = 6–10 h/w; 3 = 11–20 h/w; 4 = 21–30 h/w; 5 = +30h/w.
[**] Reading, Listening, Speaking, Writing: 9-point Likert scale from 1 = very poor to 9 = native-like.
[†] Pronunciation only: 9-point Likert scale from 1 = very poor to 9 = native-like.
[‡] Meara and Miralpeix (2015).

2.3 Viewing materials and input enhancement

Previous research has used typographical highlighting in yellow to textually enhance target words and effectively draw learners' attention to lexical forms (e.g., Lee & Révész, 2020). For the enhanced non-contrastive conditions, we highlighted both target sounds in yellow. For the enhanced contrastive conditions, we used yellow for /æ/ and purple for /ʌ/. This highlighting was applied to the stressed vowel portion of target /æ/- and /ʌ/-words, which appeared either in standard orthography (*manners, country*) or in IPA phonemic transcription (/ˈmænəz/, /ˈkʌntri/) in the captions.

The participants watched a 30-minute episode of the TV series *Ted Lasso*. Five different versions of the episode were created according to the conditions described above (C1-C5). The captions were edited with *Aegisub*, using Arial Unicode MS, font size 20. The aim of contrastive input enhancement was to help learners correctly encode a sound contrast that will help them distinguish lexical forms. Considering that vowels in unstressed syllables tend to be reduced and do not present well-defined vowel quality, textual enhancement was applied exclusively to the lexical words in the captions with the target vowels in stressed syllables. Occasionally, words considered to be unclear exemplars of /æ/ or /ʌ/ (e.g., because of the speaker's accent) were not visually enhanced (12 instances of /æ/ and 6 of /ʌ/). The episode included a total of 123 visually enhanced instances of /æ/ (lexical frequency[2] $M = 127.6$, $SD = 371.4$; orthographic length $M = 6.3$ characters, $SD = 2.5$) and 126 of /ʌ/ (lexical frequency $M = 331.5$, $SD = 544.1$; orthographic length $M = 6.2$ characters, $SD = 2.4$).

2.4   Eye-gaze recording and data acquisition

Participants' eye movements were recorded with a Tobii Pro Spectrum eye-tracker, at a 1200 Hz sampling rate equipped with a Tobii-supplied 23.8" monitor EIZO FlexScan EV2451 (16:9 aspect ratio, 1920 x 1080 resolution). Participants were seated in front of the monitor at a viewing distance of 55–75 cm, as recommended by the manufacturer for optimal recording of eye movement. Before recording, accuracy was verified using a five-point calibration and validation procedure, which was repeated if values were > 0.5°.

Using Tobii Pro Lab software, areas of interest (AOIs) were drawn as rectangles around the target words ($n = 249$) and all the captions ($n = 578$) for all video versions. AOIs were activated on the frame in the video when the caption appeared on the screen and deactivated on the frame before the caption disappeared from the screen. Measures of the number of fixations, first-fixation duration, as well as the average and total duration of fixations were extracted from the AOIs.

2.5   Testing perceptual sensitivity to the /æ/-/ʌ/ contrast

Learners' potential changes in sensitivity to the target contrast resulting from the exposure to the textually enhanced captioned video were assessed through two perception tests that used a selection of 40 words from the video: an identification test (IDV) and a forced lexical choice test (FLeC). A female native speaker

---

2. Lexical frequency per million words in the SUBLEX$_{US}$ database (Brysbaert & New, 2009).

of Southern British English recorded 20 /æ/-words (e.g., *man* /mæn/) and 20 /ʌ/-words (e.g., *club* /klʌb/) as well as their corresponding /æ/ and /ʌ/ nonwords (e.g., *clab* /klæb/, *munn* /mʌn/) created by changing the vowel (/æ/ into /ʌ/ or /ʌ/ into /æ/). The words and nonwords were produced at normal conversational speed in carrier phrases (Appendix A). These items were excised and normalized for mean amplitude for the IDV and FLeC tasks, which were administered through DmDx (Forster & Forster, 2003).

The IDV task presented the 40 test words for identification in fully randomized order. Based on the vowel they heard in the stressed syllable of the word, participants selected the correct response alternative as accurately and as fast as they could by pressing a designated response key. The alternatives were presented orthographically and in phonemic transcription (*cap* /kæp/ + a line drawing of a cap on the left, and *cup* /kʌp/ + a line drawing of a cup on the right). Trials were presented 500 ms after the participants' response or 2,500 ms after the end of the previous trial if there was no response. Accuracy (proportion correct) response latency (RT) scores were then obtained.

The FLeC test presented 40 pairs of words (1 real word + 1 nonword) in 40 fully randomized trials (i.e., 20 /æ/-words and the 20 /ʌ/-words with their corresponding mispronunciations). Participants selected as accurately and as fast as they could which of the two words in the pair, the one presented first or the one presented second, was a nonword. On every trial, participants would hear two words (e.g., *man* /mæn/ – **munn* /mʌn/; ISI = 500 ms) and selected the correct response alternative (left or right response key) according to whether the nonword was presented first or second; /æ/-nonwords and /ʌ/-nonwords appeared an equal number of times in first and second position. Trial presentation and scoring were as in the IDV task.

To test for generalization of learning to a phonetic non-lexical context, an identification (ID) and a discrimination (ABX) test with CVC nonwords targeting the /æ/-/ʌ/ contrast were administered. The ID test consisted of eight minimal-pair CVC nonwords with /æ/ (/fæʃ, mæb, ʃæd, tʃæŋ, tæz, tæm, θæk, θæt/) and eight with /ʌ/ (/fʌʃ, mʌb, ʃʌd, tʃʌŋ, tʌz, tʌm, θʌk, θʌt/) produced by a male and a female speaker (32 randomly presented trials). Using the same interface as in the IDV task described above, participants selected the correct response alternative (/æ/ or /ʌ/) as accurately and as fast as they could. The ABX test consisted of 32 /æ/-/ʌ/ test trials and 8 control /æ/-/iː/ and /ʌ/-/ɪ/ trials (40 randomly presented trials) with the same CVC nonwords as in the ID test produced by six different native speaker voices (three males, three females). Each trial presented three CVC nonwords with 500 ms ISI (ABX) to decide if the last one (X) was the same as the first (A) or the second one (B). A and B (/æ/-/ʌ/ CVC minimal pair nonwords: /fæʃ-fʌʃ/ or /fʌʃ-fæʃ/) were spoken by two different male or female voices, whereas X could be the same as A (/fæʃ-fʌʃ-fæʃ/) or B (/fæʃ-fʌʃ-fʌʃ/) but spoken by a third different male or female voice. RT and accuracy measures were obtained too.

2.6   Data analyses

RTs were computed on correct responses only and screened for extreme values (2.5 *SD*s from mean RT by participant) resulting in 1.6% data exclusion. The analysis of the results was carried out separately for each perception test in three steps. First (Analysis 1, A1), we compared the control group (C6) to the five groups who had watched the video (C1–C5). Then (Analysis 2, A2), we compared the group exposed to unenhanced captions (C1) to the 4 groups exposed to enhanced captions. Finally (Analysis 3, A3), we analyzed the effects of *Enhancement Type* (contrastive vs. non-contrastive) and *Text Type* (orthography vs. IPA symbols) on the perception of the target contrast in the groups exposed to textually enhanced conditions (C2–C5). These analyses were performed through a series of linear mixed-effects models (in SPSS 27) that included testing *Time* (T1, T2), *Condition* (A1: experimental, control; A2: enhanced, unenhanced; A3: contrastive, non-contrastive), *Text Type* (A3) and their interactions as fixed effects, as well as random intercepts for *Subject* and *Item*. Random slopes and a random intercept for Item were only included if they improved the model's fit (i.e., AIC decreased) and did not prevent model convergence. Square root (IDV) and Log10 transformations (ID and ABX) were used to normalize positively skewed data.

3.   Results

The descriptive statistics in Table 2 show that overall gains were very modest. The groups who viewed the episode generally improved between testing times and did so to a larger extent than the control group, primarily as regards reaction times. Differences between testing times by condition were not consistent across tasks. For example, in the ABX task, while both groups exposed to orthography decreased in accuracy between testing times, both groups exposed to IPA symbols improved. However, in the FLeC task, the greatest gain was made by the group exposed to enhanced non-contrastive orthographic captions (C2), and in the IDV task, all groups improved between testing times. We tested the significance of such differences through a series of linear mixed-effects models.

Table 2. Accuracy, reaction time and gains by task, testing time and condition

			IDV			ID			FLeC			ABX		
			T1	T2	Gain	T1	T2	Gain	T1	T2	Gain	T1	T2	Gain
C1	RT	M	1193	1091	−103	1021	955	−67	1215	1022	−193	1019	933	−86
		SD	288	288		318	286		350	350		311	288	
	ACC	M	0.84	0.88	0.04	0.77	0.77	0.00	0.82	0.84	0.02	0.78	0.75	−0.03
		SD	0.37	0.33		0.42	0.42		0.39	0.37		0.42	0.43	
C2	RT	M	1299	1139	−159	1084	1005	−79	1122	957	−165	1020	974	−46
		SD	339	290		319	298		335	396		305	304	
	ACC	M	0.84	0.86	0.02	0.80	0.82	0.02	0.78	0.86	0.08	0.79	0.76	−0.03
		SD	0.37	0.35		0.40	0.39		0.42	0.35		0.41	0.43	
C3	RT	M	1221	1042	−180	1012	950	−62	1077	954	−124	989	942	−48
		SD	308	312		277	278		366	380		280	300	
	ACC	M	0.82	0.84	0.02	0.75	0.75	0.00	0.87	0.84	−0.03	0.77	0.75	−0.02
		SD	0.39	0.37		0.44	0.43		0.34	0.37		0.42	0.43	
C4	RT	M	1183	1064	−119	991	914	−77	1087	948	−139	1017	965	−52
		SD	320	284		285	274		421	408		372	337	
	ACC	M	0.82	0.86	0.04	0.78	0.80	0.02	0.88	0.89	0.01	0.80	0.81	0.01
		SD	0.38	0.35		0.41	0.40		0.32	0.31		0.40	0.40	
C5	RT	M	1274	1104	−170	1075	972	−102	1170	1030	−140	1063	945	−118
		SD	353	306		298	276		365	390		299	288	
	ACC	M	0.81	0.83	0.02	0.71	0.75	0.04	0.80	0.82	0.02	0.69	0.74	0.05
		SD	0.39	0.38		0.46	0.43		0.40	0.39		0.47	0.44	
C6	RT	M	1293	1144	−149	1072	1060	−13	1155	1097	−58	1035	1013	−22
		SD	342	321		331	337		333	385		331	340	
	ACC	M	0.78	0.81	0.03	0.72	0.71	−0.01	0.82	0.81	−0.01	0.75	0.72	−0.03
		SD	0.42	0.39		0.45	0.45		0.39	0.40		0.44	0.45	

Note: T1 = pre-test; T2 = post-test; Gain = T2-T1; ACC = accuracy; RT = reaction times; C = condition (see section 2.2)

3.1 A1: Control (C6) vs. video viewing (C1–C5) conditions

For RT, the analysis revealed significant effects of *Time* in all the tasks and significant *Time x Condition* interactions in the FLeC, ID, and ABX tasks (Table 3). Pairwise contrasts (Bonferroni-corrected) showed that the main effect of *Time* in the IDV task arose because both the experimental and control conditions improved significantly between testing times ($t = −23.42$, $p = <.001$; $t = −8.1$, $p = <.001$, respectively). The *Time x Condition* interaction arose either because the experimental condition improved significantly from pre- to post-test whereas the control condition did not (ID: $t = −11.87$, $p = <.001$; $t = −0.168$, $p = .866$, respectively), or because the gains made by the experimental condition were substantially larger than those by the control group (FleC: $t = -22.16$, $p = <.001$; $t = -3.03$, $p = .002$; ABX: $t = -10.84$, $p = <.001$; $t = -1.96$, $p = .049$, respectively). The only significant main effect for accuracy was found for *Time* in the IDV task. However, although no significant *Time x Condition* interactions were found, the pre-/post-test changes for the experimental group were significant in the IDV and FLeC tasks, whereas those for the control group were not (IDV: $t = 3.21$, $p = .001$; $t = 1.5$, $p = .133$; FLeC: $t = 2.29$, $p = .022$; $t = -0.54$, $p = .587$, respectively).

Table 3. Tests of fixed effects for A1

Task	Fixed effects	RT		ACC	
		F	*p*	*F*	*p*
IDV[*]	Time	257.675	**<.001**	7.804	**.005**
	Condition	1.397	.237	2.875	.090
	Time x Condition	0.92	.338	0.001	.981
FLeC[**]	Time	119.933	**<.001**	0.214	.644
	Condition	1.122	.290	1.401	.237
	Time x Condition	28.266	**<.001**	2.127	.145
ID[†]	Time	20.486	**<.001**	0.261	.609
	Condition	1.865	.172	2.263	.133
	Time x Condition	17.753	**<.001**	0.624	.429
ABX[‡]	Time	33.417	**<.001**	0.962	.327
	Condition	0.600	.439	0.829	.363
	Time x Condition	4.500	**.034**	0.641	.423

Note: significant *p*-values marked in boldface. ACC=accuracy; *df* for RT and ACC respectively:
[*] (7082, 8636) [**] (7083, 8636) [†] (4949, 6652) [‡] (5112, 6908)

3.2   A2: Unenhanced (C1) vs. textually enhanced (C2–C5) captions conditions

The models testing the effects of enhancement revealed significant main effects of *Time* on RTs in every task (significant T1–T2 differences for both conditions in all tasks; Table 4). Significant *Time x Condition* interactions were found in the IDV and FLeC tasks due to a larger improvement in one of the two conditions. The gains obtained in the enhanced condition were greater than those in the unenhanced condition ($t = -23.28$, $p = <.001$; $t = -7.93$, $p = <.001$, respectively) in the IDV task, whereas the opposite trend was found in the FLeC task ($t = -152.48$,

$p =$ <.001; $t = -196.44$, $p =$ <.001). For accuracy, significant effects were only found for *Time* in the IDV and FLeC tasks. Tests of pairwise contrasts showed that the change between testing times was significant for both conditions in the IDV task (enhanced: $t = 2.52$ $p = .012$, unenhanced: $t = 2.06$, $p = .039$). However, in the FLeC task, the gains in the enhanced condition approached significance, but neither the enhanced nor the unenhanced condition resulted in significant T1–T2 changes ($t = 1.95$, $p = .051$; $t = 1.21$, $p = .225$, respectively).

Table 4. Tests of fixed effects for A2

Task	Fixed effects	RT		ACC	
		F	p	F	p
IDV[*]	Time	315.25	**<.001**	9.79	**.002**
	Condition	0.18	.673	0.29	.590
	Time x Condition	13.47	**<.001**	0.71	.400
FLeC[**]	Time	366.73	**<.001**	4.17	**.041**
	Condition	1.38	.240	0.24	.621
	Time x Condition	5.82	**.016**	0.02	.880
ID[†]	Time	67.31	**<.001**	0.79	.374
	Condition	0.004	.952	0.03	.856
	Time x Condition	1.22	.269	0.37	.542
ABX[‡]	Time	85.34	**<.001**	0.66	.415
	Condition	0.01	.930	0.12	.730
	Time x Condition	0.76	.384	1.10	.294

Note: significant *p*-values marked in boldface. ACC = accuracy; *df* for RT and ACC respectively:
[*] (6111, 7396) [**] (6134, 7436) [†] (4276, 5692) [‡] (4429, 5948)

3.3   A3: Effects of *Enhancement Type* and *Text Type*

Since *Enhancement Type* and *Text Type* included four conditions (orthography and IPA symbols with contrastive and non-contrastive enhancement – C2–C5), the outcome of tests of fixed effects (Table 5) will be interpreted by referring to the pairwise contrasts (Table 6) resulting from the *Time x Text Type x Enhancement Type* interaction.

In the IDV task, the RT data revealed a significant effect of *Time* and a significant *Time x Enhancement Type* interaction. Although T1–T2 differences reached significance for the four groups, this interaction arose because the groups with contrastive enhancement made larger gains than those with non-contrastive

Table 5. Tests of fixed effects for A3

Task	Fixed effects	RT		ACC	
		F	*p*	*F*	*p*
IDV[*]	*Time*	496.874	**<.001**	7.030	**.008**
	Text Type	0.438	.508	0.022	.883
	Enhancement Type	0.000	.993	0.613	.434
	Time x Text Type	1.950	.163	0.082	.774
	Time x Enhancement Type	6.203	**.013**	0.121	.728
	Text Type x Enhancement Type	3.851	.050	0.229	.632
	Time x Text Type x Enhancement Type	0.021	.886	0.397	.529
FLeC[**]	*Time*	354.129	**<.001**	3.809	.051
	Text Type	0.045	.832	0.009	.922
	Enhancement Type	0.095	.758	0.403	.526
	Time x Text Type	1.251	.263	0.097	.756
	Time x Enhancement Type	4.325	**.038**	9.228	**.002**
	Text Type x Enhancement Type	1.113	.291	2.312	.128
	Time x Text Type x Enhancement Type	3.504	.061	10.062	**.002**
ID[†]	*Time*	122.02	**<.001**	2.974	.085
	Text Type	0.574	.449	0.483	.487
	Enhancement Type	0.069	.793	4.640	**.031**
	Time x Text Type	1.899	.168	0.893	.345
	Time x Enhancement Type	0.567	.451	0.017	.897
	Text Type x Enhancement Type	3.596	.058	0.003	.956
	Time x Text Type x Enhancement Type	1.464	.226	0.614	.433
ABX[‡]	*Time*	88.831	**<.001**	0.040	.841
	Text Type	0.000	.991	0.150	.699
	Enhancement Type	0.006	.940	4.690	**.030**
	Time x Text Type	3.972	**.046**	5.411	**.020**
	Time x Enhancement Type	6.601	**.010**	0.742	.389
	Text Type x Enhancement Type	0.554	.457	2.488	.115
	Time x Text Type x Enhancement Type	1.791	.181	0.230	.632

Note: significant *p*-values marked in boldface. ACC = accuracy; *df* for RT and ACC respectively:
[*] (4820, 5872) [**] (4886, 5912) [†] (3448, 4600) [‡] (3515, 4728)

enhancement. For accuracy, the only significant main effect was found for *Time*. No significant T1–T2 differences were found for any of the groups when analyzing the triple interaction, but pairwise contrasts exploring the *Time x Text Type* interaction revealed significant T1–T2 differences for the groups exposed to IPA symbols ($t(5872)=1.973$, $p=.048$), but not for those using orthography ($t(5872)=1.656$, $p=.098$).

In the FLeC task, the RT data revealed significant effects of *Time* and a significant *Time x Enhancement Type* interaction. The T1–T2 differences were significant for the four groups, but the gains by the C2 group (orthography, non-contrastive) were superior. Focusing on accuracy, the model also yielded a significant *Time x Enhancement Type* interaction, which arose because the C2 group was the only one with significant differences between testing times.

In the ID task, only the *Time* effect on RTs reached significance because all four groups improved between testing times. For accuracy, only the *Enhancement Type* effect reached significance, as there were significant differences between non-contrastive (C2, C4) and contrastive (C3, C5) conditions already at T1 and the differences between these conditions also approached significance at T2 ($t(4600)=1.944$, $p=.052$).

The results for the ABX task for RT revealed significant effects of *Time* and of the *Time x Text Type* and *Time x Enhancement Type* interactions. The pairwise contrasts suggest that the main effect of *Time* arose because there were significant T1–T2 differences for the four groups. However, the gains made by the C5 (contrastive, IPA) group were larger than those of the other three conditions, resulting in a *Time x Text Type* interaction. Finally, the *Time x Enhancement Type* interaction arose because the gains made by the groups using contrastive enhancement (C3 and C5) were superior to those using non-contrastive enhancement (C2 and C4). In terms of accuracy, the model revealed significant effects for *Enhancement Type* and for the *Time x Text Type* interaction. The main effect of *Enhancement Type* and the *Time x Text Type* interactions were caused by the C5 group. The differences between testing times were significant only for this group, whose gain was far superior to the other three, with the two groups using orthography getting worse from pre- to post-test.

3.4   Descriptive analysis of viewing behavior

A detailed analysis of the eye-gaze data by target word is beyond the scope of the current chapter. Nevertheless, we explored the extent to which the viewing conditions implemented had had consequences for learners' viewing behavior; in particular, regarding the effect of the different types of enhancement in the captions on the total amount of fixation time spent on them over time. To this end, we computed a measure of total duration fixation relative to the number of characters (relative fixation duration) in the captions (Figure 2) and in the target words in them (Figure 3) by condition. As shown in Figure 2, captions with highlighted target words (1, right panel) obtained overall longer relative fixation durations than

Table 6. Pairwise contrasts between testing times for A3

Task		Enhancement		*b*	*SE*	*t*	*p*	95%CI	
IDV	RT	O	NC	−2.290	.213	−10.735	**<.001**	−2.708	−1.872
			C	−2.793	.205	−13.603	**<.001**	−3.196	−2.391
		IPA	NC	−1.959	.221	−8.856	**<.001**	−2.393	−1.526
			C	−2.525	.218	−11.571	**<.001**	−2.952	−2.097
	ACC	O	NC	0.017	.017	1.007	.314	−.016	.051
			C	0.023	.017	1.357	.175	−.010	.056
		IPA	NC	0.031	.018	1.732	.083	−.004	.065
			C	0.019	.019	1.016	.310	−.018	.055
FLeC	RT	O	NC	−195.19	16.90	−11.552	**<.001**	−228.31	−162.06
			C	−130.62	15.57	−8.388	**<.001**	−161.15	−100.09
		IPA	NC	−146.32	16.06	−9.112	**<.001**	−177.81	−114.84
			C	−142.93	16.80	−8.507	**<.001**	−175.87	−109.99
	ACC	O	NC	0.077	.023	3.371	**.001**	.032	.122
			C	−0.030	.016	−1.906	.057	−.061	.001
		IPA	NC	0.010	.014	0.684	.494	−.018	.038
			C	0.018	.020	0.907	.365	−.021	.056
ID	RT	O	NC	−0.033	.007	−5.072	**<.001**	−.046	−.020
			C	−0.030	.006	−4.817	**<.001**	−.042	−.018
		IPA	NC	−0.034	.006	−5.306	**<.001**	−.047	−.022
			C	−0.047	.007	−6.807	**<.001**	−.061	−.047
	ACC	O	NC	0.014	.022	0.654	.513	−.028	.057
			C	0.002	.024	0.069	.945	−.045	.048
		IPA	NC	0.019	.023	0.847	.397	−.025	.064
			C	0.050	.027	1.835	.067	−.003	.103
ABX	RT	O	NC	−0.022	.007	−3.088	**.002**	−.035	−.008
			C	−0.030	.007	−4.519	**<.001**	−.043	−.017
		IPA	NC	−0.026	.007	−3.805	**<.001**	−.040	−.013
			C	−0.053	.007	−7.307	**<.001**	−.068	−.039
	ACC	O	NC	−0.029	.024	−1.208	.227	−.076	.018
			C	−0.021	.023	−0.913	.361	−.067	.024
		IPA	NC	0.012	.022	0.554	.579	−.031	.056
			C	0.056	.028	2.008	**.045**	.001	.110

Note: significant *p*-values marked in boldface. ACC=accuracy; O=orthography, C=contrastive, NC=non-contrastive.

did the captions without target words (o, left panel). The relative fixation duration measure shows substantial differences in how much attention to the captions the enhancement conditions generated. Captions with IPA symbols and contrastive enhancement (C5) obtained the highest relative fixation durations, whereas unenhanced captions obtained the lowest, as expected. The normalized linear trends in the slopes represent learners' attentional behavior during the exposure to the video. Such linear trends indicate little attentional loss over time. The largest drop in attention seems to affect the viewing condition generating the largest amount of fixation durations, possibly indicating a limitation of the condition generating the highest potential of cognitive overload in making viewers sustain attention over time.

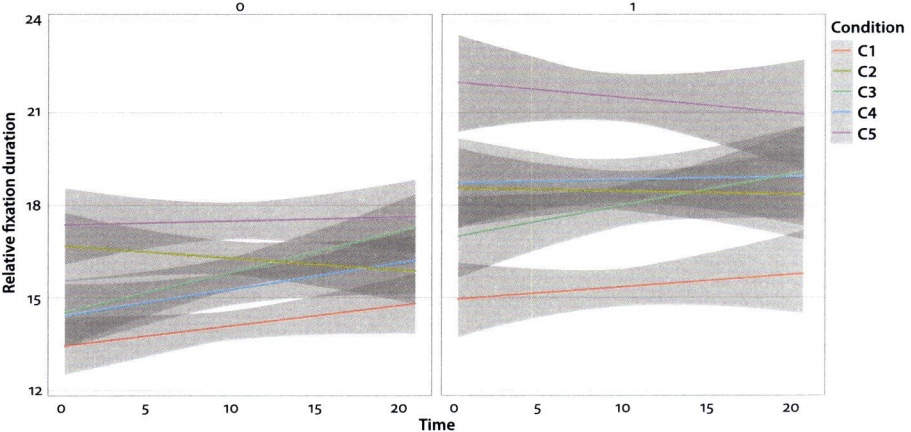

Figure 2. Normalized linear trends of relative fixation durations in captions along exposure time (in minutes)

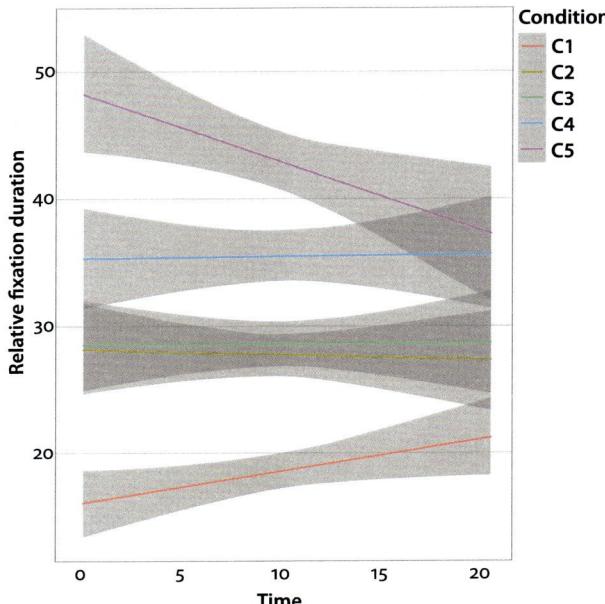

Figure 3. Normalized linear trends of relative fixation durations in the target words in the captions along exposure time (in minutes)

The same normalized linear trends computed on the highlighted target words revealed the same attentional patterns, with words presented in phonemic transcription with contrastive textual enhancement obtaining the highest relative fixation durations. Overall, these results indicate that the textual enhancement conditions implemented in the current study were effective in modifying the amount of attention learners allocated to the processing of the target words in the captions.

Finally, we related the effects of viewing conditions on individual eye-gaze behavior to individual gains in sensitivity to the /æ/-/ʌ/. To this end, we aggregated the total duration fixations the target words in the IDV and FLeC tasks had received by subject and related these scores to individual T1–T2 gains in accuracy in the same tasks both for all participants and separately by condition. None of these analyses revealed any significant correlations.

4.   Discussion and conclusion

The perception tests revealed larger gains in perceptual sensitivity to the /æ/-/ʌ/ contrast by experimental (C1–C5) than control (C6) groups, suggesting that viewing the video and the textual enhancement conditions we applied influenced L2 perceptual learning. Such gains were more noticeable for RT than for accuracy scores. This indicates that the experimental conditions affected processing speed more than accuracy, which was expected given the short 30-minute exposure. Some RT improvements were observed for the control group in some of the tasks, indicating benefits in testing driven by the single-session experimental design. However, in general, the experimental conditions led to larger gains in processing speed, which resulted in significant *Time x Condition* interactions in three of the tasks. These interactions were caused by either the gains by the experimental condition being superior or by the experimental condition being the only one for which pre-/post-test differences reached significance. In terms of accuracy, none of the interactions reached significance, but for two of the tasks the experimental (and not the control) condition obtained significant gains. This indicates that watching the video had a positive impact on the learners' perception of the target contrast, even after such a short intervention.

RTs were also found to be significantly faster in the post-test for participants in the unenhanced (C1) and the textually enhanced conditions (C2–C5) in the four tasks, with *Time x Enhancement Type* interactions being significant only in two of them, but with a different pattern. While gains in the IDV task were larger for participants exposed to textual enhancement than for those in the unenhanced condition, the opposite pattern was found in the FLeC task. This suggests that gains (or their absence) were not always consistent across tasks, which might be related to task difficulty and the different levels they tap into. For example, IDV and FLeC tap into phono-lexical processing, whereas ID and ABX tap into phonetic processing, allowing learners to identify acoustic differences between vowels better by comparing them in sensory memory without lexical activation. Also, whereas IDV scores index learners' ability to identify (i.e., label) vowel categories correctly, the FLeC task is more complex in that it requires learners to identify mispronunciations for lexical words with confusable vowel categories (/æ/ and /ʌ/) they perceptually assimilate to a single L1 /a/ vowel. In any case, we did not find any consistent trend in the results that we could unequivocally assign to specific task properties.

It is also worth noting that all participants exposed to the video – including those in the unenhanced "control" condition (C1)– were instructed to pay attention to /æ/-words and /ʌ/-words. This allowed us to measure the impact of visual enhancement on attention to form more precisely, but it likely drew participants' attention to /æ/-words and /ʌ/-words in the unenhanced condition too (Guion & Pederson, 2007). It is therefore not surprising that the C1 group also benefitted from the viewing. In fact, participants in the unenhanced condition were attentionally unconstrained and could pay attention to any /æ/-words or /ʌ/-words they could spot in the captions, whereas those in the enhanced conditions might have paid attention only to /æ/-words and /ʌ/-words when enhanced (i.e., lexical words with the target sounds in stressed syllables).

In three of the tasks (IDV, FLeC and ABX) the *Time x Enhancement Type* interactions reached significance for RT, as did the *Time x Text Type* interaction in the ABX task. The contrastive enhancement conditions were superior in two of the tasks (IDV and ABX), whereas in the FLeC task the orthography non-contrastive condition (C2) obtained larger gains. The *Text Type* effects indicated that IPA symbols were superior to orthography, but only in the ABX task. For accuracy, participants in the non-contrastive orthographic condition (C2) obtained the largest gains in the FLeC Task, whereas those in the contrastive IPA symbols condition (C5) obtained the largest gains in the ABX task. In sum, both gains in response speed and accuracy seem to be task dependent.

A relationship between learners' visual behavior in terms of amount of attention paid to form across the different enhancement conditions and gains in perceptual sensitivity to the /æ/-/ʌ/ contrast was not found. Thus, as Winke (2013), we succeeded in effectively making learners pay attention to visually enhanced input, promoting noticing, but this did not appear to result in consistent gains. Nonetheless, the gains obtained – considering the short exposure provided – suggest that it might be worth investigating the effects of the textually enhanced conditions in this study in the context of a longer treatment. Finally, the current study explored the effects of contrastive input enhancement and the use of IPA symbols on L2 perception. Following other single-session video viewing interventions (Hutchinson & Dmitrieva, 2022; Weber & Geissler, 2023), a follow-up of the current study will be to extend the current research focusing on the effects of visual enhancement on learners' ability to qualitatively distinguish /æ/ from /ʌ/ in production.

It is also important to mention several limitations of the current study that also offer directions for future research. One such limitation is the short duration of the training. While some single-session interventions have found positive effects on the participants' pronunciation (see above), for substantial gains to occur in the categorical perception of challenging phonological contrasts, longer training periods may be necessary. Future studies could explore the impact of contrastive input enhancement and the use of IPA symbols after several viewing sessions and determine what amount of exposure is needed for substantial changes to take place. Another limitation is the lack of a control condition (C0) for a group watching the video without enhancement (like the C1 group did) but without any explicit instruction to pay attention to the target sounds. Such a group would allow us to measure the effect of directing learners' attention to form (C1) relative to any incidental learning taking place without it (i.e., the way learners normally watch a TV show). Future research could study the impact of such methodological decisions in detail.

To conclude, the results of this study suggest that contrastive input enhancement is effective in attracting learners' attention to target phonetic forms and that it can have a positive impact on perceptual learning. Despite the modest gains observed, such a short intervention fostered improvements in the perception of a very challenging sound contrast. Hence, more extensive exposure to contrastive input enhancement as part of language classes or homework tasks could be a useful way of raising learners' awareness of difficult target sounds and of complementing in-class pronunciation tasks and other perceptual training activities.

Acknowledgements

This work was supported by grants PID2022-138129NB-I00 from the Spanish Ministry of Science and Innovation and 2023SGR00303 from the Catalan Agency for Management of University and Research Grants (AGAUR) to the first author. We would like to thank Miren Adrian, Cristina Aliaga, Josh Frank, Katherine Fraser, Núria Gavaldà, Ingrid Mora-Plaza, Mireia Ortega, and Gisela Sosa for their help in collecting data and Joan Borràs-Comes and the Laboratori de Fonètica Eugenio Martínez Celdrán of the Universitat de Barcelona for assistance with the eyetracking data processing. We would also like to thank the two anonymous reviewers and the editors of this volume for useful comments and suggestions on a previous version of the current manuscript.

Ethical considerations

The protocols of data collection, data anonymization, data processing, and data storage of the current study were approved by the Institutional Review Board of the University of Barcelona (IRB00003099).

References

Alsadoon, R., & Heift, T. (2015). Textual input enhancement for vowel blindness: A study with Arabic ESL learners. *Modern Language Journal, 99*(1), 57–79.

Baills, F., Alazard-Guiu, C., & Prieto, P. (2022). Embodied prosodic training helps improve accentedness and suprasegmental accuracy. *Applied Linguistics, 43*(4), 776–804.

doi Bird, S.A., & Williams, J.N. (2002). The effect of bimodal input on implicit and explicit memory: An investigation into the benefits of within-language subtitling. *Applied Psycholinguistics, 23*(4), 509–533.

doi Brysbaert, M., & New, B. (2009). Moving beyond Kucera and Francis: A critical evaluation of current word frequency norms and the introduction of a new and improved word frequency measure for American English. *Behavior Research Methods, 41*(4), 977–990.

doi Cebrian, J. (2019). Perceptual assimilation of British English vowels to Spanish monophthongs and diphthongs. *Journal of the Acoustical Society of America, 145*(1). EL52–EL58.

Chan, M.J. (2018). Embodied pronunciation learning: Research and practice. *The CATESOL Journal, 30*(1), 47–68.

Charles, T.J., & Trenkic, D. (2015). Speech segmentation in a second language: The role of bimodal input. In Y. Gambier, A. Caimi & C. Mariotti (Eds.), *Subtitles and language learning: Principles, strategies, and practical experiences* (pp. 173–198). Peter Lang.

doi Darcy, I., & Rocca, B. (2022). Comprehensibility improvements in integrated pronunciation instruction: A comparison of instruction methods and task effects. *Journal of Second Language Pronunciation, 8*(3), 328–362.

doi Derwing, T.M., & Munro, M.J. (2015). *Pronunciation fundamentals: Evidence-based perspectives for L2 teaching and research.* John Benjamins.

doi Finger-Bou, R., & Muñoz, C. (2023). The effects of regular and enhanced captions on incidental vocabulary acquisition. *ELIA, 23*, 15–50.

doi Forster, K.I., & Forster, J.C. (2003). DMDX: A Windows display program with millisecond accuracy. *Behavior Research Methods, 35*(1), 116–124.

doi Fouz-González, J., & Mompean, J.A. (2021). Exploring the potential of phonetic symbols and keywords as labels for perceptual training. *Studies in Second Language Acquisition, 43*(2), 297–328.

doi Galimberti, V., Mora, J.C., & Gilabert, R. (2023). Audio-synchronized textual enhancement in foreign language pronunciation learning from videos. *System, 116*, 103078.

doi Gesa, F., & Miralpeix, I. (2023). Extensive viewing and L2 vocabulary learning: Two studies in EFL classes with children and adolescents. *ITL-International Journal of Applied Linguistics.*

doi Hamada, Y. (2019). Shadowing: What is it? How to use it. Where will it go? *RELC Journal, 50*(3), 386–393.

doi Henderson, A., & Rojczyk, A. (2023). Foreign-language accent imitation: Matching production with perception. In V. Sardegna & A. Jarosz (Eds.), *English pronunciation teaching: Theory, practice, and research findings* (pp. 102–117) Multilingual Matters.

doi Hutchinson, A.E., & Dmitrieva, O. (2022). Exposure to speech via foreign film and its effects on non-native vowel production and perception. *Journal of Phonetics, 95*, 101189.

doi Lee, M., & Révész, A. (2020). Promoting grammatical development through captions and textual enhancement in multimodal input-based tasks. *Studies in Second Language Acquisition, 42*(3), 625–651.

doi Leow, R.P., Donate, A., & Gutierrez, H. (2019). Textual enhancement, type of linguistic item, and L2 development: A depth of processing perspective. In R.P. Leow (Ed.), *The Routledge handbook of second language research in classroom learning* (pp. 317–330). Routledge.

Levis, J. M. (2005). Changing contexts and shifting paradigms in pronunciation teaching. *TESOL Quarterly*, 39(3), 369–377.

Levis, J. M. (2020). Revisiting the intelligibility and nativeness principles. *Journal of Second Language Pronunciation*, 6(3), 310–328.

Li, P., Xi, X., Baills, F., & Prieto, P. (2021). Training non-native aspirated plosives with hand gestures: learners' gesture performance matters. *Language, Cognition and Neuroscience*, 36(10), 1313–1328.

Mathias, B., & von Kriegstein, K. (2023). Enriched learning: Behavior, brain, and computation. *Trends in Cognitive Sciences*, 27(1), 81–97.

Meara, P., & Miralpeix, I. (2015). *V_YesNo*. Lognostics. Retrieved on 28 May 2024 from http://www.lognostics.co.uk/tools/V_YesNo/V_YesNo.htm

Mitterer, H., & McQueen, J. (2009). Foreign subtitles help but native-language subtitles harm foreign speech perception. *PloS One*, 4(11), e7785.

Mompean, J. A., & Fouz-González, J. (2021). Phonetic symbols in contemporary pronunciation instruction. *RELC Journal*, 52(1), 155–168.

Mompean, J. A., & Lintunen, P. (2015). Phonetic notation in foreign language teaching and learning: Potential advantages and learners' views. *Research in Language*, 13(3), 292–314.

Montero Perez, M. (2022). Second or foreign language learning through watching audiovisual input and the role of on-screen text. *Language Teaching*, 55(2), 163–192.

Montero Perez, M., Van Den Noortgate, W., & Desmet, P. (2013). Captioned video for L2 listening and vocabulary learning: A meta-analysis. *System*, 41(3), 720–739.

Mora, J. C., & Mora-Plaza, I. (2023). From research in the lab to pedagogical practices in the EFL classroom: The case of task-based pronunciation teaching. *Education Sciences*, 13(10), 1042, 1–21.

Munro, M. J., & Derwing, T. M. (1995). Foreign accent, comprehensibility, and intelligibility in the speech of second language learners. *Language Learning*, 45(1), 73–97.

Muñoz, C. (2014). Contrasting effects of starting age and input on the oral performance of foreign language learners. *Applied Linguistics*, 35(4), 463–482.

Muñoz, C. (2023). Audio–visual input and language learning. In C. A. Chapelle & M. Sato (Eds.), *The encyclopedia of applied linguistics. Instructed second language acquisition* (2nd ed.). Wiley-Blackwell.

Pattemore, A., & Muñoz, C. (2020). Learning L2 constructions from captioned audio-visual exposure: The effect of learner-related factors. *System*, 93, 1–13.

Pujadas, G., & Muñoz, C. (2020). Examining adolescent EFL learners' TV viewing comprehension through captions and subtitles. *Studies in Second Language Acquisition*, 42(3), 551–575.

Rallo Fabra, L., & Romero, J. (2012). Native Catalan learners' perception and production of English vowels. *Journal of Phonetics*, 40(3), 491–508.

Rodgers, M. P. H., & Webb, S. (2020). Incidental vocabulary learning through viewing television. *ITL – International Journal of Applied Linguistics*, 171(2), 191–220.

Sharwood Smith, M. (1993). Input enhancement in instructed SLA. *Studies in Second Language Acquisition*, 15(2), 165–179.

Stenton, A. (2013). The role of the syllable in foreign language learning: Improving oral production through dual-coded, sound-synchronised, typographic annotations. *Language Learning in Higher Education*, 2(1), 145–161.

Strachan, L., Kennedy, S., & Trofimovich, P. (2019). Second language speakers' awareness of their own comprehensibility: Examining task repetition and self-assessment. *Journal of Second Language Pronunciation*, 5(3), 347–373.

Thomson, R. I. (2018). High variability [pronunciation] training (HVPT): A proven technique about which every language teacher and learner ought to know. *Journal of Second Language Pronunciation*, 4(2), 208–231.

Weber, J., & Geissler, C. (2023). Accommodation to passive exposure in the L2. In R. Skarnitzl & J. Volín (Eds.), *Proceedings of the 20th International Congress of Phonetic Sciences* (pp. 2681–2685). Guarant International.

Winke, P. M. (2013). The effects of input enhancement on grammar learning and comprehension: A modified replication of Lee (2007) with eye-movement data. *Studies in Second Language Acquisition*, 35(2), 323–352.

Wisniewska, N., & Mora, J. C. (2020). Can captioned video benefit second language pronunciation? *Studies in Second Language Acquisition*, 42(3), 599–624.

Xi, X., Li, P., Baills, F., & Prieto, P. (2020). Hand gestures facilitate the acquisition of novel phonemic contrasts when they appropriately mimic target phonetic features. *Journal of Speech, Language, and Hearing Research*, 63(11), 3571–3585.

Zhen, A., Van Hedger, S., Heald, S., Goldin-Meadow, S., & Tian, X. (2019). Manual directional gestures facilitate cross-modal perceptual learning. *Cognition*, 187, 178–187.

Appendix A. Test words in the IDV and forced lexical choice (FLeC) tasks

/æ/-words			/ʌ/-words		
Orthography	IPA	/ʌ/-nonword	Orthography	IPA	/æ/-nonword
absolute	ˈæbsəluːt	ˈʌbsəluːt	another	əˈnʌðə	əˈnæðə
average	ˈævərɪdʒ	ˈʌvərɪdʒ	ussie	ˈʌsi	ˈæsi
candidates	ˈkændɪdəts	ˈkʌndɪdəts	other	ˈʌðə	ˈæðə
casual	ˈkæʒjʊəl	ˈkʌʒjʊəl	bunch	bʌntʃ	bæntʃ
classic	ˈklæsɪk	ˈklʌsɪk	comfortable	ˈkʌmfətəbl	ˈkæmfətəbl
family	ˈfæmɪli	ˈfʌmɪli	country	ˈkʌntri	ˈkæntri
fat	fæt	fʌt	couple	ˈkʌpl	ˈkæpl
gaffer	ˈgæfə	ˈgʌfə	current	ˈkʌrənt	ˈkærənt
Lasso	ˈlæsəʊ	ˈlʌsəʊ	club	klʌb	klæb
landing	ˈlændɪŋ	ˈlʌndɪŋ	fucking	ˈfʌkɪŋ	ˈfækɪŋ
man	mæn	mʌn	husband	ˈhʌzbənd	ˈhæzbənd
manager	ˈmænɪdʒə	ˈmʌnɪdʒə	jump	ˈdʒʌmp	ˈdʒæmp

/æ/-words			/ʌ/-words		
Orthography	IPA	/ʌ/-nonword	Orthography	IPA	/æ/-nonword
manners	ˈmænəz	ˈmʌnəz	jungle	ˈdʒʌŋgl	ˈdʒæŋgl
national	ˈnæʃənl	ˈnʌʃənl	love	lʌv	læv
perhaps	pəˈhæps	pəˈhʌps	number	ˈnʌmbə	ˈnæmbə
practice	ˈpræktɪs	ˈprʌktɪs	nothing	ˈnʌθɪŋ	ˈnæθɪŋ
salad	ˈsæləd	ˈsʌləd	nuts	nʌts	næts
thank	θæŋk	θʌŋk	one	wʌn	wæn
understand	ʌndəˈstænd	ʌndəˈstʌnd	something	ˈsʌmθɪŋ	ˈsæmθɪŋ
waxed	wækst	wʌkst	touch	tʌtʃ	tætʃ

The role of language aptitude in learning L2 constructions from captioned and uncaptioned audiovisual input

Anastasia Pattemore,[1] Maria del Mar Suárez,[2]
Maribel Montero Perez[3] & Carmen Muñoz[2]
[1] University of Groningen | [2] Universitat de Barcelona | [3] Ghent University

This chapter discusses the effects of aptitude on learning L2 grammatical constructions from TV series with or without captions. Study 1 involved 69 Catalan/Spanish learners of English (EFL) who watched ten episodes of an English TV series, and targeted grammatical constructions learning. Study 2 comprised 30 Flemish learners of Spanish (ELE) who watched two excerpts from a Spanish TV series episode, with auditory grammaticality judgement pretest-posttest to assess their learning of subjunctive constructions. Grammatical sensitivity and inference aptitude was measured using LLAMA F in both studies. Results revealed that groups without captions relied more on aptitude to handle the demanding processing of fast-paced TV series. Successful processing of uncaptioned input appeared to require higher aptitude, whereas captions attenuated the effects of individual differences.

1. Introduction

Given the increasing evidence supporting the effectiveness of audiovisual input, such as TV series and films in viewers' second (L2) or foreign language (FL) development, it is essential to consider the factors that might promote or hinder L2 gains from this type of input. For instance, previous research suggests that captioned audiovisual content (with on-screen text in the same language of the audio) is more beneficial over uncaptioned input for improving vocabulary, grammar, and content comprehension (see Montero Perez, 2022). However, the availability of on-screen text is not the only factor that can positively affect learning. Individual factors such as viewer's proficiency (e.g. Suárez & Gesa, 2019),

https://doi.org/10.1075/lllt.61.08pat

working memory (e.g. Montero Perez, 2020), and beliefs (e.g. Pattemore et al., 2024) might influence learning from audiovisual input, too.

This chapter explores the role of language aptitude – a talent for language learning and one of the cognitive individual differences frequently discussed in second language acquisition (SLA) research (Wen, 2021) – in L2 learning from captioned and uncaptioned audiovisual input, with a focus on grammatical constructions uptake.

In this study we assign a central role to language aptitude, delving deeply into its potential effects on learning L2 grammatical constructions from TV series. To do so, we consolidate and discuss findings from two separate yet interconnected studies that implemented TV series interventions for L2 English (Study 1) and L2 Spanish (Study 2), either with or without captions.

2.   Literature review

2.1   Foreign language learning aptitude

Language learning aptitude is a specific talent or a set of abilities that predicts the capacity, readiness, rate, and speed of language acquisition (Wen, 2021). Consequently, there has been extensive research in SLA on the roles of language aptitude and learning outcomes. Carroll (1990) proposed four aptitude constructs that could be tested in the Modern Language Aptitude Test (MLAT): phonemic coding ability, grammatical sensitivity, inductive language learning ability, and associative memory. Similarly, this componential framework of language aptitude was later adopted in the LLAMA tests (Meara, 2005) that assess four constructs: the ability to learn new words (LLAMA B), the ability to recognise words in the auditory input (LLAMA D), the ability to make a connection between sounds and symbols (LLAMA E), and the ability to learn new grammar rules (LLAMA F) (Meara & Rodgers, 2019).

Drawing on the previous research on the effects of aptitude on language gains, one of the most frequently studied language feature is grammar (followed by pronunciation and vocabulary, Li, 2015). This is not surprising as one of the sub-components of the FL aptitude is language analytic ability. A meta-analysis of 33 studies on the role of aptitude on grammar gains (Li, 2015) discovered that aptitude scores were moderately associated with grammar learning. The results also unveiled that this positive effect was not universal. For instance, FL aptitude was more likely to predict the rate of acquisition at the beginner rather than higher proficiency levels. This aligns with Carroll's (1981) traditional concept of aptitude as a learner trait implicated in the initial stages of learning (originally termed 'initial readiness for language learning'), suggesting that other type of abilities may be more sensitive to advanced learning (see Li, 2019). Despite limited primary research on the influence of proficiency level on aptitude-learning associations (Li, 2019), the results of some studies seem to indicate this trend. For example, Winke (2013) found that FL aptitude was not particularly crucial for the overall language skills of advanced learners of Chinese, suggesting that language aptitude may play a more significant role with lower-proficiency learners. Indeed, several studies have confirmed the strong influence of aptitude in young school learners with a beginner proficiency level (Muñoz, 2014; Muñoz & Tragant, 2023; Suárez & Muñoz, 2011). Therefore, it is reasonable to predict that the learning process of lower proficiency learners would be more significantly impacted by language aptitude. Considering previous findings (see meta-analysis and systematic review by Li, 2015, 2019) on the impact of language aptitude on grammar learning, it may be suggested that these findings extend to the processing and learning of grammatical constructions from audiovisual input.

2.2   Aptitude effects on learning from audiovisual input

Research on audiovisual input that has taken language aptitude into account is limited, with only one study, to our knowledge, focusing on grammatical constructions (Pattemore & Muñoz, 2020), while others explored the effect of language aptitude on learning vocabulary or on enhancing comprehension from audiovisual materials.

Suárez and Gesa (2019) examined vocabulary learning of upper-intermediate level undergraduate students watching eight captioned episodes of a TV series (approximately 24 minutes per episode). The authors found that language aptitude, as measured by the LLAMA total score, did not explain the students' gains in word forms, but it had a significant impact on their meaning recall of the target words. The researchers suggested that students only drew on their aptitude to learn the word meanings because it can be considered a more challenging task that requires more cognitive effort than learning word forms.

A similar finding on the facilitative effect of cognitive individual differences was reported by Casulleras (2023) and Casulleras and Miralpeix (Chapter 1, this volume). The results of the study revealed a significant correlation between aptitude, as assessed by the LLAMA B, and word form recognition. Notably, this correlation was observed exclusively within the L1 subtitles group, where the task of word form recognition might have posed a greater challenge due to the absence of on-screen English words. Consequently, participants in the L1 subtitles group had to rely more heavily on their language aptitude than those in the L2 captions group.

Muñoz et al. (2022) explored the effects of language learning aptitude, measured by LLAMA D, which tests the ability to recognise patterns in spoken language, on vocabulary learning. Upper-intermediate L2 level undergraduate participants watched one captioned episode of a TV series (about 21 minutes) twice. It was found that the participants with higher aptitude scores performed better in the meaning recognition test, but there was no effect of aptitude on meaning recall. The latter finding, with LLAMA D, contrasts with the significant correlation with meaning recall found in the study by Suárez and Gesa (2019) above, with the LLAMA total score; using different LLAMA sub-tests in the analysis might explain the difference in findings observed.

Higher aptitude as measured by LLAMA B was also determinant in making written form-meaning connections after watching a 3-minute-long TV commercial with English audio and Polish subtitles (Miralpeix et al., 2023). This was especially the case of the more challenging words that received less than 50% correct answers, while frequency of appearance was not crucial for learning after such minimal exposure to completely unknown input.

Another study on aptitude and vocabulary (Teng, 2022) found a significant effect of aptitude on vocabulary gains but unfortunately did not examine the interaction with the presence or absence of captions. Undergraduate intermediate English proficiency students watched a 51-minute documentary with or without captions. The results suggested that the LLAMA total score had a significant effect on receptive and productive vocabulary learning, as measured by four different tests on form and meaning recognition, and form and meaning recall. While the captioned group outperformed the uncaptioned group in the posttests, the results for the effects of aptitude are not transparent as there was no interaction included in the analysis between the viewing group (captions or no captions) and aptitude scores.

The only study on learning grammatical constructions from captioned and uncaptioned audiovisual input that incorporated language aptitude (Pattemore & Muñoz, 2020) found no effects of it. That study also explored the effects of another cognitive factor, working memory capacity, which had a stronger effect on the posttest scores than aptitude, likely attenuating the influence of language aptitude. The results showed that participants in the uncaptioned group relied on their working memory more than those in the captioned group, which suggested that captions had neutralising effects on the limits of working memory capacity. However, interaction between aptitude and proficiency level was not the focus of the study, so the issue of whether aptitude was more strongly associated with outcomes among the lower-level participants remains inconclusive.

The results of the previous research on the effects of aptitude on learning from audiovisual input are mixed, and so far, no studies have looked into the interaction between the viewing mode and aptitude, especially for grammar uptake. Given that language aptitude influences grammar learning in traditional learning contexts (e.g., Li, 2015), it could be assumed that the same will apply to learning from audiovisual input. It is also expected that the addition of captions will facilitate processing and lead to higher gains (e.g., Pattemore & Muñoz, 2020). This study, therefore, aims to fill this gap by analysing learning of L2 grammar constructions from captioned and uncaptioned TV series through the aptitude perspective. More specifically, the present study consists of two independent, but interrelated studies exploring the effects of aptitude on learning two different languages (L2 English and L2 Spanish) from captioned and uncaptioned audiovisual input.

The following research question is addressed: To what extent is learning target constructions through audiovisual input affected by language learning aptitude and viewing mode?

3.   Methodology

3.1   Study 1

3.1.1   *Participants*

Sixty-nine 17-to 32-year old Catalan/Spanish bilingual L2 English students participated in the study. They were following an audiovisual communication undergraduate degree at the University of Barcelona, in Spain. The participants attended one of two intact obligatory classes on Oral and Written Communication in English that were randomly assigned to a captions ($n=39$) and no captions ($n=30$) condition. Participants' proficiency levels measured with the Oxford Placement Test (Allan, 2004) varied from A1 to C2 according to the Common European Framework of Reference for Languages (CEFR, Council of Europe, 2020), with a mean of B2 upper-intermediate level.

3.1.2   *Target audiovisual input and grammatical constructions*

The first ten episodes of the first season of *The Good Place* TV-series (Schur, 2016) were used for the intervention (227 minutes). This comedy TV-show introduces an alternative afterlife and shows how a person who does not belong in heaven learns her way around being a good person. We chose this show as it was not broadcast on Spanish TV and was unfamiliar to the participants (as was confirmed by the background questionnaire). In addition, the content of the TV-series was appropriate for classroom use as it excluded excessive swearing, nudity, and violence. The lexical profile of the ten episodes included 89% of words from the first 1000 words band, and 95% of words fell within the 3000 words band (Text Range, Cobb, n.d.).

On the basis of the ten episodes scripts, 27 frequently occurring grammatical constructions were selected (see Table 1). These constructions belonged to fully-filled constructions (e.g., *figure out*) that always appeared in the same form, partially filled constructions (e.g., *to be allowed to*) that had some variability in their presentation in the input, and fully-schematic constructions (e.g. reported speech) that could vary in their form upon each presentation in the input.

Table 1. Study 1 target constructions with frequency of occurrence

Construction form	Examples from *The Good Place*	Frequency
do for a living	What did you *do for a living*?	3
let you down	I won't *let you down*	3
N[irregular plural]	There are *shrimp* flying around	5
big deal	No *big deal*	6
say no more	*Say no more*	3
figure out	To *figure out* what's going wrong	15
to be[tense] allowed to V	I'*m not allowed to* tell you about	3
would rather V	I'*d rather* not *let* people see it	3
break[tense] DET promise	You *broke your promise*	3
the Xer the Yer	*The more* you practice, *the more* you improve	4
used to V	I *used to* just throw them in the sink	7
PRON just want[tense] to	*I just want to* be an academic	9
let's V, shall we?	So let's chat, *shall we?*	3
why don't PRON	*Why don't you* go ahead?	12
to be[tense] supposed to V	You *were supposed to* be there	18
subj belong[tense] here	You don't *belong here*	18
let's V	*Let's* move on	54
passive present continuous (subj aux VP)	Her memory's still *being rebooted*	3
future continuous (subj aux V-ing)	Later this evening, we *will be enjoying*	3
subjunctive (subj V that PRO V)	You *wish* that you *were* related	4

Table 1. *(continued)*

Construction form	Examples from *The Good Place*	Frequency
V[negative] either	You're not supposed to be here *either*?	5
passive present perfect (subj aux VP)	It *has been proven*	3
reported speech (reporting V (that) V)	Tahani *said* that you *helped* Michael	6
catenative V obj infinitive (sub V PRO to V)	You *need me to* lie	17
catenative V obj bare infinitive (let PRO V)	Should I *let her stay*?	20
future in the past (subj V[past] V)	I thought transition *would* be easier	14
emphasis (do[tense] V)	That *does* sound like me	25

3.1.3 *Language tests*

To measure the target constructions uptake, we designed a test that included productive grammar test items such as sentence transformation, fill-in-the-gap, and complete the gap with the correct form of a given word. This format was familiar to the participants as it is similar to the First Certificate Exam (Cambridge English, n.d.). Two test items per target construction were created with a total of 54 items, and both pretest and posttest consisted of the same items in randomised order. The test was scored dichotomously. A sample of the test items is presented in Figure 1. The test items were piloted with a similar group of language learners ($n = 15$) and some changes in wording were made before the test was used for the study. Cronbach's alpha showed that both the pretest ($\alpha = 0.879$) and the posttest ($\alpha = 0.835$) reached a good level of internal consistency.

The Oxford Placement Test (OPT, Allan, 2004) was administered to measure participants' English proficiency level. The test comprises two parts: Listening and Grammar, with a total score of 200 that can be converted to CEFR proficiency levels.

3.1.4 *Language aptitude test*

Given the grammatical focus of this study, language learning aptitude was assessed using LLAMA F (version 1, Meara, 2005). This aptitude test measures the analytical ability to infer and learn grammatical structures of an unknown language. LLAMA F is a computer-based, open-source, language-independent, and automatically scored measurement of aptitude. Participants have five minutes to learn the rules of a new language, followed by a testing phase. Note-taking was not permitted (see Rogers et al., 2017).

I.   Sentence transformation exercise:
     Complete each sentence with **two to five words,** *including the word in bold*
     I hate it when people ask me what my job is because I am unemployed.
     FOR I hate it when people ask me what_____because I am
     unemployed.

II. Complete the gap with a correct form of a given word exercise:
     Complete the sentences using a form of the words in brackets
     _____ (cold) it got, _____ (many) clothes they had to put on to keep
     warm.

III. Fill-the-gap exercise:
     Complete the gaps with the appropriate word:
     Let's go to the theater, _____ we?

Figure 1. Study 1 example of test items with instructions

3.1.5   *Procedure*

The viewing intervention was fully integrated into the class syllabus, and participants received points for completing the intervention-related activities. Two
weeks before starting the viewing sessions, participants filled out a background
questionnaire, completed the OPT, pretest, and LLAMA F. Subsequently, they
watched two episodes of the TV series (22 minutes per episode) per week in the
classroom. After each episode, participants answered comprehension questions to
maintain engagement with the series. This procedure continued for five weeks,
covering ten episodes. The week following the final episode, participants completed the posttest.

3.2   Study 2

3.2.1   *Participants*

The initial pool of participants for this study comprised 60 students. However, we
encountered significant data loss due to cancelled classes during the COVID-19
pandemic. As a result, the final sample consisted of 30 L1 Dutch learners of Spanish as a Foreign Language (ELE), randomly assigned to the captions group ($n = 15$)
and the no captions group ($n = 15$). These participants were second-year 19- to- 21-
year old Applied Linguistics undergraduate students at the University of Ghent in
Belgium, enrolled in a low-intermediate proficiency level Spanish course as part
of their degree. Their mean Spanish vocabulary size (Izura et al., 2014, see below)

was assessed at 20/60 (33%), roughly corresponding to a pre-intermediate level. For context, a typical beginner learner scores 12/60 (20%), while a native speaker scores 54/60 (90%).

3.2.2 *Target audiovisual input and grammatical constructions*

The Spanish TV series *Gran Hotel* (Neira & Campos, 2011) was selected for the study as it was not broadcast on Flemish TV, and therefore was unlikely to have been watched by the participants in any language. To further assure that the students had not watched the target TV series, the background questionnaire included a question about their familiarity with this series. None of the participants reported watching *Gran Hotel* before. The plot of this historical drama is about a family that owns a hotel and tries to keep its secrets away from strangers. The participants watched the first episode of the show (1 hour 11 minutes). Given that the episodes of this TV series are long, we decided to divide the episode into two parts (34 minutes and 45 seconds and 37 minutes and 39 seconds) to avoid a possible fatigue of viewing in a foreign language for too long. The episode was divided at a logical place without affecting the flow of the scenes. The lexical coverage of the episode was 85% within the most frequent 1000 words band, and 93% within the most frequent 3000 words band (MultilingProfiler, Finlayson et al., 2022).

The target grammatical constructions for this study were present forms of Spanish subjunctive mood. This grammar structure is considered as one of the most challenging for L2 Spanish learners (Collentine, 2013). In addition, it is absent in the participants' L1 (Dutch), and at the time of the intervention the participants were not receiving any formal instruction on Spanish subjunctive mood, but they were going to be introduced to it in the following month. Therefore, this target grammatical structure was perceived as unfamiliar yet within the participants' appropriate level of language learning.

Upon analysing the script of the target episode, 19 subjunctive structures were identified and were divided into ten types of subjunctive constructions (following the classifications in Alonso Raya et al., 2011, pp. 167–182). They included subjunctive mode for doubting the information, expressing wishes, evaluating the information, requests and orders, something not identified, negative imperative, and prepositional phrases that are followed by subjunctive mode (*antes de que, hasta que, para que, de que*). The examples of the target structures and their frequency of occurrence in the TV series episode are presented in Table 2.

Table 2. Target types of subjunctive mode

Subjunctive type	Example from the TV series	TV episode frequency
Doubting information	Dudo que suceda pronto.	5
Expressing wishes	Espero que todo salga bien.	16
Evaluating the information	No me alegro de que se haya ido.	12
Requests and orders	He ordenado que la envíen.	15
Something not identified	A un lugar donde me respeten.	3
Negative imperative	¡No lo hagas!	13
Antes de que	Antes de que se marche.	2
Hasta que	Hasta que me lo devuelvas.	3
Para que	Es un buen momento para que te comprometas.	6
De que	Es hora de que me retire.	4

3.2.3 *Language tests*

An auditory Grammaticality Judgement Test (GJT) was developed to assess the knowledge of the target grammatical construction. The test measured participants' ability to differentiate between grammatically correct and incorrect sentences and phrases. We chose an auditory format for the test, addressing concerns raised in audiovisual input research about test modalities that might favor captioning conditions (see Montero Perez, 2022). Since both groups were exposed to audio input, with only the captions group viewing with on-screen text, we opted for an auditory version of the GJT for both viewing groups.

To design the test, we created test items for the 19 target structures in two versions: correct and incorrect (38 test items). The pretest included 16 distractors designed to divert participants' attention from the subjunctive mood, present in both correct and incorrect forms (32 test items). Distractors featured grammatical constructions familiar to participants at their proficiency level (e.g. present and past tenses of the indicative mode). The pretest comprised four practice items and a total of 70 test items, while the postest contained four practice items and 38 test items, excluding distractors as the need to divert attention from the target items was no longer present. Test items in the pretest and posttest were the same, but were presented in a different order in the pretest-posttest for randomisation purposes. The pretest and posttest were scored dichotomously per each test item with a maximum cumulative test score of 38. Cronbach's alpha showed that both the pretest ($\alpha = 0.885$) and the posttest ($\alpha = 0.873$) reached a good level of internal consistency.

A female native Spanish speaker recorded the test items. The test, presented as an audio recording file, was played in the same version to all the participants (with distinct versions for the pretest and posttest). Participants listened to target items one by one twice with 3-second intervals, and the same interval was maintained between test items. The test, including a short 30-second break to prevent fatigue, lasted 17 minutes. Participants were required to determine whether the heard phrase was grammatically correct or incorrect; to discourage guessing, they also had the option to choose the "I do not know" option (see Figure 2; the italicised text was presented audibly; the test items were not provided in written form). The GJT was piloted with Spanish language learners of similar proficiency ($n=10$) to check the pace and the clarity of the audio before it was used for the intervention.

Instrucciones: Vas a escuchar 70 frases en español, tienes que decidir si las frases son gramaticalmente correctas o no (puedes elegir "no lo sé" si tienes dudas).
Primero hacemos una práctica de cuatro frases.

	Correcto	Incorrecto	No lo sé
Práctica			
1. *Es un chico.*			
2. *¿Qué tiempo hace hoy?*			
3. *Es una chico.*			
4. *¿Qué tiempo es hoy?*			
Prueba			
1. *Me alegro que has aprobado el examen.*			
2. *Me alegro que hayas aprobado el examen.*			
3. *Necesito que me ayudes.*			
4. *Necesito que me ayudas.*			

Figure 2. Example of the GJT instructions, items, and answer sheet

To measure Spanish vocabulary size, we used Lextale-Esp (Izura et al., 2014). To complete the test, the participants are presented with a 90-item list of existing and non-existing Spanish words and they have to decide whether they know these words or not. Test-takers are advised to choose a "no" option if they are not sure about a particular word to avoid guessing. In addition, if guessing occurs, then the score can be penalised as positive answers regarding the non-words would count as double negative. We scored the final scores manually following test creators' guidelines (vocabulary size score = number of words identified as known – 2*number of non-words identified as known).[1]

3.2.4 *Language aptitude test*

Similar to Study 1, we used LLAMA F to measure participants' grammatical inference ability. However, at the time of the data collection the LLAMA F version had been updated, and we used the newest available version (Version 3, Meara & Rodgers, 2019). The noticeable differences between the two versions are the number of test items (20 items in version 1 and 10 items in version 3), the learning phase time (five minutes in version 1 and four minutes in version 3), and the maximum score (100 in version 1 and 20 in version 3). Despite having used two different versions, for the purposes of this study, this is not a problem since we are not comparing aptitude scores across studies.

3.2.5 *Procedure*

Three weeks before the viewing, the participants received the information about the study, signed the consent forms, filled out background questionnaires, and completed the GJT pretest and the Spanish vocabulary size test in the classroom. Then, all participants received individual links to view the episodes at home (episode 1 part 1 and episode 1 part 2). The participants viewed the episodes with or without captions, depending on their experimental group. They were given three days to watch the first part of the episode, and then they received the second link to watch the second part of the episode. The episodes were viewed through the EdPuzzle platform (Sabrià, 2013) that can track the viewing progress and include comprehension questions at the end of the episodes to ensure the participants watched the episodes attentively. The week after viewing the two parts of the episode, the participants completed the GJT posttest and LLAMA F during their usual class time.

---

1. Test developers do not offer specific guidelines for interpreting scores and their corresponding CEFR proficiency levels. However, given that all participants underwent pre-course language proficiency tests and followed the same language course, the vocabulary size test results serve solely to assess comparability between intervention groups.

4. Results

4.1 Preliminary data analysis

The data analysis was conducted in JASP software (2024). For d values, the effect sizes were considered as small ($d=.40$), medium ($d=.70$), or large ($d=1.00$) following Plonsky and Oswald (2014). For partial eta square (ηp^2), the effect sizes were considered as small ($\eta p^2=.01$), medium ($\eta p^2=.06$), or large ($\eta p^2=.14$) following Cohen (1988).

First, to measure overall learning from the intervention, we ran a series of paired-samples t-tests that indicated a significant increase in the participants' posttest scores compared to the pretest in both Study 1 ($t(68)=-11.866$, $p<.001$, $d=-1.428$), and Study 2 ($t(29)=-4.409$, $p<.001$, $d=.805$). Table 3 shows the progression of mean scores before and after the interventions. Second, to ensure the comparability of the two viewing groups in both studies at pretest, a series of independent samples t-tests were run with the participant's proficiency scores (Table 4) as a dependent variable (OPT for Study 1 and Lextale-Esp for Study 2), and viewing group (captions or no captions) as an independent variable. The analysis showed no significant differences between the viewing groups in terms of proficiency for either of the studies; Study 1: $t(67)=.547$, $p=.586$, $d=.133$; Study 2: $t(27)=.235$, $p=.816$, $d=.372$.

Table 3. Pretest-posttest descriptive statistics for both studies

	Group	n	Test	Mean (SD)	Range
Study 1	Captions	39	Pretest	23.61 (11.52)	5–45
			Posttest	32.12 (10.99)	12–49
	No captions	30	Pretest	23.06 (11.77)	2–45
			Posttest	30.06 (13.18)	6–51
	Both groups	69	Pretest	23.81 (11.55)	2–45
			Posttest	31.23 (11.94)	6–51
Study 2	Captions	15	Pretest	20.12 (7.94)	7–32
			Posttest	23.20 (8.13)	7–34
	No captions	15	Pretest	20.13 (7.28)	9–34
			Posttest	24.86 (6.89)	12–35
	Both groups	30	Pretest	20.13 (7.49)	7–34
			Posttest	24.03 (7.45)	7–35

The same procedure was applied to check the comparability of the two viewing groups in terms of language aptitude scores. The distribution of language aptitude scores was similar between the captions and no captions groups in both Study 1 ($t(67) = 1.422$, $p = .160$, $d = .345$) and Study 2 ($t(28) = .416$, $p = .681$, $d = .154$).

Table 4. Proficiency scores

	Group	n	Mean (*SD*)	Range
Study 1	Captions	39	140.85 (21.20)	92–178
	No captions	30	137.87 (23.96)	94–183
	Both groups	69	139.55 (22.32)	92–183
Study 2	Captions	15	20.66 (3.69)	12–25
	No captions	15	20.21 (6.41)	6–30
	Both groups	30	20.44 (5.09)	6–30

Note. Study 1 OPT scores max = 200; Study 2 Lextale-Esp max = 60 per viewing group

However, further data exploration for both studies showed that LLAMA F scores were not linear, and therefore they were recoded with a median split into lower and higher aptitude groups (Table 5). In addition, division of scores into lower and higher score groups allowed us to tackle the issue of having different maximum scores for the two versions of LLAMA F used in this paper (see above); for comparability purposes, scores are also shown as percentages in Table 5.

Table 5. LLAMA F scores

	Group	Aptitude group	n	Mean (*SD*)	% score	Range
Study 1	Captions	All	39	56.92 (22.49)	56%	0–90
		Lower	17	37.06 (17.23)	37%	0–50
		Higher	22	72.27 (11.09)	72%	60–90
	No captions	All	30	47.50 (28.10)	47%	0–100
		Lower	18	30.56 (23.12)	30%	0–100
		Higher	12	74.17 (15.64)	74%	60–100
	Both groups	All	69	52.99 (25.22)	52%	0–100
		Lower	35	33.71 (20.44)	33%	0–50
		Higher	34	72.94 (12.68)	72%	60–100
Study 2	Captions	All	15	9.60 (3.79)	48%	5–17
		Lower	8	6.75 (1.03)	33%	5–8
		Higher	7	12.85 (3.02)	64%	9–17

Table 5. *(continued)*

Group	Aptitude group	n	Mean (SD)	% score	Range
No captions	All	15	9.00 (3.98)	45%	2–17
	Lower	6	5.33 (1.86)	26%	2–7
	Higher	9	11.75 (2.60)	58%	9–17
Both groups	All	30	9.31 (3.82)	46%	2–17
	Lower	14	6.14 (1.56)	30%	2–8
	Higher	16	12.26 (2.74)	61%	9–17

Note. Study 1 LLAMA F Version 1, max = 100; Study 2 LLAMA F Version 3, max = 20 divided into sub-groups with a median split.

4.2   Study 1

To answer the research question of this study, we fitted a series of general linear models (GLMs). The GLMs included the posttest scores as a dependent variable, LLAMA F aptitude group (lower or higher) and group (captions, no captions) as fixed factors, and the pretest scores as a covariate. The first GLM did not return a significant main effect in the model for either LLAMA F nor the interaction between the viewing and aptitude groups ($p > .05$). Although the effects of aptitude were found to be non-significant in the first model, we had predicted based on previous research (see above) that aptitude may be a more significant factor for lower-proficiency learners than for advanced learners. Therefore, we recoded proficiency scores into three different groups following the OPT scoring procedure. The three groups were distributed according to the CEFR proficiency scale: elementary (A1–A2), intermediate (B1–B2), and advanced (C1–C2); see Table 6 for descriptive statistics per proficiency group. Due to the small sample size of the elementary proficiency sub-group ($n = 14$), we also included scores of the intermediate level participants ($n = 32$) in the second model ($N = 46$), from which the advanced level participants were excluded.

To test the hypothesis that aptitude is a significant predictor of language uptake for lower rather than higher proficiency level learners, the second model included the posttest scores of elementary and intermediate proficiency participants as a dependent variable, LLAMA F aptitude group (lower or higher), group (captions, no captions) as factors, and the pretest scores as a covariate. The results showed a significant effect of viewing group ($F(1, 45) = 4.181$, $p = .047$, $\eta p2 = .093$), along with a moderate effect of LLAMA F on the posttest scores ($F(1, 45) = 3.405$, $p = .072$, $\eta p2 = .077$), with a significant interaction between the LLAMA F group and the viewing group ($F(1, 45) = 5.913$, $p = .019$, $\eta p2 = .126$).

Table 6. Study 1 scores per proficiency group

	n	Proficiency score (Max: 200)			Pretest score (Max: 54)			Posttest score (Max: 54)		
		Mean (SD)	Min.	Max.	Mean (SD)	Min.	Max.	Mean (SD)	Min.	Max.
A1–A2	14	107.71 (8.48)	92	118	10.71 (5.69)	2	20	15.57 (6.02)	6	28
B1–B2	32	136.16 (9.42)	120	149	21.16 (8.41)	7	35	30.44 (9.01)	12	44
C1–C2	23	163.65 (10.21)	150	183	35.48 (5.63)	28	45	41.87 (5.45)	31	51

The between viewing groups Bonferroni post-hoc analysis of the interaction revealed that there was no significant difference between the participants with higher LLAMA F (Mean Difference = −0.582, SE = 2.289, p > .05, d = −.111), but there was a significant effect of viewing group for the participants with lower LLAMA F (Mean Difference = 6.988, SE = 2.124, p = .012, d = 1.336), with the captions group outperforming the no captions group. As for the within groups comparison, there was no significant difference between the lower and higher aptitude group in the captions condition (Mean Difference = −0.896, SE = 2.123, p > .05, d = −.171), but there was a significant difference between the lower and higher aptitude groups in the no captions condition (Means difference = 6.674, SE = 2.289, p = .034, d = 1.276). The estimated marginal means are presented in Table 7 and the results of the interaction are summarised in Figure 3.

Table 7. Study 1 estimated marginal means (posttest) per aptitude group

Group	Aptitude group	n	Mean (SE)	95% CI
Captions	Lower	17	27.86 (1.41)	[25.01; 30.72]
	Higher	22	26.97 (1.57)	[17.69; 24.06]
No captions	Lower	18	20.87 (1.57)	[17.69; 24.06]
	Higher	12	27.55 (1.66)	[24.19; 30.91]

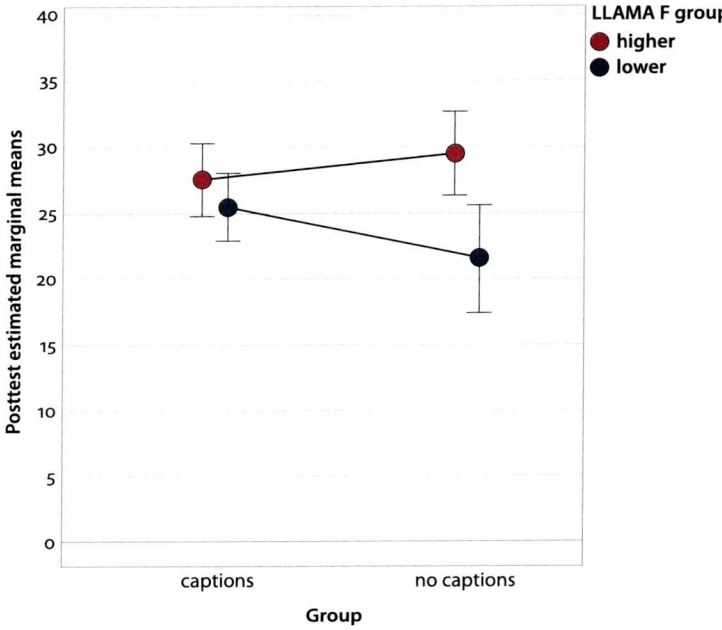

Figure 3. Study 1 interaction between the viewing and aptitude groups

4.3   Study 2

The same analysis as in Study 1 (see above) was performed on the data in Study 2. A series of GLMs with the posttest scores as outcome variable, group (captions or no captions), and LLAMA F group (lower or higher) as factors, and pretest scores as a covariate were included in the model. The model returned non-significant effects of viewing group ($F_{(1, 25)} = 0.531$, $p = .473$, $\eta p^2 = .021$) and aptitude group ($F_{(25, 1)} = 1.590$, $p = .219$, $\eta p^2 = .060$), but a significant interaction between the viewing and aptitude groups ($F_{(1, 25)} = 5.185$, $p = .032$, $\eta p^2 = .172$). The Bonferroni post-hoc analysis revealed (only) one significant pairwise comparison between higher and lower aptitude in the no captions group (Mean Difference = 5.636, $SE = 2.269$, $p = .032$, $d = 1.311$). The estimated marginal means for this interaction are presented in Table 8, and the results are summarised in Figure 4.

Table 8. Study 2 estimated marginal means (posttest) per aptitude group

Group	Aptitude group	n	Mean (SE)	95% CI
Captions	Lower	8	23.96 (1.62)	[20.82; 27.09]
	Higher	7	22.33 (1.52)	[18.97; 25.68]
No captions	Lower	6	21.48 (1.75)	[17.68; 25.10]
	Higher	9	27.12 (1.43)	[24.16; 30.07]

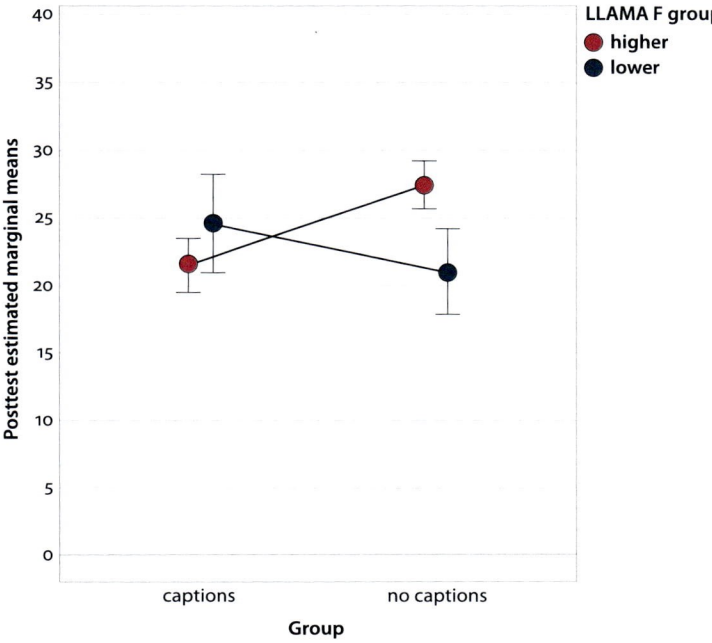

Figure 4. Study 2 interaction between the viewing and aptitude groups

5. Discussion

In this chapter we aimed to explore the effects of language aptitude, measured by LLAMA F (grammatical inference ability), on learning L2 grammatical constructions from captioned and uncaptioned TV series. The results of the two studies revealed a significant interaction between the viewing condition (captions or no captions) and language learning aptitude (lower or higher). Participants in the no captions group achieved significantly higher posttest scores when they had higher language learning aptitude, whereas aptitude did not impact scores for participants in the captions group. Despite the studies being separate, each focusing on learning grammatical constructions in different languages (English and Spanish) and using different TV series for interventions, we synthesise and discuss the findings together. The two studies aimed to answer the same research question, followed a similar pretest-posttest intervention design, and obtained matching findings, thus echoing and reinforcing each other.

The first interesting finding is the facilitative effect of aptitude on lower proficiency levels rather than more advanced learners which is in line with previous aptitude research (e.g. Li, 2015, 2019; Winke, 2013). It seems that earlier audiovisual input studies reporting no effects of aptitude on learning could at least partially be explained by the inclusion of advanced learners (e.g., Pattemore & Muñoz, 2020). The first model in Study 1 showed no effect of language aptitude on posttest scores; however, once we removed the advanced proficiency group scores and analysed only elementary and intermediate groups, a moderate effect of aptitude was uncovered. This finding is consistent with Winke (2013) who proposed that learners with advanced proficiency levels rely less on their language learning aptitude. Interestingly, the results of Study 2, which included lower proficiency participants, echoed the findings of Study 1 with a different pool of participants and a different target language. These results also align with previous research (Muñoz et al., 2022; Suárez & Gesa, 2019; Teng, 2022), where intermediate level learners with higher language learning aptitude scored higher on vocabulary posttests. It can be suggested that advanced learners do not need to rely on their language aptitude while processing audiovisual input, while those at elementary and intermediate levels depend on it more, especially when watching without captions. This is due to the higher processing demands compared to viewing with captions (Pattemore & Muñoz, 2020) as the viewers do not have an opportunity to revisit language content if they were unable to fully process the audio (Mayer et al., 2020).

The second notable contribution of this paper is the finding that captions mitigate differences in language aptitude. This conclusion is based on a significant interaction between LLAMA F group (lower and higher), and the viewing group (captions and no captions) in both Study 1 and Study 2. Participants with higher language aptitude outperformed those with lower aptitude in the no captions group, while there was no difference between the aptitude groups in the captions group. This result indicates that the no captions group relied significantly more on their language aptitude than the captions group. Therefore, not only do captions neutralise variability in working memory (Pattemore & Muñoz, 2020), but they also extend their advantage to those elementary and intermediate level learners who have lower grammatical inference ability. The finding that language aptitude facilitates learning in a more challenging condition (uncaptioned input in this study) aligns well with previous vocabulary research on audiovisual input (Casulleras, 2023; Suárez & Gesa, 2019). In Suárez and Gesa (2019), aptitude was activated when learning word meanings rather than word forms, as form-meaning pairing may have required greater cognitive involvement. In Casulleras (2023), language aptitude had a significant effect when participants had to attend to multiple languages in the input (L2 audio and L1 subtitles), which might be a more challenging condition than L2 audio and L2 captions when learning word forms, especially for young learners (see Chapter 1 in this volume). In addition, our finding is also in line with other SLA studies on aptitude and grammar learning. For example, Yalçin and Spada (2016) found that their participants relied on grammar inferencing ability while processing a more difficult grammatical structure (passive) rather than a less complex one (past progressive). Similarly, we uncovered that those participants who did not have facilitative captions and encountered themselves in a more difficult condition had to turn to their "additional source of learning" (Yalçin & Spada, 2016), aptitude.

An intriguing result is the difference in learning gains between the two studies. In particular, in Study 1, we observe a significant advantage of the captions group over the no captions group in learning grammatical constructions, while in Study 2, there was no significant difference between the two viewing groups. This discrepancy in results could be explained in two ways. First, compared to the first study, the intervention of the second study did not involve prolonged viewing. It is possible that the positive effects of captioning take some time to become visible, as observed in Pattemore & Muñoz (2022), where the captions group did not outperform the no captions group in the first weeks of the intervention, as measured by the immediate post-viewing tests. Since Study 2 had only two viewing sessions (compared to ten viewings in Study 1), it is possible that longer viewing exposure was needed for the positive effect of captions to become evident. In fact, it has been claimed that the benefits of captioned viewing on grammar acquisition may need a longer period of exposure than on vocabulary acquisition (Kuppens, 2010; Matielo et al., 2015; Van Lommel et al., 2006). Alternatively, it is possible that the test modality (Mohd Jelani & Boers, 2018), written in Study 1 and auditory in Study 2, has contributed to conflicting results. However, this congruency effect has not consistently garnered support across research findings (Montero Perez, 2022; Sydorenko, 2010), and the captions group did receive auditory input similar to the no captions group. Future research should carefully consider this test modality limitation and investigate this issue in greater detail.

Another limitation to acknowledge is that we could not fully explore the interaction between language aptitude, proficiency level, and viewing group. In Study 1 this was due to the low number of participants in the elementary proficiency group ($n = 14$), while in Study 2 we had a small homogeneous pool of participants with a similar proficiency level. Future research should incorporate comparisons between proficiency groups to determine at what point in proficiency development language aptitude may play a lesser role in learning from audiovisual input.

6. Conclusion

The results of the two studies in this chapter provide additional evidence of captions levelling the playing field, as elementary and intermediate proficiency level (A1–B2) participants who watched without captions needed to rely on their aptitude more. Greater grammar inference ability, as measured by LLAMA F, appears to be required to process TV series without captions and uptake L2 grammatical constructions, particularly for elementary and intermediate proficiency levels. Therefore, our recommendation for teacher's use of videos in a classroom or for learner's out-of-school leisure viewing is to make captions available, as the results have demonstrated their ability to mitigate variability in cognitive individual differences and allow viewers to extract more value from the audiovisual input.

Acknowledgements

This study was supported by grant PID2019-110594GB-I00 from the Spanish Ministry of Science and Innovation, grant 2020FI_B2 00179 from the Catalan Agency for Management of University and Research Grants (AGAUR), and Montcelimar 2021 mobility grant from the University of Barcelona. We also thank Patrick Goethals for making it possible to collect data for Study 2, and the reviewers for their thoughtful remarks and suggestions.

Ethical considerations

The protocols of data collection, data anonymization, data processing, and data storage of the current study were approved by the Institutional Review Board of the University of Barcelona (IRB0003099) and of Ghent University (Approval: 2021-49).

References

Allan, D. (2004). *Oxford Placement Test 1*. Oxford University Press.

Alonso Raya, R., Castañeda Castro, A., Martínez Gila, P., Miquel López, L., Ortega Olivares, J., & Ruiz Campillo, J.P. (2011). *Gramática básica del estudiante de español*. Difusión.

Cambridge English. (n.d.). https://www.cambridgeenglish.org/exams-and-tests/first/

Carroll, J.B. (1981). Twenty-five years of research on foreign language aptitude. In K.C. Diller (Ed.), *Individual differences and universals in language learning aptitude* (pp. 83–118). Newbury House.

Carroll, J.B. (1990). Cognitive abilities in foreign language aptitude: Then and now. In T. Parry & C.W. Stansfield (Eds.), *Language aptitude reconsidered* (pp. 11–27). Englewood Cliffs.

Casulleras, M. (2023). Language learning from subtitled TV series in the primary EFL classroom (Unpublished doctoral dissertation). University of Barcelona. Retrieved on 28 May 2024 from http://hdl.handle.net/10803/688923

Cobb, T. Range for texts v.6 [computer program]. Retrieved on 28 May 2024 from https://www.lextutor.ca/cgi-bin/range/texts/

Cohen, J. (1988). *Statistical power analysis for the behavioral sciences* (2nd ed.). Lawrence Erlbaum Associates.

Collentine, J. (2013). Subjunctive in second language Spanish. In K. L. Geeslin (Ed.), *The handbook of Spanish second language acquisition* (pp. 270–286). Wiley Online Library.

Council of Europe (2020). *Common European Framework of Reference for Languages: Learning, teaching, assessment – Companion volume.* Council of Europe Publishing. Retrieved on 28 May 2024 from www.coe.int/lang-cefr

Finlayson, N., Marsden, E., & Anthony, L. (2022). *MultilingProfiler (Version 3) [Computer software].* University of York. Retrieved on 28 May 2024 https://www.multilingprofiler.net/

Izura, C., Cuetos, F., & Brysbaert, M. (2014). Lextale-Esp: A test to rapidly and efficiently assess the Spanish vocabulary size. *Psicologica, 35,* 49–66. Retrieved on 28 May 2024 https://psycnet.apa.org/record/2014-24635-003

JASP Team (2024). JASP (Version 0.18.3)[Computer software]. Retrieved on 28 May 2024 https://jasp-stats.org/

Kuppens, A. H. (2010). Incidental foreign language acquisition from media exposure. *Learning, Media and Technology, 35*(1), 65–85.

Li, S. (2015). The associations between language aptitude and second language grammar acquisition: A meta-analytic review of five decades of research. *Applied Linguistics, 36*(3), 385–408.

Li, S. (2019). Six decades of language aptitude research. In Z. Wen, P. Skehan, A. Biedroń, S. Li, & R. L. Sparks (Eds.), *Language aptitude: Advancing theory, testing, research and practice* (1st ed.). Routledge.

Matielo, R., D'Ely, R., & Baretta, L. (2015). The effects of interlingual and intralingual subtitles on second language learning/acquisition: A state-of-the-art review. *Trabalhos Em Lingüística Aplicada, 54,* 161–182.

Mayer, R. E., Fiorella, L. & Stull, A. (2020). Five ways to increase the effectiveness of instructional video. *Educational Technology Research and Development, 68,* 837–852.

Meara, P. M. (2005). *Llama language aptitude tests.* Lognostics.

Meara, P. M., & Rogers, V. E. (2019). *The LLAMA tests v3. LLAMA_F v3.0 grammar rules.* Lognostics.

Miralpeix, I., Gesa, F., & Suárez, M. M. (2023). Vocabulary learning from subtitled input after minimal exposure. In B. L. Reynolds (Ed.), *Vocabulary learning in the wild* (pp. 263–283). Springer.

Mohd Jelani, N. A., & Boers, F. (2018). Examining incidental vocabulary acquisition from captioned video: Does test modality matter? *ITL – International Journal of Applied Linguistics, 169*(1), 169–190.

Montero Perez, M. (2022). Second or foreign language learning through watching audio-visual input and the role of on-screen text. *Language Teaching, 55*(2), 163–192.

Muñoz, C. (2014). The association between aptitude components and language skills in young learners. In M. Pawlak & L. Aronin (Eds.), *Essential topics in applied linguistics and multilingualism* (pp. 51–68). Springer.

doi   Muñoz, C., Pattemore, A., & Avello, D. (2022). Exploring repeated captioning viewing as a way to promote vocabulary learning: Time lag between repetitions and learner factors. *Computer Assisted Language Learning*.

doi   Muñoz, C. & Tragant, E. (2023). English at the end of primary school. In E. Tragant & C. Muñoz, *Ten years of English language learning* (pp. 29–68). Palgrave.

Neira, G. R., & Campos, R. (Creators). (2011). *Gran Hotel*. [TV series]. Bambú Producciones.

doi   Pattemore, A., & Muñoz, C. (2020). Learning L2 constructions from captioned audio-visual exposure: The effect of learner-related factors. *System*, *93*.

doi   Pattemore, A., & Muñoz, C. (2022). Captions and learnability factors in learning grammar from audio-visual input. *The JALT CALL Journal*, *18*(1), 83–109.

doi   Pattemore, A., Suárez, M. M., & Muñoz, C. (2024). Perceptions of learning from audio-visual input and changes in L2 viewing preferences: The roles of on-screen text and proficiency. *ReCALL*.

doi   Plonsky, L., & Oswald, F. L. (2014). How big is "big"? Interpreting effect sizes in L2 research. *Language Learning*, *64*(4), 878–912.

doi   Rogers, V., Meara, P., Barnett-Legh, T., Curry, C., & Davie, E. (2017). Examining the LLAMA aptitude tests. *Journal of the European Second Language Association*, *1*(1), 49–60.

Sabrià, Q. (2013). Edpuzzle. Retrieved on 28 May from 2024 from https://edpuzzle.com/

Schur, M. (Creator). (2016). *The good place*. [TV series]. Fremulon.

doi   Suárez, M. M. & Gesa, F. (2019). Learning vocabulary with the support of sustained exposure to captioned video: Do proficiency and aptitude make a difference? *The Language Learning Journal*, *47*(4), 497–517.

doi   Suárez, M. M., & Muñoz, C. (2011). Aptitude, age and cognitive development: The MLAT-E in Spanish and Catalan. *EUROSLA Yearbook*, *11*, 5–29.

doi   Sydorenko, T. (2010). Modality of input and vocabulary acquisition. *Language Learning & Technology*, *14*(2), 50–73.

doi   Teng, M. F. (2022). Incidental L2 vocabulary learning from viewing captioned videos: Effects of learner-related factors. *System*, *105*, 102736.

doi   Van Lommel, S., Laenen, A., & D'Ydewalle, G. (2006). Foreign-grammar acquisition while watching subtitled television programmes. *British Journal of Educational Psychology*, *76*, 243–258.

doi   Wen, Z. (2021). Language aptitudes. In T. Gregersen & S. Mercer (Eds.), *The Routledge handbook of psychology of language learning and teaching* (pp. 389–403). Routledge.

doi   Winke, P. (2013). An investigation into second language aptitude for advanced Chinese language learners. *The Modern Language Journal*, *97*(1), 109–130.

doi   Yalçın, Ş., & Spada, N. (2016). Language aptitude and grammatical difficulty: An EFL classroom-based study. *Studies in Second Language Acquisition*, *38*(2), 239–263.

Vocabulary learning from audiovisual input at first exposure in young adult novice learners

Imma Miralpeix, Ferran Gesa & Maria del Mar Suárez
Universitat de Barcelona

In this 'First Exposure' (FE) study, 106 Catalan/Spanish young adults proficient in English watched a short advert with the audio in English and subtitles in Polish, a language they were not familiar with. Results indicated that vocabulary learning took place, as their meaning recognition scores were significantly higher than those of a control group who had not seen the video. The most recurrent learning strategies these novice learners used were associations with imagery and with vocabulary in previously learned languages, along with attention to specific input factors such as frequency of word occurrence. Findings reveal how audiovisual input can help vocabulary acquisition at FE, as well as factors relevant for learning from video viewing at these very first stages.

1. Introduction

Recent advancements in digital technology have transformed the way we engage with new languages, and the prevalence of exposure to audiovisual materials has been steadily increasing in contemporary times (De Wilde et al., 2020). A growing body of research indicates that audiovisual input enhances second language (L2) learning (see, for instance, Reynolds et al., 2022). However, much of the existing research has predominantly focused on *en route* learners – those already in the process of learning a language. There is a dearth of research investigating whether and how audiovisual input facilitates learning for *ab initio* or novice learners – individuals encountering a language for the first time (see, for instance, Rast, 2008). We denote this area of study as 'First Exposure' (FE) research.

Conducting studies on FE holds relevance both theoretically and practically. Firstly, as highlighted by scholars like Gullberg and Indefrey (2010) or Han and Rast (2014), the initial phases of adult L2 vocabulary acquisition have often been overlooked in research, thus creating a gap in the literature investigating the nat-

https://doi.org/10.1075/lllt.61.09mir

ural processes and mechanisms underlying learners' capacity to 'break into the wild' (see, for instance, Reynolds, 2023). Furthermore, it is crucial to uncover the pre-linguistic knowledge individuals bring to the task of language acquisition, along with exploring input and learner factors that may facilitate learning during these early stages. From a practical standpoint, acquiring a core vocabulary early on is essential for effective communication (de Groot & van Hell, 2005), particularly when starting from scratch in a new language. Thus, any input source that aids in accelerating our learning rate is worth exploring, as noted by McLaughlin et al. (2004), who observed that minimal instruction can lead to rapid progress.

To date, FE studies have examined language acquisition using various types of input, primarily artificial languages (i.e., languages intentionally developed for experimental purposes, often in laboratory settings) or natural languages (typically in classroom settings). Examples of the former include studies by Cunillera et al. (2006), de Diego Balaguer et al. (2007), and Folia et al. (2010), while an instance of the latter is the VILLA project, where controlled classroom input was provided to French learners of Polish to evaluate their linguistic progress at multiple testing intervals (e.g., Dimroth et al., 2013; Rast, 2008, 2010a, 2010b; Shoemaker & Rast, 2013).

These FE investigations have revealed that lexical knowledge can indeed be acquired upon initial exposure to a completely unfamiliar language. For instance, Cunillera et al. (2006) demonstrated that both stress and statistical cues aid in word segmentation, while Shoemaker and Rast (2013) found that cognate words are recognized more readily than non-cognates, and that word recognition at FE is influenced by utterance position. However, there remains a significant gap in understanding how audiovisual input, consistently shown to promote language acquisition (e.g., Vanderplank, 2016), might contribute to intentional vocabulary learning during FE. Likewise, exploration is needed to uncover the strategies learners employ in this endeavour and their perceptions of the viewing experience.

2.   Literature review

2.1   FE studies and audiovisual input

Two studies have thus far explored learning from audiovisual input during initial exposure, both focusing on incidental learning: Gullberg et al. (2010, 2012) and Bisson et al. (2014). In the former study, speakers of Dutch as a first language (L1) viewed a seven-minute Chinese weather forecast (without on-screen text) specifically designed for the experiment, with several lexical items in the input enhanced by gestures. Results revealed participants' ability to extract both formal and semantic information from limited input, as evidenced by word form and meaning recognition tests. The impact of word frequency and syllable structure on performance was also observed. Moreover, the use of fMRIs on participants during task performance yielded neurocognitive insights: for example, the involvement of the supramarginal gyri – regions within the inferior parietal lobule implicated in phonological processing – was noted in the creation of phonological representations of potential L2 words during brief exposure, accompanied by rapid neurological adaptation.

In Bisson et al. (2014), L1 English participants viewed a 25-minute episode of *SpongeBob* in Dutch under three distinct conditions: with intralingual subtitles (Dutch audio and Dutch subtitles), with standard subtitles (Dutch audio and English subtitles), and in a reversed subtitles condition (English audio and Dutch subtitles). Additionally, a control group watched the episode with Dutch audio and no subtitles. Using eye-tracking technology, the study confirmed the processing of subtitles and images, with participants dedicating less time to reading when the audio was in English. Nonetheless, no evidence of lexical learning was found in a vocabulary auditory test, where participants were presented with 78 Dutch words and had to determine whether the translation appearing on the screen for each word was correct or not.

Thus, in incidental learning conditions, Gullberg et al. (2010, 2012) demonstrated participants' ability to extract lexical knowledge from a brief, unsubtitled video, even if the languages under examination in the study were typologically distant, stemming from different language families (L1 Dutch – L2 Chinese). However, in contrast, Bisson et al. (2014) found no incidental vocabulary acquisition when participants viewed a lengthier video, despite the languages being typologically closer (L1 English – L2 Dutch).

It is worth mentioning that Hofweber et al. (2022, 2023) have also conducted research on incidental learning from audiovisual input at FE, focusing on the acquisition of sign language. These studies yielded interesting findings, such as the impact of input properties (e.g., item frequency or degree of iconicity) on language learning abilities during FE, surpassing the influence of other individual variables examined (e.g., intelligence or aptitude). However, given the distinct modalities of expression between sign and verbal languages, we do not provide an exhaustive account of these studies within this chapter.

2.2   Factors influencing learning at FE

2.2.1   *Input and learner factors*

Several factors have been shown to influence learning in FE studies, namely input- and learner-related factors. In relation to the first ones, we can mention syllable structure or gestural cues. For instance, participants in Gullberg et al. (2012) learned disyllabic words with stress on the first syllable more easily, as they were also more usually found in their L1 than monosyllabic words. Moreover, those words highlighted with gestures were also more liable to be learned. Utterance position has also been found to influence learning: as Shoemaker and Rast (2013) have indicated, novice learners in language classes are particularly attentive to the edges of prosodic domains. In contrast, word frequency has been shown to influence learning in Gullberg et al. (2012) and in Miralpeix et al. (2023), but not in Shoemaker and Rast (2013).

In terms of learner-related factors, previous studies have primarily focused on age, aptitude, languages previously learned, and psychotypology. For instance, Ristin-Kauffmann and Gullberg (2014) categorized their participants into nine age groups ranging from 10 to 86 years old. They discovered that performance in a lexical decision task, following exposure to audiovisual input, improved with age. Miralpeix et al. (2023), in a study involving a subset of participants from the current study's sample, found that linguistic aptitude (measured by the LLAMA B test; Meara, 2005) explained 24% of the variance in meaning recognition vocabulary scores. Moreover, Carroll (2014) noted that cognate stimuli were easier to segment and learn than non-cognate items. This advantage with transparent words has also been observed by Rast et al. (2014), suggesting that language typology and psychotypology (i.e., the perceived distance between languages; Kellerman, 1979) play a role in learning from minimal input (Rast, 2010b). It should be noted that, in research on learning from audiovisual input, learners' previous exposure to this type of input or their perceptions on the task performed have rarely been considered.

2.2.2   *Vocabulary learning strategies*

While prior research has begun to explore input and learner variables that could influence learning within foreign language (FL) education, learning strategies have received relatively little attention. Griffiths (2008) defined strategies as those activities consciously chosen by learners to regulate their own learning. Even if different researchers have classified strategies in different ways – see, for instance, Oxford (1990) – a difference is often made between cognitive strategies (operations on the incoming input to enhance learning, such as chunking, visualization or association), metacognitive (involving learners' awareness and control over their own learning process, such as planning or evaluating), and affective (which involve managing emotions, attitude and motivation to facilitate learning, such as setting goals or building confidence).

Despite the abundance of studies on vocabulary learning strategies (e.g., Brown & Payne, 1994; Gu & Johnson, 1996; Pavičić Takač, 2008; Schmitt, 1997, 2000; Zhang & Li, 2011), fewer have focused on novice learners. For instance, in a study where English native speakers were tasked with reading while listening to a text in Dutch (a language they did not know), Singleton and Little (1984) observed that learners relied on their prior linguistic knowledge and input features simultaneously, and that they especially fell back on those previously learned languages typologically closer to the new one. In relation to the strategies used when exposed to multimodal input, the studies have been conducted with *en route* learners. For example, Borrás and Lafayette (1994), assessing the effects of subtitles on learner's production, posited that a low anxiety environment, as well as students' familiarity with this type of input, can contribute to the use of affective strategies. Furthermore, Thompson and Rubin (1996) claimed that learners engaging with audiovisual input can employ both cognitive (e.g., using visual cues for predictions or identifying cognates) and metacognitive strategies (e.g., setting listening objectives, planning, and establishing goals). Sydorenko (2010) found out that beginner learners were acquiring most words by associating captions with images. In extensive viewing, where learners regularly watched original version TV, Vanderplank (2016) noticed that those who made use of retention strategies (e.g., keeping record of new words) learned more than those who did not. So far, then, we lack information on what novice learners do to try to understand messages conveyed by subtitled audiovisual input and to retain the information that they may gather from it.

2.2.3   *Learners' perception of the viewing experience*

While some studies have explored learners' perceptions of the effectiveness of L2 audiovisual materials, research in FE situations is lacking. Studies involving *en route* learners have commonly found these materials to be beneficial for learning, particularly in terms of vocabulary acquisition (e.g., Kusyk & Sockett, 2012; Stewart & Pertusa, 2004). Additionally, it has been noted that learners may not always recognize that learning is occurring (e.g., Sydorenko, 2010, in the context of learning from short videos) or be aware of which viewing condition fosters better learning outcomes (e.g., Pattemore et al., 2024, comparing captions, enhanced captions, and no captions).

Despite the lack of research, the study of learners' perceptions is particularly pertinent in learning from viewing at FE. The initial exposure to a new language can be daunting for novice learners, potentially affecting their engagement with the learning material, confidence levels, self-efficacy beliefs regarding language learning, and, consequently, their overall performance.

3.   Research questions

Given the identified gaps in the literature and the abundance of audiovisual materials now available to learners in multiple languages, this chapter aims to explore the potential benefits of this type of input for novice learners. For this purpose, we pose the following research questions:

RQ1.   Can adult Catalan/Spanish native speakers establish word form-meaning connections after minimal exposure to audiovisual input with the audio in a language they know (English) and subtitles in a completely new language (Polish)?

RQ2.   In relation to vocabulary learning in the novel language:

   RQ2a.   Is it related to knowledge of other FLs learners may know or to previous exposure to audiovisual input in other languages?

   RQ2b.   Which vocabulary learning strategies do learners use?

RQ3.   How do novice learners perceive this viewing/learning experience?

   RQ3a.   Does learning depend on learners' perceptions?

4.   Method

4.1   Participants

135 Catalan/Spanish pre-service teachers pursuing studies in early childhood and primary education at the University of Barcelona participated in the study: 106 belonged to the Experimental Group (EG) and 29 to the Control Group (CG); see Table 1. At the time of data collection, they had studied English at primary and secondary school for about ten years and had a mean receptive vocabulary size of about 4,500 words, according to the V_YesNo test (Meara & Miralpeix, 2015). Moreover, there were not any significant differences between the two groups as far as their English vocabulary size was concerned, as corroborated by an independent samples t-test (see Table 1). They did not have any knowledge of Polish and had never been exposed to it either formally or informally, as was confirmed by a questionnaire that participants filled in after taking the tests (Appendix B) and by direct questions from the researchers to the participants in case of any doubt.

Table 1. Participants in the study

	N	Age M (SD)	L1	English vocabulary size M (SD)	
Experimental (EG)	106	19 (.667)	Catalan/Spanish	4,554 words (1,410.29)	$t(71.822) = .488$, $p = .627$
Control (CG)	29	18.7 (.556)	Catalan/Spanish	4,443 words (931.76)	

4.2 Instruments

4.2.1 TV advert

A TV advertisement from the renowned e-commerce platform Allegro, accessible at https://rb.gy/9phftk (Allegro, 2016), served as the stimulus for this study. The advert, lasting 2 minutes and 58 seconds, depicted the story of a resourceful Polish grandfather preparing for a trip to the UK, and learning English at home to be able to communicate with his granddaughter. The audio of the advert was in English, while the subtitles were provided in Polish. The subtitled text comprised 75 tokens and 45 types (i.e., distinct words) across a total of 34 subtitles, ranging from one to six words in length, and with a mean of 2.2 words per subtitle. In terms of the audio content, approximately 95% of the words fell within the 1k frequency band, with the remaining 5% in the 2k band, according to VocabProfile (Cobb, n.d.). This distribution aligned well with the learners' competence level, as their receptive vocabulary size exceeded by far 2,000 words.

It is important to note that the technique we use is a specific form of reversed subtitling: in reversed subtitling, the audio is presented in the viewers' L1 while the subtitles are provided in the target language (TL). Although less common than standard subtitling (where audio is in the TL and subtitles are in the L1), it has been argued to facilitate the acquisition of unfamiliar vocabulary (Danan, 1992; d'Ydewalle & Pavakanun, 1997). This method enables students to engage with content in their L1 while making connections between what they hear and the on-screen text (Talaván, 2012). In international advertisements, English is often employed in the audio. Given its status as a lingua franca, it is increasingly common to encounter it alongside less widely spoken languages, as in the present study involving Polish. Therefore, instead of referring to it as 'reversed interlingual subtitling' (L1 audio with TL subtitles), it is more accurate to describe it as 'reversed multilingual subtitling' (audio in a known language with subtitles in the TL).

4.2.2 *Polish vocabulary test*

The Polish vocabulary test was administered online and consisted of 15 target words (TW) and expressions appearing in the advert. We mainly focused on content words (nouns), instead of grammatical words, and very short phrases (e.g., *ono to jest* – it is –) as well as idiomatic expressions (e.g., *kocham cię* – I love you –). We avoided including cognates because they have already been shown to have a facilitating effect when learning from minimal input (e.g., Shoemaker & Rast, 2013) and their meanings could have been guessed just from the test. Therefore, we did not include transparent words in Spanish, Catalan, or English as TWs (e.g., *passport* – passport – or *piżama* – pyjamas –). All the TWs appeared once except for *kocham cię* and *ono to jest* (appearing twice), *cześć* – hi – (5 times) and *ja jestem* – I am – (6 times).

This multiple-choice meaning recognition test presented one word at a time to participants, who were then prompted to provide an answer before proceeding to the next item. Once an answer was submitted for a word, participants were unable to revisit previous items. Each TW (in Polish) was accompanied by three possible meanings (in English), along with the option "I don't know" (please refer to Appendix A to see the test). The two distractors were items that had also appeared in the advert. In cases where the target was a multi-word item, there were also options consisting of multiple words (for instance, refer to items 6, 7, 9, 13 and 15 in Appendix A). To mitigate any recency effects, the order of appearance of the TWs was randomized. The entire test had a time limit of three minutes, with a maximum score of 15 points – one for each correct answer. The test assessed Level 3 knowledge, as per the intake typology proposed by Rast (2008). Specifically, it evaluated items that were perceived and comprehended, but not (re)produced.

4.2.3 *Receptive vocabulary size test*

V_YesNo v1.0 (Meara & Miralpeix, 2015) was used to measure participants' receptive vocabulary size. It is an online test which aims to assess the number of words a person understands in English. It accomplishes this by presenting a series of words individually in a context-free environment. Test-takers are required to indicate whether they know the meaning of each word or not. The test covers words from the first ten frequency bands in English (1k to 10k) and provides an estimate of total receptive vocabulary size upon completion. To mitigate guessing, the test includes pseudo-words, ensuring that false alarms are factored into the final vocabulary size estimation. V_YesNo is derived from Yes/No tests initially proposed by Meara and Buxton (1987) and further developed by Meara and Jones (1988) for L2 English learners. For a comprehensive understanding of the test's functionality, the reader is referred to Meara and Miralpeix (2017, pp. 113–133).

4.2.4 *Questionnaire*

The questionnaire comprised nine questions (refer to Appendix B), designed to collect participants' demographic details, their vocabulary learning strategies while engaging with the advert, and their perceptions of this viewing experience. The initial question inquired participants about their proficiency in languages other than English, Spanish, and Catalan (the latter two being their native languages). Furthermore, to ensure participants were not familiar with Polish, the second question explicitly inquired about their familiarity with the TL and their proficiency level: beginner, intermediate, or advanced.

For the present study, several further questions are relevant: two open-ended questions prompted participants to reflect on their experience watching the Polish-subtitled advertisement and the vocabulary learning techniques they employed. The latter question facilitated the categorization of learning strategies in this study. Additionally, two further questions delved into participants' television viewing routines, specifically, whether they watched TV in Spanish, Catalan, or English. For those who indicated English, the questionnaire asked about their use of on-screen text and their subtitling preferences.

4.3 Procedure

Data from participants were collected in class by the teacher/researcher after obtaining the necessary permissions. Initially, participants in the EG were instructed to watch a short advertisement with the audio in English and subtitles in an unfamiliar language. They were directed to attempt to learn as much of this new language as possible. Following the first viewing, they were informed that they would watch the advertisement again for the same purpose, resulting in two viewings in total, that is, six minutes of exposure to Polish subtitles. Subsequently, participants were asked by the teacher to complete a vocabulary test available on the Moodle Virtual Campus of the course. They were informed that they had three minutes to answer all the questions and advised to select the "I don't know" option if uncertain, rather than guessing. Scores for this test were automatically recorded on the Virtual Campus of the course. Next, participants were provided with a questionnaire to complete, with no time limit specified, although they typically took an average of five minutes to answer it. Finally, they were debriefed about the results and explained how subtitled audiovisual input may contribute to learning new languages. The CG took the vocabulary test under the same conditions as the EG, but without watching the advert.

4.4   Data analysis

Test scores were processed and analysed using SPSS v.27. Similarly, responses to close-ended questions underwent systematic coding and analysis employing the same statistical software. Open-ended questions from the questionnaire were categorized and grouped *ad hoc* by the researchers and percentages calculated, to provide a description of participants' performance in RQs 2b and 3.

A preliminary independent samples *t*-test was first conducted to confirm there were no statistically significant differences between EG and CG in terms of English vocabulary knowledge (and that both would be equally able to understand the options provided in the Polish vocabulary test, see Table 1).

To answer RQ1, we analyzed how many questions were answered correctly in the Polish vocabulary test by participants in the EG after viewing the advert. We then compared these results with those of the CG, who had not seen the advert, using a *t*-test. This analysis helped ensure that any observed learning in the EG was attributable to the video exposure and not to random chance.

To address RQs 2a and 3, Chi-square tests were conducted. The continuous variable 'vocabulary scores' was categorized into three groups (low, middle, and high) using a *k*-means cluster analysis. In the case of RQ2a, enquiring about a possible relationship between learning from the advert and variables such as the number of known languages or previous exposure to audiovisual input in other languages, Chi-square tests were conducted between vocabulary scores and these variables. To uncover the strategies employed by learners to facilitate vocabulary acquisition (RQ 2b), frequency counts were conducted to determine the prevalence of these strategies among novice learners.

Finally, in relation to RQ3, on how participants perceived the experience, several categories were derived from the data and a difference was made between 'positive' and 'negative' perceptions. A Chi-square test was performed to assess whether learners' perceptions had an impact on vocabulary scores (RQ 3a).

5.   Results

5.1   Vocabulary learning

Results on vocabulary learning from viewing showed that participants watching the subtitled advert were able to make form-meaning connections, recognizing the meaning of about half of the target Polish vocabulary after only six minutes of video exposure (see Table 2). These scores were also significantly higher than those in the control group $t(133) = 10.682$, $p < .001$, with a very large effect size ($d = 2.24$; Plonsky & Oswald, 2014).

Table 2. Vocabulary scores in the EG and CG

	M	SD	Min.	Max.	95% CI
Experimental n = 106	7.33	2.43	2	14	[6.86-7.80]
Control n = 29	1.83	2.55	0	8	[0.86-2.80]

5.2 Variables influencing vocabulary learning

Results from the k-means cluster analysis indicated three distinct groups based on vocabulary scores: low ($n = 30$, mean = 4.57, $SD = 1.52$), mid ($n = 56$, mean = 7.60, $SD = 1.15$) and high ($n = 20$, mean = 10.70, $SD = 1.08$). The Kruskal-Wallis test revealed a significant difference among the three groups ($\chi^2(2) = 77.095$, $p < .001$) and the post-hoc analyses indicated that all groups differed significantly from each other.

Regarding proficiency in other languages, the ability to speak FLs other than English did not show a significant association with Polish scores ($X^2(2, 106) = .181$, $p = .913$). Similarly, familiarity with other Germanic languages such as German or Dutch, which were the most common languages learned after English, did not demonstrate a significant impact on Polish learning outcomes in either German ($X^2(2, 106) = 1.312$, $p = .519$) or Dutch ($X^2(2, 106) = 1.610$, $p = .447$).

When assessing the possible influence of previous exposure to multimodal input and viewing habits on vocabulary scores, it was found that the frequency of exposure to original version TV (whether never, monthly, or weekly) was not related to Polish vocabulary scores ($X^2(4, 106) = .547$, $p = .969$). Similarly, the choice of subtitles in either L1 or the L2 (or the absence of subtitles) showed no significant effect. That is, no effects were observed in those setting the subtitles in Spanish ($X^2(2, 57) = .155$, $p = .926$), Catalan ($X^2(2, 57) = 2.395$, $p = .302$), English ($X^2(2, 57) = .724$, $p = .696$); or in those that did not use subtitles at all ($X^2(2, 57) = .817$, $p = .665$).

5.3 Vocabulary learning strategies

Table 3 displays the strategies used by participants to learn vocabulary from the video, with cognitive strategies being the most prevalent. Notably, participants frequently mentioned reading subtitles in the new language and relying on visual aids or their visual memory to foster retention. They also emphasized focusing on frequently repeated words (18.68%) and, to a lesser extent, on basic vocabulary (i.e., words that students tend to learn first when they are introduced to a new language, such as 'thank you', 'I', 'dog', etc.) (6.59%). Moreover, they also attempted to draw comparisons between the new vocabulary and words they knew in other languages. Additionally, the instruction to maximize learning and the opportunity to view the video twice proved beneficial in facilitating the acquisition of new vocabulary from the input.

Table 3. Vocabulary learning strategies and percentage of use

Strategies	Percentage	Strategy type[*]
Reading subtitles in Polish	26.37	C
Use of imagery/visual memory	23.08	C
Focus on repeated words	18.68	C
Cross-language comparisons	10.99	C
Intentional approach	8.79	M
Focus on basic words	6.59	C
Repeated viewing	3.30	M
Others	2.20	–

[*] C=Cognitive strategies, M=Metacognitive strategies

5.4 The viewing/learning experience

Based on participants' responses (please refer to Table 4), 59.82% of the sample perceived the experience negatively, describing it as very difficult (resulting in feelings of getting lost), weird, challenging, or stressful. However, 40.18% of the participants perceived the task as fun, interesting, and useful for learning new words, finding it easy to navigate. Results from the Chi-square test revealed that perceiving the experience as being 'positive' or 'negative' did not impact vocabulary scores ($X^2(2, 106) = .387$, $p = .824$).

Table 4. Participants' perceptions of the viewing/learning experience

The viewing/learning experience	Percentage	Experience perception[*]
Very difficult, I got lost	26.79	–
Strange, weird	21.43	–
Fun, interesting	18.75	+
Useful to learn new words	16.07	+
Challenging	8.04	–
Easy	5.36	+
Stressful	3.56	–

[*] +: Positive experience, –: Negative experience.

6.   Discussion

Findings from the study demonstrate that making form-meaning connections for new vocabulary in a new language is possible with just very minimal information (i.e., a subtitled advert watched twice, six minutes of exposure in total). It should be considered that the audio was in a language participants knew, even if it was not their L1: this is a common scenario learners may encounter due to the widespread use of English as a lingua franca in mass media. The fact that the English vocabulary present in the advert was within the participants' level in this language made input easy to follow, minimizing the effects of not having been exposed to L1 audio. Additionally, participants were instructed to deliberately try to learn the new language, which did not happen in Bisson et al. (2014), possibly causing the difference in the two studies' outcomes. Therefore, it is probable that task orientation changed participants' focus, as suggested by VanPatten (2014), and prompted learners to make an extra effort to commit words to memory (Schmidt, 2001). As the video was shorter (it was an advert instead of an episode in Bisson et al. 2014), participants did not need to maintain attention for an extended duration, facilitating retention. Last, the fact that participants watched the same advert twice might have also assisted the learning of some TWs since learners could easily (dis)confirm the hypotheses already formed during the first viewing, in line with previous studies which have shown that repeated viewing is beneficial for language development (Muñoz et al., 2022).

Furthermore, it is noteworthy that despite similar percentages of participants perceiving the task as 'difficult/strange' and 'interesting/useful', vocabulary acquisition did not appear to be contingent on learners' perceptions. This suggests that first of all, learning occurs regardless of how learners perceive the task (similarly to Pattemore et al., 2024, where perceptions of learning in *en route* learners did not necessarily align with the actual learning). Also Sydorenko (2010) found significant vocabulary gains from short video viewing, even if many participants had not perceived any learning from the treatment. Secondly, other factors, such as individual differences, may play a more significant role in explaining learning outcomes. For instance, Miralpeix et al. (2023) observed aptitude effects when learning from visual stimuli, and Rast et al. (2014) indicated that factors such as working memory, learning style, and motivation were associated with task performance in Polish during the initial five hours of language contact in a classroom setting.

Regarding variables that may affect linguistic gains from the subtitled video, previous knowledge of other languages did not affect learning at FE. This may appear contradictory to findings by Gibson and Hufeisen (2003) or Hirosh and Degani (2018) in *en route* learners, or by Rast (2010a) in novice learners, suggesting an advantage for multilinguals when learning new languages. However, it is important to note that we did not include cognates in our test, and our participants had no knowledge of any Slavic language which was closer to Polish (they were bilingual in two Romance languages and were studying English, which belongs to the Germanic branch). It should also be noted that, if being bilingual could confer a lexical advantage in the early stages of language learning (e.g., Hopp et al., 2019), all participants in our study were bilingual. This means that they all would have an advantage in an FE experience compared to monolinguals.

Despite the non-significant results of the Chi-square test, participants indicated in the questionnaire that they were using other known languages for cross-linguistic comparisons, although this strategy might not have been helpful in achieving higher scores on the vocabulary test, as no cognate words were included. In connection with this, while the four primary languages examined in the study (Catalan, Spanish, English, and Polish) all employ the Roman alphabet, Polish exhibits a slightly different orthography compared to the other three. This includes the presence of diacritics unique to Polish, which consequently increases the learning challenge for the TWs and diminishes the effectiveness of cross-language comparisons. For example, in Polish we find the *kreska* (graphically similar to the acute accent) on the letters ć, ń, ó, ś, ź; the *kropka* (overdot) in the letter ż; the stroke in the letter ł; or the *ogonek* (little tai) in the letters ą, ę. Similarly, Polish features a syllable structure characterized by numerous consonant clusters not commonly found in the other three languages, for instance, cz, dz, sz (Orzechowska & Wiese, 2015).

Regularly watching TV in the original version, with or without subtitles, did not exhibit any correlation with learning outcomes in this study. At first glance, this may appear contradictory to Vanderplank's (2016) findings among *en route* learners, where individuals with more viewing experience tended to adopt more strategic approaches, such as making connections, comparisons, or corrections more frequently. However, exposure to audiovisual input in an FL may not automatically lead to better performance when watching videos in a completely new language, at least not within the initial moments of contact, as each new language poses its own challenges. It is possible that more time and engagement are needed for learners to get accustomed to this practice in the new language.

It is interesting to observe that the vocabulary learning strategies reported by participants in the questionnaire can be correlated with the steps students undertake when acquiring new words, as proposed by Brown and Payne (1994), also referenced in Hatch and Brown (1995). Consequently, we can categorize the actions students take when intentionally learning through viewing at FE according to the stages outlined by Brown and Payne (1994), as depicted in Figure 1. Among the five stages they propose, we will concentrate on three: 'forming a clear mental representation of the new word forms', 'grasping the meaning of words', and 'establishing a memory connection between form and meaning'. We will exclude 'accessing sources for discovering new words', which would precede the aforementioned three stages, as participants were already provided with the video source to extract lexical information. Similarly, we will omit the fifth and final stage, 'using the words', as our study did not evaluate production.

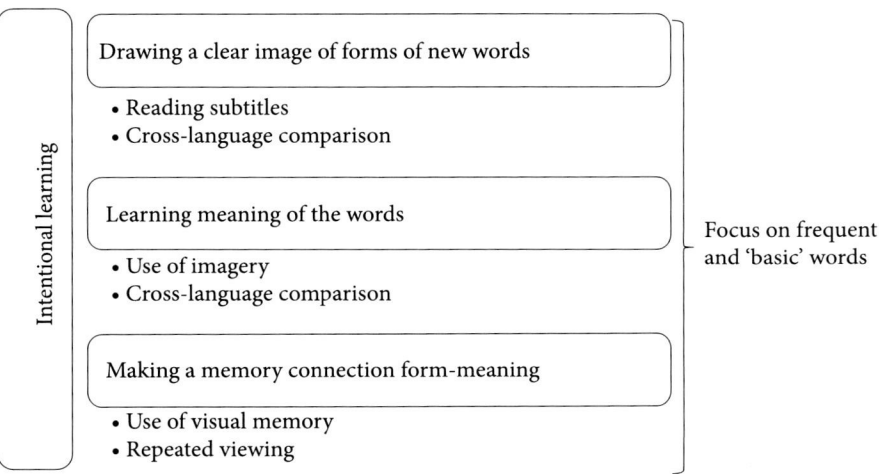

Figure 1. Vocabulary learning strategies at FE related to the steps students take when learning new words (adapted from Brown & Payne, 1994)

Therefore, participants, to form a clear mental representation of the new word forms in this type of reversed subtitling condition, would read the subtitles (a discovery strategy, according to Schmitt, 1997) and possibly engage in cross-language comparisons. Progressing to the next stage (i.e., learning the meaning of new words), they would employ imagery and potentially rely on other languages they are proficient in, seeking similarities (as in Sydorenko, 2010). In the final stage, when establishing a strong connection between the form and the meaning of words, they would use their visual memory, and repeated viewing would aid in solidifying these connections (Muñoz et al., 2022). Furthermore, at all stages, there would be a focus on frequently encountered items and fundamental words (as confirmed by the participants' responses to the questionnaire). This approximation helps us to understand how learners confront the challenge of 'breaking into the wild' when exposed to multimodal input in an unfamiliar language, allowing us to see how they possibly make sense of such input and try to turn it into intake.

7.   Conclusion, limitations, and further research

The present study confirms that intentional vocabulary learning occurs even with minimal exposure to a completely new language through subtitled videos, particularly when the audio language is familiar, facilitating the establishment of a form-meaning connection. Our findings align with Gullberg et al. (2010, 2012), underscoring adults' capacity to learn under minimal input conditions. Thus, short subtitled videos can serve as a tool to promote lexical acquisition in novice learners, aiding in the development of vocabulary from the outset. Optimal effectiveness may be achieved when the content is engaging and includes repeated vocabulary. Furthermore, starting with audio in a language learners know (not necessarily the L1, as in this case) can promote fast-mapping, while incorporating audio in the new language may facilitate recognition of written forms, as evidenced in studies with *en route* beginner learners (see, for example, Casulleras and Miralpeix, Chapter 1, this volume).

The present study has demonstrated that learning occurs regardless of task perception (whether perceived as 'easy' or 'difficult'). While direct effects of knowledge of other languages on learning were not evident, cross-language comparisons were acknowledged to take place by participants, who were already multilingual. Additionally, we have observed variations in the strategies employed to learn new vocabulary compared to those used in other contexts or with different input types. This insight holds significant value for educators aiming to support learners during their initial language acquisition stages, especially when devising instructional sequences that incorporate video viewing. Offering guidance on how to use these learning strategies can enrich the prospects for novel learning opportunities.

Addressing the limitations, it is important to note that only one specific combination of languages was investigated in this study, with a limited number of TWs and immediate testing (assessing only one intake type). To draw more robust conclusions regarding learning from viewing at FE, studies incorporating different language combinations, a broader spectrum of vocabulary, and various intake types (such as word form recognition and recall, word meaning recall, etc.) should be conducted. In addition, the intentional learning approach implemented in the current design undoubtedly influenced the processing of TWs. Therefore, it would be valuable to conduct studies on novice learners acquiring new vocabulary incidentally from short subtitled videos at FE.

Furthermore, data-driven classifications, not predetermined by researchers, were used to identify patterns in the data. However, alternative approaches, such as providing students with a pre-piloted list of potential strategies and prompting them to indicate which strategies they employed (e.g., using plot clues, identifying word categories, linking words to scenes or characters, recalling entire subtitles to make inferences, etc.), could have been employed. This approach would have enabled learners to recall actions they engaged in while watching the video, but which might not have been mentioned otherwise. Additionally, a different approach, as suggested by Meara (2009), could involve uncovering groups of participants who adopt similar strategies rather than focusing solely on strategies that frequently co-occur. We propose conducting this 'by-subjects' analysis in future research on the topic. Finally, it is recommended to improve our understanding of the roles played by individual differences (e.g., aptitude or working memory) and to advance our exploration of learning at FE through eye-tracking techniques. This will enable us to investigate potential correlations between processing and learning in these contexts.

Acknowledgements

This work was supported by grants PID2019-110594GB-100 from the Spanish Ministry of Science and Innovation and 2023SGR00303 from the Catalan Agency for Management of University and Research Grants (AGAUR).

We thank Neus Frigolé for her help with data collection, Paulina Olender for her revision of the Polish test, as well as the students who participated in the study. We are also very grateful to the chapter reviewers for their feedback and suggestions, which helped improve our work.

Ethical considerations

The study protocol adhered to the good practices of data collection, data anonymization, data processing, and data storage of the Institutional Review Board of the University of Barcelona (IRB0003099).

References

Allegro (2016, Dec.). *English for beginners*. Allegro. Retrieved on 28 May 2024 from https://rb.gy/9phftk

Bisson, M. J., Van Heuven, W. J. B., Conklin, K., & Tunney, R. J. (2014). Processing of native and foreign language subtitles in films: An eye tracking study. *Applied Psycholinguistics*, 35(2), 399–418.

Borrás, I., & Lafayette, R. C. (1994). Effects of multimedia courseware subtitling on the speaking performance of college students of French. *Modern Language Journal*, 78(1), 61–75.

Brown, C., & Payne, M.E. (1994, March 8–12). *Five essential steps of processes in vocabulary learning* [Conference presentation]. 28th TESOL Annual Convention, Baltimore, MD.

Carroll, S.E. (2014). Processing 'words' in early-stage foreign language acquisition: A comparison of first exposure and low proficiency learners. In Z.H. Han & R. Rast (Eds.), *First exposure to a second language* (pp. 107–138). Cambridge University Press.

Cobb, T. (n.d.). VocabProfile VP Classic [Computer software]. Retrieved on 28 May 2024 from https://www.lextutor.ca/vp/eng/

Cunillera, T., Toro, J.M., Sebastián-Gallés, N., & Rodríguez-Fornells, A. (2006). The effects of stress and statistical cues on continuous speech segmentation: An event-related brain potential study. *Brain Research*, *1123*(1), 168–178.

Danan, M. (1992). Reversed subtitling and Dual Coding Theory: New directions for foreign language instruction. *Language Learning*, *42*(4), 497–527.

De Diego Balaguer, R., Toro, J.M., Rodríguez-Fornells, A., & Bachoud-Lévi, A.C. (2007). Different neurophysiological mechanisms underlying word and rule extraction from speech. *PloS ONE*, *2*(11).

De Groot, A.M.B., & van Hell, J.G. (2005). The learning of foreign language vocabulary. In J.F. Kroll & A.M.B. de Groot (Eds.), *Handbook of bilingualism: Psycholinguistic approaches* (pp. 9–29). Oxford University Press.

De Wilde, V., Brysbaert, M., & Eyckmans, J. (2020). Learning English through out-of-school exposure: Which levels of language proficiency are attained and which types of input are important? *Bilingualism: Language and Cognition*, *23*(1), 171–185.

Dimroth, C., Rast, R., Starren, M., & Watorek, M. (2013). Methods for studying the acquisition of a new language under controlled input conditions. *Eurosla Yearbook*, *13*, 109–138.

d'Ydewalle, G., & Pavakanun, U. (1997). Could enjoying a movie lead to language acquisition? In P. Winterhoff-Spurk & T.H.A. van der Voort (Eds.), *New horizons in media psychology: Research cooperation and projects in Europe* (pp. 145–155). Springer.

Folia, V., Uddén, J., de Vries, M., Forkstam, C., & Petersson, K.M. (2010). Artificial language learning in children. *Language Learning*, *60*(Suppl. 2), 188–220.

Gibson, M., & Hufeisen, B. (2003). Investigating the role of prior foreign language knowledge: Translating from an unknown into a known foreign language. In J. Cenoz, B. Hufeisen, & U. Jessner (Eds.), *The multilingual lexicon* (pp. 87–102). Springer.

Griffiths, C. (2008). Strategies and good language learners. In C. Griffiths (Ed.), *Lessons from good language learners* (pp. 83–98). Cambridge University Press.

Gu, P.Y., & Johnson, R.K. (1996). Vocabulary learning strategies and language learning outcomes. *Language Learning*, *46*(4), 643–679.

Gullberg, M., & Indefrey, P. (Eds.) (2010). The earliest stages of language learning. *Language Learning*, *60*(Suppl. 2).

Gullberg, M., Roberts, L., & Dimroth, C. (2012). What word-level knowledge can adult learners acquire after minimal exposure to a new language? *IRAL – International Review of Applied Linguistics in Language Teaching*, *50*(4), 239–276.

Gullberg, M., Roberts, L., Dimroth, C., Veroude, K., & Indefrey, P. (2010). Adult language learning after minimal exposure to an unknown natural language. *Language Learning*, *60*(Suppl. 2), 5–24.

Han, Z.H., & Rast, R. (Eds.), (2014). *First exposure to a second language*. Cambridge University Press.

Hatch, E., & Brown, C. (1995). *Vocabulary, semantics, and language education*. Cambridge University Press.

Hirosh, Z., & Degani, T. (2018). Direct and indirect effects of multilingualism on novel language learning: An integrative review. *Psychonomic Bulletin and Review*, 25(3), 892–916.

Hofweber, J. E., Aumonier, L., Janke, V., Gullberg, M., & Marshall, C. (2022). Breaking into language in a new modality: The role of input and individual differences in recognising signs. *Frontiers in Psychology*, 13.

Hofweber, J. E., Aumonier, L., Janke, V., Gullberg, M., & Marshall, C. (2023). Which aspects of visual motivation aid the implicit learning of signs at first exposure? *Language Learning*, 73(S1), 33–63.

Hopp, H., Vogelbacher, M., Kieseier, T., & Thoma, D. (2019). Bilingual advantages in early foreign language learning: Effects of the minority and the majority language. *Learning and Instruction*, 61, 99–110.

Kellerman, E. (1979). Transfer and non-transfer: Where we are now. *Studies in Second Language Acquisition*, 2(1), 37–57.

Kusyk, M., & Sockett, G. (2012). From informal resource usage to incidental language acquisition: Language uptake from online television viewing in English. *ASp, la revue du Geras*, 62, 45–65.

McLaughlin, J., Osterhout, L., & Kim, A. (2004). Neural correlates of second-language word learning: minimal instruction produces rapid change. *Nature Neuroscience*, 7(7), 703–704.

Meara, P. M. (2005). *LLAMA language aptitude tests*. Lognostics.

Meara, P. M. (2009). Review of 'Vocabulary learning strategies and foreign language acquisition'. *System*, 37(3), 545–547.

Meara, P. M., & Buxton, B. (1987). An alternative to multiple choice vocabulary tests. *Language Testing*, 4(2), 142–154.

Meara, P. M., & Jones, G. (1988). Vocabulary size as a placement indicator. In P. Grunwell (Ed.), *Applied Linguistics in Society* (pp. 80–87). CILT.

Meara, P. M., & Miralpeix, I. (2015). V_YesNo. Lognostics. Retrieved on 28 May 2024 from https://www.lognostics.co.uk/tools/V_YesNo/V_YesNo.htm

Meara, P. M., & Miralpeix, I. (2017). Tools for researching vocabulary. *Multilingual Matters*.

Miralpeix, I., Gesa, F., & Suárez, M. M. (2023). Vocabulary learning from subtitled input after minimal exposure. In B. Reynolds (Ed.), *Vocabulary learning in the wild* (pp. 263–283). Springer.

Muñoz, C., Pattemore, A., & Avello, D. (2022). Exploring repeated captioning viewing as a way to promote vocabulary learning: Time lag between repetitions and learner factors. *Computer Assisted Language Learning*.

Orzechowska, P., & Wiese, R. (2015). Preferences and variation in word-initial phonotactics: A multi-dimensional evaluation of German and Polish. *Folia Linguistica*, 49(2), 439–486.

Pattemore, A., Suárez, M.-M., & Muñoz, C. (2024). Perceptions of learning from audiovisual input and changes in L2 viewing preferences: The roles of on-screen text and proficiency. *ReCALL*, 36(2), 135–151.

doi Pavičić Takač, V. (2008). *Vocabulary learning strategies and foreign language acquisition.* Multilingual Matters.

doi Plonsky, L., & Oswald, F. L. (2014). How big is 'big'? Interpreting effect sizes in L2 research. *Language Learning, 64*(4), 878–912.

doi Rast, R. (2008). *Foreign language input: Initial processing.* Multilingual Matters.

doi Rast, R. (2010a). The role of linguistic input in the first hours of adult language learning. *Language Learning, 60*(Suppl. 2), 64–84.

doi Rast, R. (2010b). The use of prior linguistic knowledge in the early stages of L3 acquisition. *IRAL – International Review of Applied Linguistics in Language Teaching, 48*(2–3), 159–183.

Rast, R., Watorek, M., Hilton, H., & Shoemaker, E. (2014). Initial processing and use of inflectional markers: Evidence from French adult learners of Polish. In Z. H. Han & R. Rast (Eds.), *First exposure to a second language* (pp. 64–106). Cambridge University Press.

doi Reynolds, B. L. (Ed.), (2023). *Vocabulary learning in the wild.* Springer.

doi Reynolds, B. L., Cui, Y., Kao, C. W., & Thomas, N. (2022). Vocabulary acquisition through viewing captioned and subtitled video: A scoping review and meta-analysis. *Systems, 10*(5), 133.

doi Ristin-Kauffman, N., & Gullberg, M. (2014). The effects of first exposure to an unknown language at different ages. *Bulletin Suisse de Linguistique Appliquée, 99*, 17–29.

Schmidt, R. (2001). Attention. In P. Robinson (Ed.), *Cognition and second language instruction* (pp. 3–32). Cambridge University Press.

Schmitt, N. (1997). Vocabulary learning strategies. In N. Schmitt & M. McCarthy (Eds.), *Vocabulary: Description, acquisition and pedagogy* (pp. 199–227). Cambridge University Press.

Schmitt, N. (2000). Issues in the emerging area of vocabulary learning strategies. In J. Arabski (Ed.), *Studies in foreign language acquisition and teaching* (pp. 107–116). Wydawnictwo Uniwersytetu Slaskiego.

doi Shoemaker, E., & Rast, R. (2013). Extracting words from the speech stream at first exposure. *Second Language Research, 29*(2), 165–183.

Singleton, D., & Little, D. (1984). A first encounter with Dutch: Perceived language distance and language transfer as factors in comprehension. In L. Mathuna & D. Singleton (Eds.), *Language across cultures* (pp. 259–270). Irish Association for Applied Linguistics.

doi Stewart, M. A., & Pertusa, I. (2004). Gains to language learners from viewing target language closed-captioned films. *Foreign Language Annals, 37*(3), 438–442.

doi Sydorenko, T. (2010). Modality of input and vocabulary acquisition. *Language Learning & Technology, 14*(2), 50–73.

doi Talaván, N. (2012). Justificación teórico-práctica del uso de los subtítulos en la enseñanza-aprendizaje de lenguas extranjeras. *TRANS. Revista de Traductología, 16*, 23–37.

doi Thompson, I., & Rubin, J. (1996). Can strategy instruction improve listening comprehension? *Foreign Language Annals, 29*(3), 331–342.

doi Vanderplank, R. (2016). *Captioned media in foreign language learning and teaching: Subtitles for the deaf and hard-of-hearing as tools for language learning.* Palgrave Macmillan.

VanPatten, B. (2014). Epilogue: Input processing by novices – Issues in the nature of processing and in research methods. In Z. H. Han & R. Rast (Eds.), *First exposure to a second language* (pp. 193–207). Cambridge University Press.

Zhang, B., & Li, C. (2011). Classification of L2 vocabulary learning strategies: Evidence from exploratory and confirmatory factor analysis. *RELC Journal, 42*(2),141–154.

Appendix A.   Meaning recognition vocabulary test

Target Word (TW)[*]	Option A	Option B	Option C	Option D
1. chleb (1)	breakfast	**bread**	fridge	I don't know
2. dziękuję ci (1)	goodbye	you are perfect	**thank you**	I don't know
3. dziadkiem (1)	wall	beach	**grandpa**	I don't know
4. ręcznik (1)	fork	bath	**towel**	I don't know
5. kapcie (1)	towel	pyjamas	**slippers**	I don't know
6. ono to jest (2)	**it is**	you are perfect	I love you	I don't know
7. szczoteczka do zębów (1)	**toothbrush**	I love you	I'm gonna fucking kill you	I don't know
8. śniadanie (1)	knife	**breakfast**	bread	I don't know
9. kocham cię (2)	you are perfect	I am gonna fucking kill you	**I love you**	I don't know
10. początkujących (1)	pyjamas	**beginners**	fork	I don't know
11. psem (1)	**dog**	beach	grandpa	I don't know
12. drogę (1)	toilet	mirror	**way**	I don't know
13. bądź dobrym (1)	can you show me	thank you	**be good**	I don't know
14. cześć (5)	**hi**	thank you	be good	I don't know
15. ja jestem (6)	**I am**	you are	you can	I don't know

* Correct answers for each TW appear in bold and TW frequency in the advert within parenthesis.

Appendix B.   Questionnaire

1. Apart from Spanish, Catalan and English, do you know any other language(s)?
   ☐ Yes   ☐ No
   If you said 'yes', which level do you have in each? (Beginner, Intermediate, Advanced)
   Language: .... Level: ....
   Language: .... Level: ....
2. Before watching the clip, did you know any Polish?   ☐ Yes   ☐ No
   If you said 'yes', which level do you have in Polish?
   ☐ Beginner   ☐ Intermediate   ☐ Advanced
3. How was the experience of watching an advert in English subtitled in Polish? Please describe it.
4. Did you notice that the language in the subtitles was Polish?   ☐ Yes   ☐ No
5. Did you expect to learn anything from the new language when seeing the advert?
   ☐ Yes   ☐ No
   If you said 'yes', what?
   ☐ grammar ☐ vocabulary ☐ morphology ☐ pronunciation ☐ fixed expressions
   ☐ others (please specify): ....
6. You have the result of the quiz. How do you feel about it?
   – I have learned <u>what I expected</u> ☐
   – I have learned <u>more</u> than I expected ☐
   – I have learned <u>less</u> than I expected ☐

7. Which strategies did you use to help you to learn new words?
8. Which language do you usually watch TV series, films and/or videos on YouTube in:
   ☐ Spanish   ☐ Catalan   ☐ English
   ☐ Others?_____
9. Do you usually watch TV series, films and/or videos in English?   ☐ Yes   ☐ No
   If you said 'yes':
   How often? ☐ Less than once a month
                    ☐ Between 1–3 times / month
                    ☐ Between 1–3 times / week
                    ☐ Between 4–6 times / week
                    ☐ Every day
   Please select the language you set the subtitles in:
   ☐ Spanish   ☐ Catalan   ☐ English   ☐ No subtitles at all

More pieces in the puzzle about language learning through audiovisual input

Carmen Muñoz & Imma Miralpeix
Universitat de Barcelona

In this concluding chapter, we bring together findings from the studies in this volume and place them within the context of prior research on audiovisual input, particularly within the broader framework of the SUBTiLL project. The findings are organized into three sections: captioned viewing, learning outcomes across various language dimensions, and individual differences. The first section addresses several concerns regarding captions, including their appropriateness for use with primary school children, a comparison with L1 subtitles, and caption enhancement. The second section delves into the observed improvements in vocabulary acquisition, content comprehension, grammar, pronunciation, and pragmatics. The third section examines individual differences, specifically focusing on vocabulary size, reading skills, language learning aptitude, and age. Finally, we discuss implications and propose future research directions.

1. Introduction

One of the fundamental assumptions in the field of second language acquisition (SLA) is the need for exposure to input (e.g., Krashen, 1987; Long, 1990). The realization that instructed learners often lack the quantity, quality, and authenticity of input required for successful second language (L2) acquisition fueled our exploration into audiovisual input (AV). The research presented in this volume investigates different facets of the language learning process and its outcomes as it occurs through viewing. An additional unique aspect of this research is that, unlike most studies in this field, which are typically one-off, our contribution within the SUBTiLL project has been to conduct extended longitudinal viewing experiences. Similarly, while most studies in this field primarily examine young adults, our research places a significant emphasis on younger learners. By examining language acquisition through viewing in primary and secondary school

https://doi.org/10.1075/lllt.61.10mun

children and teenagers, our research expands our understanding and addresses a significant gap in the literature.

In this final chapter, we bring together findings from the studies in this volume and contextualize them in relation to previous research, particularly within the broader SUBTiLL project. We organize findings into main themes, starting with captioned viewing, a pivotal characteristic of multimodal input. Questions regarding captions include their suitability for primary school, comparison with L1 subtitles, and maximizing their effects through textual enhancement. The second theme addresses learning gains across different language dimensions: vocabulary and comprehension, as well as the less studied areas of grammar, pronunciation, and pragmatics. The third theme explores learner individual differences, specifically focusing on vocabulary size, reading skills, language learning aptitude, and age. The concluding section proposes avenues for future research in this field: more pieces for the picture.

2.   Captioned viewing

In this book, we use the term "captions" or "L2 subtitles" to refer to subtitles in the same language as the audio, also known as intralanguage subtitles. On the other hand, we use the term "L1 subtitles", or simply "subtitles", to denote subtitles in the viewer's first language, that is, interlanguage subtitles or interlingual translations, which differ from the language of the audio.

The interest in captions among L2 researchers is relatively recent, sparked by evidence indicating that captions facilitate L2 learning (see Montero Perez, 2022; Muñoz, 2022; Vanderplank, 2016b) compared to other forms of on-screen text (see the meta-analysis by Reynolds et al., 2022). The supportive role of captions can be attributed, primarily, to their assistance in segmenting and decoding the continuous stream of auditory input, facilitating the linkage between written and spoken words. Furthermore, their presence on screen can effectively draw viewers' attention to new elements in the input. Additionally, through caption enhancement, students' attention may be directed externally to specific features. In what follows, we discuss three contributions of the studies in this volume concerning captions: the use of captions with primary school children, the effects of captions compared to L1 subtitles, and caption enhancement.

2.1   Captioned viewing by primary school children

Primary school children represent a relatively recent addition to the language learner population. Differences in cognitive abilities and their slower learning rate in formal educational settings highlight the need for age-appropriate teaching methodologies (Muñoz, 2007). Moreover, today's children inhabit a predominantly visual world and are exposed to digital stimuli more than ever, making AV media highly suitable for classroom use.

In the context of AV input, a common recommendation has been to use L1 subtitles with beginner learners whose proficiency level does not meet the minimum threshold required to comprehend unmodified captions (e.g., Danan, 2004). This is particularly relevant for primary school children. While simplifying captions to make them less effortful may not be feasible for busy teachers or parents at home, captions in animated cartoons are typically simple enough to effectively support learners with lower proficiency levels and to engage them throughout the video (d'Ydewalle & Bruycker, 2007; d'Ydewalle & Vanrensbergen, 1989; Tragant & Pellicer-Sánchez, 2019). Furthermore, captions in cartoons are neither too fast nor too long for children, whose reading speed may still be slow (Carver, 1990; Vanderplank, 2016a).

The three studies presented in this volume involving primary school children (Chapters 1 to 3) deepen our insight and confirm the assumption that even at this early age and proficiency level, learners can benefit from captions provided the AV material is suitable. All three studies used cartoons designed for English native-speaking children, which, despite originally targeting younger audiences, remained engaging for fourth, fifth, and sixth graders. Additionally, the duration of the episodes (around 10–12 minutes) was age appropriate.

While many studies have investigated the relationship between L1 and L2 reading (e.g., Koda, 2008; Sparks et al., 2008), this area is under-researched concerning young L2 learners in the context of subtitled and captioned videos. The studies by Casulleras and Miralpeix (Chapter 1) and by Avello and Muñoz (Chapter 2) are pioneering in exploring the influence of reading skills (such as reading speed and efficacy) on comprehension and vocabulary gains among young L2 learners, illuminating the important role played by reading in learning through AV input. Casulleras and Miralpeix explored the impact of L1 and L2 reading skills, revealing that reading speed in the learners' L1 was associated with video comprehension, while reading speed in the L2 was not. The superior reading skills in their native language enabled learners to read subtitles faster, thereby enhancing comprehension. Avello and Muñoz's study in this volume takes a step further by investigating the potential benefits of captioned video viewing for reading, a finding previously observed only in L1 reading contexts (e.g., Linebarger et al., 2010). The results indicate that, indeed, in an L2 context, learners' reading skills also improve with captioned viewing. This improvement was observed in both L2 and L1 reading skills, supporting the concept of interlanguage reading, which involves the integration of learners' L1 and L2 knowledge (e.g., Birch & Fulop, 2021)

2.2   Captions and L1 subtitles

The comparison between captions and L1 subtitles, that is, the use of L2 text or L1 text on the screen, is addressed by two studies in this volume. The results of these studies contribute to improving our understanding of the processing differences resulting from the language of the text and learner proficiency. In Chapter 1, the study by Casulleras and Miralpeix compared the effectiveness of captions and L1 subtitles, demonstrating the advantage of the former for learning vocabulary. Understandably, primary school learners who watched cartoons with L1 subtitles performed better in comprehension, as noted earlier. These findings are consistent with research by Pujadas and Muñoz (2019, 2020) involving secondary school learners, which also hinted at a potential trade-off between comprehension, favored by L1 subtitles, and attention to vocabulary drawn by pre-viewing instruction.

In Chapter 4, Pujadas and Puimège follow up on those previous studies and investigate whether pre-viewing instruction affects attention allocation to captions and subtitles among teenagers (age 13), a previously unexplored issue. Through eye-tracking, Pujadas and Puimège observed that participants who watched the video with L1 subtitles fixated on the on-screen text more frequently and for longer durations, regardless of pre-viewing instruction. This suggests that elementary-level learners relied more heavily on L1 subtitles than on captions for comprehension, corroborating similar results found in a previous study (see Muñoz, 2017). Additionally, learners in the captions group who received pre-viewing instruction had shorter fixations, indicating that teaching the target words before viewing the video facilitated the processing of those words when presented in the target language, a finding consistent with previous research involving participants of similar ages (Pujadas & Muñoz, 2020).

2.3   Caption enhancement

A new insight from the research in various chapters of this volume is that the facilitative effect of pre-viewing instruction may be compared to the facilitative effect of caption enhancement. Caption enhancement, a type of input enhancement, involves manipulations that teachers apply to the input to direct learners' attention to specific features (e.g., Sharwood Smith, 1991, 1993). Numerous reading studies have explored the effects of input enhancement, yielding mixed results. Conflicting findings may arise due to disparities between external salience and learners' internal mechanisms guiding attention at different points in the learning process (e.g., Galimberti, 2023), as well as the shallowness of perceptual salience (e.g., Leow & Martin, 2017; Puimège et al., 2024; Sharwood Smith, 1991). Additionally, learners at lower proficiency levels may struggle to allocate cognitive resources to both meaning comprehension and attending to the highlighted formal aspects via input enhancement (Ellis, 2016).

For this reason, several AV studies have investigated whether caption enhancement can counteract viewers' natural inclination to focus on meaning comprehension rather than linguistic form (see Vanderplank, 2015). Results in this area are also mixed, suggesting that various factors may mediate the effects of caption enhancement. These factors include the nature of the enhanced elements (lexical items or grammatical constructions), the timing of the test (immediate or delayed), the length of the treatment (one-off studies or extensive studies) (Pattemore & Muñoz, 2022), and the proportion of enhanced captions (Cintrón-Valentín et al., 2019).

The studies in this volume advance our understanding of the effects of input enhancement in AV input in several ways. Firstly, the study by Finger-Bou and Muñoz (Chapter 3) with primary school children demonstrates that caption enhancement increased vocabulary gains, consistent with previous studies involving older and more proficient participants. To our knowledge, this is the first study to explore caption enhancement with young learners. Additionally, the analysis of eye movement data revealed that the fixations of the enhanced-captions group were longer than those of the regular-captions group soon after the intervention began, although this difference diminished by the end. These findings challenge conclusions drawn from one-off experiments, which may not capture the dynamic and transitory nature of enhancement. Furthermore, the short-lived effect of caption enhancement, if confirmed by future studies, holds implications for pedagogical implementations.

Another insight with pedagogical implications emerges from comparing this study with a previous study by Avello (2023) using the same AV material and tests with children of the same age but with unenhanced captions and post-viewing activities. The vocabulary gains of participants with enhanced captions in Finger-Bou and Muñoz's study were like those of participants in Avello's study with regular captions and post-viewing activities. This suggests that post-viewing activities and caption enhancement may be similarly effective in directing learners' attention to unknown words in the input, at least at this age and proficiency level. This association could extend to pre-viewing activities, as evidence suggests no significant differences between pre-viewing and post-viewing tasks, both leading to higher vocabulary gains than viewing without tasks (Suter et al., 2024).

The comparison can be extended to include the results of the study by Mora and Fouz-González in Chapter 8, which investigated the effects of textual enhancement to facilitate learners' perceptual sensitivity to difficult L2 sound contrasts. While the researchers observed a general positive effect of enhancement, they also found that the participants in the unenhanced condition benefitted from the viewing as well. The authors reflect on the fact that those participants had also been instructed to pay attention to the words containing the target sound contrast. As with pre-viewing activities, such instruction promoted intentional learning.

An original contribution of the chapter by Mora and Fouz-González is the innovative use of textual enhancement. Specifically, the study tested the effectiveness of two novel textual input enhancement techniques: (color-)contrastive input enhancement and the use of phonetic symbols. Additionally, through eye-tracking, the study revealed that captions featuring phonetic symbols and contrastive enhancement had the highest relative fixation durations, as anticipated. This condition also presented the largest loss in attention, which the authors suggest could stem from the potential cognitive overload of this condition, hindering sustained attention over time. However, no correlation was observed with gains in perceptual sensitivity to the sound contrast, in line with previous studies (e.g. Winke, 2013), which similarly found that promoting noticing did not result in consistent gains. The authors propose that this could be attributed to the brief exposure duration (30 minutes) in their study, leading them to consider whether more consistent gains may arise with a longer treatment period.

3.   Learning gains in different language dimensions

The language dimensions that initially garnered the most attention from SLA researchers, as highlighted in an early meta-analysis (Montero-Perez et al., 2013), were vocabulary and comprehension. Nearly a decade later, this remains the case (Reynolds et al., 2022). Within the SUBTiLL project, we have aimed to incorporate AV studies on grammar, pronunciation, and pragmatics to obtain a more comprehensive understanding of the benefits for language learning. These pioneering studies have enhanced our grasp of the conditions needed for learning different language dimensions, such as a more extensive exposure for learning pronunciation (Chapter 8) and grammar (Chapter 9) compared to learning vocabulary.

3.1   Vocabulary

A recurring finding in vocabulary acquisition studies is the significant role of prior vocabulary knowledge in learning new words. This phenomenon is often described as "the rich get richer" or the Matthew effect (Stanovich, 1986). The vocabulary studies presented in this volume, by Casulleras and Miralpeix (Chapter 1) and by Finger-Bou and Muñoz (Chapter 3), further support the extension of this finding to the learning of new words through viewing, as those with bigger vocabulary sizes tend to obtain larger lexical gains.

Moreover, a recurring finding in SLA is that learning in incidental conditions results in smaller gains than learning in intentional conditions, at least in the immediate post-tests or in the short term. In both studies, the number of words learned by participants is relatively small. However, it is important to note that vocabulary learning is incremental, and the tests used in these studies may not fully capture the gradual word learning that occurred and that did not reach the threshold for explicit recognition or recall (Bisson et al., 2013). Likewise, as Casulleras and Miralpeix (Chapter 1) indicate, the video exposure also reactivates already known words. It is also possible that participants may have acquired words that were not specifically targeted to some extent (Webb et al., 2023).

In contrast, the study on intentional learning by Popova and Miralpeix (Chapter 5) reported higher vocabulary gains compared to previous studies, and these gains were observed in meaning recall (a skill that typically presents greater difficulty compared to other aspects of lexical learning, such as form or meaning recognition). This could be attributed to the support provided to participants, including immediate repeated viewing for one group and access to *Language Reactor* (Netflix) for the other group (see below).

Continuing with intentional learning, Miralpeix, Gesa and Suárez (Chapter 9) demonstrate that vocabulary acquisition can take place with minimal exposure to a new language through AV input, particularly when both languages (known and new) are present in the input (e.g., the audio in a familiar language and the on-screen text in the new language). This form of 'reversed subtitling' provides learners with the opportunity to connect new linguistic forms with their meanings, primarily relying on the language known in the video and contextual cues.

In the initial stages of learning a new language, rapidly expanding vocabulary is crucial, and AV input can facilitate the acquisition of word meanings after minimal exposure. This may help learners quickly master the necessary words to enable effective communication and comprehension in everyday interactions (i.e., being in command of a *core vocabulary*, according to Carter [1998]). However, it is important to note that fast-mapped words may not be fully comprehended (e.g., approximately half of the target words were learned in the study in

Chapter 9) or retained over time without additional reinforcement or repeated exposure. Thus, ensuring consolidation and continued exposure will be essential for long-term retention.

3.2   Content comprehension

Several studies have demonstrated that viewing supported by on-screen text, captions or L1 subtitles, enhances comprehension. Unsurprisingly, L1 subtitles have been shown to offer an advantage for comprehension (e.g., Pujadas & Muñoz, 2020). This advantage was confirmed by the study conducted by Pujadas and Puimège (Chapter 4), which investigated the eye movements of elementary-level learners when viewing with captions versus L1 subtitles. In their study, the group with subtitles had higher comprehension, and higher number of fixations, than the group with captions, regardless of the pre-viewing condition (with or without previous instruction). Casulleras and Miralpeix (Chapter 1) further validated this advantage with primary school learners, as previously mentioned. A notable finding from this research, however, was that comprehension varied depending on the episode, with significant differences observed in most, though not all, episodes, consistent with findings from prior studies (Gesa, 2019; Pujadas & Muñoz, 2020). This underscores the value of the results obtained from extensive studies rather than from research limited to a single video, which represents an innovative contribution of the research from the SUBTiLL project.

Another comparison was explored in the study by Popova and Miralpeix (Chapter 5), which focused on the effects of different viewing methods on plot comprehension. Specifically, they compared comprehension between a repeated captioned viewing condition and a Language Reactor condition, finding no significant difference between the two conditions. Interestingly, several participants in the repeated captioned viewing condition reported paying more attention to plot comprehension during the first viewing and to linguistic form during the second viewing. In contrast, participants in the Language Reactor condition primarily focused on language forms. This contributes to our understanding of how various viewing methods may support language learning.

3.3   Grammatical constructions

In the study by Pattemore, Suárez, Montero Perez, and Muñoz (Chapter 8), participants were assessed on their acquisition of grammatical constructions. As previously mentioned, this dimension remains understudied in research on AV input. Furthermore, in earlier studies that explored grammar learning through viewing, the results had not been particularly positive. Those studies typically involved very brief exposure, often lasting only a single session, suggesting that more extensive exposure to AV input may be necessary for grammar learning compared to learning new words through videos (Van Lommel et al., 2006).

In contrast, extensive studies conducted within the SUBTiLL project have demonstrated significant grammar learning (e.g., Pattemore & Muñoz, 2020), supporting the notion that the benefits of AV viewing for grammar acquisition may depend on the duration of the treatment. In Chapter 8, differences between learning in the captioned condition and the uncaptioned condition only emerged in the study where participants viewed 10 episodes (227 minutes), but not in the study with two viewing sessions (71 minutes). While this disparity in results may not solely be attributed to the duration of exposure, it appears worthwhile to further investigate the required exposure time for significant results to manifest across different language targets.

3.4 Pronunciation

As mentioned above, there is a paucity of studies addressing pronunciation benefits through AV input. The study by Mora and Fouz-González, in Chapter 7, shares with previous studies within the SUBTiLL project (Galimberti, 2023; Wisniewska & Mora, 2020) a concern for ways to promote attention to pronunciation when viewing captioned video. Such concern arises from the consideration that captioned video viewing is cognitively demanding in terms of information processing because auditory processing happens simultaneously with the processing of imagery and on-screen text. In such a complex input-processing situation, learners are more prone to prioritize meaning and comprehension over phonological form, which suggests that incidental pronunciation learning is less likely to happen.

In this volume's study, Mora and Fouz-González examine the effectiveness of contrastive input enhancement and the use of phonetic symbols as enhancement techniques, as seen above. Beyond its contribution to the field of caption enhancement, this chapter provides evidence that viewing the video, even without captions, positively influenced learners' perception of the target vowel contrast compared to a control group that did not watch the video, even after just 30 minutes of exposure. The short length of the treatment may also account for the more pronounced gains in processing speed compared to accuracy.

3.5 Pragmatics

The study by Barón, Celaya, and Martínez-Flor (Chapter 6) delved into the potential benefits of captioned viewing for learning pragmatics, particularly focusing on learning requests. While the chapter's focus on pragmatics represents a novel contribution, the study carries direct implications for the classroom, demonstrating how videos offer models of authentic interaction. The finding that viewing captioned video excerpts had a more positive impact on pragmatic awareness than viewing without captions aligns with previous research indicating benefits across various language dimensions. In this case, it could be argued that the presence of captions facilitated the matching of form and meaning, thereby facilitating comprehension and freeing up cognitive resources for noticing the pragmatic aspects of the interaction. Although the analysis of eye movement data did not fully elucidate the outcomes, it was apparent that while captions attracted viewers' attention, this did not pull attention away from the visual elements (such as the eyes and mouth of the characters), which were similarly attended to by students who did not have captions. Other interesting ideas from the study emerge through the retrospective interviews, where students reflected on their awareness of pragmatic aspects gleaned from the video content and recognized the importance of guidance in acquiring L2 pragmatics.

4.   Learner individual differences

The impact of individual differences on learning through visual media has been explored by a handful of recent studies. One consistent finding in these studies is the potential of captions to alleviate individual differences and create a level playing field for all learners. Previous investigations within the SUBTiLL project offered initial evidence that the presence of captions reduced individual differences, such as those related to working memory, as demonstrated in a study on grammatical constructions (Pattemore & Muñoz, 2020). Conversely, individual differences were noted to affect performance in the uncaptioned condition, which was also more challenging. Two studies in this volume support this finding, enriching our understanding of the mediating role of captions in the effects of language learning aptitude on language acquisition. More generally, research in this volume contributes to our understanding of how vocabulary size, reading skills, aptitude, and age – four key learner individual differences – affect learning through AV input.

4.1   Vocabulary size

Previous research has emphasized the importance of vocabulary size in determining proficiency in English as a Foreign Language (EFL) (Miralpeix & Muñoz, 2018), leading to its frequent use as a proxy for learner proficiency in AV studies. As seen above, a prevalent finding across the chapters in this volume is the notable correlation between vocabulary knowledge and word acquisition. Older and more proficient children with a larger vocabulary tend to exhibit greater gains compared to younger children with a smaller vocabulary, as evidenced in Finger-Bou and Muñoz (Chapter 3), Avello and Muñoz (Chapter 2). Furthermore, in the study by Avello and Muñoz, prior vocabulary knowledge emerged as the most influential predictor of improvements in English reading efficacy through the use of captioned video content. However, vocabulary size may have a varying influence depending on the viewing condition, as Casulleras and Miralpeix indicate in Chapter 1. On the other hand, vocabulary size does not seem to predict gains in pronunciation through video viewing, as indicated by Galimberti (2023), also within the scope of the SUBTiLL project. This discrepancy could stem from the specific nature of oral production skills, which are not typically assessed by vocabulary size tests.

4.2   Reading skills

The focus on participants' reading skills in two chapters represents a new emphasis in this area of research, with a double focus: how reading contributes to L2 learning through viewing and how viewing helps to improve reading. While the latter is a new endeavor with respect to L2 learning, the practice of "turning on the subtitles" has been advocated for some time to bolster reading abilities and promote reading practice in the first language. In the context of first language literacy, subtitles have indeed been considered as a means of facilitating functional literacy in many regions worldwide (https://worldliteracyfoundation.org/turn-on -the-subtitles/). Numerous advantages for children engaging in reading and listening to their L1 have been observed across various domains, including phonemic awareness, vocabulary enrichment, and comprehension.

We predicted that these benefits would naturally extend to L2 learners reading on-screen text. This hypothesis was explored in the study conducted by Avello and Muñoz (Chapter 2), which investigated the impact of captioned video viewing on reading skills. The findings not only demonstrated positive effects on young learners' L2 reading abilities but also revealed improvements in their L1 reading skills, breaking new ground in the field.

While Avello and Muñoz's study focused on using *viewing to enhance reading*, the study by Casulleras and Miralpeix (Chapter 1) probed into how *reading contributes to L2 learning through viewing*. Undoubtedly, reading skills (including speed and comprehension) are crucial for effectively using on-screen text during viewing sessions, particularly when these skills are still developing, as is often the case with young learners. This study revealed that L1 reading skills, superior to L2 reading skills, positively influenced the comprehension of young learners viewing videos with L1 subtitles, surpassing the comprehension levels of participants using captions.

4.3   Aptitude

A few studies within the SUBTiLL project have delved into the role of language learning aptitude with the aim of identifying the skills that play a significant role in learning through AV input. To achieve this, the LLAMA suite of tests (Meara, 2005; Meara & Rodgers, 2019) has been employed, either in its entirety or by selecting specific tests aligned with the skills predicted to be required in each investigation. For instance, in the research conducted by Muñoz and colleagues (2022), LLAMA D was employed to measure viewers' ability to recognize repeated sounds in spoken language, with the prediction that these skills would be more influential in viewing without captions than with captions. The researchers confirmed their prediction as aptitude effects were more pronounced in the uncaptioned condition compared to the captioned condition.

The two chapters in this volume that investigate the role of language learning aptitude in learning through AV input contribute to this inquiry, confirming our insight that the effects of language learning aptitude become apparent especially in challenging learning conditions. The study by Casulleras and Miralpeix (Chapter 1) used LLAMA B as a measure of associative memory, assumed to predict vocabulary learning. The findings revealed that LLAMA B scores were significantly related to the comprehension outcomes of both groups of primary school children, regardless of whether they viewed with L1 subtitles or captions. As LLAMA B assesses rote learning of vocabulary (helping learners recognize and recall words in isolation), this ability can contribute to comprehension. Notably, a correlation between aptitude and L2 word-form recognition was only observed in the L1 subtitles group, not in the captions group. The authors posit that aptitude may just be assisting learners in the condition that was more challenging (i.e., recognizing words without the aid of the L2-text, as was the case in the L1 subtitles group). Participants in the L1 subtitles group needed to rely more on their memory skills, as recognizing word forms in captions made the task easier for the captions group.

In the study by Pattemore, Suárez, Montero Perez, and Muñoz (Chapter 8), the effects of language learning aptitude on learning grammatical constructions through viewing were explored. Specifically, the study examined learners' inductive learning ability, measured by the LLAMA F test. A notable finding across both studies reported in this chapter is the significant effects of aptitude observed among learners in the uncaptioned condition but not in the captioned condition. Despite differences in participants' L1, target language, proficiency level, and target grammatical constructions, this consistent result provides evidence supporting the general notion in the field that language learning aptitude is more pertinent at initial stages of language acquisition than at advanced levels (e.g., Winke, 2013). As mentioned earlier, this finding is in line with previous research suggesting that captions mitigate the effects of individual differences in more demanding conditions (Muñoz et al., 2022; Pattemore & Muñoz, 2020).

Additionally, it is worth emphasizing that in these studies, language learning aptitude is linked to outcomes resulting from incidental learning (or, at least, not from an explicit teaching/learning setting), which challenges the notion that the predictive power of aptitude is limited to classroom-based learning (see Li, 2016).

4.4   Age

As is common in the field of SLA, the participants in most studies on learning from AV input are young adults. In the SUBTiLL project, we aimed to address this gap by placing a strong emphasis on young learners. This focus is represented by Chapters 1 to 3 of the present volume, which involve primary school students, and in Chapters 4 and 5, which involve secondary school students. Initially, we sought to determine whether the learning benefits associated with viewing for young adults could be extended to children (Gesa, 2019) and teenagers (Pujadas, 2019) with elementary proficiency levels in their L2. Additionally, considering that captioned viewing generally offers more benefits than L1 subtitled viewing, we wondered whether young learners could also benefit from captioned viewing. We have answered both questions affirmatively, in that research in this volume demonstrates that young learners can also benefit from captioned viewing.

Several findings from our previous studies laid the groundwork for the investigations presented in this volume. For instance, an eye-tracking study revealed that primary school learners were capable of disregarding captions they found difficult or unhelpful, a behavior potentially linked to the way they engaged with the task and their developing language learning awareness (Muñoz, 2017). However, further analysis of eye movements in Finger-Bou and Muñoz (Chapter 3) indicated that children do engage with captions written in simpler language in age-appropriate cartoons. Moreover, the study by Casulleras and Miralpeix (Chapter 1) demonstrated the advantage of the captioned condition over L1 subtitles in vocabulary learning, aligning closely with findings from research involving teenagers by Pujadas and Muñoz (2019).

Another noteworthy finding from our prior research was the observation that older learners, including young adults and secondary school students, exhibited greater learning benefits compared to primary school learners (Gesa, 2019; Gesa & Miralpeix, 2023b). While disentangling age effects from proficiency effects is unfeasible, the superior gains among older groups were corroborated by Chapter 2 in this volume, which focuses on the development of reading skills through captioned viewing. This finding is also in line with Avello's study (2023), which compared the vocabulary acquisition of children across two different primary school grades.

The findings from the study by Miralpeix, Gesa, and Suárez (Chapter 9) with adult participants support the efficiency of the adult learning mechanism, as novice learners demonstrate the ability to establish connections between form and meaning for new vocabulary with only minimal information from AV input. This result is consistent with previous studies where adults exhibit rapid learning progress after brief L2 instruction or exposure (e.g., Gullberg et al., 2010; McLaughlin et al., 2004). As Gullberg et al. (2010) suggest, it is reminiscent of the fast-mapping capacity that children seem to have in the L1 (by quickly learning the meaning of new words with minimal exposure to them), but which has not usually been attributed to adult L2 learners. Additionally, the success of learning after such limited exposure may also be influenced by other individual variables such as linguistic aptitude, as shown in Miralpeix et al. (2023).

5.   Looking ahead: *Learning while viewing* and *viewing for learning*

This chapter has gathered findings from the studies presented in this volume to paint a comprehensive picture of L2 learning through AV input. It is fitting to conclude this chapter, and indeed this book, with a few reflections on issues that deserve attention in future research.

To begin with, the studies compiled here confirm the advantages of exposure to AV for L2 learning. However, further research is necessary to shed more light on the optimal conditions for effective learning through viewing, as benefits have been found to vary depending on learner characteristics and viewing methods. Regarding learner characteristics, the influential role of proficiency and vocabulary size is well-established, while additional research is needed on learner cognitive abilities and their interaction with viewing methods, particularly with captioned viewing. Similarly, further investigation is required on learner affective factors, such as attitudes toward target language learning and engagement (e.g., Lo, 2023), where objective measures (i.e., eye-tracker, test scores) and subjective measures (i.e., retrospective interviews, students' diaries) can be triangulated. Regarding viewing methods, for example, the benefits of video repetition have been demonstrated, but research concerning the respective benefits of immediate or spaced repetition is incipient (Lo, 2024; Muñoz et al., 2022). Knowledge about optimal lags can be valuable for both teachers and for autonomous learners.

Similarly, knowledge about optimal spacing between exposures can enhance the effectiveness of learning strategies, whether in a formal classroom setting or in self-directed learning outside (see Pattemore & Muñoz, 2023).

The findings gathered from these studies shed light on important pedagogical implications, both in relation to incidental learning – *learning while viewing* – and to intentional learning – *viewing for learning*. AV input is deemed "optimal" by Long (2020) because it enhances incidental learning, which is typically insufficient in the classroom. With this aim, unobtrusive enhancements have been suggested, such as slower-paced audio and captions (Jordan & Long, 2023), though it has been argued that enhancing captions create conditions for *semi-incidental* rather than incidental learning (Pellicer-Sánchez & Boers, 2018).

As regards captioning, the possibility that text enhancement may have a fleeting effect is intriguing and warrants further research and critical consideration. Exploring the long-term retention of enhanced captions (e.g., Puimège et al., 2024) could provide relevant information into their efficacy in educational settings. Additionally, the triangulation of eye-tracking data and introspective or retrospective interviews can contribute to clarifying the potential of caption enhancement for fostering learning.

Equally important, AV input can be used to promote intentional learning in multiple ways both inside and outside the classroom (e.g., Chapter 5, this volume; Webb, 2015). The benefits of pre-viewing and post-viewing tasks for vocabulary learning are evident (e.g., Gesa & Miralpeix, 2023a), but further research is needed to understand the characteristics of tasks that promote deeper processing and enhance learning. Additionally, significant pedagogical insights can emerge from research into the most effective strategies to guide viewing for use in the classroom and for independent learning outside the classroom, which is becoming a popular activity.

Furthermore, other *viewing for learning* methods should be investigated. For instance, very few studies have paid attention to the tools provided by modern educational applications offered as support when watching videos (with exceptions such as Alm, 2021; Fievez et al., 2023 or Popova & Miralpeix, in Chapter 5). Research to date has mainly focused on the effects *of* technology. That is, we have mainly investigated the effect *of* adding on-screen text on different linguistic skills. However, as suggested by Vanderplank (2016a), we should also assess the effects *with* technology, that is, what learners do with on-screen text and other tools designed to enhance language learning. The effects *with* technology can only be analyzed when learners have a choice and take control of the technology offered (which has not happened until lately, with the use of digital technology to transmit TV programs, the increase in power of portable devices such as tablets or laptops, and the possibility to use learning apps while watching the videos). These apps often include features like interactive subtitles, vocabulary lists and pronunciation practice to support language acquisition and their effects on learning deserve further exploration.

Learners may also encounter new languages through AV input during extramural exposure (see Chapter 9) and measuring intake from viewing can provide valuable insights into how we break into a new language, as suggested by Miralpeix (2024). It is also common for students of languages typologically close to their L1 to initiate their learning journey through extensive viewing outside of formal educational settings. For instance, Portuguese speakers may watch TV series in Spanish, Catalans in Italian, or Norwegians in Swedish. Given the considerable mutual intelligibility between the learner's L1 and the target language, particularly in written form, watching subtitled/captioned videos can facilitate the comprehension of main ideas and promote language acquisition. However, empirical research in this area is limited, warranting further investigation. These future studies may yield results in line with existing research demonstrating a significant degree of incidental English learning from AV input among children before formal school instruction, particularly in countries with languages that are typologically similar to English (e.g., De Wilde et al., 2020, for Flemish; Muñoz et al., 2018, for Danish).

Last, but not least, in present-day schools, we need to gain insight into the most effective ways of presenting visual media to young L2 learners. For instance, should we expose them to videos without on-screen text when their reading skills are still very basic? And when to transition to captioned or to L1-subtitled videos? Alternatively, should we expose young learners to captioned viewing to support their L2 reading skills and to L1 subtitles to enhance their L1 reading skills while also developing their L2 listening skills?

These are only some of the issues and questions that researchers in this promising field could explore to advance our understanding of language learning through AV input and to provide valuable guidance for educators in today's classrooms.

Acknowledgements

We gratefully acknowledge the funding provided by grants PID2019-110594GB-100 from the Spanish Ministry of Science and Innovation and 2023SGR00303 from the Catalan Agency for Management of University and Research Grants (AGAUR), which made the research in this volume possible. We would also like to thank the series editors for their support and their valuable comments and suggestions.

References

Alm, A. (2021). Language learning with Netflix: from extensive to intra-formal learning. *The EuroCALL Review, 29*(1), 81–92.

Avello, D. (2023). L2 learning from captioned-video viewing in primary school students (Unpublished doctoral dissertation). University of Barcelona. Retrieved on 28 May 2024 from http://hdl.handle.net/2445/196164

Birch, B., & Fulop, S. (2021). *English L2 reading: Getting to the bottom* (4th ed.). Routledge.

Bisson, M-J., Van Heuven, W. J. B., Conklin, K., & Tunney, R. J. (2013). Incidental acquisition of foreign language vocabulary through brief multi-modal exposure. *PLoS ONE, 8*(4), e60912.

Carter, R. (1998). *Vocabulary: Applied linguistics perspectives*. Routledge.

Carver, R. P. (1990). *Reading rate. A review of research and theory*. Academic Press.

Cintrón-Valentín, M., García-Amaya, L., & Ellis, N. C. (2019). Captioning and grammar learning in the L2 Spanish classroom. *The Language Learning Journal, 47*(4), 439–459.

Danan, M. (2004). Captioning and subtitling: Undervalued language learning strategies. *Meta: Journal des Traducteurs / Meta: Translators' Journal, 49*, 67–77.

De Wilde, V., Brysbaert, M., & Eyckmans, J. (2020). Learning English through out-of-school exposure. Which levels of language proficiency are attained and which types of input are important? *Bilingualism: Language and Cognition, 23*(1), 171–185.

Ellis, R. (2016). Focus on form: A critical review. *Language Teaching Research, 20*(3), 405–428.

Fievez, I., Montero Perez, M., Cornillie, F., & Desmet, P. (2023). Promoting incidental vocabulary learning through watching a French Netflix series with glossed captions. *Computer Assisted Language Learning, 36*(1–2), 26–51.

Galimberti, V. (2023). Audio-synchronized textual enhancement in L2 pronunciation teaching and learning with TV series (Unpublished doctoral dissertation). University of Barcelona.

Gesa, F. (2019). L1/L2 subtitled TV series and EFL learning: A study on vocabulary acquisition and content comprehension at different proficiency levels (Unpublished doctoral dissertation). University of Barcelona. http://hdl.handle.net/10803/668505

Gesa, F., & Miralpeix, I. (2023a). Extensive viewing as additional input for foreign language vocabulary learning: A longitudinal study in secondary school. *Language Teaching Research.*

Gesa, F., & Miralpeix, I. (2023b). Extensive viewing and L2 vocabulary learning: Two studies in EFL classes with children and adolescents. *ITL – International Journal of Applied Linguistics.*

Gullberg, M., Roberts, L., Dimroth, C., Veroude, K., & Indefrey, P. (2010). Adult language learning after minimal exposure to an unknown natural language. *Language Learning, 60*(Suppl. 2), 5–24.

Jordan, G., & Long, M. (2023). *English language teaching now and how it could be*. Cambridge Scholars.

Koda, K. (2008). Looking back and thinking forward. In K. Koda & A. Zehler (Eds.), *Learning to read across languages* (pp. 222–234). Routledge.

Krashen, S. D. (1987). *Principles and practice in second language acquisition*. Prentice-Hall International.

doi Leow, R. P., & Martin, A. (2017). Enhancing the input to promote salience of the L2: A critical overview. In S. M. Gass, P. Spinner, & J. Behney (Eds.), *Salience in SLA* (pp. 167–186). Routledge.

doi Li, S. (2016). The construct validity of language aptitude: A meta-analysis. *Studies in Second Language Acquisition*, 38(4), 801–842.

doi Linebarger, D., Taylor Piotrowski, J., & Greenwood, C. (2010). On-screen print: The role of captions as a supplemental literacy tool. *Journal of Research in Reading*, 33(2), 148–167.

doi Lo, S. (2023). Viewing dual-subtitled videos under different learning conditions: Effects on learners' behavioural, emotional, and cognitive engagement. *Computer Assisted Language Learning*.

doi Lo, S. (2024). Vocabulary learning through viewing dual-subtitled videos: Immediate repetition versus spaced repetition as an enhancement strategy. *ReCALL*.

doi Long, M. H. (1990). The least a second language acquisition theory needs to explain. *TESOL Quarterly*, 24, 649–666.

doi Long, M. H. (2020). Optimal input for language learning: Genuine, simplified, elaborated or modified elaborated? *Language Teaching* 53(2), 169–182.

doi McLaughlin, J., Osterhout, L., & Kim, A. (2004). Neural correlates of second-language word learning: Minimal instruction produces rapid change. *Nature Neuroscience*, 7(7), 703–704.

Meara, P. M. (2005). *LLAMA language aptitude tests*. Lognostics.

Meara, P. M., & Rogers, V. E. (2019). *The LLAMA tests v3. LLAMA_F v3.0 grammar rules*. Lognostics.

doi Miralpeix, I. (2024). Vocabulary learning at first exposure: Replication of Gullberg, Roberts & Dimroth (2012) and Shoemaker & Rast (2013). *Language Teaching*, 57(1), 122–131.

doi Miralpeix, I., Gesa, F., & Suárez, M. (2023). Vocabulary learning from subtitled input after minimal exposure. In B. Reynolds (Ed.), *Vocabulary learning in the wild* (pp. 263–283). Springer.

doi Miralpeix, I., & Muñoz, C. (2018). Receptive vocabulary size and its relationship to EFL language skills. *IRAL – International Review of Applied Linguistics in Language Teaching*, 56(1), 1–24.

doi Montero Perez, M. (2022). Second or foreign language learning through watching audio-visual input and the role of on-screen text. *Language Teaching*, 55(2), 163–192.

doi Montero Perez, M., Van Den Noortgate, W., & Desmet, P. (2013). Captioned video for L2 listening and vocabulary learning: A meta-analysis. *System*, 41(3), 720–739.

doi Muñoz, C. (2007). Age-related differences and second language learning practice. In R. DeKeyser (Ed.), *Practice in a second language. Perspectives from applied linguistics and cognitive psychology* (pp. 229–255). Cambridge University Press.

doi Muñoz, C. (2017). The role of age and proficiency in subtitle reading. An eye-tracking study. *System*, 67, 77–86.

doi Muñoz, C. (2022). Audiovisual input in L2 learning. *Language, Interaction and Acquisition*, 13(1), 125–143.

doi Muñoz, C., Cadierno, T. & Casas, I. (2018). Different starting points for English language learning: A comparative study of Danish and Spanish young learners. *Language Learning*, 68(4), 1076–1109.

Muñoz, C., Pattemore, A., & Avello, D. (2022). Exploring repeated captioning viewing as a way to promote vocabulary learning: Time lag between repetitions and learner factors. *Computer Assisted Language Learning.*

Pattemore, A., & Muñoz, C. (2020). Learning L2 constructions from captioned audio-visual exposure: The effect of learner-related factors. *System, 93.*

Pattemore, A. & Muñoz, C. (2023). The effects of binge-watching and spacing on learning L2 multi-word units from captioned TV series. *The Language Learning Journal, 51*(4), 401–415.

Pellicer-Sánchez, A., & Boers, F. (2018). Pedagogical approaches to the teaching and learning of formulaic language. In A. Siyanova-Chanturia & A. Pellicer-Sánchez (Eds.), *Understanding formulaic language: A second language acquisition perspective* (pp. 153–173). Routledge.

Puimège, E., Montero Perez, M., & Peters, E. (2024). The effects of typographic enhancement on L2 collocation processing and learning from reading: An eye-tracking study. *Studies in Second Language Acquisition, 45*(1), 88–110.

Pujadas, G. (2019). Language learning through extensive TV viewing. A study with adolescent EFL learners (Unpublished doctoral dissertation). Universitat de Barcelona. http://hdl.handle.net/10803/668091

Pujadas, G., & Muñoz, C. (2019). Extensive viewing of captioned and subtitled TV series: A study of L2 vocabulary learning by adolescents. *The Language Learning Journal, 47*(4), 479–496.

Pujadas, G., & Muñoz, C. (2020). Examining adolescent EFL learners' TV viewing comprehension through captions and subtitles. *Studies in Second Language Acquisition, 42*(3), 1–25.

Reynolds, B. L., Cui, Y., Kao, C.-W., & Thomas, N. (2022). VocabularyaAcquisition through viewing captioned and subtitled video: A scoping review and meta-analysis. *Systems, 10*(133).

Sharwood Smith, M. (1991). Speaking to many minds: On the relevance of different types of language information for the L2 learner. *Second Language Research, 7*(2), 118–132.

Sharwood Smith, M. (1993). Input enhancement in instructed SLA: Theoretical bases. *Studies in Second Language Acquisition, 15*(2), 165–179.

Sparks, R., Patton, J., Ganschow, L., Humbach, N., & Javorsky, J. (2008). Early first-language reading and spelling skills predict later second-language reading and spelling skills. *Journal of Educational Psychology, 100*(1), 162–174.

Stanovich, K. E. (1986). Matthew effects in reading: Some consequences of individual differences in the acquisition of literacy. *Reading Research Quarterly, 21*(4), 360–407. https://www.jstor.org/stable/747612

Suter, L., Berthele, R., & Thomas, A. (2024). L'apprentissage du vocabulaire en français L2 avec Netflix: Effet des activités de pré-/post-visionnage. *Journal of French Language Studies.*

Vanderplank, R. (2015). Thirty years of research into captions/same language subtitles and second/foreign language learning: Distinguishing between 'effects of' subtitles and 'effects with' subtitles for future research. In Y. Gambier, A. Caimi, & C. Mariotti (Eds.), *Subtitles and language learning. Principles, strategies and practical experiences* (pp. 19–40). Peter Lang.

Vanderplank, R. (2016a). 'Effects of' and 'effects with' captions: How exactly does watching a TV programme with same language subtitles make a difference to language learners? *Language Teaching, 49*(2), 235–250.

Vanderplank, R. (2016b). *Captioned media in foreign language learning and teaching: Subtitles for the deaf and hard-of-hearing as tools for language learning.* Palgrave Macmillan.

Van Lommel, S., Laenen, A., & D'Ydewalle, G. (2006). Foreign-grammar acquisition while watching subtitled television programmes. *British Journal of Educational Psychology, 76,* 243–258.

Webb, S. (2015). Extensive viewing: Language learning through watching television. In D. Nunan & J.C. Richards (Eds.), *Language learning beyond the classroom* (pp. 159–168). Routledge.

Webb, S., Uchihara, T., & Yanagisawa, A. (2023). How effective is second language incidental vocabulary learning? A meta-analysis. *Language Teaching, 56*(2), 161–180.

Winke, P. (2013). An investigation into second language aptitude for advanced Chinese language learners. *The Modern Language Journal, 97*(1), 109–130.

Wisniewska, N., & Mora, J.C. (2020). Can captioned video benefit second language pronunciation? *Studies in Second Language Acquisition, 42*(3), 599–624.

Index